The Search for
Heinrich
Stief

A Genealogist on the Loose

LES BOWSER

Quotations from Gottlieb Mittleberger are reprinted by permission of the publisher of *Journey to Pennsylvania*, edited by Oscar Handlin and John Clive, Cambridge, Mass.: The Belknap Press of Harvard University Press, Copyright © 1960 by the President and Fellows of Harvard College.

Image on page 36: Contemporary portrait of Rev. Heinrich Mülenberg, pastor of St. Michael's Lutheran Church, Philadelphia, reproduced with permission of The Pennsylvania-German Society from Theodore Emanuel Schmauk, "Pennsylvania-The German Influence in its Settlement and Development: Part IX, The Lutheran Church in Pennsylvania 1636-1800," The Pennsylvania-German Society Proceedings and Addresses at Easton, Oct. 26, 1900, Vol. XI (The Society, 1902).

Copyright ©Les Bowser, 2001

All rights reserved. No part of this book may be reproduced, stored in a retrieval system or transmitted in any form or by any means without the prior written permission from the publisher, or, in the case of photocopying or other reprographic copying, permission from CANCOPY (Canadian Copyright Licensing Agency), 1 Yonge Street, Suite 1900, Toronto, Ontario M5E 1E5.

Nimbus Publishing Limited
PO Box 9166
Halifax, NS   B3K 5M8
(902) 455-4286

Printed and bound in Canada
Designed by Arthur Carter

Canadian Cataloguing in Publication Data

Bowser, Les
    The search for Heinrich Stief: a genealogist on the loose
    ISBN 1-55109-375-8

    1. Stief, Heinrich. 2. Steeves family. 3. New Brunswick—Genealogy. 4. Bowser, Les. 5. Genealogy—Anecdotes. I. Title.

CS90.S703 2001   929'.2'0971   C2001-901377-9

We acknowledge the financial support of the Government of Canada through the Book Publishing Industry Development Program (BPIDP) and the Canada Council for our publishing activities.

Contents

Preface   vii

Introduction   ix

Chapter 1
Heinrich Stief: The Legend   1

Chapter 2
Beginnings   5

Chapter 3
Dancing up a Terrible Storm   11

Chapter 4
A Flamboyant Speculator   15

Chapter 5
Searching for Ancestors   23

Chapter 6
"A Herd of Hogs"   31

Chapter 7
Charles Jones, his Mark   35

Chapter 8
Bedbunts and Faggathies,
Candlesticks and Chocolate   47

Chapter 9
A Crisis over Stamps   57

Chapter 10
A Loyal Englishman   67

Chapter 11
Into a Dungeon of Fog   77

Chapter 12
"NovaScosha or sum such plase"   83

Chapter 13
A Chance Discovery   101

Chapter 14
Across the Pond   112

Chapter 15
A Hidden History   116

Chapter 16
A Castle in the Sky   125

Chapter 17
In the Neckar Valley   131

Chapter 18
A Travelling Shoemaker   140

Chapter 19
Stief from Schlaitdorf   151

Chapter 20
In America   159

Chapter 21
A Walk on an Old Hill   171

Chapter 22
A Mistaken Signature   181

Chapter 23
Journey to Another World   187

Epilogue   197

Afterword
A Late-Breaking Discovery   203

Endnotes   204

Appendices   236

Bibliography   252

Acknowledgements   266

Index   270

Author's Notes

A Note about Footnotes

In history and genealogy, it has been said, footnotes are everything. As my friend Professor Rotstein at Massey College likes to put it, the study of history is essentially a matter of chasing down footnotes. In this account, all information necessary to the story will be found in the text; the notes at the end of the book have been added for technical clarification or to allow researchers to pursue subjects of their own choosing. Most of the notes will be useful only for further research.

A Note about Names

Names change over time: people's names, the name of a river, the names of a province. New Brunswick's Saint John River was once called St. John's River, and before that Rivière St. Jean, named by Champlain in 1604. The city of Moncton was originally Monckton, after a British lieutenant-colonel. The province of New Brunswick was created from the colony of Nova Scotia in 1784; in the seventeenth century it was all Acadia. Today's Petitcodiac River in New Brunswick is an extreme example of a name change—it has seen no fewer than fifty different spellings since the Mi'kmaq first called it Pet-koat-kwee'-ak.

People's names changed too. A man in Philadelphia born Valentin Müller later became Valentine Miller. Heinrich Stief's wife saw her name change from Regina Stief to Rachel Stieve in only twenty years. The two versions of the name may have sounded much the same to her.

In keeping with the spirit of the past, I have retained the contemporary spelling, while trying to keep potential confusion to a minimum. Where several contemporary versions exist, I have used the name most prevalent. If a cautionary note is in order, it is simply that one should be mindful of the fact that names change over time.

Dedication

For my mother, who drove me to cemeteries around Albert and Westmorland Counties in our family's 1958 Pontiac before I was old enough to have a driver's license.

"Let us not forget to honour the pioneer...a greater man than any who follow, for it is he who faces the terrors of the unknown."

—Arthur S. Robinson,

"The Bend," *Collections of the New Brunswick Historical Society*, No.18 (Saint John, 1963) 236.

Preface

Early on Monday afternoon, December 8, 1997, I stepped from a west-bound train in the little town of Metzingen in southern Germany, and looked around for a back-country bus to Münsingen, twenty kilometres away. I had come to this remote part of Europe to follow up an obscure genealogical clue I'd stumbled across in a Toronto library three months earlier. A quest for family origins I had begun as a teenager in New Brunswick thirty-five years before was about to reach its climax in the archives of a Württemberg church whose own history spanned more than one thousand years.

I settled into my seat as the bus wound its way through the Swabian hills and valleys. A pale sun had broken through the clouds, and long shadows slanted through the trees beside the road. New snow lay in the woods, and mountain freshets cascaded from the hills above.

With no more than a handful of German phrases in my vocabulary and only a casual background in genealogy, I was about to solve a puzzle that had baffled family historians for decades. When the bus reached the sleepy town of Münsingen, all my thoughts were centred on a couple who had left their home somewhere in Germany and emigrated to America 250 years before. The man's name was Heinrich Stief, and his exploits have become the stuff of legend.

CENTENARY STEEVES GATHERING!

A GRAND GATHERING of the STEEVES FAMILY, ---on the Pic-Nic plan,---to celebrate the ONE HUNDRETH ANNIVERSARY of their First Landing in this Country, will be held on the HEIGHTS immediately behind the Village of Hillsboro', in Albert County, on

TUESDAY, 24TH INST.,

at 10 o'clock, A. M.

Much interesting information respecting the early history of the Family and their subsequent rapid increase in numbers and prosperity will be given.

Addresses will be delivered by several Gentlemen connected with the Family.

The Committee have found it impossible to see but a small portion of the connection, but they feel satisfied that the interesting nature of this intended Gathering will bring together an immense representation of the Family.

THE ALBERT SAXEHORN BAND WILL BE IN ATTENDANCE.

---COMMITTEE:---

James Steeves, Grandson of Jacob;
Caleb Steeves, " John;
Solomon Steeves, " Christian;
Milledge Steeves, " Frederick;
Robert M. Steeves, " Ludwick;
R. E. Steeves, " Henry;
Jordon Steeves, " Matthias.

HILLSBORO', SEPT. 14, 1867. ADVOCATE PRESS.

Poster announcing the "Grand Gathering" in 1867 of the descendants of Heinrich Stief.

Introduction

I originally thought this story would take four months to write–chronicling the origins and movements of a little group of Pennsylvania-German and Welsh settlers, sailing away from colonial Philadelphia in 1766, and heading into the wilds of eighteenth-century Nova Scotia—it all looked straightforward enough. The impetus for the story was a genealogical breakthrough I had made in Germany in 1997. The story would be a combined history-travelogue—a personal account of my genealogical discoveries. After all, it was Pennsylvania-German scholar Dr. Don Yoder who posed the question: "what is genealogy if it cannot be personal?"[1]

But somewhere in the process of gathering the background material that would explain the story, I fell in love with the actors in the drama—with Benjamin Franklin, who gave his blessing but cast a distant shadow on the township-settlement project; with Deborah Franklin, Benjamin's devoted wife, whose odd, phonetic spelling left a voice that hearkens back to another time; with their loyal son, William, whose letters to his father shone a revealing light on the settlers and their predicament; with Franklin's friend John Hughes, the visionary Philadelphia merchant and land speculator who found himself at the centre of a dangerous political crisis; with Hughes' and Franklin's partner in the land company, "mad" Anthony Wayne, the young surveyor whose adventuring spirit carried him twice from Philadelphia to old Nova Scotia to establish the new settlement; with their associate John Hall, something of a mystery figure who was believed to be the captain of the unnamed sloop that made the pioneering voyage to the Bay of Fundy in 1766; with the flamboyant Alexander McNutt, the rogue speculator who could be credited with initiating the land deal, but whose unpredictability almost killed the plan in its infancy; and finally with the Philadelphia settlers themselves—Heinrich Stief and his companions—who are supposed to be at the centre of the story but who seem to stand on the sidelines of the great events of the day. And indeed, it was a time of great events. While I knew little about those settlers and their adventures, I had a personal reason for wanting to get to know them: they were my ancestors.

Four months of writing became six. Then six months became twelve, as every piece of evidence led me into another field of discovery—sometimes related to the story, more often not. Two more years went by the wayside, as I tried to transform the scattered bits and pieces of digging and collecting into a narrative that would add life to the skeletal remains of ancestral memory. Still, I couldn't picture the main subjects of my investigation. Despite all my efforts to bring the Pennsylvania settlers into the foreground, they seemed perfectly happy to occupy the faded pages of family history exactly the way they'd lived their lives: in distant anonymity.

The settlers and their families might have been content to remain in the background of Pennsylvania affairs and live their lives in peaceful solitude, but they had arrived on the scene at a turning point in North American history—at a time when the idea of revolution was only a gleam in the eyes of the rebellious Sons of Liberty. The Acadians of supposed French loyalty had been deported from Nova Scotia a decade before, and the American colonists were preoccupied with growth and the anticipation of economic and political freedom. New settlements were springing up along the eastern seaboard, and colonization was the dominant theme of the day. It was the age of sail, and every seaport and fishing camp from Newfoundland to Charles Town was bustling with traffic: single-masted sloops, coastal schooners, and ocean-going ships from European and West Indian ports.

Enter onto the stage a little group of would-be settlers who were feeling the constraints of life in crowded Pennsylvania. It was difficult to raise a family and make the best of things when land was so hard to come by. When they heard that fertile land around the Bay of Fundy was available for settlement, they made the decision to better their lives.

The agreements were signed, a sloop was lined up, and off they went to begin life anew on the Petitcodiac River in today's province of New Brunswick. The future looked promising, but there was nothing in the agreements about abandonment by their sponsors and the real possibility of starvation.

After they had struggled through the first crucial years on the Petitcodiac River, the families settled down to serious homesteading. The years came and went, and their descendants latched onto every opportunity that presented itself: improved farming, grindstone quarrying, gypsum mining, occasional ship-building, and exporting farm produce to markets in New England. They did whatever it took; survival was their uppermost concern, and any free time was spent planning a better future.

But if the descendants of the first settlers lived their lives without looking back, all that would change in 1867, when they began "to consider their history." That year, at a large family gathering, some of the grandsons of Heinrich Stief attempted to map the branches of the family tree. By then, the name Stief had evolved into Steeves, the same way the other surnames had evolved from earlier spellings—well-known names in New Brunswick today such as Somers, Lutes, and Trites.[2]

The Steeves family naturally took its name from the founder, but the majority of his descendants could also trace their roots to several of the other families who arrived with him in 1766. The gathering in 1867 heralded the earliest beginnings of genealogical research, and, soon after, family histories began to emerge—some accurately inspiring, others so faulty they would curdle the milk in your tea.

After a century of intermarriage, the descendants of the Pennsylvania families had spawned a huge, extended, Welsh-German clan encompassing Jones–Steeves–Lutes–Somers–Trites–Ricker–Wortman. Everyone was related to everyone else; everybody was a distant cousin. Today, a large percentage of the population of southeastern New Brunswick is related several times over.

The early families were so prolific—a dozen children per family was not uncommon—that the living descendants of Heinrich Stief now number as many as 150,000 people around the world. Steeves descendants live in countries from Chile to China; in cities from Coquitlam, B.C. to Corner Brook, Nfld.; in towns and villages from Steevescote, N.B. to Steveston, B.C. In the ten municipalities of the 1999 Moncton area phone directory, for instance, the name Steeves was listed 803 times. Surnames which derived from the other settlers from Philadelphia totalled 589. Even the Toronto phone book that year listed the name Steeves 63 times. The immensity of the family prompted a New England observer to comment: "It is more than a family: it is a nation."[3]

When its charter was granted on May 27, 1967, the Steeves Family became the first incorporated family in North America. Since then, several of the others, including the Lutes and the Trites families, have formed their own organizations.

The Daily Times.

MONCTON, THURSDAY, MAR. 2, 1893

HENDRICK STEEVES

And His Wife and Seven Stalwart Sons.

A REMARKABLE RECORD IN PROVINCIAL HISTORY.

Perils and Achievements in Pioneer Days in Albert County.

To the Editor of the St. John Sun:

SIR,—About two years ago a very interesting article appeared in the Sun relative to the early settlement made on the Petitcodiac river by Hendrick Steeves and his companions at the close of "the old French war."

Recently, during a visit to Hillsboro, I enjoyed the hospitality of Jordan Steeves, from whom I learned some further particulars regarding the experience of his ancestor, Hendrick Steeves, during the few years that followed his arrival in the country. Being much interested in the history of all relating to the early settlement of the province, I asked Mr. Steeves to write out a brief account of what he had related to me in conversation, with any additional facts of interest.

A few days since the following was received from Mr. Steeves, which I should be glad to see published in your columns. It is much to be desired that some printed record should be preserved of all old settlements in the province and their founders; and Mr. Steeves' interesting reminiscences of pioneer days on the Petitcodiac is an important contribution in this direction.

Yours very truly,
W. O. RAYMOND.
St. John, N. B., March 1st.

In May, 1763, three years after the taking of Quebec by the English, and shortly after the treaty of peace between England and France, six German families left Pennsylvania to settle on the Petitcodiac river. They sailed in a sloop commanded by Capt. Hall. After a long and wearisome passage they arrived at the place now called Hillsboro, July 1st, and landed at a small creek on the north side of Gray's island. Here the Steeves family, consisting of Hendrick, the father; Rachel his wife; and their seven sons, Jacob, John, Christian, Frederick, Lutrick, Henry and Matthias, whose respective ages were, 14, 12, 10, 8, 6, 4 and 2 years, built a log house and made it their headquarters.

The sloop proceeded up the river to what is now called Moncton and here the remainder of the party, Jones, Trites, Ricker, Lutzes and Sumors, with their families, landed at "Hall's creek," which was so named after the captain of the sloop. Jones, Trites and Sumors located themselves here. Ricker and Lutzes crossed over the river to Outhouse point, opposite Moncton, where they remained.

The sloop left on her homeward voyage with the promise of returning the following spring. The Steeves family commenced to clear their land and make a home for themselves. The only crop they put in the first year was a few turnips, as it was too late in the season to plant any other kind of seed.

Every year, during the third week of July, the entire population of Hillsborough, the village in New Brunswick where Heinrich Stief and some of his companions eventually settled, turns out for a week of festivities. The gathering of the family in 1867—the year of Canada's confederation—was possibly the first of such events. When they heard about a "GRAND GATHERING of the STEEVES FAMILY on the Pic-Nic Plan..." slated for the twenty-fourth day of September that year, four hundred descendants came to dinner.

Ninety-nine years later, in 1966, as Canada prepared to observe its first centenary, the Steeves family commemorated two hundred years of settled life in its adopted home. This time, ten thousand people connected by blood and marriage showed up to celebrate.[4]

Over the years since 1867, numerous descendants of the early Petitcodiac families have attempted to trace their roots to the first immigrants from Pennsylvania. Generally they've been successful. The local fascination with family history had been a long-standing tradition, but it was historian Esther Clark Wright who greatly encouraged their enthusiasm when she gathered the entire Steeves family genealogy into a 962-page book, appropriately titled *The Steeves Descendants*. That outstanding accomplishment came in 1965 after seven years of laborious effort. New Brunswick genealogy hasn't been the same since. Today, if one considers all the backgrounds together—including

Moncton Daily Times, Mar. 2, 1893. This letter was largely responsible for the erroneous mythology that came to surround the legend of Heinrich Stief in the twentieth century. The same story appeared concurrently in the *Saint John Sun*: "A Remarkable Record in Provincial History."

Acadian, American, Irish, Loyalist, Scottish, Welsh, and Yorkshire—genealogy is probably the best-loved hobby in the whole province.[5]

But why go looking for ancestors anyway? What odd force of nature compels otherwise rational beings to dig for their long-forgotten roots—as author Marguerite Yourcenar expressed it—"to burrow in registries and archives for original documents whose legal and bureaucratic jargon is devoid of all human content"? A good question, if I may put her insightful comment in the interrogative. The answer may not be so easy to find.[6]

An activity that was formerly the domain of the nobility and landed gentry who needed to verify their claims to inheritance, genealogy has become a world-wide occupation. Ask your parents something about one of your four grandparents; in that moment, you've made a tentative entry into the sometimes murky world of genealogy. No longer the "faintly ridiculous" pastime that "carried an air of quackery about it," genealogy is recognized as a "legitimate subject for study" in its own right, as well as an important investigative tool for historians.[7]

Granted, one must have a little spare time in order to pursue one's family roots. Preoccupied with the demands of daily life and having no time for the distant past, it's easy to plead an excuse. Nevertheless, an estimated five to ten million people are searching for their roots in North America alone, where the second most popular category on the Internet is genealogy.[8]

After spending a century researching their roots, Steeves family members were well ahead of the game. But while most members of the clan were aware of the family's German ancestry, the European records had been lost to history; no one could say with certainty where the first couple had originated. For decades, the city of Osnabruck in northern Germany was proposed as Heinrich Stief's home town, but without any evidence to support the idea. Although the proof was lost or non-existent, Osnabruck had worked its way into the Steeves legends, and the name stuck.[9]

Any competent family historian would agree that an unverifiable assumption warrants further questioning. The story of the Philadelphia settlers had captured my imagination as a youth, and the uncertainty of Osnabruck represented a void in family history. Was it fact or fancy? Encouraged by the challenge, I took up the quest.

But how did a single, obscure clue lead me to the European roots of Heinrich Stief? What new scientific research capabilities or advanced genealogical procedures were employed? The only answer I can give is this: In the shadowy world of genealogy, sometimes hunches just work out.

In hindsight, the solution was simple. The all-important clue had existed long before I found it, waiting to be uncovered. It wasn't so surprising that I stumbled across that small piece of information, pulled an insignificant hint out of obscurity, and followed the thread of an idea into little towns and villages deep in southern Germany. That no one else had discovered the clue and traced it back in time is the real wonder. In the arcane world of genealogy, however, surprises are not so much a wonder as they are occasionally the beginning, the middle, and the end of the whole affair.

PART 1

CHAPTER 1

Heinrich Stief: The Legend

Heinrich Stief would probably be uncomfortable with all the attention his life has garnered since his arrival in Pennsylvania in 1749. When he and his wife, Regina (or Rachel as she was later called), stepped ashore in Philadelphia, they were just one more immigrant German couple in a great, seventy-five-year-long exodus of oppressed humanity numbering as many as one hundred thousand souls. Two hundred-and-fifty years later, no one has any idea what they looked like—no portraits, no physical descriptions, nothing exists. If their descendants could see them today it is doubtful they would be recognized. Distant, vague, shuffling off an old ship—they would be just two more anonymous faces disappearing into the crowd.[1]

By all legendary accounts, Heinrich Stief was a poor man whose greatest desire was to farm in peace, and whose greatest accomplishment was to successfully raise a brood of seven sons. When he and his family left Philadelphia in 1766 for a new home at the head of the Bay of Fundy, he was apparently looking for good land on which to farm and for a quiet place where he could care for his wife and sons. In that respect, Heinrich Stief typified German immigrants living in Pennsylvania at the time. As historian Frederic Klees describes them, their "souls' desire was to till their own land or set up for themselves in business."[2]

For many poor immigrants newly arrived in America, however, obtaining their own land was not easy. English, Scottish, Irish, Welsh, German, Swiss, French, and other Europeans had been pouring into William Penn's

Quaker colony of Pennsylvania since 1683, and by 1766 the best land had already been taken. Whatever land remained was expensive or situated far from settled areas.[3]

The greatest influx to Pennsylvania in the 1700s originated in the Palatinate of southern Germany—the area around the upper Rhine River—where 150 years of war and economic collapse had devastated the countryside. By 1727, German migration to Pennsylvania had reached such proportions that one alarmed observer compared the deluge to the Saxon invasion of Britain in the fifth century.[4]

Increasingly crowded conditions in Pennsylvania in the ensuing decades of the eighteenth century eventually shifted the focus of settlement to other areas of North America. One such place was the quiet Acadian backwater of old Nova Scotia; one person who had a particular interest in land settlement was Benjamin Franklin.

It was a vacant parcel of fertile land in Acadia that brought Benjamin Franklin and Heinrich Stief into the same sphere. The first wanted to turn a profit selling land; the other wanted to make a life by farming it. They lived worlds apart. One man was destined to enjoy a life of wealth and fame; the other would eke out an unremarked existence in a remote colony in the north. The former helped found a country; the latter founded a family. One would stand in the spotlight of history, the other in the sunlight that shone on his own fields beside the muddy Petitcodiac River in colonial Nova Scotia.

But if Heinrich Stief would have shunned the limelight of historical events, sixteen years after his arrival in Pennsylvania he found himself on the fringe of a political dispute that came to have far-reaching consequences. When he landed in Philadelphia in 1749, he could never have guessed that he would one day cross paths with the famous Benjamin Franklin. And although neither Heinrich Stief, nor Franklin himself, nor anyone else knew it then, they stood on the threshold of an upheaval that would transform the heart and soul of North America.

Since the eventful decade-and-a-half between the Seven Years' War and the American Revolution, Benjamin Franklin's life has undergone much inquiry. In libraries across North America, shelf after shelf carries books about the famous inventor from Philadelphia—the man who brought lightning down from the sky. In the two centuries since his death, numerous scholars have dedicated their careers to the study of his life, each with a different story to tell.

While there aren't many books about Heinrich Stief on the library shelves of the world, his life has nevertheless attracted the attention of a multitude of his descendants. Since the family gathering in 1867 and perhaps before, family members have been collecting the anecdotes, telling the tales, and preserving the memory of the European who founded the Steeves family in North America. For a man about whom not much is known, the legends have been surprisingly tenacious and prolific.

First came the stories of the eight families from Philadelphia who prevailed in the face of adversity—the stories of men and women who braved the unknown to establish themselves in a remote wilderness. The legends speak of terribly harsh conditions with insufficient food, and of the first winter on the Petitcodiac River when they subsisted for months on little more than turnip mush.

There was the legend of the sea journey from Philadelphia to the Bay of Fundy—a disjointed chronicle that included a side trip up the Saint John River and a violent storm in the bay. The sloop was very crowded, apparently, and the captain's name was said to be John Hall. There was also the myth of a second boat from Philadelphia—the boat that was supposed to bring additional supplies to the Petitcodiac, but which never appeared.

There was the story of Belliveau, an Acadian refugee who encountered Heinrich Stief and his companions, and taught them the survival skills necessary to avoid starvation that first desperate winter.

There was the story of Jacob Treitz, Heinrich Stief's compatriot, who traded his last family heirloom, a silver plate, for a few days worth of provisions; the story of two of the settlers walking thirty miles through the snowy woods to plead for supplies at Fort Cumberland; the tale of Heinrich Stief constructing a crude dug-out canoe, and paddling the unlikely craft across Shepody Bay to the fort, on another occasion, to seek food for his struggling family. All the legends speak of men and women of courage—determined individuals who persevered in the face of seemingly insurmountable odds.

Then there was the myth of Osnabruck, the German city where Heinrich Stief was thought to have originated. It was an unconfirmed rumour which, by the beginning of the twentieth century, had become a fixture in family lore. For a genealogist, there lay the difficulty; it was a piece of the puzzle that did not seem to fit.

On the subject of European ancestry, I recalled Dr. Yoder's comment: "The principal problem faced by the Pennsylvania German genealogist is that of determining the place of origin of his European ancestor."[5] For Steeves family members, the Osnabruck problem might have been described as unsolvable. An amateur genealogist had other ideas.

But why did I bother to search for a distant ancestor whose face I would never see, whose voice I would never hear? What impulse kept me looking when the trail had grown cold, when all hope of discovery had disappeared? Perhaps it was the same drive that fosters the ingenuity of any family genealogist, particularly the one who doggedly persists with the search for the long-lost relative who refuses to be found.

On the other hand, it may have been the same yearning that would prompt an Albert County farmer, after he had worked in his fields and barns all day, to return to his house in the evening, and after supper sit with his wife in front of their fireplace, stare into the flames, and wonder about his forebears. And if they were both descended from the Pennsylvania settlers who came to the Petitcodiac River, then his wife would wonder with him: Who were they? Where did they come from? What brought them to America? What kind of people were they to have engendered such long-enduring legends, the legends that came to sustain a family's memory for eight generations?

Old Burying Ground, Fort Beauséjour, looking toward Cumberland Basin.

CHAPTER 2

Beginnings

It was my grandmother who first put me on the trail of my Pennsylvania ancestors. Always the star to my wandering barque, that kindly woman set me on a course of discovery about the time when a boy begins to investigate for himself such puzzling philosophical riddles as the meaning of life and death, and the nature of time.

One summer afternoon, she took me for a stroll along the railroad tracks to the Boundary Creek Cemetery. I must have been about fourteen years old. The railway line between Moncton and Saint John ran near the back of the farm, and we were walking along the crushed rock beside the tracks—either on our way to pick blueberries, or going to the Baptist church; I don't remember which.

We came to the little cemetery nestled between the tracks and the church. Partly fenced in, the place was bordered on two sides by evergreen trees and bushes. Grandmother led the way, and in we went.

Crooked rows of weathered tombstones were arranged across an uneven carpet of rough grass, and small mounds and depressions created a hilly effect in the yard. The grey, white, and salmon-coloured stones leaned at odd angles to each other, their irregular poses suggesting to my young mind the various dispositions of the departed. Even with it under my feet, the graveyard seemed a strange and distant place. It was the final resting place, grandmother explained, of her husband's ancestors. My grandfather's name was Abel Saunders Jones.

As I came face-to-face with the names of his ancestors carved on their lichen-covered stones, I stepped into another world. Suddenly I had a personal, seemingly uncharted history to explore—one that reached beyond my own short life into the mysterious unknown. On that summer day, the tombstones became signposts to the past.

Jane Mitton, 1808-1890, great-granddaughter of Jacob Treitz and Charles Jones.

Ephraim Steves, 1805-1883, grandon of Heinrich Stief and Matthias Sommer.

As Grandmother and I walked back to the farm, we heard the whistle of a train coming down the line. We promptly got well off to the side of the tracks and stood waiting in the bushes as a blast of smoke and steel went barrelling past, furiously blowing the trees, and shaking the ground under our feet. "Here it comes, there it goes," ventured my youthful imagination—perhaps like time itself.

Back at the farmhouse, Grandmother showed me how to arrange my new-found ancestors' names in a chart that would show their blood relationships. I had the beginnings of a time-map that could be expanded into the past like a borderless jigsaw puzzle. From that moment, my hobby took flight; I had become an amateur genealogist.

The game of collecting family names lured me into a happy routine for a long time after. And the more names I collected, the farther the branches of my family tree extended into the unknown. Interconnecting lines of generations past sprang into being, and the chart took on the look of a spider's web. Second cousins had married each other; third cousins had married third cousins once-removed. Holding the tree together were some old farmers and their wives whose odd-sounding names made up a young boy's map of family history.

Once I had found their names, the next challenge was to ferret the bits and pieces of their stories from days gone by—tales that were forgotten, long since lost, or hidden away for decades in the cupboard drawer of some distant cousin. Although they'd lived mostly quiet farming lives, far from the important events of the day, my ancestors had their own stories to tell. And, as I came to discover, their stories were not without dignity and moment.

Collecting ancestor stories wasn't the only source of excitement on the busy farm where summer days were filled with wonder and adventure. Fishing in the brook, building forts in the woods, or catching stray mice in the barn—there were countless fantasies to live out, and myriad places to explore. Meals often included those Maritime exotics, goosetongues and samphires—the wild marsh greens whose delights are known to every living soul around the Bay of Fundy. Picking greens in summer on the mud flats beside the Petitcodiac River complemented everyday farm-life: shelling peas on the porch, pulling carrots from the garden, or chewing on a piece of rhubarb out behind the barn. The sour taste of a fresh rhubarb stalk seemed a suitable balance to a life of sweet and glorious adventure.

Another early memory comes to mind: my grandmother wiping her flour-covered hands on her apron, chasing me and my brothers out of her pantry, and sending

Solomon Jones, 1802-1875.   Margaret Lutz, 1800-1886.
Courtesy of Judi Berry Steeves

us down to the river to find some greens for dinner. Characteristically, I came back with the biggest bunch of greens my little arms could carry—mud, sticks, weeds, grass, and all.

The river was a far-away place where a boy could explore to his heart's content. Where the heavy marsh grass gave way to the salt weeds at the river's edge, there grew the object of my mission. From June till September, goosetongues and samphires sprang up in the mud—the sticky, brown mud for which the river was once famous.[1] In summers, I was never alone at the river. Nearby were timid mice and other small mammals, raucous seagulls and cheerful lowland birds, and always the timeless smell of the sea.

Although my grandmother Lena was the one who introduced me to my Boundary Creek ancestors, it was author Dr. Esther Clark Wright who fired

The Ancestry of Abel S. Jones

Abel JONES
b. March 17, 1832
d. December 14, 1895

Solomon JONES
b. January 27, 1804
d. March 25, 1875

Margaret LUTZ
b. March 23, 1800
d. December 23, 1886

Calvin Abel JONES
b. December 17, 1858
d. 1948

Catherine STEEVES
b. December 3, 1833
d. February 27, 1910

Ephraim STEEVES
b. February 27, 1805
d. October 25, 1883

Jane MITTON
b. 1808
d. August 25, 1890

Abel Saunders JONES
b. November 26, 1896
d. June 15, 1985

Maude Clara STEEVES
b. March 15, 1863
d. August 25, 1934

Lewis Edward STEEVES
b. June 4, 1812
d. January 24, 1893

Lucy Anne JONES
b. 1816
d. 1896

John STEEVES
b. February 28, 1782
d. September 29, 1857

Nancy TRITES
b. May 12, 1787
d. February 21, 1848

8 The Search for Heinrich Stief

Refurbished tombstone of Heinrich Stief

Abraham Trites
1751–1810

my teenaged imagination with her life-and-death stories of early days on the Petitcodiac River and of the first Welsh and German settlers who had come from distant Pennsylvania. Dr. Wright was a locally renowned historian and genealogist whose several books about pioneer life in New Brunswick and Nova Scotia put flesh on the bones of history. Once I began reading her engrossing tales about the passage of sloops and ships on the Bay of Fundy, of pioneer adventure, and of the settlers' early survival on samphire greens, I was hooked.

The author at work in the Boundary Creek Cemetery, 1996.
Courtesy of Edith Hoar

My grandfather Jones's genealogy became a rich field of discovery for many years after my first explorations in the Boundary Creek Cemetery. Travelling to cemeteries in Westmorland and Albert Counties on the weekends, and pestering my relatives for stories, I latched onto every scrap of information about my ancestors I could find. Sifting through the collected data in my spare time after school, eventually I could trace the long connection back to Dr. Wright's original Welsh and German settlers on the Petitcodiac River. And the way those pioneer families had intermarried within their small community, my grandfather claimed descent from no less than five of the first immigrants from Pennsylvania: Charles Jones, Heinrich Stief, Michael Lutz, Matthias Sommer, and Jacob Treitz.

Those five men had signed an agreement in 1766 with a well-known Philadelphia merchant and land speculator by the name of John Hughes, himself a sometime farmer and a good friend of Benjamin Franklin. Hughes and Franklin had contracted with the British government in Halifax to procure settlers to repopulate the rich marshland at the head of the Bay of Fundy left vacant after the tragic deportation of the Acadians eleven years before.[2]

CHAPTER 3

Dancing up a Terrible Storm

The seeds were sown for the great migration to the British colony of Nova Scotia when several thousand French-speaking Acadians were forcibly removed from their farms around the Bay of Fundy and scattered to the wind. An event that today would be condemned as ethnic cleansing had suddenly changed the course of North American history. It is not a happy story. But it was that story and subsequent events that opened the way for a little group of poor farmers in Pennsylvania to make a new beginning.

As early as 1636—when Boston was a dirty fishing village and Philadelphia still a forest—the Acadians were constructing dykes and tilling the soil on the marshes around the Fundy coast until they could lay claim to what was probably the best farmland on the Atlantic seaboard. Greater things than husbandry were afoot in America, however. A century later, Acadia would become an important pawn in a more important game of conquest.[1]

The subject of deporting the entire Acadian population from their homes was debated by New England governors as early as 1711, but an idea of such magnitude had lain dormant until it took root, forty years later, "in the fertile mind of [William] Shirley," the governor of Massachusetts. Although measures of such severity were opposed by the British goverment in London, Shirley encouraged Nova Scotia's Lieutenant-Governor, Charles Lawrence, until Lawrence was convinced of the necessity of the action.[2]

Using as a pretext the Acadians' refusal to take an unqualified oath of allegiance, Lawrence carried the plan into execution. Contrary to orders from London in which Lawrence was advised "to act with caution, prudence, and tact in dealing with the 'Neutrals,' as the Acadians were called," he took matters into his own hands. In the verdict of Canadian historian George Wrong, the obdurate lieutenant-governor was also a soldier: "a stern, relentless man, without pity, and his mind was made up."[3]

Beginning in September 1755, approximately seven thousand Acadians living around the Bay of Fundy were rounded up and forcibly herded onto sea-going transports bound for the American colonies. Many were exiled to Louisiana, Europe, and the French West Indies. Of those who escaped the deportation, hundreds fled into the surrounding woods and hills. Some

A Portion of Nouvelle France, "Canada Louisiane et Terres Angloises," par le Sr. d'Anville, Novembre 1755, sous le Privelége de l'Académie.
Courtesy of Tony Steele

headed to temporary safety in Quebec. Others encamped on Northumberland Strait and on the Miramichi River, where they had a better chance of avoiding the British soldiers for a few years. A decade later, a lone Acadian refugee remaining on the Petitcodiac River came to have a life-saving impact on a little group of settlers living in Pennsylvania at the time.

It may be tempting to romanticize the great Acadian eviction, as Longfellow did so famously in his story of Evangeline: displaced families, destruction of homes, much shedding of tears—his tale is one of sorrow and woe. But while Longfellow's hero and heroine mourned on some imaginary shore, the strife in Acadia continued long after the transports left in 1755.

For their part, roving bands of Acadians in Nova Scotia sporadically attacked the British soldiers, while Mi'kmaq warriors, inspired by the notorious French priest Le Loutre, killed British soldiers and settlers alike.[4]

In 1756, bedevilled by the strength of Acadian and Mi'kmaq resistance, Lawrence, who had become governor, proffered a £25 bounty on Native scalps. With so hefty a price on their victims' heads, his soldiers were quick to include black-haired Acadian scalps in their grisly harvest. The bounties were paid despite the objections of John Huston, a New England trader and sea captain who was in charge of the military chest at the time. So offended was Huston that he declared: "the curse of God should ever attend such guilty deeds...." It was a dark period in Acadian history.[5]

Ten years later, John Hughes's Welsh and German settlers from Philadelphia would experience Huston's benevolence when they arrived on the Petitcodiac with insufficient provisions to see them through the winter. According to a subsequent chart of expenses, Huston provided the settlers with supplies valued at £34, 10 shillings—no trifling sum. From the lack of evidence, it appears Captain Huston was never reimbursed for his generosity.[6]

The expulsion was a sorry business but it was not the first time a people had been so completely devastated. By the end of the 1600s, Louis XIV of France had driven nearly half a million Protestant French Huguenots into Switzerland and the Palatinate of the Rhine—a calamity that set the stage for the great German migration to America that was to follow in the eighteenth century.[7]

In the aftermath of the heartbreaking Acadian deportation, Governor Lawrence issued a proclamation calling for new settlers to come to Nova Scotia. He and his council at Halifax were anxious to secure Acadia for the British crown at a time when French interests in America were still to be reckoned with. Lawrence's intention, states Nova Scotia archivist Thomas Akins, was "to engage such great numbers of substantial and reputable Protestant families from the neighboring colonies to settle on the vacated lands...." It's doubtful that some poor German farmers living near Philadelphia could be called substantial and reputable, but they needed land and they offered to go.[8]

Lawrence's proclamation of October 1758 announced that land grants of 100,000 acres were available to interested parties. Despite an exaggerated description of the lands, which "never fail of crops nor need manuring," the overture received only a tentative response. The promise of good land was not sufficient to satisfy prospective New England grantees who wanted assurances of religious and political freedom. Lawrence initially resisted the call to offer incoming settlers the opportunity to elect their own representatives to the legislative assembly, but the pragmatic governor had little choice. "His desire to attract settlers," wrote Esther Clark Wright, "overcame his dislike of such a democratic innovation."[9]

Three months following the first proclamation, a second was issued—one that was more to the New Englanders' liking. Regarding religious freedom, the land was available to "persons of all persuasions, Papists excepted...." The government and the courts of Nova Scotia were described as similar to those of New England, and townships of fifty inhabitants would be entitled to send two representatives to the assembly in Halifax.[10]

This time the results were more encouraging. Companies were formed in the American colonies, and agents were dispatched to investigate and survey the Nova Scotia lands. By May 1760, the first New England settlers began to arrive in the province, opening a new chapter in the long and often troubled history of Acadia.[11]

Meanwhile, France was faring poorly in the war with Britain. After several initial victories in 1755, French fortunes in America took a turn for the worse. Following a two-month siege, British general James Wolfe, with 13,000 men and officers, captured Fortress Louisbourg on July 25, 1758. On the Plains of Abraham one year later, Quebec fell to the audacious General Wolfe, who got himself killed in the attack. In the autumn of 1760, the final French holdout of Montréal was taken by British soldiers and American militia, bringing French dreams of an American empire to an end. France's claims east of the Mississippi were reduced to its former possessions in the West Indies plus the rocky islands of St. Pierre and Miquelon off the coast of Newfoundland, its final holdout in the north Atlantic.[12]

On October 11 of that year, to celebrate the victory in style, Governor Lawrence entertained the Halifax elite at a grand ball at Government House. All the gentlemen and ladies of the town were in attendance, and Lawrence danced up a storm. During the festivities, he began to perspire from so much dancing, and drank from a pitcher of cold water. He quickly took a chill, and shortly after developed pneumonia. Eight days later, the fifty-year-old governor was dead.[13]

Left behind by Lawrence's sudden death were the bright beginnings of an enterprising young province plus the shameful legacy of an uprooted Acadian people who would spend the next two-and-a-half centuries trying to regain their stolen pride and their lost sense of place in a land they loved.

CHAPTER 4

A Flamboyant Speculator

The death of Charles Lawrence in 1760 did nothing to slow the resettlement of the now vacant land around the Bay of Fundy. Once the war between France and England ended, the scheme to repopulate Acadia with Protestant settlers entered a phase that was described as "a veritable carnival of land grabbing." Would-be land proprietors—some of them honest businessmen, others unscrupulous profiteers—tried to outperform each other in their attempts to obtain the best land for themselves and their friends. Quick profits were to be made, and there was much good land to be had.[1]

About this time, there appeared at the forefront of affairs an Ulster emigrant from Virginia—an eccentric land speculator of extraordinary talents by the name of Colonel Alexander McNutt. "[H]ighly persuasive, distinctly untrustworthy"—as historian Brebner has forever marked him—he was an unrepentant schemer of the first rank. Never content with his accomplishment, McNutt was always dashing off to initiate a new land deal before the ink had dried on the one before. Although John Hughes's Philadelphia settlers would probably never meet McNutt, he was about to exert a profound influence on their lives. And while the settlers seem determined to remain hidden from view, McNutt presents a different story. The man is worthy of a book in itself, but hopefully a brief sketch will do justice to the drama that was his life.[2]

Alexander McNutt was born in Ireland about 1725, the eldest son of Alexander McNutt Senior. Twenty-five years earlier, the McNutt family had migrated from their ancestral home in southern Scotland where the name had been spelled McNaught. Alexander McNutt Jr. was looked upon as a well-educated young man of "excellent address" when he arrived in Virginia sometime before 1753. Intending to advance his standing in America, McNutt courted the friendship of Virginia's governor, Robert Dinwiddie, with whom he gained a useful alliance.[3]

A self-styled man of action, McNutt served with British troops in numerous campaigns during the French and Indian War. He fought alongside George Washington during General Braddock's disastrous battle at Fort Duquesne in 1755, and also served under Major Lewis in a campaign against the Shawnee Indians in 1756. Following that latter engagement, McNutt sent a critical report to his friend, Governor Dinwiddie, regarding Lewis's unsuccessful tactics. Unknown to McNutt, the report made its way back to Lewis, who was displeased with McNutt's appraisal. When Lewis and McNutt met one day in a street in Staunton, Virginia, some harsh words followed, and, before long, the two were down in the mud with fists flying.[4]

While the extent of Alexander McNutt's involvement in the taking of Louisbourg from the French in 1758 is uncertain, it is unlikely that he would willingly stand on the sidelines of a good fight. During the course of that historic siege, he encountered Governor Lawrence and "unfolded vast plans" to repopulate Acadia with settlers from the north of Ireland.[5]

Notable players were in no short supply at the battle of Louisbourg. General Wolfe's chief-of-staff was Lieutenant-Colonel Guy Carleton, who later served as governor of Canada. Another up-and-coming protagonist at Louisbourg was the sailing master of the supply ship H.M.S. *Pembroke*, James Cook. The thirty-year-old Yorkshireman had joined the Royal Navy only three years before and was about to launch the world-wide sailing career for which history would remember him. A third noteworthy contestant at Louisbourg was Lieutenant-Colonel Robert Monckton. Three years earlier, Monckton had commanded the capture of Fort Beauséjour in Acadia from the French. Later, he would see a new township on the Petitcodiac River created in his honour—a parcel of land that a twenty-year-old surveyor in 1765 would bring to the attention of Alexander McNutt, Benjamin Franklin, and Philadelphia merchant John Hughes.[6]

Although Alexander McNutt's numerous military adventures had gained the approbation of King George II, they were minor activities compared to his passionate schemes for colonization. McNutt's voracious appetite for land-settlement deals involved him in so many projects at the same time and put him on the move so often, that the governor and council in Halifax were flabbergasted by his grandiose plans.[7]

Canadian historian W. O. Raymond paints a vivid picture of the rogue McNutt:

> He delighted in great undertakings and his zeal and impetuosity made him at times a veritable stormy petrel....As long as he lived he wore the court costume of the reign of George II, with buckles and ornamental buttons of silver, and trimmings of gold lace, a cocked hat, powdered hair and top boots. His sword never left his side....[8]

McNutt's sword was a gift from old King George who had bestowed on him the honourary title of colonel in recognition of his enthusiastic military service. As to McNutt's shortcomings, Raymond charitably acknowledges:

> While Alexander McNutt accomplished much as a colonizer, one is amazed at the vastness of his plans and speculations which did not mature. His failure in many of his undertakings was due to attempting too much, and the consequent lack of attention to details. He was quick to think, quick to act, quick to *write*. His memorials to the Lords of Trade and the Governors of Nova Scotia are in some cases very voluminous, seemingly written with haste, not always elegant in style, and expressed with greater freedom than was customary in those days.[9]

By 1762, Alexander McNutt had crossed paths with John Hughes. Through Hughes's efforts, McNutt convinced a number of merchants and leading men to join his attempts to obtain grants from the Nova Scotia Council. When the deals in Philadelphia were concluded, twenty-two men, many of them prominent in their various circles, had formed a speculating syndicate comprising four companies, all dependent on the insidious intrigues of Colonel Alexander McNutt.[10]

The companies then began to solicit settlers to occupy the lands McNutt was to obtain. They had their work cut out: five hundred families were to be settled during four years in a 100,000-acre township. The role of the speculators, or proprietors as they were properly called, was vital:

> The proprietors were the owners of the land and were responsible collectively for the improvement of the new plantation. "More specifically they were responsible for inducing and enlisting settlers and new comers, for locating home lots and dwelling

houses, for building highways and streets, for subdividing the adjacent arable land, and subjecting the meadow and forests, for a time at least to a common management."[11]

British surveyor Joseph F. W. DesBarres set the tone for the success of Nova Scotia townships when he informed King George III:

> The great business of effectually settling such a Colony, of cherishing and fostering it during its infancy, of directing and regulating its pursuits as it advances to maturity...will afford an ample field to the most vigorous exertion of talents.[12]

Alexander McNutt doubtless believed he possessed such talent for fostering new settlements. But, just as things were getting underway, McNutt suddenly took passage to England and did not return to Philadelphia until September, 1764. By May of that year, John Hughes had lined up a number of potential settlers, his own brother included, all waiting for McNutt to make the next move.[13]

To his alarm, Hughes discovered he couldn't trust "such a fertile liar."[14] So exasperated was Hughes that he warned of a lawsuit for breach of contract. His intended settlers, he told McNutt, had:

> *put themselves in a posture for Removing this Spring... [and many had] put themselves out of Business in the way of their Trades, and many others Sold or Gave up their Little farms, being fully perswaded of the truth of our Informations....*

Hughes's settlers were threatening his arrest and were ready to tear him to pieces. He implored McNutt:

> *for God sake Sir Do not procrastinate any Longer or our plan may Miscarry and we be put to a Monstrous Expence, besides the Loss of Reputation, which as I am, not only a Merchant but a farmer, and Iron Master, will Injure me Extremely in my Business in Each Branch.*[15]

Unable to comprehend why McNutt had left him in the lurch, Hughes protested:

> *it is Realy very Extraordinary that you Shou'd Enter into Such Engagements as you have Done with me & as I have Done with others on your Credit and by Your Orders, And afterwards to Leave the place and go home to Brittain and Leave me a Sacrifice to the people, and my character as an honest man Call'd in Question....*

Sacrifice to the people, indeed. One year later, John Hughes would truly become a sacrifice to the people, although the attack would come from an unexpected quarter. Moreover, Hughes would never have imagined that the blame could be laid at the doorstep of his friend Benjamin Franklin.

Perhaps McNutt took John Hughes's letter to heart because the colonel soon came sailing back to Philadelphia. Once the unpredictable speculator had his feet on the ground, he wasted no time getting back to his favourite game—this time, pitching his land-promotion schemes to the listening ears of the pastor of St. Michael's German Lutheran Church.

Alexander McNutt exerted a tremendous influence on the recolonization of old Nova Scotia following the deportation of the Acadians. It would be difficult to imagine the shape the region might have taken without his charismatic presence. Indeed, Canadian author Thomas Raddall describes McNutt simply as "the tireless promoter of Nova Scotia settlements...." Perhaps Raymond said it best: "His was truly a chequered and eventful career."[16]

Whatever McNutt's shortcomings may have been, by the time his Philadelphia partners became aware of them it was too late to turn back. Settlers had been engaged, and plans were underway to move them to Nova Scotia.

Not a great deal is known about McNutt's land syndicate which resettled Heinrich Stief and his friends at the head of the Bay of Fundy, but certainly more than is known about the settlers. A look at some of the Philadelphia speculators might seem like a side-track from the search for Heinrich Stief, but one must go where the evidence lies. In the realm of historical investigation, it might be added, a genealogist sometimes has to go around in circles to reach the heart of the matter.

The land company headed by John Hughes included three other men: John Cox Jr., Anthony Wayne, and Hughes's close friend, Dr. Benjamin Franklin. Although their group was sometimes referred to as "Franklin & Co.," Benjamin Franklin had only a background role in the partnership. It may have been Alexander McNutt who first applied Franklin's name to the Monckton grant in an effort to feature a prominent name on his applications.[17]

From the lack of other mention, it would appear Cox played little part in the endeavour. He and his father were merchants in Philadelphia, but, other than that, little is known.[18]

A great deal is known about Anthony Wayne. Wayne acted as field agent for the group, and the young man travelled to distant Halifax in 1765, when only twenty years old, to help McNutt and three other members of their syndicate secure grants from the governor and council.[19]

A natural-born surveyor, Wayne had an eagle-eye for good land. He was an avid letter-writer, and the descriptions he sent to John Hughes during his explorations in Nova Scotia that first spring and summer were highly encouraging.

> *I do assure you the Land exceeds any Idea I ever could have formed of it before I saw it....I need say no more of the land than this — it is sufficient to produce any kind of grain whatsoever & an Industrious man may make a fortune in a few years. Do you provide Settlers & I Engage to find land that is good & well Situated.*[20]

Wayne's evaluation of the country was favourable, but his estimation of McNutt's participation was not. And although John Hughes might have been wiser to cut his losses with McNutt, he persevered. Shortly before, Hughes and some of his land-speculating associates had extracted a signed commitment from McNutt that he would live up to his agreements. But the writing was already on the wall; the good intentions professed in McNutt's commitment were empty promises. In July 1765, Anthony Wayne wrote again to Hughes from Halifax, charging that McNutt had secretly tried to supplant the interests of the speculators—the same gentlemen in whose best interests he had agreed to act.[21]

In August, Wayne wrote to Hughes again. "I am sorry to Inform you, that our affairs has not met with the Desired suckcess in this place as we Expected. I could wish Col.n McNutt had acted more Open in Respect of his Grant...."

Although McNutt was becoming a problem, Wayne hoped that the efforts of their illustrious friend Benjamin Franklin would be more helpful. "And as Mr. Franklin is in England," Wayne wrote, "we shall have a good Oppertunity of Making our terms there. I fear Col.n McNutt will fail if it be left to him as he is Concerned for too many seperate Company's."[22]

Matters only got worse. Three months after the first revelation of McNutt's double-dealing, Wayne learned that the colonel had been up to his tricks again.

> *I have been Informed by several Gentlemen of the Council, that Col.n McNutt had made Interest privately against us, & Said that we had Nothing to do with the terms, or anything Else, & was only Employed, as Surveyors under him....*

In the final analysis, McNutt's "Despicable & Unjust prosecdings" led Wayne to conclude that the colonel "has been rather a Determent than of Service to us."[23]

Anthony Wayne's energetic abilities and keen powers of observation would lead him into greater endeavours during the American Revolution. Who knows, but possibly it was the surveying expedition on the Petitcodiac River in 1765 that gave the youthful Anthony Wayne a taste for far-flung adventure—a proclivity that was to find fulfillment ten years later when George Washington came looking for generals to fight a Revolutionary War.

Wayne was a strikingly handsome man who "carried himself with a very fetching and gallant air." Despite a reputation for rowdyism, his forthright personality endeared him to the hearts and minds of his country folk. During the American Revolution, Wayne's valiant leadership and reckless manoeuvres in the face of danger would earn him the nickname "mad Anthony" by his troops.[24]

If Americans during the Revolutionary War counted themselves lucky to have the dynamic and energetic Anthony Wayne fighting on their side, Hughes's Philadelphia settlers were no less fortunate in 1765 to find young Wayne devoted to their welfare. His trip to Nova Scotia to survey the land and meet with the council was highly beneficial to all concerned.

Partly because of Alexander McNutt's devious plots against his own associates, and partly due to lengthy delays imposed by the Board of Trade in London, the Philadelphia syndicate experienced considerable difficulty obtaining title to their township. The problem was compounded by councillors in Halifax who doled out the best land to their cronies and friends.[25]

Despite the obstacles, Monckton township was finally granted to McNutt and his speculators on October 31, 1765. On the following day, a new British statute called the Stamp Act was scheduled to come into effect. The act imposed a tax on legal transactions of every kind, and thus there was sound reason for getting as much business as possible out of the way before November 1.[26]

Forming a twelve-by-twelve-mile square, Monckton township's great sweep of 100,000 acres extended back from the north side of the Petitcodiac River where the town of Moncton sprang to life in the next century. Fronting the river were endless stretches of fertile marsh backed by wooded uplands running with game. Six miles beyond, a shouldering ridge of low, dark hills stood aloof in the distance.[27]

Three months later, the participants in the colonization scheme were ready to make a formal agreement. For the Welsh and German farmers who gathered with Anthony Wayne in John Hughes's Philadelphia office on

January 27, 1766, the occasion would signal a new direction in the course of their lives. Once they had decided to leave the thriving colony of Pennsylvania and begin life anew on the banks of the Petitcodiac River, there could be no turning back. A £1,000 penalty for default was a financial disincentive against breaking their pledge. As Esther Clark Wright described the historic event, the twenty-seventh of January 1766 was their "day of decision."[28]

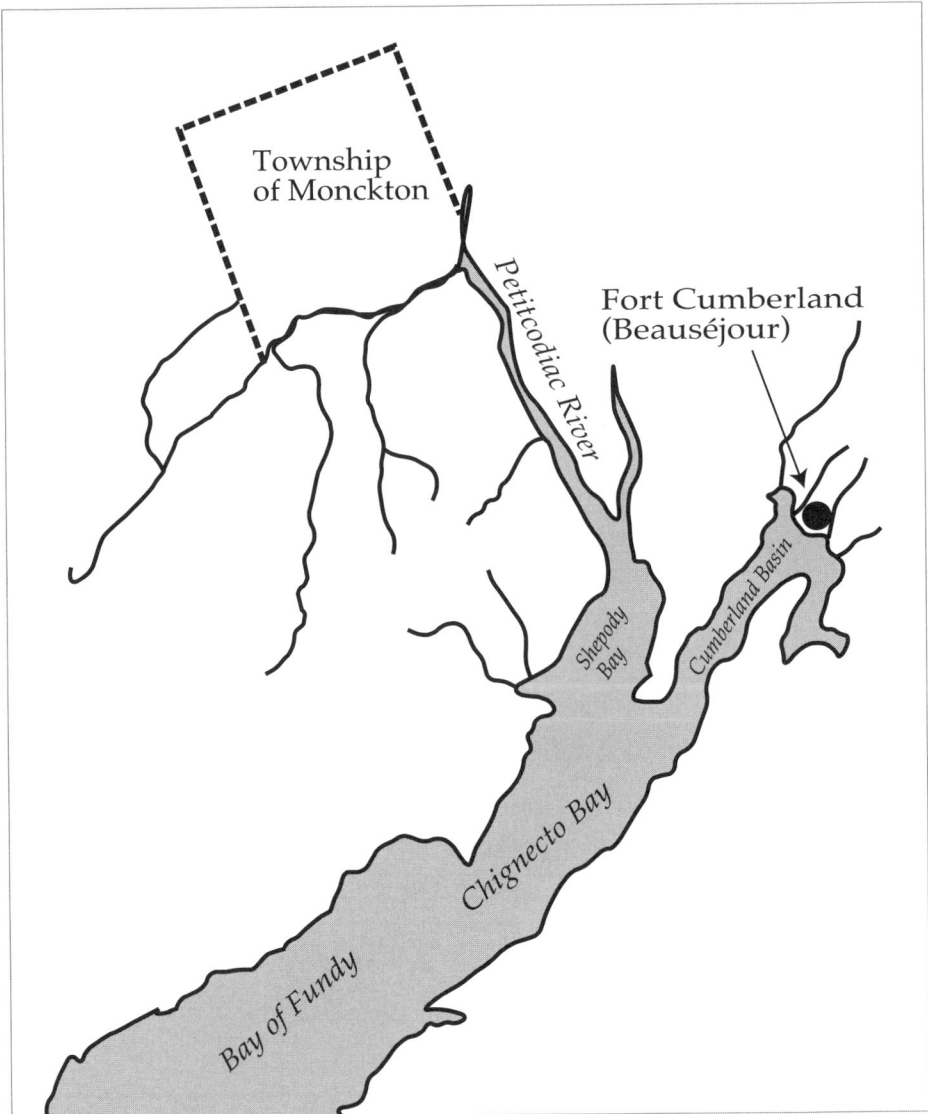

Part of old Nova Scotia in 1766.

CHAPTER 5

Searching for Ancestors

The agreement signed in Philadelphia by the Welsh and Pennsylvania-German settlers lay buried in the darkness of the Hughes family papers for a long time after that January day in 1766. The papers, including the settlers' agreement, were handed down through generations of the Hughes family until the whole lot was donated to the Historical Society of Pennsylvania sometime after 1824—the year the society was founded. Then, after that brief exposure to daylight, the papers and the agreement went back into the dark.[1]

One hundred and seventy-six years after the signing ceremony in John Hughes's office, a forty-eight-year-old historian from the Maritimes packed her suitcase and headed to Philadelphia. It was the bleak spring of 1942— that bleak year when the flames of the Second World War were spreading relentless destruction into the four corners of Europe. Esther Clark Wright's mind, however, was not focused on the violent conflagration raging throughout Europe and beyond, but rather on the comings and goings of a little group of peace-loving Pennsylvania-German settlers who had departed their European homeland some two centuries before.

In 1942, Dr. Wright held a Ph.D. from Radcliffe College, and was a professor of economics and history at Acadia University in Wolfville, Nova Scotia. By then, Dr. Wright had authored a score of articles about Maritime life and history, and in the next twenty-five years would write a dozen books on the subject. Dr. Wright had travelled to the Historical Society of Pennsylvania that spring to follow up a clue, as she later wrote, "in one of the Monographs of W. F. Ganong...." In addition to her background in Maritime history there was a personal component to the search: she was descended from Heinrich Stief.[2]

Ganong's clue, whatever it was, led to a unique discovery. One day just before Easter that year, as Dr. Wright rooted around in the collected papers of long-deceased Philadelphia merchant John Hughes, she uncovered the Articles of Agreement, signed on January 27, 1766 by the nine local farmers who had been recruited by Hughes for his company's land grant in old Nova Scotia.[3]

The agreement was of such significance to the history of the upper reaches of the Bay of Fundy that it became a focal point in *The Petitcodiac*, Dr. Wright's first book about those settlers and early life on the river. When *Samphire Greens* was published sixteen years later, the agreement again took centre stage. In the opening sentence of her book, Dr. Wright set the scene at the moment when Heinrich Stief took the quill pen in his calloused hand and signed his name "in the careful, upright German script he had learned in his homeland...."[4]

After studying those two works by Dr. Wright since my teenaged beginnings at family history, I could not deny an irrepressible urge to make the pilgrimage to Philadelphia to see the Articles of Agreement for myself.

By 1995, my first excursion to the Historical Society of Pennsylvania was long overdue. One bright September morning that year, with a touch of autumn in the Philadelphia air, I climbed the stone steps at 1300 Locust Street, expectant and hopeful. With seventeen million manuscripts and 564,000 books at my disposal, something interesting was bound to turn up. I paused momentarily on the threshold of a stately and formidable institution that contained probably the largest collection of genealogical material in the United States and possibly the world. I imagined its cavernous vaults shrouding the mysteries of the past. As I would soon discover, the task ahead of me was no less formidable than the institution I was about to enter.[5]

After registering at the front desk in the great, echoing lobby, I went on a self-guided tour of the open stacks. Once I'd got my bearings and sated my initial curiosity, I requested permission to examine the original Articles of Agreement which Dr. Wright had found more than fifty years before.

I was waiting at a designated table in the research room when the oversized document was brought to me. It was much larger than I had expected, and I had to stand up to take it in. With my hands spread flat on the wooden table, I leaned over the document, spellbound. Sentence by sentence, my eyes travelled over the lines of tidy script describing how the settlers were to establish their new community. I tried to imagine what had gone through their minds as John Hughes explained the agreement to them. I wondered how Dr. Wright reacted the day she had come face-to-face with this vibrant relic of colonial Maritime history.

Aligned near the lower right corner of the agreement were the signatures of Hughes's nine settlers, each with a red seal beside it. I was unprepared for the rich colour—the blood-red seals glowing like rubies on a mediaeval cloak.

With a magnifying glass at hand, I pored over the document. The faded, yellow paper was still in good condition two-and-a-quarter centuries after the agreement was signed. Measuring more than a foot square, the extensive agreement had been written on both sides of the page, possibly to conserve paper, but more likely to keep everything together on a single sheet. At some period in its history, the document had been folded in half three times, allowing it to be tucked away as a small, three-by-seven-inch packet. In the darkened folds of the yellowing paper, and in the red seals, cracked and chipped with age, time had left a signature of its own.[6]

The Articles of Agreement set out in much practical detail the conditions under which the settlers would create their township. A town centre was to be laid out in the proposed settlement, and each family would possess a lot 40 by 225 feet. As well, each family would receive farmland outside the future town, at the rate of two hundred acres per five persons. They were

Historical Society of Pennsylvania, containing possibly the largest collection of genealogical material in the world.

required to plant crops on the land: two acres of corn, one acre of meadow, fifty apple trees, and a quarter acre of hemp—all subject to a small quit-rent payable to the crown. The settlers were to assume the costs of surveying the lands, and were required to live in the township for a minimum of four years beginning May 1, 1766. At the end of five years, the settlers would

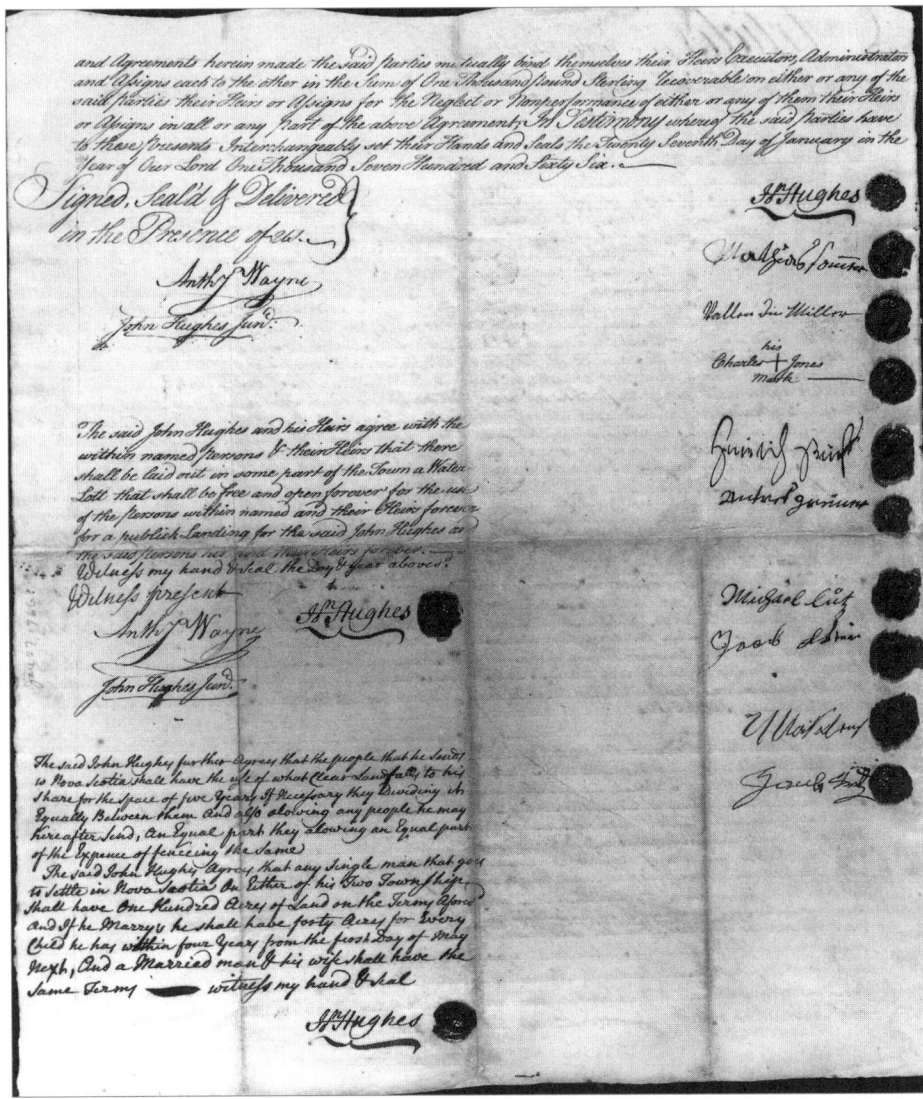

Articles of Agreement, January 27, 1766. The ten signatures, with their seals, on the right of the agreement are: John Hughes, Matthias Sommer, Valentin Miller, Charles (+) Jones, Heinrich Stief, Andrew Criner, Michael Lutz, Jacob Cline, Matthias Lentz, Jacob Treitz.

Courtesy of the Historical Society of Pennsylvania, John Hughes Papers pay Hughes and Company £5 for every one hundred acres they obtained. Once they had constructed a fence around their property and built a house with a stone or brick chimney, the land would be theirs.[7]

A clause added by Hughes at the end of the document, perhaps as a final concession, specified that the town would have common access to the river where a public landing would be built. Unallocated land would be available to the entire group for five years, or to any newcomers who might arrive at a later date. Furthermore, every unmarried male adult would receive one hundred acres of land, and those who married soon after would receive another forty acres for each child born within the first four years. This last stipulation, as Dr. Wright points out, was especially important to settlers like Heinrich Stief, Michael Lutz, and Jacob Treitz, whose eldest sons were approaching early manhood.[8]

The agreement specified that their journey to the township would commence within the month of April following—intended, no doubt, so they could arrive in time for the planting season. It was vital they get their crops planted early; their survival depended on what they could produce for themselves.

The plan was optimistic, albeit impractical given the difficult logistics required to transport entire families and their possessions from eighteenth-century Philadelphia to the wilds of Nova Scotia. Nevertheless, the underlying goal was clear. Both John Hughes and the government in Halifax wanted industrious farmers with strong backs, as well as vigorous women capable of bearing many children.

The terms of the agreement complied with Governor Lawrence's 1759 proclamation for land resettlement, and standard copies had been forwarded to McNutt's other Philadelphia land companies for their own prospective settlers to sign.[9]

The Articles of Agreement appeared to be straightforward, but I brought out the magnifying glass for a closer look; the document had a hidden story to tell.

First, the text of the agreement was not written by merchant John Hughes, as would be expected, but had been prepared in advance by Hughes's son, John Jr. The young man wrote like an artist, and his signature was easy to match to the text. With his steady hand and careful attention to detail, it was natural that the younger Hughes would be assigned the task of scripting the agreement. As early as 1762, at the age of seventeen, Hughes's son had been a partner in his father's store on Fourth Street. As well, he would be at his father's side when the Stamp Act crisis came close to wrecking their lives and almost destroying their land-settlement venture.[10]

In the days leading up to the signing ceremony on January 27, 1766, the weather in Philadelphia had been cold. Two weeks earlier, Benjamin Franklin's wife, Deborah, described the chill: "Our river is froze over. On monday morning laste it was 5 degrees Colder then aney time laste winter. I have my poor Chin froste bit with the Cold." On January 24, Philadelphia resident Elizabeth Drinker noted in her diary: "snow this afternoon, weather raw and cold."[11]

The day before the signing ceremony, however, the weather had suddenly turned mild: "fine weather," wrote Drinker in her diary that day. Maybe the settlers would have taken it as a promising sign had they read the entry in Drinker's diary for January 27: "fine Weather for Travellers."

Despite Philadelphia's mild spell, other things besides the weather were on the minds of the eight Germans and one Welshman who had crowded into John Hughes's office that day. Land near Philadelphia was becoming scarce, they knew, and political tensions with England were mounting. Just a few months before, the city had found itself embroiled in a violent political panic. Unrest was in the air.

On that January day, however, their minds were on the future, not the past. The document they were about to sign would change the course of their lives, and they wanted to obtain the best deal from the agreement.

What with all the changes they were about to make to the original plan, Hughes's son must have had a lemon handy. A few drops of lemon juice placed over the contentious passages and the corrected version would look as good as new. That is to say, almost like new. Faded over time, the original terms have remained. A closer examination revealed a host of last-minute changes.

First, the intended-settlers judged some of the requirements for settlement too difficult to fulfill. Instead of ten acres of corn land to be cultivated, the stipulation was reduced to two; three acres of meadow were changed to one; and the settlers' obligation to pay Hughes and Company for the land at the end of two years was extended to five.

Even the name of one intended settler underwent an eleventh-hour change. One signer that day was Andrew Criner, but Andrew was not the name originally listed in the opening paragraph of the document; the earlier name is now obliterated. Did John Hughes Jr. make a clerical error when he first inscribed Criner's name, or did Andrew arrive at the signing ceremony in another man's place?

One other name besides Andrew Criner's seemed not to fit with the rest. The first eight names in the body of the text were inscribed in the artistic hand of John Hughes Jr. But the name of Jacob Treitz—the last in the list—

was added later by the elder Hughes. Did Jacob arrive late at Hughes's office that day. Or, as Dr. Wright seems to suggest, were there reasons for him to hesitate until the last moment? Dr. Wright cryptically hints that Jacob Treitz might have received a disproportionately larger quantity of supplies from John Hughes because he "threatened to withdraw from the enterprise...."[12]

Although Jacob's name has never been found in any other contemporary record in Philadelphia, that short-fall would be rectified much later. Because he eventually settled on land that became the city of Moncton, Jacob Treitz would later be called "the father of Moncton."[13]

Once the agreement had been amended to the participants' satisfaction, the moment arrived when the farmers would sign their names. Their weathered hands were doubtless more used to the heft of a rake or a hoe than they were with the feel of a fine quill pen. John Hughes and Anthony Wayne had signed first. Then, a pause occurred, or perhaps another pen was obtained. Whichever happened, Matthias Sommer encountered a problem as he started to write his name: The ink in the quill had dried. Matthias got as far as "Matt," faintly scratching the first four letters of his name, but he quickly saw that it wasn't going to work. Another pause, the pen was dipped in the ink-pot, then a new start. But when Matthias went back to his name, he left the "M" unchanged, and began at the second letter. The double lettering of "att" had left an unmistakable glimpse into the past.

Of the nine farmers who made their solemn agreement with John Hughes and Anthony Wayne, only five arrived at the wharf with their families when it came time to depart on their journey north. Matthias Sommer, Charles Jones, Heinrich Stief, Michael Lutz, and Jacob Treitz had chosen to honour their commitment and throw their lots together. The other four—Vallentin Miller, Andrew Criner, Jacob Cline, and Matthias Lentz—failed to join their fellow signers for reasons that have never been clear.[14]

When their sloop left Philadelphia that spring, bound for the Bay of Fundy, Hughes's five were accompanied by three additional German families who had come on board through the auspices of two of the other Philadelphia land companies included in Alexander McNutt's syndicate. Settlers George Wortman and John Copple were contracted to Matthew Clarkson and Company, while Jacob Ricker had signed with the group headed by Dr. William Smith. Those three men brought the total number of families to eight.[15]

As well as executing the agreement with his own settlers, John Hughes needed to conclude negotiations with the two other land companies who were sending settlers to Monckton township. Moreover, they would need to engage a vessel and its crew for the passage and procure supplies. Much remained to be done.

The column of signatures on the Articles of Agreement was a compelling invitation for an inquiring genealogist to discover more about the men who signed with John Hughes. Certainly they were simple farmers, in no way destined for public life. Probably little educated, they would spend the better part of their lives providing for their families and trying to survive any way they could. But if their accomplishments do not fill the pages of history books, the same cannot be said of their Philadelphia sponsors.

At this stage, I found myself looking in strange places as I tried to understand the workings of the Philadelphia land syndicate. When the pieces of the puzzle began to merge, however, those places weren't so strange after all. The only strange thing was that John Hughes would find himself working with Benjamin Franklin's arch enemy—a nasty, drunken preacher named William Smith.

CHAPTER 6

"A Herd of Hogs"

Although William Smith's company provided only one settler for the venture, Smith's role was to be far more important than might be expected. William Smith was an Anglican clergyman at the time, and for several years was provost of the College of Philadelphia, a position he had obtained through the efforts of Benjamin Franklin. The favour was not returned, however, as Smith became a harsh adversary of Franklin. The Reverend William Smith was also an active member of Pennsylvania's Proprietary Party, which was continually at loggerheads with Franklin's ruling party of Quakers. Smith and Franklin afterwards became ardent foes.[1]

To appreciate the depth of their enmity, it's necessary to go back a few years to 1758 when the political wrangling in Pennsylvania had reached an unpleasant climax. That year, William Smith and his partner-to-be in the Nova Scotia land deal, William Moore, were jailed for libel. The Quaker-led Assembly declared Smith "a common Scribbler of Libels and false abusive Papers both against publick Bodies and private Persons...." William Smith would not soon forget the outrage.[2]

Philosophical in the face of Smith's rancour, Benjamin Franklin admitted: "I made that Man my Enemy by doing him too much Kindness." And since it was "the honestest Way of acquiring an Enemy," Franklin surmised that the unfortunate situation could best be exploited. Smith would keep him on his toes, and Franklin would "keep him an Enemy for that purpose." For Smith, tortured by jealousy over Franklin's power and prestige, the sentiment would have been galling.[3]

Historian Leonard Labaree pulls no punches in describing the irascible churchman:

> Smith was not respected or even liked, and he rarely enjoyed the confidence of leading men. He drank too much, was opinionated and unreliable. Ezra Stiles thought him "a contemptible drunken Character! of tolerable academic general Knowledge. But immoral, haughty, irreligious, and profane, avaricious and covetous, a consummate Hypocrite in Religion and Politics!"[4]

Not only was Smith difficult to get along with, he wouldn't pay his debts; by 1770, he'd earned a reputation as a bad credit risk. That year, Smith had tried to rent a house in Philadelphia, and a friend of the landlord confided: "I must do the Justice to inform thee that he is accounted so very bad a Pay Master that it might be difficult to get thy Rent from him...."[5]

As for the quarrel between Benjamin Franklin and Rev. Smith, Franklin's son, William, can be relied on for the juicy portions of the story. A year before Smith was jailed, William had gone to England with his father for an extended stay, during which the elder Franklin was granted an honorary Doctor of Civil Laws degree from Oxford University. His son received a Master of Arts degree at the same time. William Smith, who earlier had been awarded a Doctorate in Divinity by Oxford, tried to block Benjamin from receiving his degree. When Smith later caught up with the Franklins in London, they renewed their argument. Afterwards, Smith spread rumours around England that Franklin had been disowned by his friends in Philadelphia.[6]

In August 1762, through his father's influence, thirty-two-year-old William was appointed governor of New Jersey, and soon after married Elizabeth Downes of St. James Street, London. Meanwhile, Benjamin took passage back to America, and three months later the newly-weds followed, arriving safely in Philadelphia on February 19, 1763.[7]

Later that spring, comfortably settled at their new home in Burlington, New Jersey, Governor Franklin revealed his feelings about Rev. Smith in a letter to a friend back in London. "Our voyage was as disagreeable as can well be imagined & I would not wish the devil, nay Parson S. to experience a winter passage like ours." The purging nature of William's sea voyage did little to ameliorate the internecine squabbling between the Franklins and Rev. Smith, for William Franklin adds in the same letter: "Both my father and myself found our friends on our return as warm and as numerous as ever, notwithstanding the vile insinuations of a certain parson to the contrary."[8]

As could be expected, Smith was critically unflattering in his reaction to William Franklin's appointment as governor. To Rev. Smith's comments, Governor Franklin responded: "there is no more foundation for Smith's report than there is for believing him an honest man."[9]

For years, rumour had churned through Philadelphia's gossip mill that William Franklin was Benjamin's illegitimate son. The common-law marriage of Deborah Read and Benjamin Franklin around the time of William's birth did not deter Franklin's opponents from alleging that the birth mother was a privy-cleaning maidservant named Barbara. The Reverend Smith was quick to stoke the fires of animosity by writing of William Franklin: "the whole Circumstances of his life render him too despicable for Notice...."[10]

Governor and bastard—it was an odd mix of reputations for the son of the great Benjamin Franklin. But it was not so odd that the loyal son would spend time attending to his father's affairs after the elder Franklin had gone back to London in 1764. One of those affairs was the Monckton land project.

Here were men who would soon launch a co-operative land-settlement deal with a number of German farmers. How did they fail to see the potential for their political quarrel to compromise their settlement plans? As events in Philadelphia were to unfold, the explosive mix of politics and religion would bode ill for a little group of settlers who one day would find themselves discharged on the remote bank of an obscure river in a distant northern colony.

But even if Franklin and Smith could have put their personal quarrelling aside, the British government in London would soon provide them and their friends with a political bone over which they could fight in deadly earnest.

The Nova Scotia undertaking was not the first attempt by Philadelphia politicians to involve Pennsylvania Germans in their schemes. During the elections for the Pennsylvania Assembly in 1764, both Franklin's party of Quakers and Smith's opposing Proprietary Party tried to drag German voters into the fray by soliciting the support of Germans who might otherwise have abstained from voting. On his father's behalf, William Franklin had campaigned in Germantown, encouraging the Germans to get themselves naturalized, at the last minute, so they could vote.[11]

But the Germans that year were not inclined to lend Benjamin Franklin their traditional support. A decade earlier, Franklin had criticized the Germans in a wild essay on the subject of population control. Using what historian Esmond Wright described as "language that would today be labelled distinctly racist," Franklin had questioned: "Why should the

Palatine Boors be suffered to swarm into our Settlements, and by herding together establish their Language and Manners to the Exclusion of ours?" When election time arrived in 1764, Smith's Proprietary lackeys told the Germans that Benjamin Franklin had called them "a Herd of Hogs." Smith's labelling them "wicked, stubborn, and stupid enemies of the King" apparently had less effect. The Quaker Party won a renewed majority that fall, but Benjamin Franklin lost his seat in the Assembly by twenty-six votes out of four thousand.[12]

William Franklin took his father's defeat personally, but their friend John Hughes, who had retained his own seat in the Assembly, put a positive spin on the outcome by orchestrating Benjamin Franklin's appointment as colonial representative to London.[13]

No sooner had Franklin departed his beloved Philadelphia on November 7, 1764, for his new posting in England, than Chief Justice William Allen began to stir up trouble. William Franklin explains:

> *Mr. Allen, one of the principal Prop'y. [Proprietary Party] Tools in Pennsylvania, has employed that miscreant Parson Smith & two or three other prostitute writers, to asperse his [Franklin's] character in which they have been very industrious. However, they have lately received a terrible shock from Mr. Hughes, one of my father's friends, who [was] incensed at their base conduct....*[14]

When John Hughes learned of the attack on Benjamin Franklin's reputation, he acted swiftly. In a clever move, Hughes offered to pay £10 to charity for every charge against Franklin that was justified, on the condition that the accusers would pay £5 for every fabrication that Hughes could prove. The accusers responded by wagering ten pies or cakes against five pies or cakes. More insults and accusations followed, but John Hughes got no takers for his gambit.[15]

CHAPTER 7

Charles Jones, his Mark

On the Friday before Franklin's departure to London in 1764, the Pastor of St. Michael's German Lutheran Church went out for a walk. The Reverend Heinrich Melchior Mühlenberg's home in Philadelphia was a busy place with visitors coming and going at all hours. The services of the kindly pastor were much sought after, and the demands on his time were great. At his country home at Trappe, "visitors of all sorts drifted in and out: ministers, traders, government officials, Indians, troubled souls of all walks of life, wanderers, the homeless—'My house,' said Mühlenberg, 'was a sort of guest-house for the scattered.'"[1] Rev. Mühlenberg welcomed the break that Friday, and looked forward to an opportunity to socialize, however briefly. Translated from German, here is the entry from his journal that day:

> *In the evening I was invited to the home of some English friends where there was a colonel who is the king's agent for giving out the vacant land in Nova Scotia, especially in the region of Cape Sable along the St. John River, where there are 1,400,000 acres in one stretch. I was asked whether I, too, would not like to take up several thousand acres for my three sons. A thousand acres cost between £2 and £3 sterling for the surveying fee, and the land is free of ground rent for ten years; however, some building must be done upon the land within three years. It is in a cold climate, like that of the kingdom of Sweden, and it is very hard to cultivate anything in such a terrible wilderness, but in a very short time the said agent has already disposed of 300,000 acres to prominent Englishmen here in Philadelphia. The agent's name is Mr. McNutt.*[2]

The untrustworthy Colonel McNutt had resurfaced in Philadelphia, pushing his favourite schemes. But Pastor Mühlenberg was not so worldly a man as to jump at McNutt's offer to get involved in Nova Scotia land speculation. The colonel would have to rely on Philadelphia businessman John Hughes to further his ambitious plans.

It was a few months later when John Hughes came calling on Pastor Mühlenberg. Hughes's visit had nothing to do with land settlement, however. Hughes wanted to talk politics. Behaving like a gentleman, as always, Hughes wanted to find out why the German voters in the election had shifted their support to the opposition. Mühlenberg had a low regard for politics, and wished to take no part in the dispute. He explained simply that the members of his congregation feared they might lose the rights granted by the King if the Quakers pressed for a revocation of Pennsylvania's charter. Such a change to Royal government would terminate the Penn family's stifling control of Pennsylvania government—the same control the Assembly's agent in London was trying to end. *Their* agent's name was Benjamin Franklin.[3]

Henry Melchior Muhlenberg, whose pastoral duties brought him into close contact with countless German immigrants.

Courtesy Pennsylvania German Society

Hughes did his best to engage the pastor in a political discussion, but Mühlenberg felt "no desire to have anything to do with their bitter strife." After an hour, according to Mühlenberg, they parted on a cordial note.[4]

Heinrich Melchior Mühlenberg was certainly no stranger to John Hughes's prospective settlers. The Philadelphia pastor's duties at Lutheran churches in Pennsylvania had brought him into close contact with countless numbers of German immigrants since his arrival in the Quaker colony more than twenty years before. Mühlenberg's organizational skills were such that, by 1750, twenty-three Lutheran churches and ten ministers were established in Pennsylvania. A decade later, the number of Lutheran churches in the colonies had grown to two hundred.[5]

Two weeks after Rev. Mühlenberg's introduction to Alexander McNutt in 1764, Heinrich Stief's eldest son, Jacob, turned fifteen. Jacob had been baptized in Mühlenberg's church of St. Michael's on November 16, 1749, only two days old. Jacob's birth-date of November 14 is fundamental because it is the earliest known irrefutable record of the Stief family in North America. For genealogists, the date becomes an anchor—a point in time, as it were, around which other events can pivot.[6]

The record of Jacob Stief's birth and baptism remained unknown to family researchers until 1986, when it was discovered by James Wood of Virginia, and made known that same year by William Oulton, a resourceful family historian whose work contributed significantly to Steeves family history. Along with that vital baptismal information came the name of Heinrich's wife: Regina.[7]

Sometime after the family's early years in Philadelphia, Regina's name changed to Rachel. No one knows why or how it changed, beyond the likelihood the transformation echoed the widespread anglicization of German names. Throughout Pennsylvania, German names and customs were slowly disappearing. The surname Müller became Miller; Gärtner became Gardner; Holtz became Wood; Zimmerman became Carpenter.[8]

Regina's name changed so thoroughly that, two centuries later, Steeves descendants were still struggling to come to terms with the fact. Even Esther Clark Wright was not immediately reconciled to the apparent contradiction. As she explained to fellow historian William Hoar in 1987, "I had written to him [William Oulton] suggesting that Regina was the mistake of an English clerk but he is determined to adopt it."[9]

Confusion over names in the Steeves family was evident as long ago as 1867. At the Steeves centennial gathering that year, some debate ensued as to the correct names of the first couple. James Steeves, who was Jacob's grandson, insisted that the founder's name was Jacob rather than Heinrich. Apparently, Regina was subject to the same confusion. At the time, her name was thought to be Margaret, as recorded on an old monument in the Hillsborough cemetery where Heinrich and his wife were laid to rest.[10]

In all the family records in New Brunswick today, the matriarch of the clan is known only as Rachel—there's no mention of any Regina. Thus, one might wonder if the name Rachel was the mistaken hand-me-down of her nineteenth-century descendants. Any doubts about the authenticity of the name Rachel, however, are put to rest by an itinerant Methodist preacher named James Mann who visited the Hillsborough area in 1790.

When Rev. Mann arrived on the Cumberland circuit, he preached up and down the Petitcodiac River while collecting donations to support his work. That fall, Mann began his sojourn in Monckton township at the bend in the river, then passed through Salisbury at the head of the tide where he crossed over, eventually making his way down the west side of the river to

Hillsborough. Regina Stief's contribution to Rev. Mann is recorded in the church steward's book for that year: "Rachel Stieve—5 shillings." Her name by then had become anglicized from the original German, Regina.[11]

And what survives of the Philadelphia church where Regina and Heinrich Stief's first child, Jacob, was baptized in 1749? That was the question I asked myself, as my days at the Historical Society of Pennsylvania in 1995 stretched into a week. Although St. Michael's was demolished in 1872, it was within the realm of possibility that some lasting trace or even a token reminder might still exist.

Putting aside the manuscripts and record books one afternoon, I fled the confines of that redoubtable institution to go on a mini-excursion to the north-east corner of Fifth St. and Appletree Alley in old Philadelphia—the place where St. Michael's Church once stood. The city was infused with sunny weather, and the trees along the street hinted at the season ahead. I welcomed the chance to take a break from my research so I could rejuvenate my eyes and take in some Philadelphia air. By then, my vision was somewhat deranged from looking at endless metres of microfilm and scrounging for obscure footnotes in dusty old volumes.

I walked the half-dozen blocks along the length of Locust Street between the Historical Society and Washington Square, one of William Penn's original public squares in his city of brotherly love. Cutting across Independence Park, I went past Franklin's Philosophical Society, and continued up Fifth until I came to Arch Street. In Franklin's day, Arch was called Mulberry Street, and in the cemetery on the corner are buried the bones of the old philosopher and his wife. Tourists had been tossing pennies on his tomb.[12]

But any hopes to become inspired by the remains of St. Michael's were quickly dashed when I discovered that the former site of the church—in fact the entire block—is occupied by the U.S. Mint. Appletree Alley is gone, supplanted by six-and-a-half acres of windowless concrete. One wouldn't know St. Michael's had ever existed. Pastor Mühlenberg would be shocked. I would have to rely on history books and church records for any inspiration.

Following their earlier beginnings under the leadership of J. Caspar Stoever in 1733, the parishioners of St. Michael's Church were re-organized by Mühlenberg in 1743 as the "German Evangelical Lutheran St. Michaelis congregation." Services were begun in the church at Fifth and Appletree Alley before the building was completed, and as late as 1749 the windows were still unglazed. St. Michael's enjoyed great popularity among the Germans, and the church soon proved inadequate for the large numbers of devout worshippers who tried to squeeze themselves into the building for services. Because of the crowding, many were forced to stand outdoors where they hoped to hear the service through the open windows. During winter storms, the pastor would occasionally have to brush the blowing snow off the Bible as he read the scripture to the people.[13]

St. Michael's Lutheran Church, 1790, north-east corner of Fifth St. and Appletree Alley, where Heinrich Stief's first son was baptized.
Courtesy of The Library Company of Philadelphia

In 1766, St. Michael's expanding congregation began construction of Zion Church in the next block at Fourth and Cherry Streets. Zion was consecrated three years later, and the combined congregation of the two churches was subsequently termed "St. Michael's and Zion Lutheran Congregation." Dr. Yoder informs that it was the "leading German Lutheran congregation in the Colonies [and] its twin churches formed a kind of joint Lutheran cathedral. Its clergy were among the great spiritual and intellectual leaders of eighteenth-century America."[14]

St. Michael's Church had seen other signers of the Articles of Agreement besides Heinrich Stief enter through its welcoming doors. One daughter of

Michael Lutz and his wife, Anna Walburga, passed through the kindly arms of Pastor Mühlenberg and his church assistants. That child was Anna Margretha Lutz, born March 4, and baptized March 10, 1755. Margretha would later marry Heinrich Stief's second son, John. In the baptismal record, the Lutz family were noted as living "4 miles out of town."[15]

Also, Matthias Sommer, the first settler to sign the Articles of Agreement, married Christina Null on October 23, 1749 in St. Michael's Church. And two of that couple's many daughters were baptized there: Anna Catharina, born October 10, baptized November 18, 1750, and Eva Magdalena, born February 6, baptized March 11, 1753.[16]

Years later, Matthias Sommer would encounter Rev. Mühlenberg again, when he moved to Barren Hill, north of Philadelphia, a few miles west of Germantown. He and his friend Valentin Miller, another signatory to the agreement, became trustees of St. Peter's Lutheran Church in Barren Hill, the congregation having been created out of a schism at the Lutheran church in Germantown. Valentin and Matthias, along with others of their church brethren at St. Peter's, met on several occasions with Rev. Mühlenberg to discuss church business. In 1765, seven years after initially forming, the members of St. Peter's congregation found themselves unable to repay the costs of constructing their church, and they wanted to send members to Europe to solicit dona-

St. Peter's Lutheran Church, Barren Hill, ca. 1850. Sketch by Benjamin J. Lossing. *The Pictorial Field-Book of the Revolution*, Vol. 2, published 1859; subsequently published in Theodore W. Bean, ed. *History of Montgomery County*, Vol. 2, (Philad: Everts & Peale, 1884).

Courtesy of the Historical Society of Montgomery County

tions from friends and relatives there. Mühlenberg described Valentin and Matthias as poor men with no property to their names: "Christopher Raben was the only one who possessed some property[.] Muller, Kolb and Sommer did not possess anything."[17]

In the Articles of Agreement, Valentin Müller's surname had been anglicized to Miller, while Matthias Sommer's own surname had become Summer. At the same time, Heinrich Stief's name had become Henry Stief.[18]

Even Charles Jones, the one Welshman in Hughes's group of intended settlers, may have been acquainted with Pastor Mühlenberg. On July 24, 1761, Henry Müller, Thomas Tindal, and a Charles Jones witnessed the marriage of John Matthew and Anna Radford in St. Michael's Church. Perhaps Henry Müller was related to Valentin Miller, and perhaps this Charles Jones was the same man whose name appeared on the Articles of Agreement. Previous to January 27, 1766, was it possible that all nine signers of the agreement had known each other through their membership in St. Michael's Lutheran Church? The idea seemed plausible; to me, it made a lot of sense.[19]

Family lore in New Brunswick has long believed Charles Jones to be of Welsh descent. In 1977, family historian Geneva Jones Emberley stated in her fifty-four page, referenced report: "It was in a Welsh Quaker section of a Quaker township (Marion) the first proven history of our ancestor Jones began. Charles Jones along with eight others had been in the office of John Hughes to sign the papers of agreement...." Dr. Wright cautiously agrees: Charles Jones was "possibly born in Wales." Historian Pincombe seems certain of the fact: "this family was Welsh."[20]

Presumably of Welsh descent, Charles Jones was a singular member of an otherwise-homogeneous group of German farmers. The only one with a non-German name, he was also the only man who couldn't write. When he signed the Articles of Agreement, Charles Jones made his "X" after John Hughes Jr. inscribed the name below Valentin Miller's signature.

Who was Charles Jones—the man behind the mark—and how did he fit into the story of John Hughes and Benjamin Franklin's settlement project involving a group of German farmers? Any probing genealogist would consider the question worthy of pursuit. An astute genealogist would propose the best explanation was kinship.

Esther Clark Wright was probably the first to suggest the existence of a family relationship between Charles Jones and John Hughes. Attempting to explain why Charles Jones had received an unusually large share of supplies from Hughes, Dr. Wright postulated: "Charles Jones may have been specially favoured because he was a relative of John Hughes's wife, whose maiden name had been Jones." According to the amount charged for provisions, Charles Jones received his allotment at a rate proportionate to a family three times larger than his own.[21]

Several questions could be posed about an illiterate Welshman named Charles Jones. Did Charles speak German, or had his fellow settlers learned to speak English during their tenure in Pennsylvania? Were any of them neighbours? The possibility that Charles Jones and his German friends were members of the same congregation in Philadelphia at one time presents as many questions as answers. Even if Charles was related to John Hughes, how did he become so intimately involved with a party of Pennsylvania-German settlers?

Was there a plausible theory hidden in this conundrum—an explanation that might answer these several questions about Charles Jones? The wheels of my genealogical mind began to turn.

If Charles Jones attended St. Michael's Lutheran Church (conceivable according to the Matthew-Radford marriage record), perhaps he was acquainted with some of the Germans who signed the Articles of Agreement with him. If his sister had married John Hughes (suggested though not proven), then surely Charles would have been aware of his brother-in-law's struggling efforts to find hardy settlers for his Monckton township. If Charles Jones had conversed with his fellow churchgoers (a perfectly natural occurrence), perhaps he had mentioned his brother-in-law's colonization plans. Was it Charles Jones who convinced the others that a marvellous opportunity awaited them in a province where fertile land was plentiful and cheap? By the middle of the eighteenth century, good land near Philadelphia—indeed anywhere in the settled colonies—was in short supply. Perhaps the settlers simultaneously came to the conclusion that the offer had good prospects. Was Charles Jones the key to the whole operation?

How difficult would it be to track down a man named Charles Jones—a man who'd had, through Hughes's Nova Scotia venture, a passing connection with the great Benjamin Franklin? Would a search for Charles Jones advance my search for Heinrich Stief? I paused long enough to ask myself those questions, then plunged in.

But it wasn't long before an amateur genealogist found himself entangled in a maze of vast proportions. Looking for a single Jones family in eighteenth-century Pennsylvania compares with trying to find a lone Murphy family somewhere in the whole history of Ireland; the Joneses were everywhere.

Soon after Dr. Edward Jones of Merionethshire in Wales emigrated with the original William Penn settlers in 1682, the Jones name began to multiply exponentially. By 1750, several thousand Jones families were already living in Pennsylvania.

My first encounter with the card catalogues at the Historical Society of Pennsylvania in 1995 was, to say the least, dismaying. Of the hundreds of cards that referred to the name Jones, many contained cryptic notations for obscure sources—journals and documents that would have to be requested from the staff, retrieved from the archives, and painstakingly examined for clues, one by one. I was having enough trouble coping with the punctilious staff, and I didn't want to push my luck. Other cards in the catalogues referred to books and collections in the open stacks, and some looked promising. After an hour of selecting likely possibilities and eliminating the redundant ones, I'd composed a list of forty-seven sources to look up in the society's open stacks.

I struggled through a volume called the "Genealogy of David and Letitia Jones" and found nothing. I slogged my way through a manuscript named the "Jones Family notes" and came up with zilch. I plowed into some old Welsh collections before retreating to safety. I waded helplessly through the eminent James J. Levick collection of Jones families with its sobering reference to Levick's ancestor who had lost twenty-three of his twenty-four sons in a fifth-century battle against the Strathclydes of northern England. Without reward, I admired a lovely hand-written document titled "The Ages of Francis Jones Senior's Sons"—a brief pedigree of the family who had emigrated from Pembrokeshire, Wales about 1700. In one obscure record of Jones marriages in southeastern Pennsylvania there appeared, without further comment, the unhelpful notation: "very few Jones brides info 'taken off.' Available if needed."[22]

In a jumbled collection simply named "Jones Bible Records," I came across the genealogy of a Welshman named John ap Thomas, another partner in William Penn's grant. Thomas was a prominent settler in his day, and his descendants had married into the Jones families of Pennsylvania. The old fellow's genealogy of no less than 108 generations extended all the way back to Noah and Adam. Now there was a man with a pedigree![23]

Many pointers to Jones genealogy quickly led to dead ends. Others took longer to come to the same end. My Jones ancestor was not to be found. Apart from the Matthew-Radford marriage in St. Michael's Church, there seemed to be no sign of anyone named Charles Jones who was preparing to leave Philadelphia in 1766. After two days of digging, I had found nothing conclusive.

In addition to the millions of original documents hidden in its vaults, the Historical Society of Pennsylvania keeps an open library of 10,000 volumes devoted to family history. In that giant assemblage, side by side with the multifarious genealogies of America's greatest families, a multitude of lesser-known works can be found: books, monographs, and essays—the love-labours of countless family historians. For a first visit to Philadelphia, the family history room seemed a commendable place to tackle the mysteries of an ancestral past.

Arranged alphabetically by family name, the books would transform my search into an inspiring field trip. After achieving little progress with the Jones families, and recalling Dr. Wright's suggestion of a familial relationship between Charles Jones and John Hughes, I gravitated to the family history room one morning and turned my attention to the name Hughes.

Among a number of unrelated books about Hughes families, I came across a slim, recently published volume by D. Michael Hughes of Ingram, Texas. In the introduction to his *Hughes Family History*, wherein the author described the work-in-progress, there was a brief mention of some "other Hughes families." Included was a single paragraph describing "John Hughes... 'stamp officer'...who is probably not related to us." This John Hughes was just the fellow I wanted to hear more about. If I'd been thinking clearly, I would have phoned Michael Hughes on the spot. It would have saved me a lot of wasted time later.[24]

My first visit to the Historical Society of Pennsylvania drew to a close. I gathered what I'd found—my observations from the Articles of Agreement; entries from St. Michael's Church; my introduction to Rev. Mühlenberg—and headed home. With me were twenty pages of notes on Pennsylvania Jones families.

When I got back to Toronto, I phoned Michael Hughes to inquire about the stamp officer in pre-revolutionary Philadelphia. What I really wanted was John Hughes's family genealogy. Mr. Hughes elaborated on what background he could remember, his information having come from an outline located by a researcher at the Lancaster Historical Society. In my mailbox a week later I found a copy of a typed, two-page genealogy summary by a Marion Steelman Hughes Brown titled:

EARLIEST RECORD OF ANCESTORS************HUGHES.

According to Marion Brown's undated summary, Sarah Jones married John Hughes, the future stamp officer, in 1738. Hughes and his wife lived at the family's country home of Walnut Grove where they raised eight children. Their sixth child, Isaac, born December 1, 1747, married Hannah Holstein, daughter of Matthias Holstein and Magdalena Hulings of Sweden. About the year 1800, according to Marion Brown, Hannah had written a book called *Family History Holstein*.

More compelling, John Hughes's father, Hugh, had married Martha

Jones of Lower Merion. The evidence that Hughes had Jones blood in his veins gave me a second reason to anticipate a family connection with Charles Jones.

In the summary, a line of descent traced from John Hughes's grandparents, through Marion Brown, and eventually down to her grandchildren. Despite a complex series of events including death, remarriage, adoption, a name change, and finally another marriage, the last adult in the Hughes blood line was the author's daughter, Patricia Steelman (Walz) Brown. Patricia had married a Robert Braun of Chestnut Hill, Pennsylvania. There was no mention of a Charles Jones, nor anything that would advance Dr. Wright's hypothesis about John Hughes's wife, Sarah Jones. If Charles Jones was related to Sarah, it wasn't mentioned.

I phoned Michael Hughes again, to ask about the book *Family History Holstein*. I wanted get in touch with Mrs. Brown, the compiler of the outline. By then, Mrs. Brown would have been eighty-five years old, but possibly still living and able to assist my investigations. Mr. Hughes had no idea what direction the search should take, but suggested I try to locate some of the descendants who might still reside around Chestnut Hill. Maybe one of them would be familiar with the book or might know the whereabouts of Mrs. Brown.

Following his advice, I made repeated enquiries to directory information in Philadelphia, and was soon phoning around the area, trying to track down the author of the Hughes document. Most of the calls led nowhere. Each time, I explained that I was looking for a descendant of John Hughes, the colonial stamp officer who had transacted a land deal with a group of Welsh and German farmers in 1766. After a week of sporadic calling, I had worked through the names and phone numbers, eliminating them one by one, until I came to the last one on my list: Robert Braun, the husband of Patricia.

My call was answered by a pleasant-sounding man who listened politely to my story. Finishing my tale and crossing my fingers, I heard him take a deep breath.

"Yes, my wife's name is Patricia," he confirmed, "but I don't think she could be related to you"—and he paused—"she's Chinese!"

I was utterly at sea. I thought I'd done my homework carefully, but obviously I was mistaken. Whatever the explanation, I'd exhausted all my leads and the search had reached an impasse. It seemed the genealogical trail of John Hughes and Charles Jones had come to an end.

Back-street scene in Philadelphia near the Historical Society of Pennsylvania.

CHAPTER 8

Bedbunts and Faggathies, Candlesticks and Chocolate

In April 1996, when I returned to Philadelphia to continue the search for Heinrich Stief, Charles Jones, and their German friends, it was with some hesitation (plus some air-sickness on the flight). My trip the previous autumn had yielded many interesting clues, but during the ensuing winter months I'd been unable to put those clues together and come up with anything definitive about the inter-relationship among John Hughes's Pennsylvania settlers. Except for Matthias Sommer and Valentin Miller, the settlers appeared to be complete strangers. But the records of St. Peter's Church in Barren Hill predating 1765, I'd learned in the meantime, were destroyed by fire in 1899. That angle wouldn't work.[1]

Charles Jones was still the odd man out. My twenty pages of notes on Jones families had taken me nowhere. In the mass of accumulated evidence, there seemed to be nothing that would explain how a lone Welsh family had become so profoundly involved with a group of German farmers.

My rental car was waiting when I arrived at the Philadelphia airport, and I drove directly to the Antique Row guest house where I'd made a reservation. My conversation with Mr. Hughes that winter had left me with a hunch I might need a car this time. After dealing with the practicalities of accommodation, I walked the two blocks to the Historical Society of Pennsylvania to begin a new phase in my explorations of eighteenth-century Philadelphia.

The let-down came quickly. Despite my initial enthusiasm, I could make no headway. The search became an unyielding chore as I retraced my steps from the previous fall, trying to find a new opening, a flicker of light in the darkness of the past. In seven months, the Jones lines had become no less confused.

Finally giving up, I looked beyond Philadelphia. Michael Hughes had mentioned that Mrs. Brown's outline was uncovered by a researcher at the Lancaster Historical Society. Maybe Lancaster would yield a clue to the identity of Charles Jones.

The next morning, I drove one hundred kilometres west to Lancaster through the rolling hills of Pennsylvania-German farmland. Ploughed fields were sprouting green, and song birds were on the wing. I stopped at a couple of old German cemeteries to look around. The Joneses were here too.

In Lancaster, I found the historical society located in a low building situated on the far side of town. An invigorating spring wind blew across the adjoining lawn of Wheatland Estate, and the April grass grew fresh and green. At the doorstep to the building, hyacinths and tulips blossomed in the bright sunshine.

Many of Lancaster's files were available to the public, stored in a wall of cabinets aligned under the windows. With an afternoon breeze streaming through an open window, I dug through the files, looking for every name on the Articles of Agreement. I found but one. In the "H" file was a slim folder labelled "Hughes." Inside was a single document: Marion Steelman Hughes Brown's original typed manuscript, a copy of which Michael Hughes had mailed to me the previous fall. My search for Charles Jones had come full circle and I was no further ahead.

The next day, a long and futile search of birth, death, and marriage abstracts left me dazed and confused. Numerous entries for Hughes and Jones families were scattered through the records, but I found none to link John Hughes to Charles Jones.

At the Maison Rouge guest house where I had lodged, I changed into more comfortable clothes. Then I escaped into the late-afternoon sun, to try to shake some of the eighteenth-century dust from my brain. Neighbourhood gardens had been tilled and seeded, and young plants poked their heads into the warm sunshine.

A few blocks beyond the guest house, I came to the last row of houses where an old cemetery was wedged between the street and a set of railway tracks. The scene was vaguely reminiscent of my own family cemetery in Boundary Creek where I had begun the search for my ancestors. I walked in.

A few hundred stones occupied the graveyard, many commemorating the early German settlers of Lancaster County. Without any pretence of a systematic search, I wandered along the rows of old stones, not expecting to find anything relating to my own pursuits. It was a comforting ritual any genealogist would recognize. I'd worked my way over to the far side near the tracks, reading the names on the stones like a sleepy school boy who quickly forgets what he had just read.

Suddenly, an odd inscription made me stop: "In Memory of Elizabeth Funk." The stone was small with plain letters. The epigraph brought to mind a favourite rock 'n' roll song of the seventies called "In Memory of Elizabeth Reed"—a song that was supposedly inspired by a gravestone in a cemetery deep in the American south.[2]

This little stone in Lancaster County stood beside that of Elizabeth's husband, Jacob Funk. Elizabeth had died on April 21, 1896. The date gave me a jolt when I realized I was only two days away from the one-hundredth anniversary of her death. I walked out of the cemetery scratching my head in surprise at the weird occurance. My search had reached another dead end.

In the Maison Rouge's guest book the next morning, I wrote a short eulogy to my new acquaintance, Elizabeth Funk—the woman with the small marker who had provided an odd and useless highlight to the quest for Charles Jones.

Back in Philadelphia that afternoon, I tried to make some progress uncovering the identity of Charles Jones, the ancestor whom I hoped would provide the key to the story of Hughes's group of settlers. But again, the tangled lines of the Pennsylvania Jones families revealed nothing. Sitting at a table in the research room at the historical society, I tried to stifle a great yawn. Discouragement was beginning to rule the day; I was ready to give up the hunt.

Wandering into the family history room, I roamed about, the many thousand books seeming to beckon from their shelves. Refusing to admit I was completely adrift (as I was), I went to the section containing the Hughes families. As I'd done seven months before, I picked up the book by Michael Hughes. I opened it to the single paragraph describing John Hughes, the Philadelphia stamp officer.

Reading it, I recalled my conversation with Michael Hughes about a book called *Family History Holstein*. Without stopping to think, I replaced the book on the shelf, and looked around for the name Holstein. If there were any books on that family, they wouldn't be far from the name Hughes. On the next shelf above, not six inches from the Hughes books, I spotted a likely volume: *Swedish Holsteins in America 1644-1892*. Its wonderfully protracted subtitle made it clear I was finally getting somewhere.[3]

After all the phoning and searching around Philadelphia and Lancaster in the months leading up to that moment, I could sympathize with the poor fellow who spends half an hour looking for his glasses, only to find them propped on top of his head. Holding the old book with both hands as if it might abruptly fly away, I withdrew to a table in the research room to explore my new discovery.

While *Swedish Holsteins* wasn't the book written by Hannah Hughes in 1800, it did prove to be a rich source of genealogy and biography for the Holstein family of colonial Pennsylvania. It took me some time to reach the passages relating to the Hughes family.

> # SWEDISH HOLSTEINS
> ## IN AMERICA
> ### FROM 1644 TO 1892.
>
> COMPRISING MANY LETTERS AND BIOGRAPHICAL MATTER RELATING TO JOHN HUGHES, THE "STAMP OFFICER," AND FRIEND OF FRANKLIN,
>
> WITH PAPERS NOT BEFORE PUBLISHED RELATING TO HIS BROTHER OF REVOLUTIONARY FAME, COLONEL HUGH HUGHES OF NEW YORK.
>
> THE FAMILIES OF
> DeHAVEN, RITTENHOUSE, CLAY, POTTS, BLACKISTON, ATLEE, COATES,
> AND
> OTHER DESCENDANTS OF MATTHIAS HOLSTEIN OF WICACO, PHILADELPHIA, ARE INCLUDED.
>
> THIRTY-FIVE FAMILY PICTURES AND FAC SIMILE OF LETTERS OF BENJAMIN FRANKLIN AND REV. NICHOLAS COLLIN, D. D. ARE GIVEN.
>
> BY
> MRS. ANNA M. HOLSTEIN,
> UPPER MERION, MONTGOMERY COUNTY, PENNSYLVANIA.
>
> NORRISTOWN, PA.:
> 1892.

Title page of *Swedish Holsteins in America from 1644 to 1892.*[3]

Confirming Mrs. Brown's outline, the book's author, Anna Holstein, stated that Isaac Hughes, a son of John Hughes, had married Hannah Holstein of Swedish descent, thus connecting the Hughes family with the Holsteins of Sweden.

Swedish Holsteins had been published in 1892—about one hundred years after *Family History Holstein* was apparently composed. Whatever the correlation among the works of those three women—Anna Holstein, Hannah Hughes, and Marion Brown—I had found a book that might reveal the family relationship between John Hughes and Charles Jones. My convoluted search for the stamp officer of Philadelphia had finally opened a new chapter.

The Hughes ancestry "from the earliest dates known in America" began with the stamp officer's grandparents, John Hughes and Jane Evans, who originated in Merionethshire, Wales. When they came to Pennsylvania, they settled in Upper Merion, north-west of Philadelphia.

Their only son, Hugh, was born in 1671, and later took up residence on Third Street in Philadelphia. There, he worked as a tanner. Hugh married Martha Jones, whose parents had also come from Wales—this time from Pembrokeshire. In 1712, the couple's first child, John, was born. Here was a potential clue: If Charles Jones was related to John Hughes's maternal grandparents, he might have lived in Pembrokeshire.[4]

John Hughes, the future stamp officer, married Sarah Jones in 1738. Five years later, the couple were living at the family farm of Walnut Grove, fifteen miles up the Schuylkill River beyond Philadelphia. Here was another clue, this one pointing to Heinrich Stief's connection with Hughes. A nineteenth-century Steeves legend states that Heinrich "left the Rhine in the year 1749 [and settled] on the Schuylkill, about 12 miles above Philadelphia." Heinrich Stief and John Hughes were possibly neighbours.[5]

Sometime later, Hughes moved to Philadelphia where he and Sarah were living in 1751, on the west side of Fourth Street above Market. Fifteen years after, when anti-British sentiment began to fester in Pennsylvania and Philadelphians were making life difficult for him and his family, it was to Walnut Grove they would retreat.[6]

The author of *Swedish Holsteins* described John Hughes favourably.

> He was a man of remarkably pleasing address and deportment, affable and genial. While yet a young man he seems to have been prominent in his own neighbourhood as well as among the noted political and distinguished men of Pennsylvania, where his presence and council were eagerly sought.[7]

Years later, the Honourable Jonathan Roberts, whose father had been a close friend and neighbour of Hughes, remarked: "He was an intellectual man, of high feelings, and fashionable manners. He was now a man of leisure, & his manners were social. He look'd round for intercourse, and in the search call'd on my father."[8]

It was all very interesting, but *Swedish Holsteins* refused to divulge any family relationship between John Hughes and Charles Jones. Other than a reference to Benjamin Franklin's related debt to Hughes, the only mention of Monckton township was in the copies of letters between Hughes, Anthony Wayne, and Alexander McNutt. His letters to McNutt indicated that negotiations with the settlers were well advanced.[9]

Family relationship or not, by 1765 John Hughes had become an important figure in the lives of the Petitcodiac settlers. Finding *Swedish Holsteins* motivated me to look at other sources at the Historical Society of Pennsylvania—newspapers and books on local politics and history—until a picture began to emerge revealing the life and character of John Hughes. Moreover, Hughes's central role in a coming political affair would almost bring their colonization plan to ruin.

John Hughes's name appears early in Pennsylvania history with his appointment in 1748 as a captain in the Provincial militia. His military career was apparently brief, for in October of that year Britain and France signed the Treaty of Aix-la-Chappelle, bringing to a conclusion another bloody episode in the long series of wars in North America.[10]

Soon after, Hughes began to establish himself in Philadelphia business circles when he took over the bakery of the late Mr. Duval on Market Street "near the sign of the Indian King." Benjamin Franklin's newspaper, *The Pennsylvania Gazette*, announced that Duval's former customers "may be supply'd with bread as usual."[11]

Peace between Britain, France, and their native allies was short-lived. Late in 1749, Hughes was organizing a local militia for the defence of the inhabitants of Upper Merion on the west side of the Schuylkill River.[12]

In the fall of 1755, as thousands of Acadian refugees began their wandering exodus through the colonies, John Hughes and Benjamin Franklin entered into a political partnership that would endure for ten eventful years. Franklin had set himself a large agenda for transforming Pennsylvania society, and his numerous friends, Hughes included, readily offered their support.[13]

Perhaps John Hughes was emulating Franklin's spirit of civic altruism when he ventured into the arena of public transportation in 1757, proposing a stagecoach-and-boat service between Philadelphia and Annapolis, Maryland. That same year, John Hughes led a foray into the wilderness to build cabins for the friendly Delaware Indians, during which time he exhibited the same strength of character that would carry him through the troubled waters of the Stamp Act crisis a decade later. In 1759, as the French and Indian War intensified, Hughes became involved in procuring wagons for the British army.[14]

When the Pennsylvania Assembly endeavoured to wrest control of land registry from the Penn family that year, John Hughes was chosen to oversee the project. With immediate access to a vast inventory of property records, it was predictable that Hughes would soon be buying and selling land. Before his career in land speculation had come to an abrupt end, he would amass a fortune in real estate.[15]

John Hughes's venture into the dry-goods business, soon after, would visibly benefit the citizens of Philadelphia. By 1762, he had drawn his son John Jr. into the business. Judging from their advertisement in the *Pennsylvania Gazette*, the two presided over one of Philadelphia's more comprehensive selections of fabric, hardware, spices, and food staples. At their storefront on Fourth Street, customers could obtain everything from ozenbrigs and ticklenburg to snuff boxes, wig springs, and whalebone—items which every well-to-do Philadelphian might need. The store also carried goods of a more practical nature—those a common farmer would need.

Situated just a couple of blocks from St. Michael's Church, the store would be a natural stopping place for German farmers needing supplies. Perhaps some of Hughes's customers were potential settlers whose greatest need was more land. Possibly they included the same Welsh and German families who would one day found a new settlement on the Petitcodiac River. Was John Hughes's store the catalyst that brought the settlers and their sponsor together?

If I thought it would be impossible to see the settlers, I was wrong. They can easily be pictured—Heinrich Stief, Charles Jones, and their male compatriots judiciously eying the hardware: the razors, pruning knives, horsewhips, and gun flints. The women would appreciate the vast assortment of fabric and clothing, as well as needles, thimbles, and thread. An iron candlestick might be affordable. A small brass kettle might be worth saving for. Maybe the flowered ribbons would catch a young girl's fancy, while the boys might be attracted to the mariners' compasses or the spike tomahawks. The chocolate would appeal to all.

> To be Sold, wholesale or retail, by,
> JOHN HUGHES, and SON,
> At their store in Fourth-street, above Market-street,

RAVEN duck, ticklenburg, ozenbrigs, princes linen, buck-ram, check, Irish linens, muslins, cotton romals, tandems, tandem garlix, spotted and long lawns, cotton chints, calicoes, stamped linens, cross bar and striped combless, jeans, thicksets, flannels, halfthicks, bedbunts, shaloons, tammins, durants, faggathies, duroy, clouting diaper, diaper table cloths, Leghorn hats, mens and womens worsted and thread hose, calimancous, hair and worsted plush, everlastings, kenting and silk handkerchiefs, linen ditto, cutteaus, pruning knives, knives and forks, razors, scissars, sleeve buttons, mohair and silk and hair, metal and hair buttons, sattin, paduasoy, flowered and plain ribbons, silk serrit, gartering, womens leather and silk mitts, silk caps, sewing silk, Scots thread, coloured ditto, breaches patterns, knee garters, mens gloves, pipe and spike tomahawks, iron candlesticks, pewter, pins, needles, thimbles, snuffboxes, awl hafts and blades, shoe tacks, snuffers, shoe and knee buckles, watch keys and seals, Holman's ink-powder, mariners compasses, spectacles, cotton and silk laces, womens fans, horsewhips, cart boxes, curtain rings, writing paper, shirt buttons, wig springs, small and large brass kettles, gun flints. Also West-India and N. England rum, melasses, loaf and muscovado sugar, rice, tea, coffee, chocolate, ginger, pepper, alspice, French indigo, resin, brimstone, bar iron, whalebone, fine salt, train oil, starch, nutmegs, cloves, mace, cinnamon, copperas, brazil, cottons and wool cards, and sundry other things, at the most reasonable rates, as usual.

The advertisement also included a reminder of the relationship between Hughes and Jones. But who was Jones?

N. B. All trade that stand indebted to the late company of Hughes and Jones, or to John Hughes, upwards of twelve months, are desired to settle immediately, or their accounts will be put into an attorney's hands.[16]

John Hughes's account books reflect the popularity of his products and the resulting success of his business. Philadelphia citizens of every sort passed through the store at one time or another. In the winter of 1763-64, for example, a Jacob Criner purchased two pairs of hinges and some nails, while a Jacob Cline from Germantown paid off his debt of £10:9s:6d. The surnames Criner and Cline, I reminded myself, appeared on the Articles of Agreement two years later: Andrew Criner and Jacob Cline. Was this another clue?

Prominent politicians joined the ranks of farmers and tradesmen. Benjamin Franklin settled a small account, as did fellow assemblyman Joseph Galloway. Another noteworthy customer was Israel Jacobs, a Philadelphia inn-keeper who was soon to become a member of Alexander McNutt's Nova Scotia land syndicate.[17]

Upwards of three hundred names, with amounts ranging from one shilling to £243:16s:6d, were listed on the books, all indebted to Pennsylvania assemblyman and successful Philadelphia merchant John Hughes.

It was fast becoming obvious that I needed to dig deeper into colonial history and biography if I wanted to understand what was happening at the time.

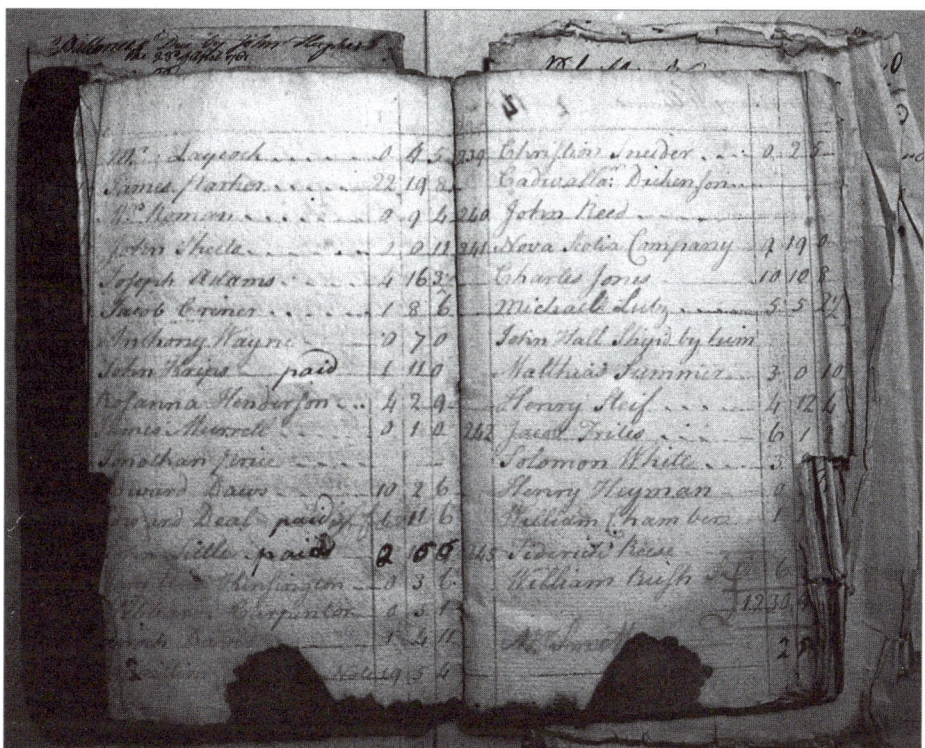

Undated page from "An Account of Outstanding Debts," John Hughes Papers. The subsequent page in the account book bears the date May 15, 1768.
Courtesy of the Historical Society of Pennsylvania, John Hughes Papers

The deeper I dug into the past, moreover, the more I found was happening. Although the Petitcodiac settlers continued to be elusive, I was sure that a look at the background of the times would allow a patient observer to experience some of the same places and people they had known.

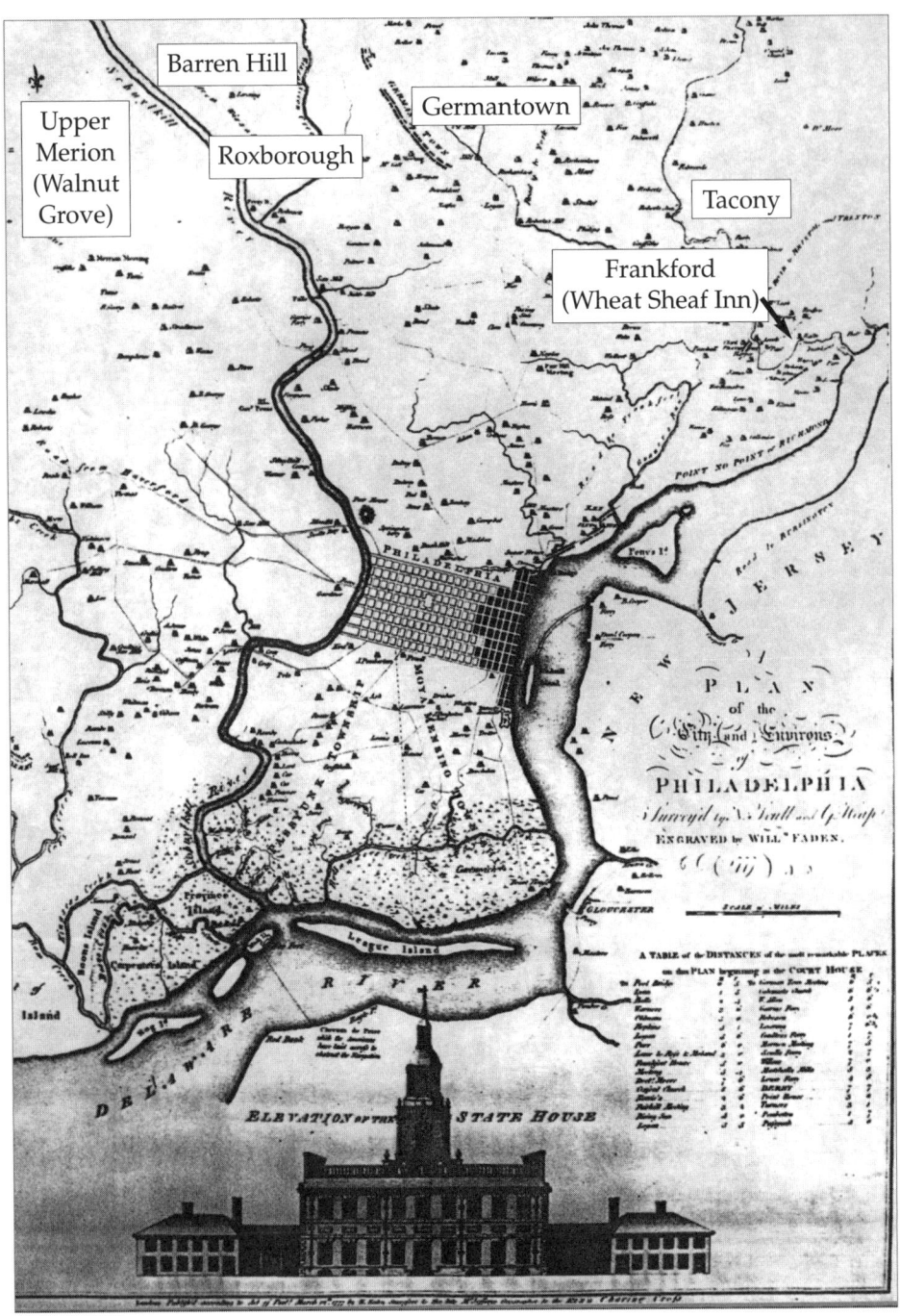

Scull and Heaps's contemporary map of Philadelphia area, the first home of German emigrants in the new world.

CHAPTER 9

A Crisis Over Stamps

It was probably during John Hughes's early residence in Philadelphia that the foundation was laid for his deep and life-long friendship with Benjamin Franklin. For any astute politician or energetic businessman living in the American colonies in the middle of the eighteenth century, Philadelphia was the place to be. By 1750, the city had more than 2,000 houses and a population of nearly 13,000 citizens. Ten years later, with a total of 18,756 residents as well as three libraries, three newspapers, a college, and the only hospital in North America, Philadelphia had become the "largest, most prosperous town in English America."[1]

Founder William Penn had laid out the city on a near east-west axis, with public squares proportionately situated at each corner of his new settlement. The streets of Philadelphia were straight and broad, unlike those in many European cities whose congested passageways encouraged fire and disease. At certain times of the year, the light from the rising and setting sun would flood down the boulevards, bathing all in glorious splendour. Philadelphia would be "a greene Country Towne," declared Penn—with orchards and gardens, "and allways be wholsome."[2]

In 1765, an English visitor described Philadelphia as "perhaps one of the wonders of the world... [a city] that bids fair to rival almost any in Europe." By that year, the Germans living in Pennsylvania numbered more than 60,000.[3]

Philadelphia boasted whale-oil street lamps, cobble-stoned streets with sidewalks, and policemen patrolling at night. The second largest city in the British empire, Philadelphia had become a thriving centre of commerce and

57

an important place of learning for America's great thinkers, the greatest of whom was Benjamin Franklin. While his rivals felt differently, Dr. Franklin's Quaker friends in the provincial Assembly were honoured to send him to London in November of 1764, to represent Pennsylvania's best interests.[4]

In March of that same year, the British government had introduced legislation that would have an impact on every person in America—Benjamin Franklin, John Hughes, and their intended Welsh and German settlers included. To finance the various expenses incurred by the British government in America, Lord George Grenville had presented Parliament with the Stamp Act, his comprehensive taxation scheme. Although the act was only one of numerous attempts by Britain to make the colonies pay for themselves, this time the undertaking would shatter the historic relations between the mother country and her precocious offspring.[5]

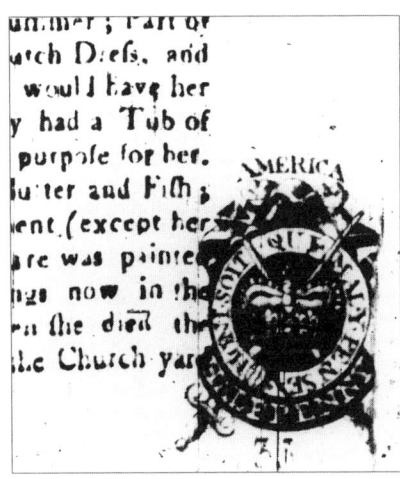

Stamp from the *Halifax Gazette*, Nov. 21, 1765.
Courtesy NSARM

Stamp duties were nothing new. Massachusetts had tried a stamp tax ten years before, and the British had been paying stamp taxes since the reign of William and Mary in the previous century. But even Benjamin Franklin failed to anticipate the consequences of the Stamp Act of 1765, a statute that would herald the beginning of the end of British rule in the American colonies. In the decade to follow, careers would collapse, and prominent men would tumble from their positions of wealth and power. For the nine settlers about to sign the Articles of Agreement with John Hughes, the Stamp Act would almost destroy their plans to migrate to a new township on the Petitcodiac River. Amid the violence and turmoil that came to surround the Stamp Act, Hughes's would-be settlers waited for their chance.

After a year spent moving through Britain's Parliament, the Stamp Act was passed in March, 1765, and was scheduled to come into force on the first day of November. The act required that legal documents and publications in America, including Quebec and Nova Scotia, be embossed with an official government stamp.[6]

More than fifty items were to be taxed, including commercial contracts, bills of lading, court documents, licenses, almanacs, newspapers, pamphlets, and playing cards. The price for mortgages and deeds was set at two shillings three pence; a ship's clearance, four pence; an insurance policy, five shillings; a retail liquor license, £1; playing cards, one shilling per pack; a single copy of a newspaper, one half penny per sheet. Even the act of dying was to be taxed: a will would cost sixpence. School books and prayer books were exempt. The list of fines for evading stamp duties was longer than the list of items to be taxed. The penalty for counterfeiting stamps was death.[7]

No doubt the settlers preparing to leave for the Bay of Fundy voiced their concerns about the added cost of land surveys: a one shilling tax for every two hundred acres of granted lands. As well, some of them might have heard about or seen in Heinrich Mueller's German newspaper the unsettling reports of a pending double tax on foreign-language papers.[8]

The Stamp Act placed a heavy burden on anyone involved in colonial trade or publishing, and its effects would be widely felt among the merchant class. The *Quebec Gazette* calculated that stamped paper would increase the cost of its newspapers by four hundred percent.[9]

When Benjamin Franklin was appointed colonial representative to London in 1764, his original assignment to convert Pennsylvania to Royal government was soon eclipsed by the Stamp Act.

With Franklin preoccupied in London, the Petitcodiac settlement would be left to John Hughes and Anthony Wayne to develop. But if Benjamin Franklin remained in the background, his interest in land speculation continued to be a driving force. Land speculation was the best business of the day, and the Nova Scotia venture was not Franklin's first attempt to make a handsome profit. The largest of the land companies in America was the Walpole Company, formed by ten prominent Philadelphia businessmen including John Hughes and Benjamin's son, William. That group set its sights on no less than ten million acres of virgin territory, for which they offered to pay London £10,000—less than half a penny per acre. Through a second land company called the Charlotiana, Benjamin Franklin and his partner Sir William Johnson bargained for most of Illinois and Wisconsin.[10]

The speculators' activities were not restricted to the western frontier, of course. When Governor Lawrence issued his proclamation following the deportation of the Acadians from Nova Scotia, that northern province attracted their attention. Whether it was through Alexander McNutt's activities or otherwise, by May 1764 Benjamin Franklin had expressed interest in obtaining a grant in Nova Scotia. His popularity in America, he wrote, would be useful "in procuring Settlers."[11]

Like Alexander McNutt, Benjamin Franklin probably never met any of his intended settlers. Nevertheless, the settlers had felt Franklin's presence in many ways. Everyone in America had heard of his greatness, and his ideas exerted a powerful influence. In science, politics, and the humanities, Franklin stood like a beacon on a dark hill.

Two-and-a-half centuries later, we take for granted many facts of life that originated in his humane and artful mind. His eminent biographer, Carl Van Doren, thought him "a great and wise man moving through great and troubling events." Historian Leonard Labaree, who laboured over Franklin's papers for a decade, wrote: "It is part of Benjamin Franklin's legacy that two centuries after he lived his name continues to evoke a magical response."[12]

Franklin, then, was a great and wise man who had a vested interest in the Nova Scotia land-settlement project, but whose political misjudgment almost stopped the plan dead in its tracks.

Benjamin Franklin was born January 6, 1706, the son of Josiah Franklin by his second wife, Abiah Folger. Benjamin was the youngest boy in a large family of nine brothers and sisters in addition to five step-siblings from his father's previous marriage. The lower-class family lived a frugal but happy life in Boston, where Benjamin was apprenticed to his brother James in the printing business. He loved reading, and quickly became a prolific writer; by the age of sixteen, his fluent essays were appearing in his brother's newspaper. But James treated his younger brother badly, and Benjamin looked for his chance of escape. Believing that employment might offer itself in Philadelphia, he fled to that fair city to establish himself and make his genius known to the world.[13]

The time-honoured story of Benjamin Franklin begins in 1723 with his arrival in Philadelphia at the age of seventeen—a story which every American school child learns by heart. Coming ashore at Market Street wharf, he walked up the street carrying a large roll of bread under each arm, while eating a third. Extra stockings and a shirt were stuffed into his pockets. As fate would have it, one Philadelphian who took particular notice of the scruffy lad that day was Deborah Read, his future wife. Franklin later agreed with Deborah's observation that he made "a most awkward ridiculous Appearance."[14]

Noted for his prowess at swimming, Franklin was an odd duck at a time when deep water for most people meant their monthly bath. During his first visit to London, at the age of twenty, Franklin demonstrated his aquatic abilities to some friends by swimming down the Thames River from Chelsea to Blackfriar's—a distance of nearly three miles—while performing along the way, as he wrote later, "many Feats of Activity, both upon & under Water...."[15]

Franklin wasn't long establishing himself in Philadelphia. As his scientific discoveries and popular inventions proliferated, his fame spread far and wide. While in the printing business, he made all the various components for himself, including the press, the type, and the ink. In his house at 141 Market Street, a lightning rod was connected to a series of bells that would ring and throw off sparks during electrical storms. Franklin loved music and was especially proud of his self-made instrument—a glass-and-water apparatus called an armonica which was reputed to delight his audiences with sweet sounds. Included among his many inventions were bifocal glasses, a street lamp, and a sea anchor designed to alleviate the problem of a storm breaking a ship's anchor chain. His Franklin stove, which today would be applauded for its environmental efficiency, generated more heat than the traditional fireplace.[16]

Benjamin Franklin had a particular interest in land speculation in old Nova Scotia.

Franklin did much to re-organize colonial society. Among the institutions he founded were a philosophical society, a lending library, a fire company, and a hospital. Franklin was instrumental in establishing the first postal service in America, and he proposed the academy which later became the University of Pennsylvania.[17]

With his many interests in various and sundry fields of life, it's no surprise that Franklin was drawn to the mysteries of his own genealogy. He seems to have picked up the bug from an uncle who, he said, shared "the same kind of Curiosity in collecting Family Anecdotes...." During their sojourn in England in 1758, Benjamin and William travelled to Ecton, Northamptonshire, where their ancestors had lived for two hundred years. The two met with the church rector and found family records in the Ecton Parish registers beginning at the year 1563. With the rector's wife in the lead, the party visited the church cemetery where they located the time-worn gravestones of Franklin's grandfather Thomas and other relatives. With a brush and a bucket of water, Benjamin's Black servant, Peter, got down on his knees and scrubbed the moss from the stones. William copied the inscriptions. When all the records had been gathered together, Benjamin was surprised to find that he was the youngest son of the youngest son of the youngest son—back five generations.[18]

A Crisis over Stamps 61

His many scientific discoveries, practical inventions, business undertakings, and societal improvements all taken together, Benjamin Franklin was truly a self-made man. But while Franklin made it clear to his friends that he needed no man's patronage in life, he was happy to assume the role of patron with his friend and admirer, John Hughes.

By 1765, John Hughes had made a name for himself as a prominent Philadelphia merchant and a member of the Pennsylvania Assembly. Furthermore, his reputation as a former judge of the Court of Common Pleas was enhanced by his close friendship with Benjamin Franklin. Years before, Franklin had told his wife Deborah, "I think nobody ever had more faithful Correspondents than I have in Mr. Hughes and you."[19]

No doubt Franklin believed he was awarding his friend John Hughes a generous favour when he nominated him to be the distributor of stamps for Pennsylvania and Delaware under Lord Grenville's new Stamp Act. For both Hughes and Franklin, the move was one they would come to regret in a most eventful and regrettable year.[20]

On April 18, 1765, the text of the Stamp Act was printed in the *Pennsylvania Gazette*, and immediately the colonists began to voice dissent. People were encouraged to exercise frugality as a way of lessening the demand for foreign products; English lamb and beer were to be avoided; funerals were to be conducted without ostentation. Inspired by a plan from Massachusetts, delegates from nine of the colonial assemblies prepared for a general congress, subsequently called the Stamp Act Congress, to meet in New York on October 7. That fall, more than four hundred Philadelphia merchants and traders, including four women, agreed to boycott the importation of any English goods and to revoke all outstanding orders.[21]

The arguments against the Stamp Act were based on the principle that the colonists had the inherent right to tax themselves; anything else would run contrary to the English constitution. The Americans even called on the rights guaranteed by the Magna Carta. The Stamp Act had been imposed without the consent of their own assemblies, and threatened public liberty and happiness.[22]

Up from every town and village street in America went the rallying cry—*No taxation without representation!* In every tavern, up went the glasses to the toast—*Liberty, Property and no Stamps!*[23]

When John Hughes's appointment as stamp distributor was announced in Philadelphia on May 30, he quickly became the focus of unrelenting hostility. If Hughes didn't have enough on his hands with his various activities as iron master, merchant, land speculator, and member of the Pennsylvania

Assembly, the stamp commission would stretch his capabilities to the limit. Although he would never be allowed to perform any of the functions of the office, the appointment would become the curse of his career. Benjamin Franklin knew how much resentment had been created by the imposition of the Stamp Act, but he badly underestimated the extent to which the legislation would inflame his fellow citizens.[24]

Throughout the Thirteen Colonies, a great swell of animosity against the stamp distributors was kindled in the minds of the populace. Secret associations of Americans calling themselves the Sons of Liberty organized to fight back. Demonstrators lit bonfires in the streets of Boston, and violent riots were staged in New York. Government officials saw their houses destroyed and their property carried away.[25]

A German engraving depicting the tax rebellion in Boston (with incorrect date).

In the words of historian John Miller, writing two centuries later:

> The stamp masters found themselves the most hated men in America; their best friends refused to speak to them.... Upon their heads descended the full weight of guilt for the Stamp Act. [In every colony, agitators tried to] terrify the stamp masters out of their wits, wreck their houses, drink their liquor, and finally chase them across the border into a neighboring province to make sport for the Sons of Liberty. Most stamp masters probably did not suspect when they received their appointment that it was to be a travelling job—usually with a mob at their heels.[26]

But if the Sons of Liberty could coerce most of the stamp distributors into resigning their commissions, they would encounter a determined opponent in Philadelphia. John Hughes was well aware of the violence caused by the Stamp Act in the other colonies, but he had a great deal to lose by abandoning his office. His honour as a gentleman and his loyalties to Benjamin Franklin and their King demanded that he stand his ground. He was not about to give up without a fight.[27]

On August 14 in Boston, the protests began in earnest. Led by a southside gang member named Ebenezer MacIntosh—a shoemaker of Irish extraction—rioters broke into the house of Andrew Oliver, the local stamp officer, and ransacked the place. That same night, the house of his brother-in-law, Lieutenant-Governor Thomas Hutchinson, was "wrecked by the mob and the manuscript of his *History of the Province of Massachusetts Bay* scattered in the mud outside his door." Hutchinson's manuscript included a collection of historical documents over which he had laboured for thirty years.[28]

Skull and cross bones from the *Halifax Gazette*, Dec. 12, 1765, meant to parody the official stamp.
Courtesy NSARM

In Philadelphia, newspapers embellished with skull and crossbones proclaimed: "Liberty at an End!" and "The Folly of England and Ruin of America." The Sons of Liberty distributed crude handbills which warned, "The first Man that either distributes or makes use of Stampt Paper, let him take care of his House, Person, & Effects."[29]

Even in distant Halifax, opposition to the Stamp Act made itself known when the appointed stamp distributor, Archibald Hinshelwood, found his effigy hanging on the town gallows.[30] As well, Nova Scotia's official newspaper, the *Halifax Gazette*, printed several inflammatory articles and sported its own version of a skull and crossbones. The two men responsible—printer Anthony Henry, and his sixteen-year-old journeyman from Boston, Isaiah Thomas—were sternly reprimanded by the provincial secretary.[31] Matters in Halifax came to a head when the *Gazette* appeared with the drawing of a horned devil stabbing his great pitchfork into the half-penny stamp which had been irreverently positioned upside down. Above the fiery collage, and blocked in heavy, black ink, were the words, "Behold me the scorn and contempt of AMERICA, pitching down to Destructions...." It was an obvious act of sedition (and a clever play on words).[32] The authorities in Halifax acted decisively, but the outcome differed from what might have ensued in New England. This time, the printer lost his job, and his young assistant was sent home to Boston on the next ship.³³

All the colonial agents in London vehemently opposed the Stamp Act, yet even Benjamin Franklin's clear and eloquent criticisms were rejected by the British government. Franklin spent long days writing letters to the English newspapers and lobbying any politician who would lend an ear. The British government, however, was not listening.

Once Franklin had acquiesced to the act becoming law, he reasoned that the colonists would eventually submit to it. While continuing to oppose the act, and warning of the consequences that would follow in America, he confided a somewhat different sentiment to John Hughes that riotous summer of 1765. Franklin was unhappy with the way the colonists had rebelled, and advised his friend to stay the course "with Coolness and Steadiness" until the people showed their consent. Then Hughes would profit from the situation:

> *In the meantime, a firm Loyalty to the Crown and faithful Adherence to the Government of this Nation, which is the Safety as well as the Honour of the Colonies to be connected with, will always be the wisest Course for you and I to take, whatever may be the Madness of the Populace or their blind Leaders, who can only bring themselves and Country into Trouble, and draw on greater Burthens by Acts of rebellious Tendency.*³⁴

It was sound advice from one loyal British subject to another, but highly dangerous should it fall into the hands of their rebellious opponents. Luckily for Franklin, the inflammatory letter stayed hidden in John Hughes's personal papers throughout the Stamp Act crisis. In fact, it remained undisclosed for 127 years until *Swedish Holsteins in America* was published in 1892. In a book review of *Swedish Holsteins* printed in *The Pennsylvania Magazine of History and Biography* in 1893, the reviewer pounced on the secret letter.

> Franklin expresses his dissatisfaction with the rebellious opposition to the Stamp Act, advises Mr. Hughes to hold on to his stamp office, until the people get used to him, pays his fees, sends him his commission, and shows his genius as an able 'trimmer' in this transaction, against which the tocsin of revolt sounded from Boston to South Carolina. Hughes bore the odium. It is not too much to say that this letter, published in the lifetime of Franklin, would have ruined his political career forever.³⁵

If the letter had been exposed in 1765, both Hughes and Franklin would have faced an impossible situation. Credit and credibility demolished and their reputations destroyed, their Nova Scotia land scheme would have come crashing down around them. Without John Hughes's dogged perseverance, Monckton township might never have come to be. Benjamin Franklin was in the clear, but more danger lay ahead for John Hughes.

The colonists did not become reconciled to the Stamp Act, as Franklin had hoped. The citizens of Philadelphia took out their vengeance on Hughes, while Franklin continued in his role as colonial agent in London. Franklin's handling of the Stamp Act had put him under some suspicion regarding his own motives, and there were pointed accusations in America that he had wanted Hughes's commission for himself.

The late summer of 1765 was a troubling time for John Hughes. His position at the centre of the Stamp Act controversy would severely strain his several business endeavours. On top of that, the Philadelphia syndicate's attempt to secure a land grant from the Nova Scotia Council was coming unglued, due, in some measure, to the questionable efforts of the unpredictable McNutt. Hughes's settlers had made preparations to depart from Pennsylvania and they were disgruntled with the endless delay.

CHAPTER 10

A Loyal Englishman

In the autumn of 1765, the protests in Philadelphia turned ugly. On Sunday, September 15, reports arrived in the city of a change of government in London and a possible repeal of the Stamp Act. The news stirred up the citizens like a hot stick in a hornet's nest. The next night, bonfires were lit in the streets and Hughes was burned in effigy. With much "whooping and hallooing," a mob congregated around his house, "threatening violence, and causing him to load his gun for defence." A mutual friend of Franklin and Hughes wrote that they had nearly lost their houses during the riots that night.[1]

> *In the Evening, a large Mob was collected at the Coffee House, and the Party declared, That your House, Mr. Hughs's[,] Mr. Galloways and Mine should be leveled with the Street; for that you had obtained the Stamp Act and We were warm Advocates for the carrying [of] it, into Execution.*[2]

Even Deborah Franklin felt sufficiently threatened that evening to barricade herself, with friends and relatives, inside the Franklin home on Market Street.

> *...sum time to words night I sed he [Benjamin's nephew] shold fech a gun or two as we had none. I sente to aske my Brother to Cume and bring his gun all so so we maid one room into a Magazin. I ordored sum sorte of defens up Stairs such as I Cold manaig my selef...."*[3]

The mounting crisis didn't slow their letter-writing. During that wild week in Philadelphia, John Hughes kept a running account as events unfolded, even as the turmoil peaked on September 16. He begins his narrative to Franklin on September 8:

> —*You are now from Letter to Letter to suppose each may be the last that you will receive from your old Friend, as the Spirit or Flame of Rebellion is got to a high Pitch amongst the North Americans; and it seems to me that a Sort of Frenzy or Madness has got such hold of the People of all Ranks, that I fancy some Lives will be lost before this Fire is put out. I am at present much perplext what Course to steer.... I cannot in point of Honour go back, until something or other is done by the People to render it impossible for me to proceed: But perhaps when a Mob is on foot, my Life and Interest may fall a Sacrifice to an infatuated Multitude.... I fancy I shall not escape the Storm of Presbyterian Rage. And as Captain Friend is expected everyday, my Doom will soon be known, but whether I may live to inform you, is yet in the Womb of Futurity.*
>
> *Sept. 12. Our Clamours run very high, and I am told my House shall be pull'd down and the Stamps burnt. To which I give no Answer than that I will defend my House at the Risque of my Life. I must say, that all the sensible Quakers behave prudently.*
>
> *Sept. 16. in the evening. Common report threat[ens] my House this Night, as there are Bonfires and Rejoicings for the Change in Ministry.... I for my Part am well-arm'd with Fire-Arms, and am determin'd to stand a Siege. If I live till tomorrow morning I shall give you a farther Account, but it is now about 8 aClock, I am on my Guard, and only write this between whiles, as every Noise or Bustle of the People calls me off.*
>
> *9 aClock. Several Friends that patroll between my House and the Coffee House, come in just now, and say, the Collection of Rabble begins to decrease visibly in the Streets, and the Appearance of Danger seems a good deal less than it did.*
>
> *12 aClock. There are now several Hundreds of our Friends about the Street, ready to surpress any Mob, if it should attempt to rise, and the Rabble are dispersing.*
>
> *Sept. 17. 5 in the morning. We are all yet in the Land of the Living, and our Property safe. Thank God.*[4]

Not long after that fearful night, John Hughes fell deathly sick. He was "critically ill for twenty-five days," writes Hannah Holstein, "and his life was despaired of." From another of Deborah Franklin's letters, written three weeks later, it can be surmised that he suffered from a carbuncle—a severely inflamed abscess beneath the skin.

> ...our Good Mr. Hughs has bin in the moste Deplorables Condishon that ever man was in this world with a disorder that is Coled [called] a burning Cole and it is this day 3 weeks senes he has bin not abel to stir or be helpe att all[.][5]

To further complicate matters, elections for the Pennsylvania Assembly began on the first day of October. As they had done the previous year, the opposing political parties solicited the German vote, again encouraging potential voters to get naturalized so they could cast ballots for the respective candidates. Unwilling to rely solely on their powers of persuasion, the parties sprinkled a little bribery into the process—the Quakers offering to pay the Germans' $2 naturalization fee, and the Proprietary Party granting charters of incorporation to Lutheran churches. The Proprietary Party falsely told the Germans it was Benjamin Franklin who had recommended the double tax on German-language newspapers.[6]

This time, Hughes's settlers were there. Just one week before—on September 22—Heinrich Stief, Michael Lutz, Matthias Sommer, Andrew Criner, and possibly others living at Roxborough and Whitemarsh near Germantown, had taken the sacrament, the first step to becoming naturalized British citizens. And, as British citizens, they could, probably for the first time in their lives, exercise their democratic right to vote.[7]

John Hughes had drawn so much indignation that he was not renominated for the elections that year. His Tory tendencies had made him a political liability, and his party reluctantly withdrew its support. Possibly the final insult came when his membership in the volunteer Heart and Hand Fire Company was revoked. Ironically for Hughes, "Stamp Act radicalism was rejected by big majorities," and the moderate Quaker Party was returned to power with more votes than ever.[8]

On Wednesday, October 2, the *Royal Charlotte* entered the Delaware River with Pennsylvania's first consignment of stamps. Vociferous demands that Hughes resign his post as stamp officer prompted him to send a letter to the ship's owner stating that he had not officially received his commission, and could neither accept any stamps nor resign a post he did not hold. The letter, all formal and polite, was written and signed on Hughes's behalf by his nineteen-year-old son, John Jr. That day, Hughes languished in his sick bed, too ill to hold a pen.[9]

It was a short-lived ploy. Three days later, the *Royal Charlotte*, escorted by

His Majesty's gunship *Sardine*, arrived at Philadelphia bearing the dreaded stamps. Accompanying the stamped paper was Hughes's official commission as stamp distributor.

Muffled church bells were set ringing, and muffled drums were sent into the streets—a prearranged signal for the mob to gather. Deborah Franklin elaborates that the drums were sent through Philadelphia:

> *...to raise the mobe and send them under Mr. Hughes window then send meisegers to tell him that they was a Coming and wold be thair in a minit and all moste terreyfi his wife and Children to deth....*

Lutheran pastor Heinrich Mühlenberg refused to participate in the fracas, and the bells of St. Michael's were silent that day.[10]

Despite Hughes's continuing illness, the mob gave him no rest. With the son of Chief Justice Allen at their head, a crowd collected at the State-house on Saturday evening and prepared to march to Hughes's house, threatening to pull it down around him. According to Pastor Mühlenberg, "a single spark would have been able to kindle and set the whole dry, inflammable mass in flames and the houses of the stamp-master and others would have been demolished and not one stone left upon another." In an event similar to what Hutchinson had witnessed in Boston two months before, Hughes might have seen his letters from Anthony Wayne, Benjamin Franklin, and Alexander McNutt lying in the dirt outside his house on Fourth Street.[11]

But Philadelphia decorum prevailed, and a deputation of seven men was selected to demand his resignation. Calling themselves the "committee of safety," and led by James Tilghman and coffee-house operator William Bradford, they soon arrived in the street outside Hughes's house. With them was John Cox, the father of Hughes's land partner, John Cox Jr.[12]

Inside his house, Hughes sweated out the hour. Undeterred by his grave condition, the seven men came to his bed and made him promise not to implement the Stamp Act.

Back at the State-house, news of Hughes's qualified resignation gained "the approbation of Three Huzza's" from the noisy crowd. On learning that Hughes was on his death bed, they agreed to allow him two more days to provide a full resignation in writing.[13]

On Monday, the committee of safety was back at Hughes's bedside. Seven men confronted another near death, and they had to bully and whine for his resignation. In the end, they got from Hughes only what he was willing to give: his written promise not to execute the act unless it was also enforced in the other colonies. Technically, Hughes still had not resigned, but, with that, they left him alone.

That week, John Hughes might have concurred with 30,000 United Empire Loyalists who, states Nova Scotia historian Margaret Ells, would later regard the rebel patriots as "a number of cheering, law-breaking, firebrand, political opportunists."[14]

John Hughes recovered slowly from his illness and from the insults of the mob. Three weeks after the rampage in Philadelphia, Deborah Franklin found Hughes "a littel better and a bel to stir himsele...." By early November he was still far from well. Deborah observed, "he dus go a brode a littel now but is but verey poorley yit."[15]

Describing the tumultuous events of the autumn of 1765, Hughes recounted that the Quakers, Baptists, and Anglicans were civilly disposed toward the Stamp Act, but the "Presbyterians and proprietary-minions spare[d] no pains to engage the Dutch and the lower class of people." Historian Scharff says the Deutsch were violent. If John Hughes needed another reason to abandon his Nova Scotia land venture, this was surely it. But a man of principle does not easily forsake the things in which he believes. Perhaps Hughes understood how important the settlement project was to a little group of landless farmers.[16]

And where, one must wonder, did Hughes's settlers stand in the face of the turmoil engulfing their sponsor? Later that winter, as they prepared to leave for the Bay of Fundy, was there any discord within their group in the aftermath of the Stamp Act riots? Was an anxious farmer tempted to reconsider his commitment to now disgraced John Hughes and a new life in far-off Nova Scotia? Did any of them think twice about throwing in their lots with a man who had been the centre of so much controversy only a few months before? Perhaps, instead, they were so disturbed by the riots that they could think of little else but escaping from Philadelphia to a distant province where they could farm in peace.

Even after Hughes had effectively resigned his commission as stamp distributor, he continued to receive anonymous threats that "a mob of several thousand people, from the Jerseys, New York, and New England," would one day finish what the local rioters had started. Hughes stoically suffered the affront to his dignity for several months longer while he remained in Philadelphia. There, states historian Morgan, "he could sometimes be seen in the streets and coffee houses arguing with the men who opposed him."[17]

Benjamin Franklin, busy in London lobbying for repeal of the Stamp Act, was strangely silent about Hughes's dilemma. And although it was Franklin who had landed Hughes in the great mess, not once did Hughes point an accusing finger at his friend. With Franklin's own political career in the balance and his star soon to rise over America, coming to John Hughes's defence would have spelled political suicide.[18]

Franklin remained in England as Pennsylvania's agent for ten more years. After signing the Declaration of Independence in Philadelphia in 1776, he went back to Europe to negotiate the alliance with France. When the Revolutionary War ended and the treaty had been signed in Paris, Franklin returned again to Philadelphia from London in 1785, arriving at Market Street Wharf—the very place where he had landed as a friendless boy from Boston sixty-two years before. This time he was greeted by half the population, who saluted him with great fanfare and an official discharge of artillery. John Hughes might have managed better through the Stamp Act affair had he remembered one of Franklin's maxims: "The first mistake of public business is going into it."[19]

Four months after the autumn riots, an unhappy Philadelphia merchant met with a group of would-be settlers to decide their collective future. John Hughes's one Welsh and eight German families would soon be heading into the wilds of Nova Scotia to put down the roots for a new settlement—or so they hoped. Little did they know that some of them would never leave Philadelphia.

On January 27, 1766, however, all was looking up. An agreement was about to be concluded, a commitment was soon to be made, and a new adventure was in the offing. For the nine intending settlers, the future was all that mattered. Once they had signed their names to the Articles of Agreement, their every thought would be toward their new home on the Petitcodiac River. Supplies would need to be obtained and a vessel engaged. Soon, it would be time to say goodbye to friends, and give heirlooms to family members whom they might never see again. The Pennsylvania chapter of their lives would soon be coming to a close.

A few weeks after the signing ceremony in Hughes's office, an advertisement appeared in the *Pennsylvania Gazette*. The Stamp Act was still in force and the boycotts were still in place, but the Philadelphia land speculators continued to pursue their goal. Matthew Clarkson had called for a meeting of the proprietors of Monckton township.

> The Grantees in the two Townships of MONCKTON and FRANKFURT, in the Province of Nova-Scotia, are desired to meet at the House of Israel Jacobs, in Elbow Lane, on Friday the 14th of February, at 6 o'Clock. MATTHEW CLARKSON[20]

Israel Jacobs owned the White Horse Inn, close by, where the thirsty speculators would find congenial surroundings. It's unknown what they discussed that February day, or even how many of the twenty-two members of the syndicate came to the meeting. Any minutes they might have kept have yet to be dredged from the murky depths of history.

Elbow Lane can still be found in the old section of Philadelphia, near Market and Third. I came across the little alley one rainy afternoon after wandering for an hour along the riverfront docks of the Delaware, reminiscing about Heinrich Stief and his companions who had departed the scene in 1766. All the flurry and bustle of eighteenth-century shipping was gone, the docks that day consigned to a few solitary tourists.

Elbow Lane, Philadelphia, where the proprietors of Monckton township met on February 14, 1767.

The excavated remains of Franklin's house are just around the corner from Elbow Lane—a big attraction for camera-wielding tourists and flocks of school children out on a field trip. White Horse Inn is nowhere to be seen, and a few of the dilapidated buildings in the neighbourhood likewise appear to be headed into oblivion.

Things are quiet in Elbow Lane these days. Boxed in by the surrounding buildings, the little street is barely wide enough for one small car. Bluish-coloured cobblestones line the upper part of the lane, later named Biddle Alley and today Bodine St. The posts are still in place, refurbished to withstand the assaults of twentieth-century vehicles. Originally erected in the 1700s to keep horse and carriage traffic off the sidewalks, the posts are reminiscent of another era. The old buildings seem to brood patiently over the alley, as if their silent vigil might somehow revive a forgotten fragment of the past.

A Loyal Englishman 73

When the settlers finally set sail that spring, John Hughes likely appeared at the wharf to see them off. Two years had passed since he had written his frantic letter to Alexander McNutt complaining that his people were ready to string him up because of the long delay. Their departure from Philadelphia represented the culmination of his efforts in the Nova Scotia venture: securing the land grant, lining up clients, procuring supplies, and negotiating with the other speculators. His settlers were now heavily in his debt, and they were about to sail away to the Petitcodiac River to found a new township. He would not want to miss the event.

As their vessel passed slowly out of port and headed down the Delaware River, perhaps a solitary figure could be seen standing on the wharf, gazing seaward at the sloop as it grew tiny in the distance. Perhaps it was an erstwhile stamp master giving thanks he could now turn to the task of putting his own life back in order. Perhaps John Hughes wished he were leaving with them.

But Hughes's troubles were not over yet. He stayed in touch with Franklin in London, advising him about the situation in Philadelphia, and offering his pro-British thoughts about the repercussions of the Stamp Act. Although no one else could see what was in store for the colonies in America, it was John Hughes who admonished the Stamp Commissioners:

> *If Great Britain can or will suffer such kind of Conduct in her Colonies to pass unpunished a Man need not be a Prophet or the son of a Prophet to see clearly that her Empire in North America is at an End.*[21]

Intending to educate the British government about the true state of affairs in America, Franklin confidentially shared extracts of Hughes's letters with the Ministry in London. Somehow, the contents of the private letters to Franklin and the Commissioners leaked out and wound up, several months later, in the pages of William Bradford's *Pennsylvania Journal*. And, to Hughes's mortification, the damning parts of his letters were read out in Bradford's coffee house. Once again, the citizens of Philadelphia found cause to make his life miserable.[22]

That summer, while the settlers were getting themselves established on the Petitcodiac River, a letter arrived in Philadelphia from Alexander McNutt. John Hughes was taking abuse on all sides, and here was the colonel announcing in his hurried scrawl that he had obtained another two million acres of prime Nova Scotia real estate. Hughes was invited to forward £200 for each township he might want. John Hughes might have rolled his eyes.[23]

His situation did not improve. Sometime later that year, and still under a cloud, John Hughes abandoned his business in Philadelphia and withdrew with his family to their farm in Upper Merion. Two years later, according to his friend Joseph Galloway, he was still living in a state of depression, "disgusted with his Friends and all the World.... This Conduct has given his friends real pain, who still wish him well and would serve him, would he permit it. I have Seen him once this twelve Months...."[24]

Benjamin Franklin's son, William, also writes that Hughes was not reconciled to his losses: "I hear nothing now a Days of Mr. Hughes, except that he shuns all his old Friends and Acquaintance, lives entirely upon his Farm and continues writing his Letters of Advice to the Ministry."[25]

Historians Edmund and Helen Morgan picture Hughes at Walnut Grove:

> ...he could be seen playing the farmer, an old man with a hoe hacking away at the weeds in his fields. Bewildered but unbowed, he would occasionally visit his Quaker neighbors, who still knew him for a friend, if not a Friend, and enjoy the kind of bantering conversation in which he excelled.[26]

In a letter to William Franklin, John Hughes confided the pain he felt from the betrayal of "certain gentlemen" and the loss of faith. Philosophical about his predicament, his script is neat and steady, the tone of the letter easygoing. After all that had happened, Benjamin Franklin was still his friend. Hughes expressed hope of joining him in London that fall. "As to myself," he wrote, "all I shall say is, that, let what will happen, Loyalty to my King, truth to my trust, and sincerity to my friend shall be my endeavor whilst I live."[27]

And just to let the world know that his political stripes hadn't changed, he went about, said his neighbour Mrs. Roberts, wearing "a fire red coat, like a loyal Englishman."[28]

From the "Isthmus of Nova Scotia," J. F. W. DesBarres, *The Atlantic Neptune* (1777). National Archives of Canada; New Brunswick Legislative Library

CHAPTER 11

Into a Dungeon of Fog

When John Hughes cleared out of Philadelphia in 1766, he may have looked back with regret on his troubles during the Stamp Act crisis the previous fall. Troubles for his settlers, however, were only beginning. They had arrived in their new township on the Petitcodiac River with insufficient food and supplies to see them through the winter. The adventure nearly came to a tragic end.

No log of their journey has ever been found, and of the voyage itself nothing certain is known. Esther Clark Wright may have been the first to speculate about the actual date of the settlers' departure from Philadelphia in the spring of 1766. From the minutes of the Second Presbytery of Philadelphia, Dr. Wright ascertained that the Reverend John Eagleson, another passenger on their sloop, had left Philadelphia sometime between April 14 and May 14. Parson Eagleson had got himself into hot water with his Presbyterian congregation, and decided he would do well to perform his ministerial duties in other parts. A servant girl had accused him of "indecent conversation."[1]

Along with Rev. Eagleson, the settlers were accompanied by John Hall—one of the partners in William Smith's company. Hall is long believed to have been the captain of their sloop. In addition to getting his settlers established, Captain Hall had a second reason for travelling to old Nova Scotia that spring. He and fellow syndicate-member Matthew Clarkson each had private interests on the St. John's River—today's St. John River—and Clarkson wanted Hall to inspect his land. On Saturday, April 26, Clarkson wrote instructions to John Hall, stating that Hall would locate the property

77

"[by Cons]ulting the Draught of St. John's River delivered you by the Company's in whose employ you are now going." On April 26, Hall, Eagleson, and the settlers were still in Philadelphia, preparing to leave.[2]

In normal sailing weather, the Bay of Fundy lay about two weeks distant from Philadelphia. Anthony Wayne's trip to Halifax the previous spring was "a somewhat stormy and tempestuous passage of thirteen days." Three years earlier, the vanguard of the future city of Saint John had left Newburyport, Massachusetts, situated about half way between Saint John and Philadelphia, arriving at the mouth of the St. John's River in eight days.[3]

But as the settlers' sloop began to penetrate the first fog banks of the Bay of Fundy that spring, the story itself enters an historical dungeon of fog. Any records of the actual voyage have long since disappeared, and the surviving tale has been twisted and tortured by subsequent narrators until the families' collective memory of the journey has become a confused tangle of half-truths and vain imaginings.

Nevertheless, every legend contains at least a grain of truth, and the Steeves legends are certainly no exception. Adding to those same legends scraps of information from disparate historical records, a scenario of the voyage can be cobbled together. Keeping in mind that parts of the legend may be mere fantasy, any account will involve some guesswork.

Although some versions of the legend include Anthony Wayne in the voyage, the evidence suggests instead that Wayne departed Philadelphia on another vessel so he could procure additional supplies in Halifax. Sloops and schooners were sailing between Philadelphia and Halifax almost every week, and Wayne could have taken passage on any of them. One such vessel was the schooner *Leopard*, commanded by Captain Thomas Church, which arrived in Halifax from Philadelphia on June 4. On June 8, Wayne began billing John Hughes for his time in Nova Scotia.[4]

Furthermore, one of Wayne's many biographers wrote that the young surveyor's efforts in Halifax were compromised by gouging merchants who refused his promissory note drawn on Philadelphia currency, demanding payment in "the best Burlington pork." True enough, a solitary bill of lading in the Wayne Family Papers indicates that after Wayne returned to Philadelphia he sent twelve barrels of cured pork to his creditors in Halifax.[5]

To the clue about the barrels of pork can be added the fact that on October 18, 1766, the sloop *Elizabeth*, commanded by Captain Lebot Harmon, departed Halifax, destined for the Bay of Fundy. The *Elizabeth* was loaded with: "Sundry Provisions for the Garrison & Settlers." Was the

Elizabeth headed for Fort Cumberland and Monckton township with Anthony Wayne aboard? Did it ever reach its destination? I have found no record of the *Elizabeth* ever arriving at Fort Cumberland or ever returning to Halifax. It was Parson Eagleson who later recounted that the settlers "were disappointed of the Provisions purchased for them by Mr. Wayne at Halifax." What did Eagleson mean by that statement? Did the *Elizabeth* reach Monckton, or did it run aground en route and fail to deliver Wayne's supplies? Or, did the sloop sail into the sunset on the horizon of the Bay of Fundy, never to be seen again?[6] All very strange.

Whatever the answer about Anthony Wayne's whereabouts that summer, by mid-May the settlers' sloop from Philadelphia was approaching the coast of Nova Scotia. They had been at sea for one or two weeks, the sloop tossing about on the Atlantic Ocean, buffeted by spring squalls and who knows what kind of weather. Without the sloop's logbook, one can only imagine how they fared. Were they seasick? What did they eat? The adults were probably anxious to set eyes on their new township, having dreamt about their future for two years or more. Spring was wearing on, and they would want to get the ground ready for planting. In the mind's eye, one can picture some of the children congregated at the rail of the crowded sloop, talking excitedly and peering into the distance, waiting to catch their first thrilling glimpse of the rocky coast of the Bay of Fundy.[7]

As much as the families wanted to reach their township and set themselves up, they did not proceed directly to Monckton. All the legends state they first went up the St. John's River to Frankfort, located on the north side of the river above St. Anne's, the future site of Fredericton. Frankfort was the second township granted in 1765 to McNutt's Philadelphia speculators, and was situated several miles upriver from Matthew Clarkson's property at Washademoak. Apparently, the settlers had a choice as to whether they would settle at Frankfort or Monckton.

As well, they may have stopped at John Hall's private stake in the settlement of Maugerville, located mid-way between Clarkson's land and Frankfort. Sometime earlier, it seems, Hall had transported cattle to his property there. A year later, Maugerville resident Francis Peabody was writing to Hall: "your Cattle are all alive at St. John's & in good order."[8]

It seems John Hall was planning to settle at Maugerville where he could be closer to his cows. In the same letter Peabody says, "Sir I am sorry you did not come as we talked of for we want you to be a Justice of the Peace...." Peabody also informs Hall that the government in Halifax had granted them two thousand acres of land for ironworks.

But why would John Hall, a sloop's captain, be interested in iron?

Equally strange was the notion that the captain of a sloop would think of settling on the St. John's River, seventy miles from the sea.

If the settlers did travel to Frankfort, that township was not to their liking. Perhaps, as Dr. Wright suggests, those former residents of Philadelphia were disturbed by lingering signs of Acadian habitation—grim reminders of the deportation eleven years before. The sad sight of burned houses and derelict fields at St. Anne's would have offered little encouragement for them to put down new roots. Then again, perhaps it was the Wolastoqewiyik Indians, always at home on the broad, blue river, who caused them some alarm. Who knows, but maybe they watched the evening sun as it set behind the hills of today's Keswick and took it as an inauspicious sign. Whatever they saw or felt that spring, Frankfort was not to be their final destination. Down the St. John's River they sailed, and on towards Monckton they came.[9]

As soon as they were back on the Bay of Fundy, according to legendary accounts, a terrific storm arose and snapped the mast on their sloop. They limped to shelter at Annapolis Royal on the south Fundy coast to repair the damage. Days or weeks passed while a new mast was cut and erected, and the sloop refitted. This part of the legend is probably true. The explicit story of a sloop's broken mast is not the kind of tale anyone would likely invent.

Seaworthy again, they sailed up Chignecto Bay to lie at anchor in the basin below Fort Cumberland. There, supposedly, they loaded up with supplies. And it was there, presumably, that Rev. Eagleson disembarked so he could take up his new ministerial duties in the fledgling communities scattered beside the marshes. It wasn't the last the settlers would see of Eagleson, however. They would meet him again, years later, when they needed a minister to perform marriages and baptisms and to help them bury their dead.

Next, ready to strike for Monckton township, they sailed back down Cumberland Basin, swung round the headland at Cape Marangouin,[10] and headed into Shepody Bay. Watching for the incoming tide, they soon arrived at the lower reaches of the Petitcodiac, only twenty miles from their destination. Finally, at the conclusion of the lengthy voyage, the settlers landed at the junction of Panaccadie Creek and the Petitcodiac River on Tuesday, June 3, 1766. It was the end of one adventure, but just the beginning of another.

Travel-worn from a long voyage, they must have looked a motley crew. Eight poor families, upwards of thirty children, some of them less than a year old, everyone bedraggled and hungry after being cooped up for a month on board their sloop—one might wonder if they entertained any doubts, at that point, as to what they had got themselves into. Devout religious folk, the families must have taken time to thank God for their safe arrival. The legends say they got down on their knees and prayed.

Thankful to have their feet on dry ground, the families probably didn't spend much time celebrating their arrival. But a celebration of sorts was underway on the south shore of Nova Scotia that same day, and it was an event that might have put the settlers in mind of the previous autumn in Philadelphia.

After months of protests and trade boycotts, the government in London had finally given up trying to force the stamp tax on the Americans. The act was repealed on February 23, 1766, at two o'clock in the morning during a late-night session of Parliament. Royal assent was granted on March 18—four days short of a year since King George III had signed the ill-fated bill into law.[11]

When the ship *Minerva* reached Philadelphia carrying news of the repeal, there was wide-spread rejoicing. The welcome news reached the little port of Liverpool three weeks after. Local shipbuilder Simeon Perkins describes the festivities on June 3:

> *Day of rejoicing over the repeal of the Stamp Act. Cannon at Point Laurence fired, colours flown on shipping. In the evening the Company marched to the home of Major Doggett, and were entertained. People made a bon-fire out of the old house of Capt. Mayhew, a settler here, and continued all night, and part of next, carousing.*[12]

Perkins wasn't the only individual in Nova Scotia to note historic events that month. Ten days after their sloop nosed its way into the mud of the riverbank at Monckton, John Hall wrote a long letter to one of his partners back in Philadelphia, Rev. William Smith, describing the landing day. Despite atrocious grammar and sometimes incomprehensible spelling, John Hall has left behind a charming and possibly accurate account of the settlers' first few days in their new homeland.

> *Deare Sir:*
> *We landed safe at Petitcoodiac the third Day of June, and our people was well pleased with the Land but most tired out with a long passage & have eate up 2 barrel of Flower on Borde which I Bought of Corronal Dickson or tha mus a broke up the Bed stid or a sufferd. I like wise got a hoghead of petatoes for them to plant as tha told me theirs was hurt & some had none for our depend on must be on what petatoes, we can rase & I believe tha are all planted by this time....*[13]

By then the planting season was well-advanced, Hall wrote, and the marsh grass would have to be cleared in order to plant grain. But, he states, "the Inglish grass is a bove our neese.... so long & green that it will not burn & the dead grass amoungst the green makes it bad moing." Their best chance for plowing the ground and planting grain had passed, so they would "try for turnup" instead. According to the legend, the turnips grew abundantly and may have been all that saved the families from certain starvation in the winter months ahead. How they ever managed to survive, one can hardly guess. Ask anyone who has spent a winter in a shack in the woods of New Brunswick and he or she will confirm that it would take more than a pile of turnips to get by.

John Hall goes on to inform William Smith that he'd purchased a yoke of oxen and "3 fine cows & 2 calfs," apparently for the whole group. For each of John Hughes's own settlers, Hall had obtained "a cow and calf." And, rather than a mare and a colt, as Hughes had instructed, Hall had purchased "a fine young bull."

From the tone of John Hall's letter, the outlook was hopeful. The settlers had safely reached their new township on the Petitcodiac River after a long journey; Hall had procured animals and supplies at Fort Cumberland; and the settlers had planted their potatoes. Almost apologetically, John Hall tells Rev. Smith:

> *I have drawn on Mr. Hugh, & you for Seventy Eight Pounds ten shillings payable to Charles Dickson...thirty 2 pound a 11: & 3 is for Frate which in part will some what surprise you, but I have sent you a copey of his Account & then you can do as you please....*

It was to be an ominous note.

CHAPTER 12

"NovaScosha or sum such plase"

When John Hall got back to Philadelphia, he soon discovered he had a big problem on his hands. If the Reverend William Smith was surprised by the bill that Hall had racked up, Hall would be even more surprised by his partners' reaction. They weren't happy. That much of the story and a lot more can be gleaned from a letter that William Franklin, governor of New Jersey, wrote to his father seventeen months after the settlers' arrival on the Petitcodiac River.

Sometime near the end of August 1767, William met with John Hall, whom he mistakenly refers to as Jacob. Despite that apparent slip, William Franklin has captured the essence of a dispute between the Philadelphia proprietors. The letter is lengthy, but it warrants careful reading. In his tasselated prose, William tells his father in London that all is not well with Monckton township.

Burlington, Oct. 23rd, 1767 — Fryday

Honrd Father

I wrote to you Yesterday in a Hurry on hearing that the Packet was to sail from New-York Tomorrow but my Letter got over to Bristol too late for the Post, who it seems missed his Tuesday's Stage and did not get into Philad till Wednesday, & the Postmaster kept him till Thursday Morning, & then dispatch'd him early, whereas in common he is not dispatch'd till Thursday Afternoon. I shall therefore send my Letter to Cousin Davenp[ort], to be forwarded by some Vessel that is going to England from Philad.

I forgot to mention before that I had received the Copy of the King's Grant to you of 20,000 Acres in Nova Scotia. I have not the least doubt but something handsome might be made of it if well managed, which, if I am well informed is far from being the Case with the Lands in which you & Mr. Hughes are concerned. Mr. Jacob Hall, (who keeps Tavern at the Wheat sheaf near Frankford, & has been lately at Nova Scotia with Settlers for your Company of which he is likewise a Member) complains heavily of the narrow spiritedness & Mismanagement of Mr. Hughes and the other Members. They impowered him it seems to conduct there a Body of Settlers, & to furnish them with such Necessaries as they should have Occasion for till they could subsist themselves; but tho' he gave them Nothing but what was indispensably [necessary] they refus'd on his Return to all[ow his acc]ount. This put it out of his Power to return again to Nova Scotia, he having bought Provisions, &c. there on his own Credit. By this means[,] Numbers who had engag'd to accompany Mr. Hall on his Return, were deterr'd from going, which has greatly retarded the Settlement. And the poor People who were left there last Fall, & who, as they were not yet able to raise any Thing for themselves, rely'd on a further Support to be brought by Mr. Hall were during the whole Winter in the greatest Distress imaginable, & must infallibly have starv'd had it not been for Lieut. Gov.^{no} Franklin & Capt Houston an old Settler in that Province, taking Compassion on them. These Gent.^{n} sent them Supplies from Time to Time in Confidence that the Company were Gent.n of too much Honour not to repay them. However, I am told by Hall, (of whom I had this Intelligence about 2 Months ago,) that the Company are averse to paying a Farthing, & he believes will not. — Some Settlers, I understand, engag'd to transport themselves at their own Expense, but others were, on Acct of their present Poverty, to be transported at the Expense of the Company, who were to be repaid as the Settlers grew able. Part of the former Sort, however, were not able to comply with their Engagements; nevertheless Mr. Hall (who seems to have very just Notions, & a proper Spirit for new Settlements) says the Company ought cheerfully to advance every Thing for the Settlers, till the Settle[ment is we]ll establish'd, and take the Peoples's Bonds [and Mortg]ages for the Repayment of what ought to be repaid. The People too complain on their Part, that the Company have not comply'd with their Engagements in having the Portion of the Land allotted to the Settlers survey'd to them, which was to have been done immediately after their arrival. In short, it appears that the Company want a Head to contrive & conduct Matters for them, & that they are too parsimonious and contracted in their Views *for such a Design. I much doubt if you don't meet with Difficulty in getting repaid the Fees you have advanc'd to the Clerk of the Council in their Behalf. —Mr. Hall tells me that the Lands which have fallen to your Share are very valuable, [being] some of the best in the Patent. He wishes that you had been present at the Meeting of the Comp[any] for then, he says, Matters w[oul]d have been conducted more properly. — I intend calling on him soon, to learn all the Particulars. As to Mr. Hughes, I never see or hear from him. I believe he lives altogether in the Country. I shall make it my Business soon to see him & hear his Acct. of the Matter....*[1]

A long letter it is, and one that bears much intelligence pertinent to the story. A closer look will be enlightening.

John Hughes was certainly living altogether in the country. The fall-out from the Stamp Act had taken its toll, and Hughes had escaped the political heat in Philadelphia for the saner atmosphere of Walnut Grove. By then, the former Pennsylvania Assemblyman had earned himself a bad name in Philadelphia business circles, and some of the members of the land syndicate may have been reluctant to deal with him. Still, Hughes had secured more settlers than all the other proprietors combined. His continued participation in the project was essential.

William Franklin's "Jacob Hall who keeps Tavern at the Wheat sheaf" can be none other than John Hall, the sloop's captain and land-company member who escorted the eight Philadelphia settlers to Monckton township the previous year. It seems Franklin simply got the name wrong. His confusion is understandable, however, since it was John Hall's brother, Jacob, who did keep the Wheat Sheaf Tavern, described as "a famous inn on the road between Philadelphia and Bristol." The popular tavern was located near Frankford, a few miles up the Delaware River beyond Philadelphia. Jacob and John were sons of Joseph and Rebecca (Rutter) Hall, and the Hall brothers had married sisters Mary and Sarah Parry.[2]

John Hall himself may have operated the Wheat Sheaf Inn for a time. According to historian John C. Mendenball writing in 1937, the tavern was "opened in 1757 and kept by a member of a family then very well known, one John Hall; this was called the Sign of the Sheaf of Wheat."[3]

But who were William Franklin's "Numbers who had engag'd to accompany Mr. Hall" on his anticipated return to Monckton but were prevented from going? Were they Vallentin Miller, Andrew Criner, Jacob Cline, and Matthias Lentz—Hughes's four would-be settlers who failed to make the journey when the sloop sailed away from Philadelphia in the spring of 1766? If so, then these four men and their families remained behind not because they defaulted on the Articles of Agreement, but because they were fully expecting Hall to take them to Monckton on a future voyage.

Traditional stories agree that the sloop was very crowded. Taken all together—men, women, and children, plus John Hall, Parson Eagleson, and the captain and crew—approximately sixty people filled up the one-masted coastal vessel. Of course, some of the children were very small, yet they all needed room to sleep and eat and move around. Assuming that the sloop was indeed too small to carry all the contracted families in one voyage, how was it decided who would travel on the first trip and who would follow later? Was an arbitrary decision made? Or, did the men meet one day in Philadelphia and draw lots? Did a length of straw decide that Heinrich Stief, Michael Lutz, Matthias Sommer, Charles Jones, and Jacob Treitz would be the ones to found the Petitcodiac settlement? And what about the other three families? Jacob Ricker was William Smith's only settler, and George Wortman and John Copple were contracted to Matthew Clarkson. Were these three men also included in the choosing? Did Smith's and Clarkson's companies have additional settlers lined up? The answers are unknown.

In the next part of his revealing letter, William Franklin explains that the speculators were unwilling to cover Hall's expenditures for supplies. John Hall had laid out some large sums to establish Monckton township with cows, oxen, potatoes, flour, and so on. As well, if Anthony Wayne's experience in Halifax can be believed, avaricious merchants may have overcharged Hall in outfitting his settlers. Did Hall's partners object to the amount spent for supplies, and did they simply refuse to pay his bills as William Franklin claims? Possibly true, but some of the records tell a different story.

Contrary to what Franklin states, John Hughes did accept Hall's claim, allocating to his own company one third of Charles Dickson's two bills of £20:5 and £58:5, as well as one third of Samuel Wetherhed's bill of £75. Presumably the rest was to be paid by Clarkson and Smith. Hughes also accepted the entire amount of John Huston's bill of £34:10, plus the bills of a Mr. Walen and a Mrs. Grayson, two unknown participants. Dickson and Wetherhed were local traders at Chignecto, Dickson being a half brother of Major Thomas Dickson, an officer stationed at Fort Cumberland. Captain John Huston was the man who, years before, had called for a curse on Governor Charles Lawrence and his post-deportation scalp hunters. Without the assistance of Captain Huston and the lieutenant governor, according to William Franklin, the families would have starved to death that first winter.[4]

The Nova Scotia settlement project was a real family affair for John Hughes and Company, and they weren't afraid to spend money on their settlers. Anthony Wayne's personal draft "for Flower" came to £23:18:2. Wayne's father had advanced £8 to the project, and John Cox Jr. contributed £6:5s. As late as 1772, Benjamin Franklin still owed John Hughes £28:10 "on N. Scotia business," and Anthony Wayne had an outstanding note of £30. Even Deborah Franklin had got into the act. After Wayne returned to Philadelphia following his first surveying expedition in 1765, Deborah advanced the hefty sum of £53 to cover one of his related debts:

> *Mr. Hughes ses he shall write to you a bought it as he Can tell you better than I can but this I have paid to wordes [towards] the land I beleve it is in NovaScosha or sum such plase but to be shorte I have paid 53 pounds to young Wain be fore the Deades is dun but he had borrowed the money of a man that was a going ought of town so you see that I am a raile Land Jober.*[5]

Was, then, the speculators' refusal to accept Hall's expenses simply a matter of him overspending himself, as Franklin states? Or did Smith and Clarkson object to an equal proportioning of some of the expenditures? Someone had to pay for the supplies that Hall had purchased, but evidently it wasn't going to be the tight-fisted paymaster, William Smith.

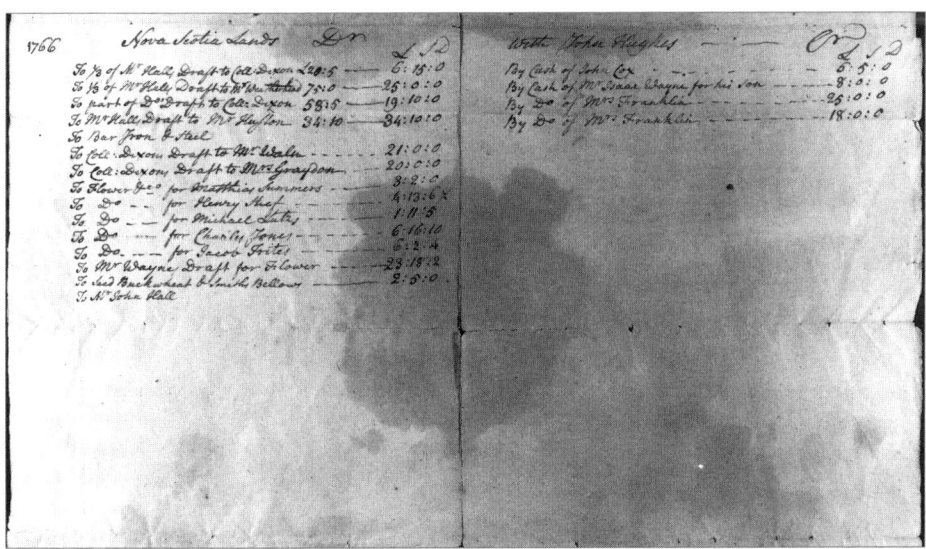

1766 Nova Scotia Lands. John Hughes's account of the participants in Monckton township include his settlers, Anthony Wayne, John Hall, John Cox, and Deborah Franklin.

Courtesy of the Historical Society of Pennsylvania. John Hughes Papers

Here was John Hughes still smarting from the insults he had suffered at the hands of his political opponents, some of whom numbered among his partners in the land syndicate. Here were William Moore and William Smith who previously had been jailed for libel by Hughes and Franklin's Quaker-led Assembly. Here was William Smith who had a reputation for not paying his debts. Here was John Cox Jr. whose father had shown his hand against Hughes during the Stamp Act riots the previous October. Here was Anthony Wayne whose own father was involved in a perennial feud with their neighbour, William Moore. Rebellious Americans versus loyal tories; hot-headed Presbyterians and upstart Anglicans at odds with staunch Quakers; to that prickly concoction add a dollop of colonial mercantilism and a heated squabble over money. For the settlers, it was a disaster in the making.[6]

Their queer accounting methods didn't help. Regarding William Smith's company, a crazy collection of information is scattered through the Jacobs Papers at the Historical Society of Pennsylvania—debits and credits transferred back and forth among the members, plus muddled receipts scribbled on little scraps of paper. The eleven members of William Smith's group would spend the next several years trying to sort out their affairs. Here are a few examples from a time before calculators and computers were at hand:

> *Rec'd Septem.r 23d 1766 of Joseph Jacobs one pound fourteen Shillings for Benj.m Jacobs, being his part of a Bill drawn by Mr. John Hall in favor of Capt. Church for £50—Halifax money amout 75 — Pensylvany Courcy. John Bayly*[7]

> *Receiv'd February 7th: 1767 of Captn. Joseph Richardson by the hands of Benjamin Jacobs the sum of Three pounds Fourteen Shillings and Twopence being his quota of the last payment of my Exps. to Novascotia. rec'd [by] John Hall*[8]

> *Receiv'd Nov. 24th 1768 from Joseph Jacobs Eighteen Shillings and 8 for himself, & 18/8 for his brother Benjamin Jacobs, and four shillings & 8 he advanced for Jos. Richardson being for a draft of Mr. Barzilles [Bryzelius] in Nova Scotia for Sundrys he advanced for the settlers of Dr. Smith & Com. William Craig*[9]

Benjamin Franklin's presence at the speculators' meeting might have made a difference, as John Hall believed, but politics were to keep the colonial representative in England for many years to come. Besides, it appears that Franklin was already losing interest in the unwieldy Philadelphia syndicate. The 20,000-acre grant mentioned by his son was a private matter between Franklin and the Privy Council and certainly not part of Monckton. Early in 1766, as John Hughes and his settlers were signing the Articles of Agreement in Philadelphia, Franklin had applied to the Board of Trade in London for an additional 20,000 acres of land in Nova Scotia. Approved the next year, the private grant was to be located "in such part on the Continent of the said Province as the said Benjamin Franklin or his Agent shall Chuse...." With other important matters demanding his attention—domestic, political, and scientific—Franklin never found time to act on his private grant, and nothing came of it.[10]

Whatever may have been the state of Benjamin Franklin's enthusiasm for land ventures in Nova Scotia in 1766, they faded a few years later. Numerous obstacles were encountered with wilderness settlements in general, and it became increasingly difficult to entice settlers in the more-populated colonies to relocate to distant climes. By 1772, Franklin was informing the Commissioners for Trade and Plantations:

> ...*many principal persons in Pennsylvania...have, several years since, been convinced of the impracticability of exciting settlers to move from the* middle colonies *and settle in that province; and even of those who were prevailed on to go to Nova Scotia, the greater part of them returned with great complaints against the severity and length of the winters.*[11]

The greatest complaint of the Petitcodiac settlers, however, was not the severe winters, but that Franklin and his partners had failed to support their settlement. The former Pennsylvania farmers were no strangers to inclement weather. During the winter of 1764-65, a year before their departure to the Bay of Fundy, Philadelphia had seen the worst weather in decades.

The storms began at Christmas, and the fierce weather had quickly shut down the city. Pastor Mühlenberg recorded in his diary that the rain and snow kept many of his congregation away from church services. On December 30 he wrote: "we had such penetrating cold weather as we have not had in many years...." The following day, the "cold continued until midday, when a heavy snow fell." There was no improvement on New Year's Day, 1765, when the "cold was more piercing than ever...."[12]

A week later, the snow fell continuously for forty-eight hours until the drifts were six feet high. The *Pennsylvania Journal* reported "our river continuing froze over." A Philadelphia business associate of Franklin bemoaned the fact that no mail had come from the east in a fortnight, and all movement had halted. "Delaware River and Brunswick all close—the Ferry to New-York extremely difficult, the Bay full of Ice."[13]

And while Benjamin Franklin was enjoying the relatively balmy weather in London, his attentive wife was shivering in Philadelphia, writing to him about

> *the coldest day I ever felte. we air all blocked up Could. I donte think we have had so much Snow this thirty years one Can hardly see the Topes of the postes now it is two deep to go a Slaying*[.][14]

As he intended, William Franklin met again with John Hall, although it was eight months after his first encounter with Hall in 1767 that he wrote to his father about the second meeting. The Monckton proprietors had asked William to help them sort out their differences. He explains:

> *...they laid before me a State of their Transactions. They seem to have taken a great deal of Pains in adjusting each Man's Share, &c. but not much in Settling the Lands. However, they have lately advertis'd for Settlers, & seem determin'd to carry on the Settlement with more Spirit for the future.*[15]

This time, William names "Mr. Jno. Hall" who had given him some papers. Those papers, William says, would provide his father with "some Idea of what has & may be done with your Lands in Nova Scotia. He has some disputes with the Company at Philad. which I am told are left to Arbitration." Almost two years had elapsed since the landing at Monckton, and John Hall had not yet settled his differences with his fellow proprietors. Hall's papers, which William sent to his father, have never been found.

The proprietors' advertisement appeared in the *Pennsylvania Gazette*:

> To industrious FAMILIES who want land.
> WHEREAS the undersigned persons, and sundry others in company, have obtained grants of two townships, in the province of Nova-Scotia, one of them called Monckton, on the river Peticoodiac, and the other called Franckfort, on St. John's River, containing one hundred thousand acres each, universally allowed to be some of the best lands in that province, having good navigation to each of said townships, and large quantities of meadow ground, already made and imbanked in the first mentioned township, where a considerable number of families from this province, have been settled for two years past, and who have expressed the highest approbation of the lands, in letters to their friends; and whereas the proprietors of said town-

ships, intend to provide a vessel, and send out a number of families this spring, with a surveyor to lay out the lands for the said settlers, and those who are already settled, any industrious persons, who may want lands for themselves and families, are desired to apply to Michael Hillegas, Edward Duffield, William Craig, and John Bailey, of the city of Philadelphia; the Rev. Mr. Thomas Barton, of Lancaster; William Moore, Esq; and Anthony Wayne, in Chester county; John Hughes, of Upper Merion; and Benjamin Jacobs, of New Providence, in Philadelphia county, who will make known the terms of settlement, enter into articles, and give all reasonable encouragement.[16]

The proprietors were obviously trying to revitalize their Monckton venture, but they seem to have overlooked their first group of settlers who were facing starvation on the banks of the Petitcodiac River. Meanwhile, the proprietors' monetary disputes were unresolved. Three years later, the members of Smith's company were still trying to settle their affairs:

> *Receiv'd Sep't: 25th 1771 of Benjamin Jacobs twenty five Shillings for 1/10 of Charles Bakers Acct. for Surveying Monckton Township in Noviscotia for Doctor Smith & Com: Share the whole of which is twelve pounds ten shillings and thirteen Shillings. & Six pence for 1/10 of £6-15.2 Wm. Craig advan.d for provisions for the Settlers. William Craig*[17]

By October 14 of that year, Joseph Richardson had bailed out of the syndicate when he received £75 from Benjamin Jacobs for "all the Lands that I have any right title or interest in or to lying within the Province of Novascotia...."[18]

William Franklin seems to have cleared up the earlier discrepancy about who travelled to the Petitcodiac with the settlers—Jacob or John Hall. But how did John Hall, a sometime tavern keeper at the Wheat Sheaf Inn, find time to be a sloop's captain? It would have been an unusual combination of jobs. As well as captain and tavern keeper, John Hall was likely a farmer, as anyone with a few square perches of earth to plough would have called themselves at the time. The emphasis Hall conveyed in his letter to William Smith about their settlers' chances to plant grain and turnips in June has the ring of any farmer's perennial concern about unpredictable weather.[19]

Farmer, captain, tavern keeper—John Hall, it seems, was a man of many talents. A cherished part of the Steeves legend names John (or Jonathan) Hall as the captain of the sloop in which the settlers came to the Petitcodiac River. All the histories of the area persistently refer to Hall as the captain, and even the Moncton Museum names "Captain Jonathan Hall" on a large brass plaque dedicated to settler Jacob Treitz. Picking up on the family yarn, numerous historians, storytellers, myth-makers, and newspaper reporters and their ilk have fed the fable over the years to the point where it would be heresy to state that John Hall was anything other than a captain.

Was something said about genealogy and surprises? John Hall was indeed a captain, but not the captain of a sloop. In 1748, John Hall was commissioned a captain in the provincial militia organized for the defence of Pennsylvania during King George's War between England and France. John Hughes and Hall's brother Jacob received their commissions the same year.[20]

Bronze plaque commemorating Jacob Trites.
Courtesy of Moncton Museum / Musée de Moncton

John Hall, in fact, was a blacksmith by trade, having inherited the ironmaster's profession from his maternal grandfather, Thomas Rutter, a smith who had come to Pennsylvania with the first wave of William Penn's Quakers in 1682. Hall lived near Frankford in Tacony, Oxford township, north-east of Philadelphia, and operated a foundry in the city. In light of that information, Francis Peabody's letter about their land grant for ironworks on the St. John's River makes perfect sense.[21]

Hall's interests in iron and steel were shared by his comrade in the militia, John Hughes.

To be SOLD by
JOHN HUGHES and SON,
At their store in Fourth street, above Market street.

The best of STEEL, Wholesale or Retail, at the most reasonable Rates. It has been tried by several Smiths both In Town and Country, and allowed to be equal to any heretofore imported into this Place. The Purchasers of this STEEL will have this great Advantage, viz. that if any Part of it proves bad, and is returned, they shall receive an equal Weight of good STEEL for it.[22]

But how did John Hall come to be known as a sloop's captain? Perhaps the settlers were aware of Hall's service in the militia and designated him captain as an honourific. His military experience would likely have equipped him with the skills needed to organize and lead an expedition—leadership skills that he could have brought to good advantage as their sloop headed north into unfamiliar territory. Whatever the answer, the title of captain has stuck like glue to John Hall's name in Maritime histories since 1766.

John Hall, the captain who was not a captain, never went back to the Petitcodiac River, apparently, but he doubtless spent time wondering how the settlers fared without his help. At the same time, the settlers wondered when they would see their friends who were left behind in Philadelphia with the badly needed supplies.

Although the settlers felt deserted by the Philadelphia proprietors, Anthony Wayne had not been idle. Like John Hall, he never returned to Monckton after 1766. But when he went back home to Pennsylvania, he dug out his surveying notes from the summer before, and went to work on a new map of the township. Wayne's exemplary surveying skills are plain to see on a large map which now hangs on a wall of Waynesborough Museum—the old stone house where he was born and raised and where he developed his early career as a surveyor.

While Anthony Wayne's speculating partners had no further success in settling the lands, as William Franklin observed, by 1767 they had reached an agreement about how the township would be divvied up. On his map, Wayne marked out the 100,000-acre township into thirty-six parcels, each one allocated to a member of the syndicate. As well, a town plot was demarcated on the riverside near the spot where the settlers landed on June 3.

The proprietors had high hopes for their township; every square perch of land was assigned. One portion of Wayne, Hughes, and Franklin's land extended from Hall's Creek to present-day King Street in downtown Moncton, and up through the Sunny Brae marshes. William Smith's company was to get the land between King Street and Church Street. Matthew Clarkson's share included the site of the former railway Hump Yard at the outskirts of the city. And of course, Alexander McNutt could not be forgotten. The eccentric colonel got three large tracts for his own use, one of which today includes Moncton's second most-famous tourist attraction, Magnetic Hill.[23]

Anthony Wayne's estate remained in the family's possession for two centuries after the young surveyor created his map in 1767. The old house is now a private museum, located near the town of Paoli, thirty kilometres west of Philadelphia. In his 1941 biography of Anthony Wayne, Harry Emmerson Wildes had suggested that papers in the family archives held information about Wayne's Petitcodiac River expeditions. Naturally, I wanted to see those papers.[24]

It was a vintage stone mansion which greeted me when I pulled my rented car off the highway south of Paoli and drove down Waynesborough's gravel lane. I parked in the driveway next to an adjoining barn. A guided tour was scheduled to get underway in an hour, and I poked around the grounds while I waited, enjoying the sights and smells of a country afternoon, trying to imagine Anthony Wayne gallivanting across his fields in search of adventure.

The tour guide was a knowledgeable woman named Rosalie Zimmermann, and at the appointed hour she and I were joined by a retired couple from Florida; we started in a dimly lit room in the oldest part of the house. Revolutionary war memorabilia adorned the walls, and Wayne's desk reposed in a corner of the room, seeming to await its owner's reappearance from the days of yore.

Mrs. Zimmermann began her lecture by telling us the story of Wayne's boyhood days and of his beginnings as a surveyor. He travelled to distant parts, our guide informed us, where he surveyed land for future development. She pointed to a far wall. "Over there is an example of one of Wayne's 'subdivisions.' At least that's what we'd call them today." We all looked over to an old map on the wall.

"Now in this next room," she continued, turning to lead the three of us out.

I veered over to the map, and leaned past the felt rope to get a closer look. The lighting was poor, and I'd left my reading glasses in the car. I had to screw up my eyes to make out the writing:

A
Map of the Township of
Monckton in the Province of
Nova Scotia by
Anthony Wayne
1767

Instantly I was transported to an eighteenth-century summer on the Petitcodiac River. Snaking across the bottom of the map was the muddy Petitcodiac with its little creeks emptying into the river from the north side. The numbered plots of the township stretched back from the river, and Hall's Creek ran up the right-hand edge, cutting through the old map like a dull knife. I had stumbled onto Wayne's map, unaware of its existence.

Later, under the guidance of Waynesborough librarian Fran Gleason, I sifted through the library's small collection of papers. The library held a good assortment of books on Wayne's life, as well as several boxes of old papers. But the only item I could find relating to the Petitcodiac River was a copy of Wayne's bill of lading for the barrels of pork which he had sent to his creditors in Halifax.

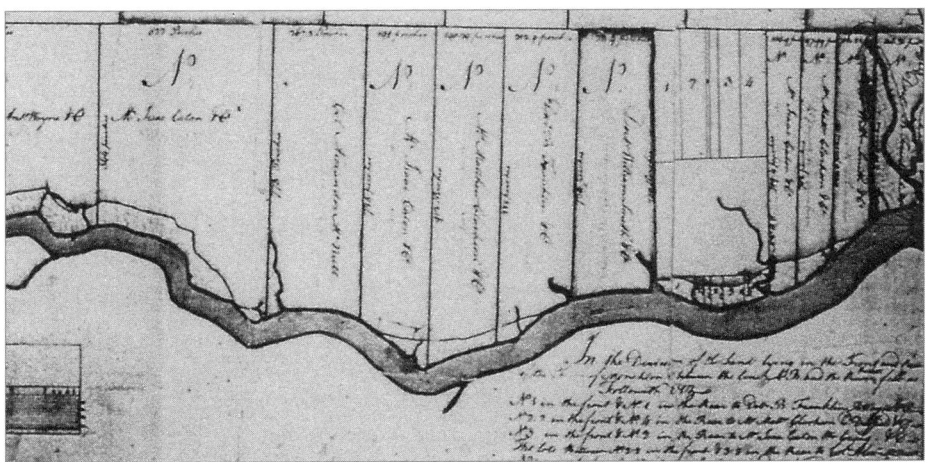

A portion of Anthony Wayne's 1767 map of Monckton Township
"In the Division of the Land lying in the Front and Rear of the township of Monckton between the line and the river fell as followeth VIZ
No 4 in the front and No 4 in the rear to Dr. Benjamin Franklin & Co...."
Courtesy of Waynesborough Museum

The settlers never saw Wayne's map. Unaware of their sponsors' intentions, they spread out along the north side of the river, willy-nilly, after they landed on June 3, establishing themselves wherever they pleased. With support from Philadelphia being tentative at best, and no shelters built and few crops planted, they soon went into survival mode. They had no choice; there were no neighbours to rely on, and in five months they might be up to their necks in snow.[25]

John Eagleson, the Presbyterian minister who travelled with them from Philadelphia, provides a glimpse of the situation. In 1767, Eagleson wrote from Halifax to a former colleague in Philadelphia, the Reverend Dr. Francis Alison, regarding the settlers at Monckton. Eagleson advised Alison that Mr. Wetherhed, the Chignecto trader, had borrowed "supplies for them out of the King's Stores when they were disappointed of the Provisions purchased for them by Mr. Wayne at Halifax." That would have been late in the season of 1766, and the weather had already turned cold. Regarding the men who transported Wetherhed's supplies up-river to the settlement, Eagleson grieved that "one lost his Life & ye other was so much frost bit in his feet that he is not able of doing any thing to procure himself a subsistence." Who these men were, or what became of the one with the frost-bitten feet, no one knows.[26]

Like John Hall, Eagleson had concerns about the welfare of the settlement. As to the proprietors, Eagleson wanted Dr. Alison to inform William Smith: "by not properly considering the difficulties naturally attending a young Settlement...they run the Hazard of loosing all...." Dr. Alison, it should be noted, was a Presbyterian minister and one of Benjamin Franklin's political enemies. By association, Alison was also an enemy of John Hughes, and not likely to offer much support for their settlers.[27]

Perhaps there was something at work in the air on October 23, 1767, when John Eagleson sat down in Halifax to write his letter to Dr. Alison in Philadelphia. By a peculiar coincidence, on that very same day William Franklin was sitting in the governor's mansion in Burlington, New Jersey, writing to his father about his meeting in August with John Hall.

If Benjamin Franklin had earlier lost interest in Monckton township, by 1769 John Hughes followed suit. He had endured enough abuse in Pennsylvania, and sometime that year left the province to accept a post as collector of customs for the Piscataqua district in New Hampshire.[28]

It was to be an exile of sorts. His wife, Sarah, stayed behind at Walnut Grove with the children, while Hughes took room and board in Portsmouth at fourteen shillings per week. It was a sad reversal for a gentleman who had previously been a wealthy Philadelphia merchant and, for ten years, a leading member of the Pennsylvania Assembly. He never did go to London.

In the face of all his troubles, perhaps it was no great wonder that John Hughes failed to keep closer contact with his settlers on the Petitcodiac River. He was a man possessed of much integrity, and doubtless intended to see the venture through to a satisfactory conclusion. Whatever may have been Hughes's differences with William Smith and Company, how much did his conscience later bother him for neglecting his stalwart pioneers? If he was related to Charles Jones, either by birth or by marriage, was he further bothered by his desertion? As for Benjamin Franklin, his partnership with Hughes may have been silent, but did Franklin himself bear any responsibility for fulfilling agreements signed on his behalf? The pioneer families waited in vain through many a long winter, hoping to see a promised second boat from Philadelphia that never came. Abandoned by John Hughes and his land partners, the families were forced to fend for themselves in a strange and lonely place, with few tools at hand beyond their own resources.

In the meantime, the Philadelphia syndicate was finally getting around to having the township surveyed as it should have done when the settlers arrived. Surveyor Charles Baker had been hired to lay out the property, and in the course of his work he became familiar with the settlers and their problems. Baker wrote to John Hughes in the summer of 1769, describing the deplorable state of the three-year-old settlement.

> *They beg that you would let them have some Working Cattle and Some Cloaths and Provisions untill they will be able to Raise it to themselves which they think will not be long. I think it is a Very Great Pitty that they should be lett Suffer so much as they have done ever since they went there as they are a Set of the Best Settlers in them Parts it has Surprised every one that knew them to see how they have lived since they went there Mostly on Herbs which they gathered in the Marsh in the Spring &c.*[29]

John Hughes may never have seen the letter. Even if he had wanted to help his settlers, he was fast fading from the picture. By then, it seems, he had already gone to Portsmouth. The following year he and Sarah moved together to Charles Town, South Carolina, where he was again collecting customs duties, a position arranged by Benjamin Franklin.[30]

But the damp, southern weather of the Carolinas did not agree with him. "This Country is Certainly the pisspot of the world," he wrote to Jonathan Roberts, his friend and former neighbour in Upper Merion, "for it Rains without Intermission...."[31]

Hughes was by then in failing health, and he pined for news of home. "Be sure to write every opportunity," he encouraged his son Isaac during the winter of 1770-71. In March, he sent Isaac seven ounces of the best imported silk worms with advice about how to feed and care for the worms. On May 24, he pleaded, "I long to hear from you and so does your mother." At the same time, he inquired about the state of farming at Walnut Grove and about the worms. "We have vessels often from Philadelphia," he wrote, "but not a scrape of a pen from any of you. Your mother is by no means pleased with your conduct, nor am I...."[32]

By 1771, the fortunes of both John Hughes and his settlers had finally improved. Discouraged by the lack of support from Philadelphia, Heinrich Stief, Michael Lutz, and Jacob Ricker had moved down-river to Hillsborough township the previous year and were farming successfully.

The census record for 1770 reported Heinrich Stief to be the owner of "two oxen, four cows, five young neat Cattle, and eight sheep." Michael Lutz and Jacob Ricker between them reported nine head of cattle.[33]

Matthias Sommer had died in the meantime, along with Jacob Ricker's wife, and Ricker had married Matthias's widow. Charles Jones, Jacob Treitz, George Wortman, and John Copple had stayed at Monckton, the only settlers to remain behind.[34]

In Charles Town, John Hughes had regained the respect he craved. He informed his son:

> *Whatever may be the sentiments of Pennsylvania Relative to me, I have now the pleasure to say in the Greatest of my Popular Credit in that province I was not by any means as happy as I am now. It is true while I sacrificed my time and Consequently my fortune, to support a party, I was a Clever fellow. But when it became me to discharge my Duty to my Sovereign, I was then with both parties a very bad man. Here I have the pleasure to know that from the Governor to the meanest merchant I am highly esteemed, Nor is there a single man in the Province but heartily wishes me to remain amongst them.*[35]

Reflecting on his resignation from the stamp distributor's job, Hughes must have thought himself weak having failed to protect the rights of his King. But, in the end, practical necessity outweighed political loyalties; he was only one man.[36]

Poor health was now becoming Hughes's greatest burden. He added in his letter to Isaac that he'd been sick for the previous three or four weeks.

In September, John Hughes wrote what may have been the last letter of his eventful life. The end is near, but he looks to the future.

> *As to my health it is but very Indifferent being Reduced to a Skelliton, but hope to Recruit when the Weather Comes Moderate, but if I shou'd not, it is not very Material, my Children are all Settled for themselves, and I have seen & known, as Much of this world, as can give a Rational being, any Pleasure, and when that is the case, what Matter how Soon we proceed to Survey the boundless Universe, and with Wonder & Amazement, Admire the Great Creators works, not only in this, but in Numberless other worlds, and Gain perhaps, an Acquaintance with, Innumerable other beings of much Superior knowledge, Ability and Sincerity.*[37]

Four months later, on February 1, 1772, at the age of sixty, John Hughes turned his back on both his pleasures and his trials, and left this world behind. In an old Bible, according to author Hanna Holstein, his son-in-law

Lindsay Coates left a touching tribute:

> *In the various stations of a public and active life He conducted himself with Stability[,] Integrity, and displayed a Strength of mind never to be acquired by Education, but which is always the Gift of Heaven. His private character was truly amiable and exemplary in every Relation.*[38]

Less than three years later, Hughes was followed by his faithful wife, Sarah, when she passed away in October 1774. In his eulogy to her, Mr. Coates was no less admiring.

> *Her Temper was mild, averse to affectation and shew. Her attention was confined to its proper sphere, Domestic Life. She was eminent as an affectionate wife, a tender mother, a kind mistress, and benevolent neighbor. Throughout this tedious and painful Illness she was all Gentleness and Patience, cheerfully expecting the welcome summons, being assured that — 'The Day of Death is not a Fatal Day....'*[39]

But if John Hughes had found liberation in death, his settlers had undergone hardship from the first day they arrived on the Petitcodiac River. They had left their problems behind in Philadelphia, only to face new troubles in a God-forsaken wilderness.

Having fallen on difficult times, the settlers at Monckton might have sympathized with William Franklin, who had shown such interest in the outcome of their settlement. Franklin now had big troubles of his own. As governor of New Jersey, William Franklin was nothing less than a King's loyal servant; when the Stamp Act came to America, Governor Franklin did his loyal best to see it properly implemented. To his misfortune, however, he found himself on the losing side of a revolutionary struggle against British rule.

Identified as a loyalist spy by American patriots, Governor Franklin was placed under house arrest in 1776. The following year he was imprisoned for eight months in Litchfield, Connecticut—in what was for him, "the very worst gaol in America." While confined to prison, he was refused permission to visit his ailing wife who, he said, "died of a broken heart." After two grievous years in custody, he was released in a prisoner exchange.[40]

In British-held New York, William became instrumental in organizing loyalist resistance against the patriots, but his efforts to aid the British army were stymied at every turn by its incompetent commanders. Although by 1779 General Washington's army had been reduced to 10,000 men—most of them half starved and mutinous—the British were unable to win the day.

Meanwhile, Benjamin Franklin had committed himself to the side of the patriotic revolutionaries, and he now considered his son an enemy.[41]

In 1782, William was shipped to England where he wrote long, plaintive letters to his father in Paris attempting to forge a reconciliation. Benjamin Franklin refused to reciprocate. In the end, Franklin effectively cut off William's inheritance, bequeathing his only son little more than the Monckton lands over which he had shown so much filial concern. By then, Benjamin Franklin's status as an American rebel had rendered the land worthless. For William it was the final, bitter blow to a life of loyal devotion.[42]

Many other Americans besides William Franklin saw their lives overshadowed by the coming Revolutionary War. The Philadelphia proprietors lost interest in their Nova Scotia grant, and their land-settlement efforts were abandoned. Commenting on the apparent failure of Monckton township, American historian Glen Tucker mistakenly surmises: "the war came on, the settlers came home...and the dream was forgotten." For the intrepid Welsh and German pioneers who landed on the muddy bank of the Petitcodiac River on June 3, 1766, however, a new dream was about to begin.[43]

Petitcodiac River at Moncton with the settlers monument on the left, erected in 1983. To the right is Outhouse Point.

PART 2

CHAPTER 13

A Chance Discovery

*of Sampyre, to excite
His dull and sickly taste, and stirre up appetite.*[1]
Michael Drayton (1563-1631) Polyolbion, xviii, 763, 764

It wasn't until more than two centuries after the event that the actual landing date of the Philadelphia settlers on the Petitcodiac River became known to family historians in New Brunswick. In 1983, John Hall's letter, written ten days after the landing, was found, through the efforts of Muriel Lutes Sikorski, in the William Smith Papers at the Historical Society of Pennsylvania. Mrs. Sikorski was a Moncton businesswoman, noted genealogist, and a descendant of four of the first Philadelphia settlers: Matthias Sommer, Heinrich Stief, Jacob Treitz, and Michael Lutz.

That key discovery of Hall's letter came hard on the heels of another of Mrs. Sikorski's finds, made a few months earlier in Florida, where she had been searching for the European roots of her Lutz ancestor. The story of that discovery, as I remembered it years later, went something like this: Mrs. Sikorski had finished her investigations for the day and was preparing to leave the Florida research facility when she noticed a journal lying open on a table. As she glanced at it, the name Lutz jumped out at her. Looking more closely, she saw that a Michael Lutz and his wife and two children had come from Wertheim in Germany. Mrs. Sikorski and her niece hopped on a plane to Europe and headed directly to the town of Wertheim situated at the junction of the Main and Tauber rivers in south-central Germany. Their discussions with a local archivist sent them across the river to the neighbouring village of Kreuzwertheim where they found the birth records of Michael Lutz and his family. It was the first time any of the signers of the Articles of Agreement had been traced to the old country.

Posing several questions, as it did, the tale would appeal to anyone's genealogical curiosity. First, what was the journal in which Mrs. Sikorski had seen Michael Lutz's name? No one in Moncton genealogy circles whom I spoke with seemed to know. And why in Florida? It would make more sense that the record of an eighteenth-century German immigrant to Pennsylvania would be found somewhere near Philadelphia—unless of course the journal was a published work or even a self-published history, and Mrs. Sikorski had been searching in a library or possibly one of the Mormon Family History Centres scattered across North America and abroad. If such a work could be found in a Florida collection, I surmised, then perhaps copies would be available in other libraries as well. Who could guess what other useful information it might contain? Since it yielded the European roots of Michael Lutz, perhaps it would do the same for Heinrich Stief. It was an idea that transformed my quest into one of intercontinental dimensions.

But first, back to June 3, 1766 on the Petitcodiac River.

When the settlers from Philadelphia landed at the muddy creek adjoining Monckton township, they gave it the name Hall's Creek, in honour of their sponsor, John Hall. None of them was aware that the small tributary of the Petitcodiac had already been given the Mi'kmaq name Panaccadie by the Acadians.[2]

Although the Acadians had been ruthlessly driven off the marshes in the decade before, signs of their many years of habitation were still to be seen in 1766. The dykes they had so expertly built and maintained were visible to the Philadelphia settlers. Without the long-suffering care of the Acadian farmers, however, the earthen dykes were likely in ruins. Here and there, the remains of a solitary Acadian dwelling could be seen, the foundations crumbling and the charred boards poking through the long grass. A short distance from the landing place, the settlers may have come upon the sorrowful sight of the derelict wooden chapel in which the Acadians had worshipped. Up and down the river in both directions, broad expanses of fertile marsh stretched into the distance, like a distant dream stretching into the sunlit world of the mind.

It was a wild and wind-swept place. Former Philadelphia pastor John Eagleson would confirm that description when he wandered up and down those same marshes, looking for young couples to join in holy matrimony and for their children to baptize. In 1774, Eagleson visited Hillsborough and

Monckton townships, where he "read prayers and preached two Sundays to a Considerable Audience of English & Dutch settlers and Baptized 14 Children."[3] (How New Brunswick genealogists today would like to get their hands on those records!)

Some years afterward, Eagleson described one of his trips across the marshes of the Petitcodiac River:

> *I Baptised Eleven Children and Married two Couple.—I this spring paid them Another Visit & Baptised 5 Children & one Adult—these Visits are more laborious & fatiguing (not to Mention the Expence) than I chuse to describe, & None but those who know this Country can have any Idea of;—Marshes to Cross of not less than 12 or 14 Miles: & then a River Rapid, & dangerous to go up in a Logg Canoe, for about 30 Miles.*[4]

Rapid and dangerous was the Petitcodiac River for the settlers as well as for John Eagleson—an extraordinary wall of water surging up the muddy channel twice a day, followed by a flood that could easily swamp a poorly moored boat and carry off an unwary fisherman. A half-century later, surveyor Joseph Bouchette would comment on the power of the tidal bore: "the waves attain a considerable perpendicular height, when they rush forward with an incredible velocity and irresistible force, their roaring noise striking terror in the animals near the shore, who fly to the highlands in awe."[5]

The settlers weren't terrified by the bore, of course, but it's impossible to know exactly what they felt and saw when they landed on June 3. Still, they're sure to have noticed the edible marsh greens growing on the banks of the creek and the river. But the settlers had no idea what they were looking at. It would take an Acadian to make the introduction.

Opposite the landing spot, where Hall's Creek enters the Petitcodiac River, a vast, marshy point of land unfolds as far as the eye can see. Washed twice daily by the tides, the river's edge in 1766 produced a great harvest of marsh greens. Situated near today's Bore Park in Moncton, where the river makes its famous bend, the marsh is named Outhouse Point, after Simon Outhouse Jr. who owned a farm there in the nineteenth century, and who started up the first ferry service across the muddy Petitcodiac to Moncton in 1841. For many years, until the Petitcodiac River became silted in by the upriver causeway, a select few residents on the Albert County side of the river kept a closely guarded secret that, on Outhouse Point, right at the bend, grew the choicest goosetongue greens for miles around.[6]

Much has been made of the greens that grow on the salty marshes of the Petitcodiac River. Any inquiry into early life around the Bay of Fundy and its tributaries would seem incomplete if it failed to mention the greens' culinary appeal. Goosetongues and late-summer samphires are native to the whole area and well beyond, and those herbs came to play a vital role in the lives of the Philadelphia settlers. From mid-June until September, the nutritious greens were an important part of their summer sustenance; pickled in salt or vinegar, they may have been the key to their winter survival.

A locally known story about marsh greens can be found in an early Steeves legend—a foggy fable which centres on an Acadian known simply as Belliveau. He had escaped the deportation in the previous decade, according to the tale, and when the settlers arrived on the Petitcodiac he was surviving there, unknown to the British soldiers at Fort Cumberland. It was the Acadian Belliveau, apparently, who showed the settlers how to gather the marsh greens that grew in great profusion along the mud flats beside the Petitcodiac River.[7]

During the century before, Acadian farmers had used the greens. Historians have occasionally speculated whether or not those herbs were known to their distant ancestors who originated on the Atlantic coast of France. But such knowledge would have made little practical difference. The Acadians would have easily discovered that the uncooked greens are edible, arousing the taste buds with a chewy texture and a salty flavour. Boiled or steamed on a spring day, a nice mess of greens can uplift the spirit as well as nourish the body.

Goosetongue greens on the Petitcodiac River near Hillsborough, 1999. These herbs came to play a vital role in the lives of the settlers.

Many Acadians in New Brunswick and Nova Scotia have kept alive the traditions associated with samphire and goosetongue greens—called *les tétines de souris* and *la passe-pierre*. No doubt modern Acadians enjoy their salty feast every bit as much as do their English-speaking neighbours.[8]

Not too long before I was tramping around the marsh at Outhouse Point in search of greens, an Acadian chap named LeBlanc was doing the same thing, a few miles away, on the banks of the Memramcook River, another tributary of Shepody Bay. But that fact didn't become widely known until much later, when, on February 8, 1995, during his installation speech to Parliament, His Excellency the Right Honourable Roméo LeBlanc, the twenty-fifth Governor General of Canada, spoke memorably of his own experiences while picking greens on the marshes near his home at Cormier's Cove.

For the Governor General, the summer ritual of gathering marsh greens on the Memramcook River had evolved into a poignant metaphor for the shared heritage of all Canadians—not only those living around the Bay of Fundy. His Excellency provided examples of how the first English, Acadian, and German-speaking settlers had much in common: the land, the forest, "and especially...the water."[9]

One body of water they shared was the Petitcodiac—a muddy river that brought people together as well as kept them apart. Like all tidal rivers, day after day the Petitcodiac River flowed back and forth, century in and century out, as it moved in harmony with the celestial rhythm of the moon and the ceaseless flow of time.

If samphire greens became a common heritage for the descendants of both the Philadelphia settlers and the early Acadians, perhaps credit can be given to the legendary Belliveau. According to the rest of the story, it was either Belliveau or the Mi'kmaq living nearby who taught the hungry families sufficient skills to survive their first desperate winter—how to set weir traps in the riverside creeks and how to spear the salmon and shad that came upriver with the tide.

It seems a remnant of the age-old art of spearing fish survived into the twentieth century. When my grandfather Jones went haying on the marsh in mid-summer, we kids were often stationed on top of the loaded hay wagon where we could stay out of harm's way. From our imperial vantage point, we surveyed the neighbouring fields of long, uncut grass tossing in the breeze. The comforting smell of salt mud wafted across the marsh to our adolescent nostrils, and we could see the Petitcodiac River beyond the dyke. From the seat of his tractor, Grandfather called for us to keep a sharp eye out for salmon coming up behind the bore. A long-handled pitchfork was always ready if the opportunity arose.

With six generations of farmers spanning the decades between my grandfather and his ancestor Charles Jones, it's difficult to say for sure which customs were passed down, and which ones were picked up along the way. Six generations is a goodly length of time for things to change. Charles Jones survived only a few years after his arrival on the Petitcodiac

River, and it can only be guessed what folklore he handed on to his sons and daughters. Nothing is known about his wife, and the number of his children is uncertain. No one knows exactly when he died, or even where he is buried. Six generations is enough time to forget many things.

Margaret (Jones) Trites, ca. 1761–1806.

If Charles Jones was a mystery figure, it only encouraged me to find out more about him. But where could I look that I hadn't looked already? Next to nothing is known about his eldest son, John, beyond the likelihood that he was a teenager when his family arrived at Monckton township in 1766. It is believed John married a daughter of settler Jacob Treitz. Not much is known because evidently no records survive.

A little more is known about John's three siblings. His brother, Henry, was born in 1758, according to his massive gravestone which stands in the Salisbury Pioneer Cemetery near the upper reaches of the Petitcodiac River. Henry married Christina, apparently a daughter of Matthias Sommer. John and Henry's two sisters, Margaret and Catherine, married brothers Abraham and Christian Treitz, sons of Jacob Treitz. According to the information on her cracked and weathered tombstone, Margaret died April 16, 1806, "in the 46th year of her age." Thus, she was born sometime in the twelve months before April 16, 1761. Catherine died April 1, 1854, aged 88 years. Thus, she was born sometime during the twelve months previous to April 1, 1766. Those few clues constituted the extent of my genealogical evidence regarding the Philadelphia family of Charles Jones.[10]

Catharine (Jones) Trites, ca. 1766–1854.

Charles Jones and the other Pennsylvania settlers had a deeper connection while they lived in Philadelphia—that much seemed clear. With a name like Jones, it was impossible that Charles was related to any of the Germans, unless through his wife. Did any of them farm together? Were they neighbours? Did they own any land at all? So many questions.

Perhaps, I told myself, the source of Muriel Sikorski's discovery might provide details about Charles Jones, Heinrich Stief, or some of the others who emigrated with them to the Petitcodiac River in 1766.

During periodic business travels in 1996 and 1997, I kept my eyes open for a copy of the nameless book Mrs. Sikorski had found in Florida.

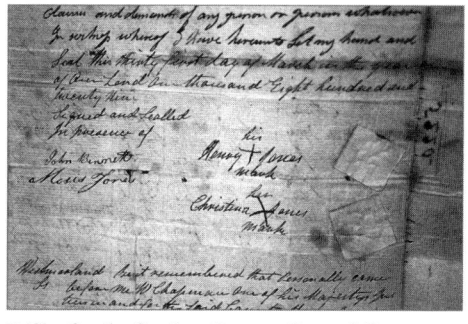

Bill of sale for land transferred from Henry and Christiana Jones to brothers Ephriam and Daniel Steeves, March 31, 1829. £110. Like his father Charles, Henry Jones never learned to write.
Courtesy of Jane Wood.

There was always an opportunity to escape the frenzy of a foreign trade show or slip away between business meetings to become immersed in the genealogy section of a local library.

Naturally, I also searched in genealogy collections closer to home. The archives at both Moncton's Public Library and the Lutz Mountain Museum had much to offer, but nothing that would connect Michael Lutz to Muriel's discovery. I looked farther afield in Toronto institutions, including the history stacks at York University Library and the North York Public Library. In the latter institution, I was pleasantly surprised to find a wealth of resources on Maritime history. But no sign of Michael Lutz.

At the University of Toronto's Robarts Library I was more optimistic. Expecting that the largest university library in Canada would offer some background on the Petitcodiac settlers, I was not disappointed. In the course of my explorations of the social and political history of colonial Pennsylvania, I accumulated much useful information about Benjamin Franklin, John Hughes, Pastor Mühlenberg, and the upheaval brought on by the Stamp Act.

The genealogy section at Robarts Library was no less useful. Together with my gleanings in Maritime history, I had soon amassed a wealth of data. Much of Esther Clark Wright's work was available, as were a few thousand other family histories, each one begging to be explored by an inquisitive and easily distracted genealogist.

In Strassburger's monumental work, *Pennsylvania German Pioneers*, I encountered Michael Lutz's name on the passenger list for the 1752 voyage of the *Phoenix*. In 1934, Ralph Strassburger and William John Hinke had published the existing lists of passenger arrivals at the port of Philadelphia between 1727 and 1808. Although their accomplishment is recognized as a cornerstone in Pennsylvania-German genealogy, none of the other German settlers to the Petitcodiac were to be found in any of the lists. And nowhere was there any mention of Michael Lutz's German home of Kreuzwertheim. The only other name in Strassburger I thought could be related to the Petitcodiac settlers was a Jurg Fredk Sthieff who had arrived in Philadelphia in 1753 on the ship *Richard and Mary*. There was no further information.[11]

Well into 1997, I was making little headway in the search for my Pennsylvania forebears. The search for their European roots—if it could be called a search at that point—was as unproductive as the hunt for their Philadelphia background.

Even the Internet revealed almost nothing, although by that year it was overflowing with genealogical information. The solitary Stief listing on the entire "Roots Surname" list of many thousand researchers was that of a William Steeves of Cincinnati, Ohio. Mr. Steeves had been involved with his own branch of Steeves family genealogy for some time, as evidenced by his occasional contributions to the family newsletter, the *Steeves Family Register*. I sent an e-mail to my distant cousin to find out where his research stood. But he too was at a loss when it came to the German origins of Heinrich Stief.

Several months passed while I tried to find the source of Mrs. Sikorski's Florida discovery. Nothing surfaced. At Ancestor Quest genealogy conference in Moncton that August, the surname-interest list revealed only one participant who was researching the Steeves family. That name was my own. Although my search for the Pennsylvania background of the Steeves family had met with limited success over the previous two years, and my search for the European background none at all, I had included that surname primarily from a sense of duty. Maybe another researcher would spot the name and offer some unsolicited advice. But, even in Moncton, it seemed the trail had grown cold.

Nothing came to light as to the source of Mrs. Sikorski's discovery until one muggy afternoon later that summer, as I wandered absent-mindedly amid the fourth-floor genealogy stacks of the Toronto Reference Library. August had brought the dog days of summer for which the city is famous, and because of which most of the city's rich and famous leave town. I was stuck in the city for the weekend and had gone to the library to day-dream about the past. In the stacks, an elderly couple conferred intently over their recent find, and at the end of the aisle, summer students were sprawled over their books.

My eyes scanned the titles on the shelves as I looked for something to lift me from an impending state of lethargy. So many books, so many names. Quite by chance, I picked up a blue-bound volume: *Pennsylvania German Immigrants, 1709-1786*. I had never seen it before.

Edited by Dr. Don Yoder, whose name I'd come across in the past, the book was an American edition of earlier German records compiled by Adolf Gerber in the 1920s, and previously published in the *Yearbooks of the Pennsylvania German Folklore Society*. A pioneering spirit in the realm of German genealogy, Gerber had solicited information from parish churches in the south German state of Württemberg in order to assemble a history of German emigration in the 1700s. Years later, Dr. Yoder took Gerber's lists and added information from Switzerland, the Palatinate of the Rhine, and the neighbouring county of Wertheim.

Dr. Yoder then cross-referenced his information with Strassburger's ship passenger lists, and also relied on subsequent Pennsylvania church and land records to identify many of his immigrants. In the end, Yoder had produced a comprehensive and revealing collection of 1,675 Pennsylvania-German families spanning seventy-seven years of immigration from 1709 to 1786. Dr. Yoder's book was published in 1980, only two years before Mrs. Sikorski had made her find in Florida.

My interest aroused, I turned to a section named "From the County of Wertheim." On page 227 were the names Georg Michael Lutz and his wife Anna Walburga. They had come from Kreuzwertheim, and had arrived in Philadelphia on November 22, 1752 on the ship *Phoenix*. The entry left no room for doubt. I had found Muriel Sikorski's ancestor.[12]

My attention was awakened from the doldrums of that Toronto afternoon. Was this the source, I wondered, of Mrs. Sikorski's Florida discovery in 1982? After fully digesting the entry for Georg Michael Lutz, I began looking for names of the other Pennsylvania families who had landed with the Lutzes on the bank of the Petitcodiac River on a late spring day in 1766.

Although immediate identification was impossible, several comparable surnames called for a second look. A Joseph Sommer of Oberboihingen arrived in Philadelphia on another ship named *Phoenix* in 1752—the same year in which Michael Lutz had arrived. Possibly Joseph Sommer was related to Matthias Sommer who signed the Articles of Agreement with Michael Lutz and the others. A Hans Michel Beck of Sachsenhausen and a Johannes Beck of Kredenbach were also named. Although Martin Beck, the King's baker at Fort Cumberland in 1767, had not come to Nova Scotia with the other German pioneers from Pennsylvania, his family became so intimately involved with the Petitcodiac settlers that it was conceivable he had known some of them previously. Hans Michel Beck had arrived with Joseph Sommer in 1752, and Johannes Beck arrived on the *Phoenix* two years later. Moreover, both Becks had originated in Michael Lutz's county of Wertheim. What these coincidences seemed to suggest I couldn't guess. As I suspected would be the case, there was no one named Charles Jones.[13]

In the chapter called "Emigrants from Wuerttemberg," one name in particular stood out: Georg Friedrich Stieff. On September 17, 1753, he and his family had arrived in Philadelphia on the *Richard and Mary*. Obviously, he was the same Jurg Fredk Sthieff I'd seen on Strassburger's passenger list. This time, the information was more revealing. According to Dr. Yoder's entry, Georg Friedrich had come from a place called Schlaitdorf. He was a *schuster*, or cobbler, the husband of Catharina, née Haubensacker. The couple and their five children later settled in Reading Town, Berks County, Pennsylvania.[14]

When Heinrich Stief signed the Articles of Agreement in Philadelphia, he had spelled his surname with only one "f." But no matter on that point—one quickly gets used to variant spellings when digging through lists of German immigrants.

There were several similarities between Georg Friedrich Stieff's family and that of Heinrich Stief. First, Georg Friedrich would be about the same age as Heinrich. As well, two of his children's names were repeated in Heinrich's family: Heinrich's wife Regina and their son Jacob. Georg Friedrich's own son Jacob was born just six months before Heinrich's son Jacob was christened in Philadelphia. Four years later, Georg Friedrich Stieff arrived in Pennsylvania.

The similarities were possibly coincidental, of course, but maybe not. Children's names were often repeated through several branches and generations of the same family. Perhaps the two families were related. The evi-

---

STIEFF, GEORG FRIEDRICH (1)—Schlaitdorf (1753)
Cobbler [*Schuster*]. Wf: CATHARINA, née HAUBENSACKER. Ch: (1) Regina, b. 10-7-1744; (2) Georg Friedrich, b. [?]-23-1746; (3) Anna Maria, b. 12-9-1747; (4) Jacob Friedrich, b. 5-5-1749; (5) Maria Catharina, b. 8-22-1751. Ludwigsburg Protocol, 1753. // JURG FRED'K STHIEFF (GERG FRI[E]DRICH STIEF), *Richard and Mary*, September 17, 1753, Hinke, I, 531, 533-4. 3PA, 18, 7: FRED'K STEEF, shoemaker, Reading Town, Berks Co., Pa., 1767.

Entry for Georg Friedrich Stieff from *Pennsylvania German Immigrants*, Don Yoder, ed.

Courtesy of Genealogical Publishing Co.

dence was meagre, but it seemed I had made a new start in my search for the roots of Heinrich Stief. I registered a mental note to look for the village of Schlaitdorf in my atlas when I got home.

Then I headed straight for the library photocopier to duplicate the relevant passages from Yoder's book. Finishing up, I turned to the title page, remembering the importance of noting the details of publication. It was a necessity that had been impressed upon me the previous spring at a Mormon genealogy library in West Los Angeles—the second largest family history centre in the United States—where an elderly fellow had been waiting patiently beside me at the copier. Observing that I had neglected to copy the title page of the book I was using, the old boy launched into a lecture about his own experiences with failing to make careful note of sources. He repeated parts of the story to ensure I had fully absorbed his admonition. After that experience, I recall his advice almost every time I copy a document.

I was thinking of him as I opened to the title page. Near the top of the page was the library stamp and the call-number of the book. At the bottom was a date stamp. I nearly jumped out of my skin when I saw the date: June 3, 1981. It was 215 years to the very day since the Pennsylvania settlers had landed at Hall's Creek. The coincidence seemed to defy logic, but, just the same, I took it as an encouraging sign.[15]

It may have been the sleepy Toronto weather that afternoon that caused me to make a small mistake—one that would cost me precious time later, when I needed it most. I did indeed look for the village of Schlaitdorf in my atlas, but was unable to find such a place. From Yoder's book, I knew only that it was located in the state of Württemberg, and I assumed I would be able to find it when the time came. But by neglecting to provide myself with a location and reliable directions, I had committed one of the seven deadly sins of the genealogist: failing to make detailed notes of sources. Although the rule would normally be applied quite differently, as my elderly friend in West Los Angeles would confirm, that mistake would nevertheless complicate my search for Heinrich Stief in the days ahead.

Chapter 14

Across the Pond

With the information about Georg Friedrich Stieff now added to my genealogical inventory, the time had arrived to begin a new phase in the hunt for the eighteenth-century Pennsylvania settlers on the Petitcodiac River. It was now late October, 1997. Granted, the Schlaitdorf clue wasn't much to go on, but it was all I had.

I'd been planning for some time to take a short leave of absence from my Toronto-based business to do some genealogical exploring in Europe—a combined business and genealogy excursion in which I could cover some of my travelling expenses while at the same time go on a self-directed history adventure. After placing my distribution business in the capable hands of my employees, I booked a flight to London, packed some clothes and my Macintosh PowerBook, then took off across the Atlantic.

Fresh on the ground, and jet-lag behind me, I was ready to tackle the search in earnest. Once my London business affairs were out of the way, I set my sights on a few days of explorations at the Society of Genealogists, a large, privately run institution near the Museum of London situated in a little dead-end lane—a seemingly appropriate location for a genealogy facility. Although I wasn't expecting to find much information relating to Georg Friedrich Stieff or any of the Pennsylvania Germans, I entertained hopes of turning up some evidence of their illiterate Welsh friend, Charles Jones. I had invested so much time looking for him in Philadelphia that I was more determined than ever to track him down.

Esther Clark Wright's allusion to a probable family connection between Charles Jones and John Hughes seemed to be a reasonable starting point.

From *Swedish Holsteins*, I had learned that Hughes's grandparents Hugh and Martha Jones had originated in Pembrokeshire, south Wales.

The Society of Genealogists was a veritable gold mine of resources: old documents, family histories, parish records, and dusty collections of crumbling testimony which probably hadn't been looked at in half a century. The daily admission charge seemed extravagant, but the staff were a most charming and interested assortment of characters. Naturally, I couldn't resist the temptation to look in their English collections for my Yorkshire ancestors while I had the chance. The sheer immensity of their holdings made it difficult for an untrained researcher to concentrate on a particular name, and repeatedly I found myself straying off down some dusty road, as I followed the trail of a related surname, the bearer of which, I eventually realized, had no connection to my ancestry whatsoever.

Of course I was happy to see Dr. Wright's *Steeves Descendants* standing on the loaded shelves. But in that giant institution there was next to nothing about the German emigration to Pennsylvania.

Once I had run down all possible leads in the society's Pembrokeshire records, there seemed to be only one thing remaining to do before I began my excursion into southern Germany to look for Heinrich Stief. If I was going to find any trace of Charles Jones in Britain, I convinced myself, it would be at the National Library of Wales in the town of Aberystwyth.

With a long journey to Aberystwyth ahead, I welcomed the chance to stop for the night in Shrewsbury, an old city with Saxon roots, located near the border of Wales on a loop in the Severn River. More than anything, I wanted to look up an old friend of mine named Brother Cadfael. The romantic adventures of that lovable twelfth-century monk have been so vividly brought to life by his creator, Ellis Peters, that I felt I knew him intimately. And because I was searching for ancestors, it seemed to make sense that I should go looking for one of the antecedents of my imagination. At least I imagined it made sense. At worst, it would be but a short diversion.

I arrived in Shrewsbury on a damp Saturday afternoon, and took overnight accommodations at the Glynndene, a small bed-and-breakfast place situated in the Abbey Foregate. Across the street stood Cadfael's age-old Church of St. Peter and St. Paul, a large house of worship where the biers of long-dead patrons gather dust beside its ancient, grey-stone walls. Before the abbey was founded in 1083 by a cousin of William the Conqueror, a wooden Saxon church had occupied the site.[1]

Today, St. Peter and St. Paul's Church is nearly all that survives of the abbey, destroyed in 1539 by King Henry VIII during the dissolution of the monasteries. In the centuries before, the church had served as a parish church as well as an abbey church, and for that reason it was allowed to escape the king's wrecking ball and his soldiers' torches.

Without any apologies, the twentieth century had miraculously transformed the former abbey precinct into a parking lot. Gone is the chapterhouse, where the assembled monks discussed the business of the day, and where Brother Cadfael could often be found slumbering in his seat in a darkened corner of the room. Gone is the guest-house, where world-worn visitors were lodged during their stay at the abbey. Gone is Cadfael's workshop, where ailing brother monks sought his healing remedies, and where they listened to his fatherly advice about how to ease their troubled minds.

Despite the incessant march of progress, over on the far side of the lot, past the rows of parked cars and the monster tour buses, the little Meole Brook continues to flow happily on its way to the nearby Severn River. Somewhere near the brook, Cadfael's pease fields once thrived in the warm, mediaeval sunshine.

It was early in the evening when I walked over to the bank of the brook and scrambled down the muddy slope. Wet bushes and bare trees afforded a partial curtain to keep the vehicles behind me at bay. The sun had set, and heavy clouds hung in the sky.

Twenty or thirty paces upstream, a small stone bridge over the brook had formed a tunnel of darkness into the distant beyond. The dark, the quiet, and the evening mist together had created a perfect opportunity to renew an old acquaintance. Sure enough, Brother Cadfael was there, waiting to give me a personal welcome. There were no words to speak; the gentle sound of the water flowing through the misty gloom said it all.

The following afternoon, the train coach from Shrewsbury to Wales coursed its way through the green English countryside of the border marches. Somewhere near Welshpool, I knew from my map, we passed Offa's Dyke, an enduring reminder that one is about to enter another country. That ancient wall was built by the Mercian King Offa in the seventh century to keep the cattle-stealing Welsh hill-dwellers in their place.

At Newtown, the train left the broad Severn valley, and headed into the rocky terrain of central Wales. The sight of steep-sided mountains and deep gorges in the heart of the country made it easy to understand why the Mercian, Saxon, and English kings had never completely subdued the Welsh. Every hill was a potential fortress, every valley a place to hide.

By mid-afternoon, we had reached the River Dovey—in Welsh, the *Afon Dyfi*—where late-season asters bordered fields of tall, yellow grass standing in the November sun. Near the village of Machynlleth, the great sweeping marshes at the Dovey's estuary stretched to the south-west, and the smell of the sea came stealing around the misted windows of the train. If Charles Jones had lived anywhere near this place in the years before his time in Pennsylvania, he would certainly have felt at home on the Petitcodiac River in New Brunswick. Above the mud flats that flanked the river, seagulls careened on the wind. Had it not been so late in the year, I might have left the train to go looking for samphire greens. Not long past Machynlleth, we rolled into the hilly seaside town of Aberystwyth.

Admittedly, I had arrived at the National Library of Wales not very well prepared for a dig into Welsh family history. The Genealogy Department looked promising at first, but without a useful starting point my quest quickly degenerated into an exercise in futility. I could not, for the life of me, decipher the system of the card catalogues. Where I had expected to find a main compilation of holdings, I was greeted with numerous card files, some apparently cross-referenced to others and some not. In the microfilm room, nothing made sense. After an hour or two of loading film I didn't want, I gave up in frustration.

To further confound my search, many of the genealogical terms in the library were a total mystery: armigerous families, Bishop's transcripts, manorial registers, Burgess lists, muniments, visitations—what did it all mean? Should I have been looking in the manor court records, the chancery records, or the episcopal consistory court records? How was I supposed to deal with the tithe maps, the apportionments, and the hearth tax returns? And I mustn't forget the quarry records, the records for Petty Sessions, and the quarter-session records. For all my efforts, I might as well have been researching in ancient Greek.

I had settled in at the Helmsman Hotel, an old, satisfactory guest house located on the promenade overlooking the Irish Sea. It was a big, plain house with a creaking circular staircase and heavy doors that locked with skeleton keys. Along the plate rail that ran around the upper walls of the breakfast room, model boats and painted ships reminded guests of seafaring days gone by. Drifting off to sleep each night, with thoughts of my Jones ancestor for company, I was lulled by the roar of the sea as the waves surged over the breakwater beside the hotel, spilling sand and seaweed across the road.

My stay at the Helmsman was more satisfactory than my investigations at the National Library. In the end, I had no more luck looking for a solitary Charles Jones in Wales than I did searching for him in Pennsylvania. In terms of discoveries, I departed Aberystwyth no differently than I had arrived, that is to say, empty-handed.

Chapter 15

A Hidden History

It was late in November when I finally packed my bags and headed out of London. The cold, damp weather seemed to call for sober second thoughts about the prospect of spending two weeks traipsing around southern Germany, where the weather wasn't likely to be any better. My fall trench coat was beginning to feel flimsy against what probably lay ahead. The search in Wales had been a disappointment, and I was reluctant to embark on another wild-goose chase in a foreign country whose language I didn't understand.

From the inner deck of the ferry to Holland, I watched the English coast grow dim in the distance, and felt the vastness of Europe loom ahead. Gazing out to sea, I worried that my single clue about a lone Stieff family from Schlaitdorf might lead me into another tangled and unproductive dig into the past. I had to wonder if I really knew what I was doing. Despite my apprehension I felt obligated to pursue the challenge that presented itself. After hearing for decades that Heinrich Stief had originated in Osnabruck, the opportunity had arrived to put my divergent hunch to the test.

I intended to stop in Amsterdam for a few days, where some business prospects awaited me, and where I could briefly amuse myself as a vacationing tourist. Half the population of Europe seemed to share my recreational intent. I had timed my arrival in that cosmopolitan port city to coincide with the opening of the tenth annual Cannabis Cup, an international, multi-faceted event promoting all aspects of the hemp plant—its many industrial uses for fibre, rope, oil, textiles, paper, and food, as well as its role in the realm of medicine and its less respectable use in the exploration of human consciousness.[1]

I had read so many fascinating accounts about the production of hemp in colonial North America, and particularly in old Nova Scotia, that I wanted to get a first-hand look at what had become of the plant in the two hundred years since my ancestors had grown it on the Petitcodiac River. That is, they were supposed to have grown hemp. The Articles of Agreement, drafted between John Hughes and his prospective settlers, had included hemp-growing as a condition of settlement. After the second year in their new township, each family was required to cultivate one-quarter acre of hemp annually for the subsequent thirty years. The reason for this seemingly odd stipulation, I discovered, was far from odd.

Hemp was of such importance to the British government of the day that German farmers were placed in Nova Scotia expressly to catch fish and grow hemp for Britain's burgeoning empire. The "Cultivation of Hemp" by "these people," declared Council secretary Richard Bulkeley in 1765, would provide "many advantages" to the young colony.[2]

The Germans' reputation as good hemp farmers had apparently preceded their arrival in Nova Scotia. As early as 1712, Palatine farmers who'd been brought into Ireland "were reported as having employed themselves very industriously in raising flax and hemp." By 1720, farmers in Lancaster County, Pennsylvania, were bringing indentured servants to their farms to work on the hemp crops.[3]

Hemp had been around many years before a little band of Pennsylvania Germans landed on the bank of the Petitcodiac River in 1766. Since ancient times, the hemp plant had been an essential ingredient in the manufacture of paper, rope, and cloth. As long ago as 4500 B.C., the Chinese were using hemp to make fishing nets and rope.[4]

Four thousand years later, in the fifth century B.C., Herodotus, the first known Greek historian, wrote favourably of hemp in his *Histories*. From Herodotus's day down through the centuries, hemp competed only with flax for the distinction of being the world's most important source of fibre.[5]

According to American author John Roulac, writing in more recent times:

> From the sixteenth to the eighteenth centuries, hemp and flax dominated among fibre crops of Asia, Europe, and North America. French, Dutch, Spanish, British, German, and Russian trading ships-including those that brought the first explorers and colonists to America-were rigged with ropes and sails made from hemp.[6]

The sailing ship became so important to Europeans in their battles for supremacy in America that the eighteenth century came to be "the Age of Hemp."⁷

Naturally, hemp was included in Governor Charles Lawrence's 1758 proclamation for the resettlement of Nova Scotia. Alluding to the Acadians whom Lawrence had subjected to much misery, the proclamation stated that hemp and other produce had been successfully cultivated "for more than a Hundred Years past."⁸

Three years later, chief surveyor Charles Morris added weight to Lawrence's claim by issuing a favourable assessment of hemp's prospects. Compared to the warmer New England colonies, Morris advised, the cool weather around the Bay of Fundy was more conducive to a good yield:

> The raising of Hemp in the Southern Colonies has fail'd principally from the excessive Heats of the Summer which Stunt it and prevents its growing to a suitable Length.... But the Air of this province [Nova Scotia] being more moderate in the Summer and more subject to Rain and Damps from the Seas surrounding it, there is great Reason to hope, This useful material will succeed here...⁹

J.F.W. DesBarres (1722-1824) Lieutenant-Governor of Cape Breton 1784-1787, who promoted hemp-growing in eighteenth-century Nova Scotia. Courtesy NSARM

Though the summer of 1761 had been "uncommonly dry," the hemp crop on the St. John's River that season grew ten feet high.

Morris's confidence in hemp culture was echoed by Joseph F. W. DesBarres, the British government surveyor whose maps and charts have left a living picture of the eighteenth-century landscape. In his preface to *The Atlantic Neptune*, DesBarres professed that Nova Scotia's "vales and Marsh-lands are well adapted for the Culture of Flax and Hemp, for Sails and Cordage."¹⁰

Montague Wilmot, appointed governor three years after Lawrence's death in 1760, so earnestly wanted to see industrious German farmers growing hemp in the province that he petitioned the Lords of Trade in London on the subject. Although the New England merchants were, he said, "at a loss to procure Fish and Hemp for the British market...nothing is wanting in Nova Scotia but a sufficiency of labouring people."¹¹

Of course, the proprietors of Monckton were very much interested in the possibilities for growing hemp in their new township. During his surveying expedition to Nova Scotia in 1765, the ever-observant Anthony Wayne wrote to John Hughes from Halifax:

> *the gentlemen who have Estates in the Cuntry, say's the land is very good & Capable of Producing any kind of Grean, they Raize Excellent Spring wheat, which Yields 60 or 70 Bushells to the acre, & Likewise hemp in all their dike Lands....*[12]

Nor was the indefatigable Colonel Alexander McNutt to be left out of the picture. After his initial introduction of 250 Irish families to Nova Scotia in 1761, McNutt returned to Londonderry where another 700 settlers awaited him. Along with obligations to his Irish farmers, according to the Lords of Trade, McNutt had "also contracted for 500 bushels of Hemp seed, with a view to encourage the production of that valuable material of manufacture in that Province." The enterprise was deemed of such importance that King George III was made aware of McNutt's hemp seed.[13]

When the Philadelphia settlers landed at Monckton township on June 3, 1766, their sponsor, John Hall, had his eyes open for good hemp land. Hall told his partner William Smith: "our land is strong enough even for hemp...."[14]

The following year, census returns revealed that hemp was already growing in several townships. In Cumberland, Horton, Maugerville, and Sackville, the average yield was twelve-and-a-half bushels of hemp seed for the season. The greatest producer was Maugerville, where McNutt's Massachusetts immigrants reported an impressive yield of 1,200 pounds of hemp fibre.[15]

Because the settlers at Monckton township had arrived unprepared for extensive farming that first year, they were unable to report any produce. Apparently, their turnips weren't worthy of the census return. Nevertheless, a number of farm animals were counted: two horses, five oxen, fifteen cows, and six pigs. The crops would come later.

The next three years were lean, but by 1770 Heinrich Stief was true to the agreement he had signed in Philadelphia. His name by then had been anglicized on the census return to Henry Steeve, and he had moved a few miles down-river to his new location in Hillsborough. That year, Heinrich harvested half a bushel of hemp seed and a hundredweight of hemp stalk, the only settler in Hillsborough to grow such a crop. It seems his farming abilities had progressed beyond potatoes and turnips.[16]

While hemp was obviously an important commodity in the 1700s, I entertained no illusions that the Petitcodiac River crop was grown for any purpose other than its oil and fibre. Certainly the settlers had transformed the long bast fibres of the plant into rope and twine. Perhaps they had made even finer materials such as sails and cloth. In the thirteen years between 1787 and 1800 alone, more than 700 sea-going vessels were built in the Maritimes, and hemp products were in constant demand.[17]

Several grandsons of Heinrich Stief and Michael Lutz were involved in the boat-building trade. About 1819, three sons of Jacob and Catherine (Lutz) Stief—John, George, and Leonard—built a schooner of fifty-eight tonnes, appropriately named the *Three Brothers*. A few years later, Heinrich's

Remains of a wharf near Hillsborough, N.B., with the Petitcodiac River beyond.

youngest son, Matthias, built the *Sophie*, a schooner which was tragically lost with its entire crew in the Bay of Fundy in 1828. Four years after that mournful event, the *Mary Jane* was constructed by Heinrich's grandson Joseph. A few years later, another grandson, John, launched the *Hillsborough*, a schooner of 163 tonnes. Before claiming fame as a Father of Confederation, William Henry Steeves, a great-grandson of Heinrich Stief, had been a successful Albert County lumberman and ship merchant.[18]

Through the ensuing decades, as the shipping industry expanded and the requirements for hemp increased, the descendants of the first German pioneers on the Petitcodiac River continued the boat-building tradition. Hemp's anti-mildew and anti-microbial properties made it particularly well suited to ocean-going vessels which would naturally be outfitted with hemp sails and rigging. Ships of the day depended heavily on hemp for their entire operation, to such an extent that an entire fleet could be quickly disabled without a steady supply.[19]

But all good things, it seems, must come to an end. Early in the nineteenth century, hemp took a back seat in the competitive world of fibre—a decline brought on by the invention of the cotton gin. The dawning of the steamship age during the War of 1812 signalled the end of the age of sail, and, soon after, the end of hemp's importance on the world stage.

Until it was outlawed, with little debate, by an incurious United States Congress in 1937, hemp probably had been the most widely used source of fibre on the planet. It was not a coincidence that many of the collaborators in the prohibition campaign against hemp were the same individuals who benefited most from the resulting market dominance of synthetic fibre.[20]

Only in the past decade has there been a reappearance of the old friend of mankind. Hemp's comeback has been so profound that, at the end of the twentieth century, several thousand products were being created from the versatile plant.[21]

As Amsterdam's Cannabis Cup proclaimed, a brand-new industry—or perhaps the reinvention of an old one—catered to environmentally minded consumers. Creative manufacturers and entrepreneurs were offering their North American and European customers a wide variety of fashionable articles: hemp hats, hemp knapsacks, hemp shirts and pants, hemp shoes and sandals, hemp paper, hemp lip-balm, hemp salve, hemp skin-lotion, hemp soap, hemp oil for cooking and salads, hemp seeds for baking, even hemp bedding for pets and hemp shingles for roofs. The list seems endless.

To what extent did the pioneer settlers on the Petitcodiac River turn their fields of hemp into similar products? Would they recognise today's hemp creations-so many hemp purses and satchels; a plethora of colourful hemp scarves; a multitude of durable hemp belts? What would Heinrich Stief make of a tasty hemp-seed snack bar?

Such were my musings, as I wandered through the narrow Amsterdam streets. In every direction, tall houses stood shoulder to shoulder, presenting a serene uniformity of mood and colour. Dignified hues of beige, white, and black were broken occasionally by a blue door or a solitary red flower box. Countless canals intersected the streets in endless geometric repetition, and the narrow streets around my hotel mirrored one another.

The maze of similar-looking streets and seemingly identical canals was too confusing to figure. In short, I was lost much of the time. My small hotel was located on Leidsekruisstraat beside the Prinsengracht canal—not far from the Spiegelgracht, and just around the corner from Lange Leidsedwarsstraat. It was close to Leidsestraat, but if I reached the Lijnbaansgracht, I knew I had walked too far. The hotel's exact location was a continual puzzle, yet I always managed to find the place by wandering in ever-diminishing circles until I arrived at the familiar front door.

Life in Amsterdam was wonderfully disorienting, but after five days of wandering introspection I grew restless. I was impatient to proceed with the prime reason for my expedition to Europe: to follow up Yoder's clue and find the home of Georg Friedrich Stieff. My genealogical pursuits had been put aside for the better part of a week, and I was eager to get on with my search for the Württemberg village of Schlaitdorf.

On a cold but sunny Saturday afternoon, I rode a city tram to Amsterdam's *Centraal Station*, where I booked a seat on the six o'clock Inter-City train to southern Germany. On the way to Württemberg, I intended first to call on a friend from Toronto, Wiltrud Steinacker, who was now living in the Austrian town of Landeck, just beyond the German border. My itinerary to Württemberg would be slightly roundabout, but the side trip would provide an opportunity to re-orient myself in another culture, and acclimatize my Anglo-Saxon ears to the German language.

After obtaining a ticket, I stowed my baggage in a computerized locker in the station, and then set out to pass the remainder of the afternoon in one of the upbeat coffeeshops nearby. Amsterdam attracts visitors from around the world, and its artfully decorated coffeeshops have become international meeting places for like-minded spirits. I chose a little place where a glassed-in patio extended onto the broad sidewalk. It was a quiet and tidy café, nearly deserted at that hour of the day. The few patrons relaxing at the tables on the patio exchanged curious glances with

Amsterdam near the *Centraal Station*.

pedestrians strolling by. The atmosphere was agreeable, and I settled into a chair at a small table near the front. I would be content to wait out the next few hours.[22]

With few distractions, it seemed a good chance to mull over the quest for my Stief ancestor. I wondered what the next two weeks would bring. Was I about to disprove the foggy legend that Heinrich Stief had come from Osnabruck?

I anticipated spending a few days in Austria, after which I would use the return portion of my ticket to travel to Württemberg. The plan would leave me a week to explore before returning to Amsterdam and then travelling on to England for my return flight to Canada.

What would I find in Schlaitdorf? Would there be any records from the 1700s or even a church remaining from that time? If I did find evidence of Georg Friedrich Stieff, would it put me any closer to Heinrich Stief? Heinrich had arrived in Philadelphia by 1749, I knew, and Georg Friedrich Stieff had landed there in 1753. The time-frame was perfect, and their surnames were similar. Beyond that, my quest was going to be a big gamble.

With the last, lingering concerns about my Toronto-based business fading away, the approaching adventure seemed to put me on the edge of the world. Two-and-a-half centuries ago, when Heinrich and Regina Stief passed near this place on their way to America, did they too feel like they were on the edge of the known world? Their journey down the Rhine River to Rotterdam would have taken them not very far from the spot where I was passing the afternoon. If they could, what would they think of the changes to the world in the ensuing 250 years since they had gone to Pennsylvania? How would they respond to the cars and traffic lights?—to skyscrapers built of steel and glass?—to neon lights as far as the eye can see?—to cellular phones?—to so much apparent wealth around every corner? Those eighteenth-century emigrants were leaving behind a world vastly different from ours today. Theirs was a world of animals and work and family and the mysteries of life. If modern man seems mesmerized by what he thinks he knows, they were more keenly aware of what they knew not.

Late in the afternoon, as my hour of departure drew near, I brought my thoughts to bear on the impending trip through the winding Amsterdam streets, now becoming gloomy in the fading light. It was imperative I fully appreciate my placid state of mind, brought on by the expansive atmosphere in the little coffeeshop. The *Centraal Station* was only a few blocks away, but I didn't have time to get lost in the unfamiliar terrain. I bade farewell to the shop's youthful proprietors, and went outside to join the flow of humanity.

I purposefully walked the darkened blocks to the station where I collected my baggage from the terminal locker. Then, on Saturday evening, November 29, 1997, a return ticket in my hand, I boarded an Inter-City night train bound for Austria, leaving Amsterdam, the city of civility, behind.

Chapter 16

A Castle in the Sky

In the train compartment to which I had been assigned, a compact, middle-aged woman was sitting in the far corner by the window. The room looked inviting in the subdued light, and I welcomed the trip ahead. After placing my largest bag on the overhead rack, I took a seat near the door. Then, in an attempt to be hospitable to a fellow traveller, I ventured a few words to the woman, in the best of my New Brunswick college French: *"Bonjour, comment ça va, ce soir?"*

My friendly overture was met with a startled look of incomprehension. I tried again. "I'm sorry," I said to her, "you don't speak French?" To which she instantly shot back in perfect English: "Of course I speak French."

Then she proceeded to stare severely at the empty seat across from her. I wondered if my gregarious introduction was too bold for her stoic demeanour. I gave up trying to make idle conversation, preferring instead the stony silence of the little compartment. But the woman continued to hold the tension in her small frame, as her eyes burned holes into the opposite seat.

Uncomfortable with her artificial stillness, I got up and stood in the vestibule while passengers sorted themselves out for the impending ride. After ten or fifteen minutes idling the time and trying to keep out of the way, boredom set in. I went back to my seat, only to find that the woman had disappeared with all her belongings. I was left alone in the compartment.

My solitude was not to last, of course, but my next two companions were considerably more amiable. The first was a strange-looking bloke—a thin fellow with scraggly hair and long whiskers on his chin—a Rasputin look-alike who had aged beyond his years. His clothes spoke of scholarly pursuits, and he had the air of a cleric. In thick English, he explained that he was Austrian, travelling to Nüremberg, Germany. With a measure of success, we tried some simple conversation on each other. I told him that my own destination was Landeck, Austria, pronouncing the name just as it's spelled. But he failed to understand immediately, and we each repeated, back and forth, the name of the little town.

"Landick?" he questioned. "Yes, Landeck," I answered. "Landeck?" he queried again, skeptically.

Yes it was Landeck I emphasized, speaking very slowly. Was he hard of hearing or had he lived his life in some monastic retreat, far from the modern world? Suddenly he got it.

"*Landick!*" he shouted, saying it exactly the way he had the first time. He repeated the name confidently to himself and then sank back in his seat, seeming to muse over his revelation with dreamy satisfaction.

A plump, young Dutch woman entered the compartment to join us. She was as sociable as the previous woman had been unfriendly, and the two of us engaged in small talk while waiting to depart.

Soon, the train crept out of the station, gained momentum, and rumbled down the tracks, destined for southern Germany. After an hour or so, a young female conductor in a neat blue uniform came to collect our tickets and help us get ready for bed. She spoke Dutch with the woman, German with Herr Rasputin, and English with me. The whole affair of processing our tickets and getting us arranged in the bunks would have been complicated enough in one language. Without our trilingual conductor, the undertaking might have ended in hopeless confusion.

The beds were simple contraptions—little more than cushioned slabs, arranged in two tiers. With the sleeping shelves built tightly into the compartment, sleep was the only option. The plain bunks were a far cry from the deep, comfortable beds and crisp sheets offered on overnight trains in Canada. But, in the end, the difference mattered little. Despite the Spartan accommodation, I was soon fast asleep.

Sometime in the night, the train passed through Nüremberg, where I presume my Rasputin friend departed. When I awoke, both he and the Dutch woman were gone. Who knows, perhaps they'd left together.

About 6:30 in the morning, the train came into München where I managed to stay awake long enough to change trains. The next train passed through Innsbruck, then climbed up the winding valley of the Inn River and into the western reaches of the Austrian Alps. In practical terms, the border between Holland and Germany had been non-existent, so I was surprised to find myself questioned, albeit perfunctorily, by an Austrian immigration officer. But after a quick glance at my Canadian passport, he went matter-of-factly about his business.

Finally, late on a Sunday morning, fifteen hours out of Amsterdam, the train rolled into the frosty, mountain-side town of Landeck where I disembarked.

I had a short but lovely Austrian holiday, wandering with my friend Wiltrud along the snow-dusted pathways that wound up from the village into the mountains above the Inn River. The mountainsides were thick with evergreen trees, many the same kinds we'd known in Canada, and she and I identified the various species, testing each other's imprecise knowledge of botany.

Perched on a little promontory on the side of the north mountain were the ruins of a small mediaeval castle, the Ruine Schrofenstein, built about the year 1200. It is believed that the castle was occupied at the close of the Third Crusade, just about the time when Richard the Lion-Heart had passed through Austria on his way home to merry olde England. The fearless king was abducted by Duke Leopold in 1192 and held for ransom in an Austrian castle.[1]

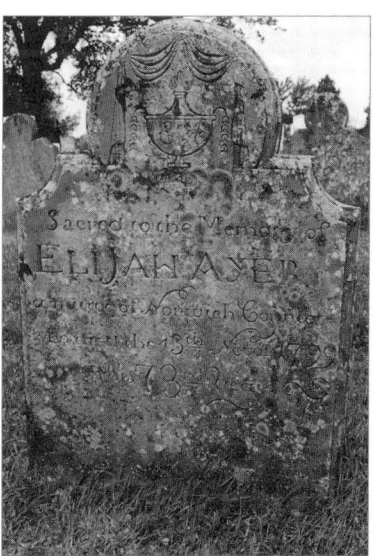

Sacred to the Memory of Elijah Ayer a native of Norwich, Connecticut who died the 13th Nov. 1799 in his 73rd year.

It wasn't the first time I had encountered adventuresome King Richard during the course of my genealogical endeavours. If the chronicles can be trusted, a very distant ancestor named Humphrey le Aire had fought alongside King Richard during the Third Crusade, in the year 1189.[2]

Five-and-a-half centuries after that heroic campaign, Humphrey's descendant, Elijah Ayer, left his home in Norwich, Connecticut, and arrived at Sackville, on the Isthmus of Chignecto in today's New Brunswick. That was in 1759, just a few years before Heinrich Stief and his friends came sailing up the Petitcodiac River to establish the township of Monckton. A granddaughter of Elijah Ayer, herself a sixteenth-generation descendant of the crusader, married Simon Outhouse Jr., noted

A Castle in the Sky 127

Noah Steeves died Sept 18, 1895, Aged 77 Y'rs. his wife Lucretia died Feb. 19, 1908 aged 79 years.

Ruine Schrofenstein.

for his 1841 Petitcodiac River ferry service. Then in 1848, Simon's daughter Lucretia married Noah Steeves, a great-grandson of Heinrich Stief, thus linking some of Heinrich's descendants to a soldier of the Third Crusade.³

With its connotation of crusader epics and Alpine adventure, the Ruine Schrofenstein quickly became an enticing destination for a modern-day descendant of Humphrey le Aire. The site had even greater allure because of its apparent inaccessibility: the tiny structure appeared to be situated almost half a mile straight up the mountainside.

Day by day, winter drew inexorably nearer to Landeck. Every morning when I awoke, the snow line had descended a little farther down the sides of the mountains. Another year was coming to an end, another century drawing to a close, as mother nature enveloped the town in a hushed embrace.

One cool and quiet afternoon, I hiked alone across the bare, hillside fields above the town. Following steep pathways through the pine woods, I climbed higher and higher to where the Schrofenstein castle stood like an ancient fortress in the brisk Alpine air. At the edge of the trees near the base of the castle, a narrow wooden walkway stretched from the cliff to a great timber door set in the stone wall. A large padlock on the door halted any further progress.

Stepping back, I gazed up at the parapets above the castle walls. I looked down at the houses below—tiny matchboxes in the distance—then across the valley to the mountains on the other side. Lingering in thought, feeling suspended in space and time, I imagined my crusading ancestor, Humphrey le Aire, returning from the Holy Land with King Richard on their long journey back to England. Perhaps they had travelled down the valley below me, and had passed through the Alps near this place. Perhaps Humphrey and his companions had taken shelter at this very same castle, and had slept and supped within these ancient walls. Possibly they had replenished their spirits here, and had tended to their wounds sustained in the valiant fighting at the walls of Acre.

It was a total fantasy, of course, but there was no one around to disillusion me. So high up the mountain had I come, I felt closer to the sky above than to the valley below. At that moment I felt certain the spirits in heaven would commend such flights of my imagination.

Back in Landeck, I marvelled at the beauty of the village children as they poured out from the school where Wiltrud taught—their bright, inquiring faces full of the vigour of life in the Austrian Alps. Wiltrud and I enjoyed each other's company over four peaceful days, and we talked about my crusading forebear and about the quest for my Pennsylvania-German roots. I retold the intriguing story of the Stief pioneer couple who had long ago left their homeland somewhere in Germany, and had taken ship to America.

After several days of quiet relaxation, however, I became anxious to continue my search for Heinrich Stief. It was then that my mistake from the previous summer in the Toronto Reference Library suddenly revealed itself: I didn't know where to find the village of Schlaitdorf, where I hoped to uncover a record of Georg Friedrich Stieff. I knew only that the place was located somewhere in the south-German state of Württemberg.

A trip to the local bookstore turned up a few large-scale road maps of Württemberg, but none showed the village I wanted. Wiltrud's colourful school atlas identified neither Schlaitdorf nor even Kreuzwertheim, Michael Lutz's former home in the neighbouring county of Wertheim. I began to wonder if an eighteenth-century village called Schlaitdorf still existed.

Feeling desperate after a whole day of searching, I cranked up my Macintosh PowerBook one evening, and prepared to send some e-mail calls for help. At the same time, Wiltrud began making inquiries on her telephone. From directory information, she obtained the phone number of the Lutheran church office in the Württemberg village of Schlaitdorf, and started calling.

Then my lack of preparation revealed a further problem: my computer wouldn't connect to Wiltrud's telephone line without an Austrian adaptor. Neither of the ones I had purchased in London or Amsterdam would fit.

With no response coming from the church office, I plodded through the Landeck cold the next day, going from store to store, trying to track down the needed plug. Invariably, a secondary search ensued in each store for someone who could understand what I wanted. A salesman in an electronics shop was convinced I needed a state-of-the-art cell phone. At a hardware store overlooking the Inn River, the clerk insisted that the nearest store to stock the product was located six miles up the adjoining Rosanna River. I kept looking. Finally, at about four o'clock in the afternoon, my persistence paid off. With the 149-shilling adaptor in my pocket, I went back to Wiltrud's apartment to get thawed out and connect my Mac to the Internet.

The following day, three responses to my e-mails had come through—two from my Internet group of Dobson cousins, and one from my brother Bob in Moncton. We Dobsons were a group of genealogists all descended from Yorkshire couple George and Mary (Barker) Dobson who had come to Chignecto in 1773. Our group regularly corresponded electronically about genealogical matters.[4]

Of the three sets of directions to Schlaitdorf, my brother's was the most precise. His message included the name and e-mail address of Schlaitdorf's mayor, and the Internet directions began at the Stuttgart airport:

> Head west on E52 until you see the exit for B27. Take that south (left), then follow B27A (the road to Tuebingen) south until it hits B312. Take that south/east (left), 2km through Aichtal, then continue a further 2km. The road to Schlaitdorf (L373) will be a right turn, hopefully marked. It's about 3km down the road from there.[5]

It appeared that things were falling into place. I sent a short inquiry to Mayor Gurrbach, but, not getting any reply, concluded that my message got lost in cyberspace. Wiltrud had not received any response from the Lutheran church office, so, with time slipping away, and directions in hand, I decided to head towards Stuttgart to see what I could find.

On a chilly Saturday morning, Wiltrud and I bade farewell, and I headed to the Landeck train station. I was due back in Amsterdam in six days.

CHAPTER 17

In the Neckar Valley

Like a wonder-struck child with its nose pressed against a windowpane, I stared up at the snow-crusted Alps, wide-eyed. All my thoughts were swept away by the dramatic beauty of the mountains. The train crept uphill through tiny snow-bound settlements where large piles of wood were stacked beside the houses. Smoke from the chimneys drifted into the clouds—white on white. Emerging from their chalets, Alpine skiers trudged expectantly toward the slopes. Winter was on their doorstep.

After a half-hour of the train's steady climbing, the Rosanna River valley narrowed to a steep gorge, hemmed in by the mountains on both sides. Suddenly, day became night—the train was swallowed by the blackness of a tunnel in the Arlberg Pass. A long ride in the dark beneath the Alps followed, during which the train began its descent to the other side. The darkness and the rocking of the train put me in a drowsy state of mind. I must have dozed for a spell. When I came to my senses, the darkness had given way to daylight, and the train had emerged into the fields and flatlands of southern Germany.

As the train sped across the broad expanse of south Württemberg, Dr. Yoder's descriptions in *Pennsylvania German Immigrants* came to mind. Although comprising only 3,150 square miles, or a tenth of present-day New Brunswick, the little dukedom of Württemberg had sent the third largest number of all the immigrants arriving in Pennsylvania, a colony whose area was many times larger. Württemberg emigrants were outnumbered only by those from neighbouring Switzerland and the Palatinate.[1]

In the three-year period between 1747 and 1750, for example, well over two thousand people made the long and difficult voyage across the Atlantic Ocean to America. Each ship was crammed with hundreds of passengers headed for a new life in the new world. In 1753, one such ship, the *Richard and Mary*, had sailed to Philadelphia with Schlaitdorf cobbler Georg Friedrich Stieff and his family.[2]

The rolling clickety-clack of the train now put me in a pensive frame of mind. I got out my brother's directions to Schlaitdorf which started at the Stuttgart airport. Because I was coming from another direction and by train, however, they were not immediately practical. Nevertheless, I knew I was getting close. Attempting to pinpoint my intended destination, I translated Bob's descriptions into a rough sketch on the back of a train schedule. Scaling it with a regional Stuttgart train map posted in the vestibule, I calculated that the village lay about fifteen kilometres south-east of the airport. If I went all the way to Stuttgart, I would have to double back. Instead, I would need to leave the train twenty or thirty kilometres before reaching the city.

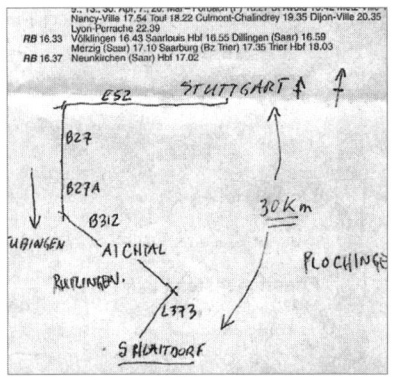

My sketch on the train schedule.

Casting about for some help from my fellow passengers, I had soon recruited a young German fellow who thought he had an idea where Schlaitdorf was located. When his difficulty with English became apparent, we tried French. Understanding each other well enough, we had soon brought a train conductor into the conversation. At that point, the two of them switched to German. The best place to stop would be the town of Nürtingen, the conductor informed us, with my new acquaintance translating into French. Before long, I was walking across the station platform in Nürtingen, as my friend waved a satisfied goodbye through the window of the train.

Outside the station, several taxis waited in a queue. I asked the first driver about Schlaitdorf. She knew the place well, or so she said; the fare was 32 Deutsche Mark. I dropped my bags into the back seat of the little car and we drove off. Before long we had reached the outskirts of Nürtingen, and were headed into the rolling hills along the Neckar River.

The Neckar is a tributary of the Rhine, yet here outside of Nürtingen it is hardly big enough to be called a river. Large or not, eighteenth-century emigrants from these parts had travelled down its valley on their way to the

Rhine River, one hundred miles distant. Once they were on the Rhine, their route took them through the Palatinate and on to the seaport of Rotterdam where they would eventually embark for America.[3]

And why did so many people leave their homes to venture to a far frontier? Their reasons were many and the same: They wanted a better life.

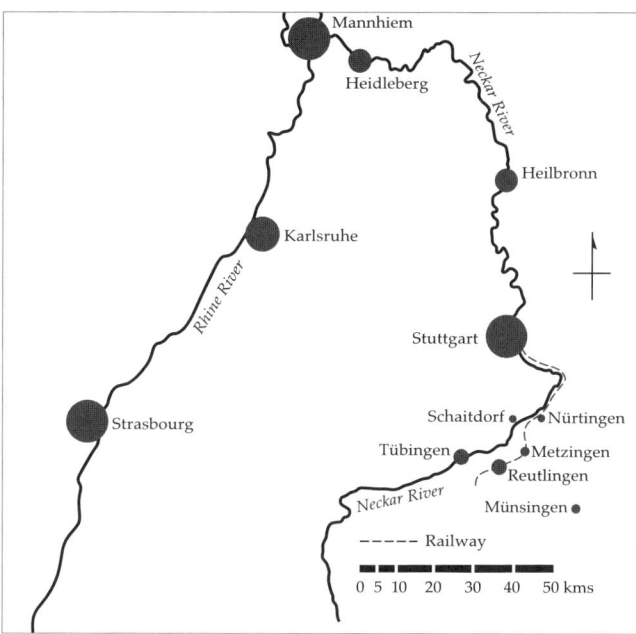

Map of the Neckar and upper Rhine Rivers.

During the two centuries previous to the great exodus, both Württemberg and the Palatinate had seen continual upheaval brought on by French and German princes struggling for control. The discord began with the religious battles that followed from the Reformation in 1534, and, for the next one hundred years, war was waged with unparalleled "cruelty and ferocity."[4]

The fighting intensified in 1618 with the coming of the Thirty Years War. During that catastrophe, states historian Kuhns, "the whole intellectual, moral, and religious character of the German people received a shock that almost threatened it with annihilation." In 1674 came the killing raids of King Louis XIV and the French Marshall Turenne. The people had not recovered from the strife when the War of the Palatinate, from 1688 to 1697, brought nine more years of misery, destruction, and death. It was a history, writes Beidelman, "written in fire and blood."[5]

The many decades of violence caused severe economic dislocation, daily hardship, and general desolation to the Palatinate. "Villages and farmhouses were burned," says Klees, "and the people driven from their homes in the dead of winter." In 1689, the cities of Mainz, Worms, Mannheim, Speyer, and Heidelberg were plundered and burned. People were slaughtered en masse, Pennypacker adds with horrifying detail, and the "fumes from their burning bodies went up into the air from every city and village along the Rhine."[6]

Beyond the Rhine valley, neighbouring Württemberg and Wertheim did not escape the widespread devastation. In those two regions, the tragedy was intensified when German rulers, attempting to imitate the extravagant splendours of the French court of Versailles, imposed excessive taxation on their subjects. The high taxes weighed heavily on the shoulders of the common folk, forcing many into bankruptcy. In Michael Lutz's county of Wertheim, situated to the north of Württemberg, the peasants were subjected to as many as two dozen taxes, including a chimney tax, a water tax, a plowing fee, the Prince's personal tax, and a tax on the second crop of hay.[7]

In 1708-09 there came a brutal winter. The cold was so intense that "firewood would not burn in the open air [and] wine and spirits froze into solid blocks of ice." On the coast of Europe, heavily laden carts could be driven across the frozen sea. In Württemberg, the weather was deadly—"'so cold that the birds froze in the air and the wild beasts in the forests.' It was then that men looked in one another's eyes and said, 'Let us go to America; and if we perish, we perish.'"[8]

In the mid-1700s, during the years of greatest emigration, new troubles were visited upon the poor folk of Württemberg. Farmers endured repeated crop failures in the vineyards, and the little food that grew in the fields was eaten by wild animals. The dukes revoked grazing and wood-gathering rights in the forests, and the already hard-pressed farmers were required to perform compulsory service to their overlords. The situation evoked a dismal observation from a contemporary writer: "These days the farmer is the most miserable of all creatures.... The barns are empty, the dwellings threaten collapse, the inhabitants appear miserable and ruined."[9]

By that time, news of William Penn's colony in America had spread widely through the German states. No doubt his generous offer of justice, good land, and religious freedom sounded like a gift from heaven. Once the movement had caught on, people left in droves. The ducal authorities did their best to limit the exodus, but the movement would not be stopped. Emigrants were required to dispose of their property, pay off any back taxes, and give up their citizenship before they were granted permission to leave. Usually, they were supplied with a certificate of good behaviour, or, for some, a document attesting to their church membership.[10]

By the late 1740s, emigration had reached epidemic proportions. In 1752, in Wertheim county, a decree disparaging the chances of survival in America was read from every church pulpit. The people were told that all manner of calamity awaited them—that the trip was so dangerous that eighty percent of the passengers died at sea; that their money would be exhausted by expenses, resulting in slavery; that families would be separated forever;

Cercle de Souabe (Swabia), Vaugundy map from the *Atlas Portatif*, 1749.
Original in the author's collection

that no religion was available in Pennsylvania; that the land was expensive, and described as "wretched and a desert." Still the people of Wertheim went—to join their fellow sufferers from Württemberg, Switzerland, and the Palatinate.[11]

Of the 272 families from Wertheim county listed by Yoder, thirty had come from the town of Wertheim. The individuals' occupations reflected a melodious range: a butcher, a baker, a button-hole maker; a tailor, three tanners, and two cabinet makers; one farmer, one saddler, and one shoemaker; and a shoemaker's apprentice. From Michael Lutz's Kreuzwertheim, across the Main River, came a baker, a weaver, and a musketeer, as well as one Nicholaus Dinkel who was so poor he was almost a beggar.[12]

South of Wertheim, numerous inhabitants of Georg Friedrich Stieff's village of Schlaitdorf departed to America. Swelling the list were a farrier, a butcher, a baker, a cobbler, a blacksmith, a cooper's daughter, a cowherd, a stonecutter, a cartwright, a member of the village council, and three farmers, plus their spouses and all their children.

By February 12, 1753, the authorities in Wertheim were so desperate to stop the depopulation of the countryside that they forbade all further emigration. By the following year, emigration from the county had stopped completely. Michael Lutz, who left Wertheim with his family only a few months before, had departed just in time.[13]

Here in Württemberg, at the end of the twentieth century, the cobblers, the coopers, and the cartwrights have disappeared. The millers, the saddlers, and the musketeers have all gone. Yet the farmers remain. Past the plowed fields and the now-dormant gardens, the modern little taxi sailed over smooth roads, and soared across the hills. Twenty minutes beyond Nürtingen, we rolled into the tiny village of Schlaitdorf.

Grey and white stuccoed buildings stood close to the road, and in the centre of the village an old, grey-stone church rose up among the houses. I had presumed the place would offer some sort of accommodation, however modest, but my driver only looked at me aghast when I asked her for a hotel. Putting aside any concerns about my immediate future, I paid the fare, grabbed my bags, and headed for the church.

Partly obscured by a line of bushes, a stone pathway led to a side door at the back of the church. Everything was quiet, and my knocks went unanswered. But as I turned to leave, an elderly fellow approached from around the corner. We entered into a stumbling conversation, partly aided by hand signs (plus some nodding and grunting), in which he informed me that no one was around who could help me that day. Confirming my hopes, he assured me that I had indeed found Schlaitdorf's Lutheran church. I would be welcome, he said, to return the next morning for the Sunday service. We experienced momentary confusion about the hour of the service until he rolled back his sleeve to point to the corresponding numbers on his watch.

Back at the street, two teenaged boys communicated in broken English that the nearest hotel could be found in Neckartenzlingen, a few kilometres distant. The strange-sounding name of the village echoed with the same name I had seen in Yoder's *Pennsylvania German Immigrants*. Johannes Siglin—judge, senator, and owner of the Stag Inn in Neckartenzlingen—had gone to Pennsylvania with Georg Friedrich Stieff in 1753. There seemed little chance the Stag Inn would be offering accommodation two-and-a-half centuries later, but I intended to deal with that prospect if the time came.[14]

According to Dr. Yoder, many villages in this region of the Neckar valley saw significant numbers of their citizens depart for America. In 1753, at least two other Schlaitdorf families accompanied Georg Friedrich Stieff and Judge Siglin. One family included the mayor, Johann Caspar Gajer, his wife, Anna Maria (née Walther), and their three children. With them went the village watchman, Hans Jacob Adam, along with his daughter, Anna Barbara, plus her farmer-husband, Johannes Kuhn, and their four children.[15]

Neighbouring Neckartenzlingen had likewise bidden farewell to many of its villagers. From that hamlet went a tailor's son, a fisherman, a cowherd, a stocking weaver, a baker, a butcher, a farm hand, and the son of a vine dresser—again with their spouses and all their children.[16]

One might wonder how these two agricultural villages, or *dörfer*, survived the repeated exodus in the mid-eighteenth century. It might also be wondered how the good people of Schlaitdorf reacted when their mayor, watchman, innkeeper, and cobbler all departed together.

Many of the emigrants were related one way or another, and many were friends. They had lived and worked in the same communities in the old country, and when they crossed the Atlantic, they often travelled together. Naturally, when they arrived in America, they often settled near each other. It was another instance of "chain migration"—a pattern of movement that often allows modern genealogists to piece together the past when little evidence has survived.[17]

There is a persistent notion that most of the emigrants were farmers. In fact, only one-fifth of all the heads of families emigrating from Württemberg were farmers by trade. The rest were craftsmen and tradesmen of every kind, all necessary for the harmonious functioning of eighteenth-century society: fourteen percent were weavers; fourteen percent were tailors and shoemakers; nine percent were masons and carpenters; eight percent were cabinetmakers, coopers, and cartwrights; seven percent were blacksmiths; six percent were butchers and bakers.[18]

I was still standing in the Schlaitdorf cold when the bus to Nürtingen pulled up. I took my cue from the two teenagers and climbed aboard. We three were the only passengers. A few minutes later, somewhere down along the Neckar River, we were joined by a middle-aged woman and her small child. They took a seat across from me. Soon after, we picked up a young woman carrying a satchel and some books. I guessed she was a student. She sat directly behind me. The boys had chosen the front-row seats opposite the driver.

The bus crossed the river and ascended the hill on the far side of the valley. As we came closer to Neckartenzlingen, I noticed that the other passengers had started a lively dialogue. The two teenagers and the student were chattering back and forth in German with the driver, discussing something far beyond my comprehension. We were approaching the village, according to the road signs, when the woman across from me joined the conversation. Her child and I were the only ones keeping quiet.

As we drove into the village of Neckartenzlingen, the five members of this impromptu discussion group suddenly fell silent. It seemed they had reached a consensus about something. The bus came to a stop. The boys were looking back at me, and with a glance in the driver's rear-view mirror I could see he was doing the same. Then the girl behind me explained.

"We think you should go to Nürtingen," she said to me in English. "There will be more hotels to choose from." They were all looking at me now. The boys nodded their heads in agreement.

"OK," I rejoined, looking at the driver's face in his mirror, "Nürtingen it is." Lodgings closer to Schlaitdorf would have been preferable, but I thought it more prudent to accept their collective suggestion. Yoder's other passengers on the *Richard and Mary* would have to wait. I hoped that, in the intervening centuries, the people of Neckartenzlingen had found a new owner for the Stag Inn to replace the one who had gone to America in 1753.

We continued our journey along the Neckar River, now in silence. Before long, the bus entered Nürtingen and pulled into the station yard. As we alighted, the student pointed to a group of pale-coloured buildings a short distance away.

"There is a large hotel over there," she informed me, "and another, the Hotel Pflum, is farther on."

Hoisting my bags onto my shoulder, I walked the half-block to where the girl had pointed. It was a garish, corporate version of a twentieth-century hotel, and much contrary to my tastes. First, it was near impossible to find the entrance since I didn't have a car; the door to the lobby was situated on the ramp to the parking lot. At the registration desk, I was taken aback by the exorbitant rate of 195 Deutsche Mark per night ($150 Cdn.)—far more than I had paid at any of the overpriced hotels in Amsterdam and London. I made a quick calculation and informed the clerk that I would look around the town and perhaps return later.

Carrying my heavy bags back into the cold, I put in a futile search for the Hotel Pflum. An hour later, after walking down the same street for the third time, I gave up the hunt; I went back to the corporate hotel and checked in.

The room was clean and tidy, but seemed empty and bland. My frustrating walk through the streets of Nürtingen had left me feeling tired and cold. Now I was lonesome as well. I flicked on the ubiquitous TV and was surprised to see my name on the screen with a message welcoming me to the hotel. It was a clever touch, but the techno-magic quickly dissipated into the emptiness of the room. I unpacked, freshened up, then went looking for a meal.

Later, back in my place of solitude, I found it impossible to sleep. My expectations regarding Schlaitdorf would not let me rest. I lay awake for hours, listening to the distant sound of heating pipes in the walls, hammering and clicking in the night. I tried watching some German television, but soon gave that up. About two o'clock in the morning, with the pipes rattling in the background, I pulled the queen-size mattress onto the floor, trying to get away from the irritating din. It was a night of intermittent sleep. I didn't know it would be only the first of several restless nights to follow.

Schlaitdorf's Wendelinkirche.

CHAPTER 18

A Travelling Shoemaker

After an elaborate self-serve breakfast in the hotel dining room the next morning, I checked out, but left my luggage in their storage room to be picked up later. There was no need to drag the extra weight to Schlaitdorf and back. On the way to the front door, I passed the one redeeming feature of the big hotel: a giant fish pond built into the stone-tiled floor of the lobby. Beside the pond, leafy tropical plants grew in their enormous pots. Large, smooth rocks lined the sun-dappled pond, and every possible breed of goldfish swam blissfully about, flashing jewel-like colours at the world.

In a focused attempt to take in the first and possibly only service in Schlaitdorf that Sunday morning, I walked to the bus yard and stood in the chilly air. It was December 7. So far, I thought I had located the right town of Schlaitdorf; soon, I would know if I had found the right church. If it was the same church where Yoder's Georg Friedrich Stieff and Catharina Haubensacker had wed, then perhaps their marriage record would yield a clue as to whether he was related to Heinrich Stief who had arrived in Philadelphia by November, 1749. The bus left Nürtingen on schedule and dropped me off in Schlaitdorf at 9:30. The village was wrapped in the cold morning sunlight of a sleepy winter day.

With an hour to wait until the service began, I walked through the narrow streets, moving to keep warm. Grass-covered lanes led into tiny gardens, still green despite the approach of winter. Stretching back from the houses and barns, broad fields lay fallow under a pale sun. At the edge of the village, just a couple of blocks from the church, I stopped to absorb the panorama of low hills frosted with snow, and the Neckar River lying tranquilly in the distance. All was calm, and scattered streams of chimney smoke rose into the morning air.

Looking south from Schlaitdorf. Neckartenzlingen and the Neckar River on the left; Alternriet to the right; the Swabian highlands in the distance.

There were about two dozen worshippers in the congregation of the Lutheran Church of Saint Wendelin that Sunday morning in Schlaitdorf. The plain, bright interior of the Wendelinkirche emphasized a simplicity and directness of devotion—a feature that has become the hallmark of the Lutheran Church. No doubt Martin Luther, the founder of Lutheranism and Protestantism, would be content.

Martin Luther was born on November 10, 1483 in Saxony, the son of a miner. After joining an order of Augustinian monks, he entered the priesthood at the age of twenty-four. For thirty-eight years, the devout biblical scholar studied and taught at the University of Wittemberg, where he received a doctorate in 1512. Five years later, Luther broke with the Roman Catholic Church in response to a structure which he saw as artificial and contrived. His observations of the selling of indulgences as well as numerous other abuses perpetrated by the Church led him to a new understanding of the natural relationship between God and man. Man and God, he believed, needed no intermediary. As author D. H. Lawrence expressed it four centuries later: "The heart was free to be alone with God."[1]

Out of Luther's beliefs emerged his famous "ninety-five theses," which he posted on the door of Wittemberg Castle Church on October 31, 1517. The Protestant Reformation was effectively born.

Luther's ideas spread far and wide, but his challenge of the Pope's supreme religious authority came at a heavy cost. In Europe, a massive religious upheaval followed, and would not end until several generations of German people were confronted with the possibility of complete cultural exhaustion.[2]

The tenacious idea that all German emigrants were persecuted for their religious beliefs and that they abandoned their homeland for that reason alone is not entirely correct. During the warfare in the 1600s, religious conflicts forced the residents of the Palatinate to change their religion with nearly every change of ruler. Restrictions were placed on their form of worship, certainly, and Reformed Lutherans often had to share their churches with orthodox Lutherans and Roman Catholics. Those who survived the hardship were the lucky ones. Their less fortunate friends and neighbours were killed in the incessant fighting between opposing factions.

East of the Palatinate, however, the dukes of neighbouring Württemberg remained Lutheran, by and large, and thus its citizens were spared some of the religious turbulence experienced in the Rhineland. By the year 1709, when south-German emigration began in earnest, religious oppression in Württemberg could not be considered a predominant factor. Non-conformists such as the Moravians and the Reformed Lutherans, as well as sects like the Plain People and the Mennonites, continued to face discrimination. For these non-adherents to the German mother church, religious persecution continued to influence their decision to emigrate. But most inhabitants of Württemberg were Lutherans, and when they emigrated to Pennsylvania it was not necessarily for religious reasons.[3]

Apart from the baptismal records in St. Michael's Lutheran Church in Philadelphia, there apparently survives only one piece of evidence to suggest Heinrich Stief's religious affiliation: his 1747 edition of the Lutheran Bible which he brought with him to the Petitcodiac in 1766. The giant book still survives, weighing a hefty five kilos.[4]

Heinrich's Bible has remained a puzzle in Steeves family history. Whether it actually came with him to Pennsylvania or whether it was obtained in America, no one knows. The Bible narrowly escaped destruction in the nineteenth century when the Hillsborough house of his second son, John, burned to the ground. The Bible survived only because it was on loan that day. And whether or not the Bible's immensity suggests the importance the family placed on religious devotion, again, no one can say.[5]

Heinrich Stief's Lutheran Bible which he brought with him to the Petitcodiac River in 1766.

Courtesy of the Provincial Archives of New Brunswick and the Moncton Museum

Here in Schlaitdorf's Wendelinkirche, the tradition that Martin Luther began in 1517 lives on. The service was gracefully moving, even if I didn't understand a single word. The melancholy but beautiful old hymns were easy to follow, and I hummed along to the music as loudly as I dared, hoping not to raise any German eyebrows. I'd neglected to pick up either a hymnal or a prayer book on the way in, and my pew-mate—a quiet old woman dressed all in black—shared hers with me. Ensconced in the choir was a charming brass band comprising six teenagers, a few sporting *nouveau* North American hair styles. On the walls of the church were wood-carved likenesses of the saints of old.

After the service that morning, I lingered near the door, in order to make inquiries of the minister. He was a visiting clergyman, I was told, and the church pastor, or *Pfarrer*, was by then at home in the *pfarrhaus*, just a few paces away. I thanked the young preacher and walked across the cobble-stoned courtyard to the parsonage.

Pfarrer Kristina Reichle answered the bell herself and happily showed me into her office. She was a young woman with a gentle disposition and a friendly smile. Although the name Georg Friedrich Stieff meant nothing to her, she understood my objective at once and disappeared into the next room. In a few moments she returned with an old book called the *Famlien-Register Schlaitdorf*—the register of Schlaitdorf families.

More than two years had passed since I had begun the search for the European origins of the Stief family. Throughout the time leading up to that moment, I had lived with the possibility that the German records I sought had been lost, were destroyed by fire, or had suffered the bombing of wars past. I knew that at any moment I might be walking out the door into cold sunlight and heading back to Canada with nothing to show for my trouble. My tenuous clue from *Pennsylvania German Immigrants* would be transformed into one more dead end in the search for Heinrich Stief.

On a table in front of us, Pfarrer Reichle opened the book. It was an early compilation of several church records, and the families were arranged alphabetically. We went straight to the letter "S."

Eureka! Neatly inscribed in clear, black script at number 553, was the entry for Georg Friedrich Stieff the shoemaker. Included was the name of his wife, Maria Katharina Haubensack, and the names of their five children—the same ones I had seen in Dr. Yoder's book the previous summer in Toronto.

Entry 553 from Schlaitdorf's *Famlien-Register*. Courtesy of the Wendelinkirche

The entry in the *Famlien-Register* was not identical to Yoder's description, however. Dr. Yoder's Catharina Haubensacker was now Maria Katharina Haubensack, and the couple had married on February 4, 1744. Of the five children listed by Yoder, I now saw that three had died young. Only the eldest and youngest daughters—Regina and Maria Katharina—had actually emigrated to America with their parents in 1753. The birth-dates for those two girls matched Yoder's, and in the place of their death-dates were the words "Penns," and "Pennsylv." The mention of the former British colony here in the record of Württemberg's distant past seemed to be proof positive that this was none other than the Stieff family who had gone to Pennsylvania 244 years before.

Georg Friedrich Stieff was a *schuster*, or cobbler, just as Dr. Yoder's entry had stated. His wife was the widow of Michael Stumpp, also a *schuster* of Schlaitdorf. Perhaps the two shoemakers had been acquainted through their trade, thus explaining how the couple had met. On the other hand, maybe the two had met under other circumstances, and Georg Friedrich Stieff had entered the shoemakers' guild only after marrying the widow of one of its members.[6]

The widow Stumpp was the daughter of Martin and Anna (Auckberlin) Haubensack, and was born in Schlaitdorf on April 6, 1712. For Georg Friedrich Stieff's birth-date there appeared only the word Münsingen. Below his name was written his father's name—Augustin Stieff, "*viehhirte in Münsingen.*"

I read the information with Pfarrer Reichle, who interpreted the meaning of Augustin Stieff's old German occupation of *viehhirte*. "Someone who looked after the cows," she ventured; "perhaps a cowboy." It was an odd choice of words, and we had to laugh at the impossible idea of a wild-west character with a lasso and six-guns, sitting high on an eighteenth-century German horse. Other interpretations for the word *viehhirte* were hinted at, but cowherd seemed the most appropriate. More important, Georg Friedrich hadn't come from Schlaitdorf at all, but from somewhere called Münsingen.

Here, at last, was new information about Dr. Yoder's Stieff family. Yoder's source was Adolph Gerber's German lists which had originated in Württemberg parish records. Had Gerber's information on Schlaitdorf somehow come from another source, I wondered, and had these particular records never gone beyond the village gates? Was I now searching on fresh ground? Whatever the answer, one thing was clear: Georg Friedrich Stieff had a history that went beyond Schlaitdorf—to a place called Münsingen.

Though there seemed to be no other Stieff entries in the *Famlien-Register*, Pfarrer Reichle wanted me to return the next day when her secretary could look further into the records. I didn't seem to be getting very far in locating the home of Heinrich Stief, but there was nothing else to be done. I would come back on Monday. We said our goodbyes, and I walked across the courtyard to find transportation back to Nürtingen.

The world has been wholly transformed in the two-and-a-half centuries since Georg Freidrich Stieff and his family departed to America. Although those former residents would recognize little now, Schlaitdorf has remained a farming community. And, like their counterparts in much of the western world, the twentieth-century inhabitants of this Württemberg village have made an earnest attempt to modernize their surroundings. But maybe the efforts in Schlaitdorf were only half-hearted. Everywhere about the place, remnants of a former life came peeking through the modern veneer. In spots where the stucco had fallen from the buildings, the old half-timber-and-stone *Fachwerk* emerged from the past. Heavy wooden barn doors were fastened to their weathered frames with rusted, ornate hinges. Curious-looking weather vanes topped the peaks of the barns.

Barnyard scene. "I dreamt I was beckoned by strange doors."

As well, signs of Schlaitdorf's present-day farm life were abundant. Boot scrapers were a popular addition to many a modern doorstep, and the pungent smell of farm animals permeated the air. The sound of a goat resonated from somewhere close by.

Not far from the church, ice-cold spring water poured into a stone trough. A tin cup and a clean towel were at hand. The streets were empty, and the only sound to mark my passing was the racket of a farm dog barking up a storm.

Building wall with *Fachwerk*.

Back in Nürtingen, I retrieved my bags from the goldfish hotel, and moved to the Hotel Pflum. The small inn was easy to find once I knew where to look. On the way, I passed through the busy town square, where festive decorations hailed the approach of Christmas, two weeks away. Artisans had erected booths to peddle their crafts, and food sellers in their mini-kitchens were serving sausages and strong mulled wine to a crowd of hungry shoppers. Bundled up against the bitter cold, the revellers were joyfully entertained by a brass band—this one larger and somewhat more accomplished than the youthful ensemble in Schlaitdorf. Circled around the musicians, the townspeople huddled with rapt attention, their spirits kept warm by the soulful music.

The Pflum was a small, family-run hotel with a well-appointed dining-room located next to the bar. Herr Werner Pflum was proud owner, bartender, and head chef. A faded oriental carpet welcomed patrons, and lace curtains in the windows screened the diners from traffic in the street. Ticking away the time in a corner, a grandfather clock added to the peaceable charm.

For dinner that evening I was served a colourful medley of no fewer than nine vegetables: carrots, green beans, broccoli, cabbage, peas, squash, potatoes, collards, and turnips. Thoughts of my German ancestors prompted me to wonder whether they had cultivated any of those vegetables when they lived in the old country. Certainly, they grew some of them during their tenure in Pennsylvania. Gottlieb Mittelberger, who travelled from Württemberg to Philadelphia in 1750, observed that the people in Pennsylvania grew "chiefly rye, wheat, barley, oats, buckwheat, flax, hemp, cabbage, and turnips."[7]

That last vegetable, the lowly turnip, put me in mind of what is perhaps Heinrich Stief's only reported utterance, spoken to two of his sons a year or so after the families had arrived on the Petitcodiac River. According to legend, they had suffered a hard winter without the additional supplies expected from Anthony Wayne and John Hall. Desperate for a change from their scant winter diet of wild game and turnips, Heinrich and his two sons loaded their dug-out canoe with furs one spring day, and paddled out to a passing boat on the river, intending to trade their trappings for food. Unhappy with the captain's paltry offer, but refusing to be taken advantage of, Heinrich turned to his sons and announced: "Well, boys, let's go back to our turnip mush."[8]

However true the legend may be, this much is certain: the pioneer families did survive the early winters on the Petitcodiac River. According to the rest of the legend, those first families persevered with not much more than marsh greens and turnip mush for nourishment.

By an odd turn of events, turnips were also the centre of interest on the other side of the Atlantic in 1767. An English farmer named John Reynolds, living in Kent County, had heard that the Society of Arts in London was offering a prize for the cultivation of kohlrabi, a turnip-like cabbage. The society was noted for its agriculture-promoting schemes, and in 1761 the chairman of its newly formed "Committee of Colonies and Trade" was none other than Benjamin Franklin.[9]

Reynolds sent to Holland for seeds, since no supply was available in England. But instead of kohlrabi, he received seeds of rutabaga, or Swedish turnip. Reynolds grew the turnips anyway, sent samples of his crop to the society, and was awarded a prize of £50 for his efforts.

The families on the Petitcodiac received no prizes for their turnips, but they survived one way or another. And the descendants of Heinrich Stief did more than just survive; for the next two centuries, they flourished. Their prolific growth prompted Esther Clark Wright to muse, "Was it the turnip mush or the samphire greens that proved so potent?"[10]

Encouraged by the legend of Stief fortitude, I polished off the last of Herr Pflum's turnips, confident the sustenance would see me through to another day.

Retiring to my room on the second floor, I composed myself for a night of rest. But again, sleep would not come. I was too tightly wound up anticipating the possibilities in Schlaitdorf. I wondered if tomorrow would finally bring me face to face with the name of Heinrich Stief, my ancestor who had departed his German home long ago. It seemed incredible that I might be able to find what had eluded Maritime genealogists for decades, simply by chasing down a vague hunch about the name Stieff that I had seen in Yoder's book in the Toronto Reference Library. The sensational nature of such a discovery—at least in New Brunswick genealogy circles—overwhelmed my already frazzled sense of equanimity. In bed, I lay awake for hours, trying to turn off my thoughts. When sleep finally came, it was fitful. I dreamt I was lost in a maze of darkened passages, beckoned by strange doors, and distracted by mysterious objects on the walls. It was an appropriate analogy, perhaps, for all the blind alleys I had wandered down during the previous two years.

I woke early, feeling as if I hadn't slept at all. Thoughts of Heinrich Stief pressed in on me again. The hotel's continental breakfast was nourishing fare, and I devoured the food expecting a full day ahead. Then, without any dawdling, I packed up my things and checked out of the room, but left my bags with Herr Pflum. If there were sufficient discoveries in Schlaitdorf to keep me another day, I could move back into the hotel. But I was now ready to continue my journey, if necessary. I didn't want to consider the possibility that the search might come to an abrupt end, and that journeying on would mean travelling back to Canada. Still, my enquiries the previous day for the record of Georg Friedrich Stieff had been successful. It appeared I was headed in the right direction.

In Schlaitdorf, Pfarrer Reichle greeted me at the door of the *pfarrhaus*, and showed me inside straight away. It seemed she had mentioned my anticipated arrival to her secretary, Ella Speier, who now came hurrying out from the back. After the introductions were made, Pfarrer Reichle translated my request. We three discussed the church records and the little-known background of Georg Friedrich Stieff and his family. On the subject of Schlaitdorf's *Famlien-Register*, neither Pfarrer Reichle nor her secretary knew when or by whom it had been created. Then, Frau Speier left to examine some registers in her study, while Pfarrer Reichle and I talked about the history of her church.

The Wendelinkirche is the namesake of Saint Wendelin, the patron saint of herdsmen and farmers. Born a Scots-Irish prince, he left Ireland about the year 570, and lived as a shepherd in the Saarland near the town which bears his name. Today, the festival of Saint Wendelin is celebrated on October 20. The pride of the Wendelinkirche is its magnificent stained-glass window, whose origin dates to the year 1466, and whose subject is derived from the Book of Revelation:

> And there appeared a great wonder in heaven; a woman clothed with the sun, and the moon under her feet, and upon her head a crown of twelve stars: And she being with child cried, travailing in birth, and pained to be delivered.[11]

Frau Speier soon returned to inform us that the only Stieff family listed in the records of Schlaitdorf was the one we had found the previous morning. We went back to the *Famlien-Register* entry to look for more clues. The single hint pointing to further development was the name of the place relating to both Georg Friedrich and his father, Augustin Stieff: Münsingen.

Pfarrer Reichle then offered to phone the church office in Münsingen and make an enquiry. I gratefully accepted her offer.

Sonja Bader, archivist for the Martinskirche—the Church of St. Martin—was in her office, and answered in the affirmative. Many Stieff families were listed in Münsingen's own *Famlien-Register*. Pfarrer Reichle reported the news.

As we discussed my options and the route to Münsingen, Pfarrer Reichle made another offer: she would ask the archivist to fax us the information regarding the Stieffs. She reasoned that if the information wasn't useful I would save myself a cold day's journey into the countryside. Her way would be "more comfortable," she added, with intended understatement.

A second call was placed and soon the pages began to emerge from the fax machine. We perused the sheets as they appeared, one by one, trying, at the same time, to maintain a semblance of order. Twenty-two pages later, the last one came out marked *"ende!"* Arranged before us was a wonderful assortment of late eighteenth- and early nineteenth-century family information with more than one hundred names.

This time, the name Stief was spelled with a single "f." There was an abundance of Johannes, Jacobs, Heinrichs, and Fredrichs. But in all those Münsingen families, the one other name I hoped to see evaded me. In none of the records was there any mention of the name Regina, though it was a popular girl's name of that period. And Regina was the name of a woman who had married Heinrich Stief sometime before the year 1749 when their names first appeared in Philadelphia. It was Regina who had gone with Heinrich to far-off America, never to return.

Pfarrer Reichle and I surveyed the records again, this time looking for dates previous to 1749. There was a Joh. Heinrich Stief born in 1752, the son of Joh. Heinrich Stief (*siehe 484*); also a Johañ Heinrich Stief, born in 1744, son of Joh. Heinrich Stief (*siehe 487*); a Jacob Friderich Stief born in 1752, son of Johañne Stief (*siehe 478*); and a Johañ Conrad Stief born in 1754, the son of Johañne Stief (*siehe 481*). Those families had passed on their names just as they handed down their clothes, their tools, and indeed every item that might have some possible value to the next generation.

Regrettably, nearly all the dates were too late to include my roving Stief ancestor. The earliest date appeared to be that of the marriage between Johannes Stief and Rosina Barbara on April 18, 1747 (*siehe 477*). But, while I had not found Heinrich and Regina Stief, my situation had changed completely. Whereas my search in Germany had begun with a single entry from *Pennsylvania German Immigrants*, now I was looking at more Stiefs than I could believe. With the name Heinrich appearing repeatedly though the records, my intuition told me that I might be on to something.

My mind was made up; I would go to Münsingen to see what more I could uncover. Studying her modern road map, Pfarrer Reichle advised me to travel back to Nürtingen, catch a train to Metzingen, and then take another bus to Münsingen. The total distance was about forty kilometres.

She copied the name of the archivist at the Lutheran church office, located at 30 Karlstraße. Then we said our goodbyes. I sensed her disappointment that the source of my quest lay elsewhere.

CHAPTER 19

Stief from Schlaitdorf

It was nearly one o'clock by the time the bus dropped me off in Nürtingen. The streets were busy with Monday traffic, and workers were headed back to their offices after lunch. I could feel my Friday appointment in Amsterdam lurking beyond the horizon. There was no time to waste. I stopped for a quick bite in a small café, then walked straight to the Hotel Pflum to pick up my bag.

When my affable host learned that my new destination was Münsingen, he responded with a knowledgeable flourish. "Ah yes! It is thirty kilometres from here. You must take the train." I wasn't sure if he was being pragmatic or prophetic, but, either way, I intended to take his advice. It never hurts to heed a hotel owner who knows his way around.

The train trip from Nürtingen to Metzingen lasted a grand total of ten minutes. I didn't have time to do much more than find a seat before the train pulled into the little station. Several buses were lined up outside. Stepping from the train, I walked to the first platform and scanned the array of schedules posted on the board. Locating the town of Münsingen, I headed to the designated platform, where a bus was loading passengers. I jumped aboard, bought a one-way ticket from the driver, then settled into my seat for the ride.

It wasn't far to go—as the crow flies. But the bus began to travel round and about, over every back road and through every little town and village the driver could find. Whenever we came to a sign pointing to Münsingen, the bus veered off in the opposite direction. I tried to follow the route with my inadequate map, but the scenario was too baffling. I put my destiny in the driver's hands and sat back to enjoy the scenery of the Swabian highlands.

The landscape of rolling hills and farmland near Schlaitdorf now gave way to a more dramatic vista of steep slopes wooded with oaks and beeches. Yellow-brown leaves tinted the hillsides, and patches of fresh snow dotted the terrain. I caught a glimpse of a limestone outcropping where a mountain stream rushed beside the road, then disappeared from view. We passed through a string of modern communities that sported strange names: Neuhaussen, Dettingen, Bad Urach, Seeburg, Trailfingen. The countryside appeared quiet but prosperous, and everywhere were signs of German enterprise. A little less than an hour from Metzingen, the bus coasted downhill into the town of Münsingen and pulled up to the curb.

I had already decided to go directly to the Martinskirche archives and look for a hotel later. An elderly woman with grocery bags in both hands

Downtown Münsingen, with the Hungerberg Hill in the background.

directed me to Karlstraße, just a block away. In a few minutes I arrived at number thirty.

The building was a large stone structure separated from the street by a high wall. I walked through the open gateway in the wall, climbed the steps to the door, and tried one of the door bells. Someone from beyond buzzed me in.

As I went past the big wooden doors and into the inner lobby, an inquisitive, efficient-looking woman came to greet me. Unsure if this was the archivist, Frau Bader, I tried something in English about my genealogy quest. But my explanation only seemed to puzzle her.

"Stief from Schlaitdorf," I added, hoping it would explain everything. It seemed to work, for she smiled with recognition and showed me into her office.

The room was large and bright—equipped with a computer, a fax machine, and two phones; a desk was loaded with papers. After I described my mission, Frau Bader showed me into an adjoining room so I could get started with my search. It was already three o'clock, and the day would soon be over.

In the centre of the small room was a large wooden table and a few chairs. On the table, several old maps and leather-bound books lay to one side. A tall wooden cabinet lined one wall, and a giant photocopier stood in the far corner of the room. Beyond the open doors of the cabinet, I could see many books of different sizes, all bound in black.

Frau Bader pulled a pair of old volumes down from the cabinet shelves, while I removed my coat and placed my notebook on the table. She then took a few moments to explain what each book contained.

The first was a marriage register, or *Ehebuch*, which had been in use between 1662 and 1785. The other was a *Taufbuch*, an early book of baptisms covering the years 1631 to 1736. Frau Bader then wished me good luck with the search, and returned to her desk in the next room. I was left to explore on my own.

I suspected that the baptism of Georg Friedrich Stieff would be found in the *Taufbuch*, but I had no way of guessing the year of his birth. Because he had married in 1744, he could have been born in any year during the first quarter of the 1700s. That approach seemed daunting. In any case, I still didn't know if Georg Friedrich Stieff was related to Heinrich Stief. Even if I could track down Georg Friedrich's birth-date, it might not help me find Heinrich, whose name was possibly listed among the many Münsingen Stiefs.

Still wondering how to begin, I reflected that the earliest known record of Heinrich and Regina Stief in Pennsylvania is that of their eldest son Jacob's birth in Philadelphia on November 14, 1749. Instead of looking for Georg Friedrich's baptism, I would tackle the *Ehebuch*. If Heinrich and Regina had wed here in Münsingen, their marriage would be recorded in the *Ehebuch*, sometime before mid-February 1749.

I was eager to begin immediately, but I paused to reflect on the task ahead. I had reservations about how much of the old German script I could decipher—a script modern German speakers would be unable to fathom. Even if Heinrich and Regina's marriage had occurred in Münsingen, would I be able to find the entry? I gave brief thanks that I wasn't working with microfilm, remembering how often the process had left me dizzy with motion sickness. But here in the pleasant archives, surrounded in solitude by the old books, the peace and quiet of some distant past seemed to drift serenely through the room. Afternoon sunlight filtered through a window. Drawing a deep, satisfying breath, I opened the *Ehebuch* of the Martinskirche—the marriage register of the Church of Saint Martin—and began a search for the forebears of all the Steeves descendants in the world.

I began at the year 1749 and traced backwards. Unable to comprehend most of the script, I was forced to look only at the names of the individuals who had married. The task was not impossible, but success hinged on keeping a sharp eye on the sometimes erratic handwriting of the pastor who had made the entries two-and-a-half centuries before.

The pages of the *Ehebuch* were strong and clean, and the ink was mostly dark and clear. Some years later, probably long after the events were recorded, someone had carefully underlined every surname with a coloured pencil—blue for the males and red for the females. The coloured marks made quick work of picking out the names from the rest of the German script. Though initially the intrusion of the marks seemed a sacrilege, I soon came to accept the probability that, without them, I might have spent half an hour on each page instead of a few minutes. Added to that cheerless prospect was the likelihood that many of the names would otherwise elude me completely as they silently disappeared into the apparent pandemonium of the old script.

Many of the names were impossible to make out, but I tried not to get bogged down, examining each one in turn. Each year had seen roughly a dozen marriages. I saw no Stieff names for the years 1749 or 1748. At the entry for January 23, 1747, I came to the name Augustinus Stieff. The surname looked like "Flintt," and he had married a woman named Anna Barbara. The Latinized name Augustinus brought to mind the Augustin, father of Schlaitdorf's Georg Friedrich Stieff.

On April 18 of the same year, a Johannes Stieff had married Rosina Barbara. Obviously, he was the same Johannes Stief whose name had come through the fax machine in Schlaitdorf. Whereas the faxed information had originated in the transcribed family record—the *Münsingen Famlien-Register*—now I was looking at the original marriage record. And here, the spelling of the surname had reverted to a double "ff."

At the entry for January 11, 1746 was the name Michael Stieff, son of Augustin Stieff, *kälberhirte*. He had married Anna Barbara Walter.

I tried to read slowly and methodically, but my excitement urged me on. I arrived at the year 1745. Suddenly, at February 25, I saw the name I had come thousands of kilometres to find: *Heinrich Stieff*! I practically shouted

The seven marriage entries from the *Ehebuch*, 1745. February 25 is the middle entry.

Courtesy of the Martinskirche, Münsingen

the name Heinrich into the room. By now, I was sitting bolt upright in my chair. I tried to read the rest of the entry, most of which was incomprehensible. Then came another name I recognised at once: *Regina*! I shouted again. I glanced through the open doorway into the next room to see if my outbursts had caused alarm, but apparently I had not been noticed. I turned back to the entry and sifted through it once more.

I read the entry a third time and then a fourth. Though most of the words meant nothing, the names Heinrich and Regina called from across the centuries, loud and clear. I wanted to run into the street, waving my arms.

I read the entry again. Then I sat back in my chair and stared out the window, wondering what to think. For a few moments, time seemed to stand still. Was this really the missing link—the long-lost record that would connect my ancestors to their former home in Germany? Possibly not, but my

Stief from Schlaitdorf 155

genealogical sixth sense told me otherwise. Outside, the light was fading, and all was quiet except for the muffled noise of a few cars passing in the street. The only other sound to reach my ears was the steady tapping of Frau Bader's competent fingers on her keyboard in the next room.

I tried to put aside the tremendous thrill I felt at that moment and continue the search. Concentration was difficult. Could there have been more than one Heinrich Stieff in all of Germany at this brief period in the middle of the eighteenth century who had married a woman named Regina? It was not impossible, of course, but such a scenario was most unlikely. If, in fact, I had found the same couple who had emigrated to Pennsylvania, perhaps further evidence could be uncovered. It was time to get help.

I carried the *Ehebuch* to Frau Bader's desk to ask her advice. Though many of the words in the marriage entry gave her difficulty, she was able to translate a few. The word *kälberhirte*, Augustin Stieff's occupation, she thought meant "a cowboy." It reminded me of the same interpretation in Schlaitdorf the day before, where the word had been *viehhirte*. I dug out my copy of the Schlaitdorf document for comparison. But the words were similar, Frau Bader explained, both terms denoting a person who herds animals. Then she suggested possible meanings of one or two other words, as well as pointing out the fact that Regina's father was a farmer in the village of Honau in the county of Pfullingen.

I put together what I had found so far: On February 25, 1745, Johann Heinrich Stieff, son of Augustin Stieff, cattleherder, married Regina Stalegger, a farmer's daughter from Honau in Pfullingen county.

A past that for decades had been vague and obscure was suddenly looking very bright. That is, of course, if the couple I had found were the same Heinrich and Regina Stief who had emigrated to Pennsylvania. I was almost certain I had found them, but proof was lacking.

I returned to the table in the adjoining room to pour over the facts from the *Ehebuch*. The name Augustin Stieff had cropped up again. Augustin was the father of both Michael and Heinrich Stieff—that much seemed certain. But was Georg Friedrich Stieff their brother, and, if so, how did he wind up in Schlaitdorf?

I wanted to continue searching for additional clues to the Stieff family's background, but there wasn't time to do much more. The afternoon was almost over, and Frau Bader was now anxious to depart for her next engagement which, I understood, was a women's group. "There are twenty women waiting," she emphasized, to make sure I didn't tarry over my discovery. Tomorrow would come soon enough. I requested copies of some of the pages from the *Ehebuch* which she kindly provided.

Rolling the oversized copies into a tube, I gathered my bags together and went out into the cool air. The sun had gone for the day, and darkness would soon descend on the town. Kite-high from my discovery, I fairly floated past the stone wall to the sidewalk. Then, in a momentary lapse into second childhood, I brought the tube of photocopies up to my mouth and trumpeted into the makeshift instrument: *"Tah-dut-ta-tah!"*

Now I began a new search—this time for a comfortable hotel. From the size of the town, I suspected I would have better luck finding accommodation than I'd had in Schlaitdorf. Signs near Karlstraße announced the Gasthof Herrmann, and I followed them until I came to a modest hotel—a half-timber-and-stone building situated beside the town square.

Several times during the next two days, my references to the square were met with denials. "Münsingen doesn't have a town square," I was told; but I would not be convinced. In the middle of the cobble-stoned space beside the hotel, surrounded by sturdy buildings, an old stone fountain occupied a prominent position.

The Gasthof Herrmann fit my needs perfectly. It was clean with a modern feel, and the charge for the room was only 75 Deutsch Mark per night—an excellent deal compared to the excessive rates I had often paid in Europe. After settling the business with the desk clerk, I withdrew to my room.

In the corner of the room was a small desk where I spread out my notes and photocopies. Directly outside the single window, an imposing church steeple dominated the view. From the ancient look of the steeple, I judged that the church was none other than the Martinskirche, in whose archives I had made my recent find.

The church was only a few houses distant, and built on raised ground so that it towered over the neighbouring rooftops. Daylight had vanished, and now the stone steeple was illuminated by a flood-light situated somewhere near the base of the church. Directly above the windows of the belfry, the gold-coloured hands of a red-and-black clock announced the time. It was six o'clock.

Just then, a bell struck the hour. Four sharp rings of the quarter-hour bell echoed from the stone chamber; then came the clanging peal of a larger bell: Clang-clang-Clang-clang-Clang-clang-Clang.... It resounded for ten minutes.

Later, I changed into fresh clothes and went looking for some supper. At a small tavern, a block from the hotel, I was soon seated in front of a tasty-looking plate of spaghetti and a mug of German lager. It was my luck to arrive on a Monday evening when the pasta dish was offered at the unbelievable price of one DM per plate. At 80¢ Canadian, it was an offer I could not refuse.

Afterwards, I wandered around the town, attempting to acquaint myself with my new surroundings. Houses and shops fronted the narrow sidewalks, and half-melted mounds of dirty snow were piled in the streets, all but deserted. Here and there, timber-and-stone *Fachwerk* was offset by stuccoed walls. Nestled, as it seemed to be, deep in the Swabian highlands of southern Germany, Münsingen felt far removed, both in time and space, from the bustle of Europe.

In the lane-ways around the Martinskirche, wet cobblestones reflected light from the neighbouring houses. A solitary tree stood close to the church—the last of its yellow leaves tentatively hanging from the branches. Two powerful flood-lamps shone through the branches of the tree, bathing the spire in golden light.

The Martinskirche steeple, Münsingen.

Eventually I went back to my hotel room to get some sleep. But again I tossed and turned all night, the day's events crowding my thoughts. The tantalizing prospect of success was overwhelming, even as the possibility of failure nagged at the edge of my thoughts. When I finally dropped off, sleep was sporadic. I rose several times in the dark to look out the window at the church steeple rising above the rooftops like a beacon in the night. The bells were silent, and the street below my window was dead quiet. I crawled back into bed and slept a little more. Sometime after five o'clock, I gave up the effort and got dressed.

The photocopies from the *Ehebuch* held my attention for a few hours as I compared the names and dates on the copies with those in the Schlaitdorf faxes. Unable to find anything genealogically substantial, I went downstairs to the Herrmann's complimentary breakfast. It was Tuesday morning. I would have to depart for Amsterdam in two days.

CHAPTER 20

In America

With a good continental breakfast under my belt, I was ready to continue the search for traces of my Stief ancestors. I walked through the little streets to archives on Karlstraße—called the *Dekanatamt*—and prepared to take up the hunt where I had left off the previous day.

That morning, I began with the *Taufbuch*—a record of baptisms for the years before 1736. Steeves family tradition has postulated 1725 as Heinrich Stief's approximate birth-year, but without any supporting evidence. If Heinrich did in fact marry here in Münsingen in 1745, as I now believed, he would possibly have done so at any age between eighteen and forty. Based on those two extremes, his birth-date would be somewhere between 1727 and 1705.

I began at the year 1700 in the *Taufbuch* and went forward, looking for Johann Heinrich Stieff, son of Augustin Stieff, *Kälberhirte*. At the same time I kept my eyes open for a Regina Stalegger, although I suspected her birthplace would be closer to the village of Honau.

On each page of the *Taufbuch*, the columns were headed *Mensis et Dies* (month and day), *Infantes* (children), *Parentes* (parents), and *Patrui* (godparents). As was the case in the *Ehebuch*, the surnames were underlined in blue or red.

Again, as it had in the nineteenth-century faxed records, the name Heinrich proliferated. In 1716, an Anna Catherina was born to parents Heinrich and Barbara Stief. In 1717, a Johann Heinrich Stief was born to parents Johann Heinrich and Maria Barbara Stief. Eight years later, the same couple gave birth to a son, Augustin, who died young. As the facts accumulated, the relationships between these several Heinrich Stiefs and Augustin Stiefs would no doubt become clear.

During the first decade of the 1700s, the script was markedly different than in subsequent years, making it plain to see when the church had changed pastors. Some had made their entries in clear, neat script, while others had entered the names with a wild scrawl. I searched through every year from 1700 to 1729 without seeing any trace of the Heinrich Stief who had married Regina Stalegger in 1745. If his name was there, it had eluded me completely.

At that moment, I became aware of someone else in the room. Looking up, my glance was met by the inquiring face of the current pastor of the Martinskirche, Pfarrer Siegfried Fischer. I rose to shake hands. Once Pfarrer Fischer had learned the reason for my visit to his archives, he was glad to discuss the history of the venerable church.

Ancient may be a better word to describe the Martinskirche. The earliest documentary evidence of the church's existence has been tentatively traced to the shadowy darkness of the year 804. For the next 700 years, the church was Roman Catholic, until the Reformation brought Protestantism to Württemberg in 1534. Like the rest of Württemberg, Münsingen and the Martinskirche have been Lutheran ever since. Although the church building was a solid structure, Pfarrer Fischer explained, time had taken its toll on the old steeple, in need of extensive repair.[1]

The Martinskirche is named for its patron saint, Martin of Tours, who was born about the year 316 in Sabaria in the Roman province of Pannonia—the modern town of Szombathely in Hungary near the Austrian border. Martin grew up in Pavia, near Milan, and was conscripted into the Roman cavalry when only a teenager. By the time he turned twenty-two, however, the young soldier made it known to the world that he had a different calling. Riding outside the gates of Amiens in Gaul one winter day, he came upon a half-naked beggar suffering in the cold. Martin removed his own cloak, cut it into two pieces with his sword, and gave one half to the poor man. That night in a dream, according to his friend Sulpicius Severus, Martin saw Jesus Christ wearing the same piece of cloak he had given to the beggar.

After he had passed beyond the military, Martin devoted himself to contemplative study and prayer. He lived for several years in a hermitage off the coast of Italy, and in another near Poitiers. Later, Martin became Bishop of Tours in Gaul. He died at Candes-St. Martin on November 11, 397, at the age of eighty-one.

Severus described the saint as constant, humble, and kind. Martin performed miracles, healed the sick, and converted the unbelieving. With "his mind ever fixed upon heaven..." wrote Severus, he was a "truly blessed man...." So popular is St. Martin in France today that more than five hundred villages are named in his memory.[2]

Sixteen centuries after St. Martin's death, a family genealogist from Canada stood in the modern archives of a Württemberg church that today bears the saint's name. He and the pastor of the Martinskirche were conferring about the search for his Stief ancestors who he believed had wed in that same church in 1745—a recent event when juxtaposed with the life of a Roman soldier who shared his cloak with a beggar in AD 338.

Back at the table in the research room, I put aside the earlier *Taufbuch* and turned to a later register of baptisms—the *Taufregister* for the years after 1736. Beginning at the year 1745, I searched for any children born to parents named Heinrich and Regina Stieff. Although tradition holds that their first child was born in Pennsylvania, perhaps other children were born in Münsingen. But if I found any children born to these two after 1749—the year of Jacob's birth in Philadelphia—then I would have the wrong couple. I was totally unprepared for what I saw next.

Statue of St. Martin in the Fuentidueña Chapel, The Cloisters, New York.

Permission of the Metropolitan Museum of Art

Still at the year 1745, I'd only reached July 28, when I came to the baptismal entry for Katharina Barbara, daughter of Johann Heinrich Stieff and Regina Stalegger. I counted the months on my fingers: February 25 to July 28. The child had been baptized only five months after their marriage. How was this possible? Perplexed, I scrutinized the entry and discovered the words *"ex premat: concub:"* below the child's name. My high-school Latin told me the phrase might explain the problem.

I took the *Taufregister* to Frau Bader, and together we guessed that the Latin phrase might translate as "born prematurely." Children at the time often did not survive the first few days beyond birth. Perhaps Katharina Barbara had died during childbirth. When a new-born succumbed to the harsh rigours of eighteenth-century life, the death was noted in the birth-record by the insertion of a cross beneath the child's name. Occasionally a date was added. But no cross had been entered beneath the name of Katharina Barbara Stieff. Unless the pastor had failed to record a death, the girl had lived. But there could be no possibility that this child was delivered four months premature. Born long before the invention of incubators and intensive-care units, she would never have survived.

What became of this mystery child, who seems to have vanished from subsequent records? Down through the decades, the Steeves family has had notable success at keeping its legends alive. Thus, if Heinrich and Regina had spoken to their seven sons about a girl named Katharina Barbara, a vague memory at least would survive today. But does such a memory exist?

In *Samphire Greens*, Dr. Wright described a girl named Rachel, stating, "Nothing is known of her except that she died young." This third-generation girl was supposedly a granddaughter of Heinrich and Regina—a child of their eldest son Jacob Stief and his wife, Catherine Lutz. Dr. Wright mysteriously added: "Later generations, having heard rumours of a daughter who died young, were apt to attribute her to Heinrich's family....there was much confusion among later generations regarding Jacob and Heinrich."[3]

Was this the surviving shred of family memory that might resolve the dilemma? Did the girl Rachel belong to the second generation rather than the third? When the family lived in Pennsylvania, were the young boys told stories of the sister they had never known—a sister who had died back in the old homeland? Years later, when the prospect of a new home on the Petitcodiac River loomed large in the boys' lives, would they put the tale aside, and consequently forget some of the details? Would it be left to later generations to confuse the story? If there was confusion about young Rachel's parentage, perhaps there was also confusion about her name. Was the Rachel who died young actually the infant Katharina Barbara?

The possibility also exists that the child perished on the voyage across the Atlantic. Those arduous eighteenth-century crossings claimed the lives of more passengers, both young and old, than anyone might want to imagine. When her parents departed for America, the child would have been at most four years old—a tender age at which to face the physical and mental horrors of the passage.

According to Gottlieb Mittelberger who was a passenger on the ship *Osgood* in 1750: "Children [under] seven seldom survive the sea voyage; and parents must often watch their offspring suffer miserably, die, and be thrown into the ocean...." On his ship, Mittelberger witnessed the deaths of thirty-two children.[4]

Could other circumstances explain little Katharina Barbara Stief's seeming disappearance? Did she survive the voyage to America after all, despite Gottlieb Mittelberger's dire prognostications? If the child survived to adulthood, she would have been nearly twenty-one years old when her family moved to the Petitcodiac River—none too early for a girl to marry. When the rest of her family pulled up stakes in Pennsylvania, did Katharina Barbara stay behind with a husband and a young family of her own?

With so many contradicting possibilities, I began to question whether the Heinrich and Regina Stieff I had found were my ancestors who had gone to Pennsylvania.

Whatever the answer about young girls named Rachel or Katharina Barbara, I left the questions and continued to move forward in the *Taufregister*, looking for evidence of other children. Examining the years as far as 1770, I saw no more. There were many other children born to Stieff parents in Münsingen, of course, but none born to Heinrich and Regina.

Still not positive I had found my Stief ancestors, I turned my attention to the *Totenregister*, the record of deaths from 1737 to 1785. If either member of this couple had died in Münsingen, they could be eliminated as candidates. I searched with care, but found no names that matched. Heinrich and Regina had neither died in Münsingen, nor were any more children born to them there.

I tried to take up the thread of where I had left off in the *Taufregister* of baptisms, but found myself ploughing through the same ground. Most of the German script was impossible to understand, and I knew I would soon need professional help. At Frau Bader's suggestion, I placed a telephone call to Dr. Rudolf Bütterlin, a local genealogist, whom she thought might be interested in my search.

After several calls between Frau Bütterlin, myself, and Dr. Bütterlin's tax-accounting office in Bad Urach, it was arranged I would join them for dinner that evening. Dr. Bütterlin would pick me up at the Gasthof Herrmann at seven o'clock. It appeared I was going to get a taste of German hospitality and some Württemberg genealogy at the same time.

Frau Bader also suggested I visit Münsingen's tourist office to obtain some historical background on the town. Perhaps I could also find something about Honau, the place where Regina had lived.

I found the Münsingen tourist office located a few blocks from the Gasthof Herrmann. A four-storey *Fachwerk* building was set off by itself, surrounded by a wide expanse of lawn now wet and dull under a cloudy sky.

In the reception area, a young woman got up from her desk to help me. I explained that I was looking for a place called Honau, and I showed her my photocopy of the marriage record. After a glance at the entry, she responded with a knowing smile.

"Ah—just a moment," she said. Then she left the room. Was a more formal explanation required? Was Honau some sort of local shrine?

The receptionist soon returned with a bespectacled young man in tow. Of medium height and light build, he had the surprised look of someone who had been buried in an old journal and was suddenly propelled into the light of the present. Roland Deigendesch, *Stadtarchivar*, archivist for the town of Münsingen, introduced himself. I showed him my photocopy, pointing to the entry for February 25, 1745.

With the receptionist looking on, Herr Deigendesch read the entry to himself. Then he explained: Honau was a little village located a few miles to the west of Münsingen, near the city of Reutlingen. But he was now curious to find out what had brought me to Münsingen, and asked me to elaborate. I briefly recounted the story of my Stief ancestors who had emigrated to Pennsylvania in the mid-eighteenth century, and who had eventually moved to the Petitcodiac River in colonial Nova Scotia. Interest sparked, he beckoned me to follow him down a hall to his office.

In the compact office, the shelves were bursting with books. A large desk took up a quarter of the room. Piled on top of the desk were books and papers—evidence of his recent pursuits into the past. He took my coat and offered a chair. Then we conferred—about my search, about the history of the town, and about German records in general. Even before I learned that he was an expert in local German history, I felt fortunate to have found such an obliging fellow. Herr Deigendesch then took my copy of the *Ehebuch* record and translated the passage into English:

> On February 25th, 1745, the former *beyschlafer*, Johann Heinrich Stieff, legal and unmarried son of Augustin Stieff, cattleherd, with the profession of a brickmaker, was married in a praying hour with Regina Stalegger, a farmer's daughter from Honau, county of Pfullingen.

Without explaining, Herr Deigendesch excused himself and left the room. I glanced around the crowded office at the books and papers lying about, and at the many volumes aligned on the shelves above his desk. I wondered if any of the books might hold my ancestors' forgotten stories. Which ones might reveal their passions, their struggles, the minutiae of their daily lives? Would any of them explain how Regina Stalegger, a farmer's daughter from Honau, had met Heinrich Stieff, a Münsingen cattleherder's son?

I gazed out the office window at the overcast sky. In the distance, overlooking the houses, a flat-topped hill was cloaked with a mantle of evergreen trees.

Soon, Roland (as Herr Deigendesch was now insisting I call him) returned with a large black book under his arm. He placed the book on a table under the window. It was the *Steuermessbuch von 1720*, he explained, an assessment book used to determine the taxes owing on pieces of land in Münsingen. The book had been started in 1720, but, after fifty years of use, a new system of taxation was devised. By 1772, the *Steuermessbuch* and its early method of collecting taxes had been discontinued. He opened the *Steuermessbuch* to a rudimentary index—one that had likely been compiled when the information was transferred to a subsequent tax book.⁵

Roland Deigendesch, archivist for the town of Münsingen, in the Stadtarchiv.

We looked through the list of names in the index. He had a quick eye and was well versed in eighteenth-century German penmanship—writing that, to me, often looked like so many chicken scratches. He pointed to number 253 and the names, *"Friderich und Heinrich Stief."*

As he turned the pages to the corresponding entry, I could almost hear the pieces of the old Steeves family puzzle gently falling into place. We came to the original record for the parcel of land that had once been owned by the two Stiefs. The tract had seen several owners, and the names were jammed together. Among them, cramped and nearly illegible, was the confirming entry:

Friedrich Stief } *in America*
Heinrich Stief

Here was the convincing proof I had found the Heinrich Stief who had

Land record for the Hungerberg Hill: *Steuermessbuch von 1720.*
Courtesy of Stadtarchiv, Münsingen

emigrated to Pennsylvania with his wife Regina; the same Heinrich whose first son Jacob was born in Pennsylvania in 1749 and baptized in St. Michael's Lutheran Church; the same Heinrich who, together with eight of his Philadelphia neighbours, signed the Articles of Agreement with John Hughes in the winter of 1766; the same Heinrich who, on the third day of June that year, landed with his family and friends on the muddy bank of the Petitcodiac River, ready to begin a new life in a strange land. The question of Osnabruck was finally laid to rest.

Roland and I weighed the evidence and concluded that Friedrich and Heinrich were brothers—sons of Augustin Stieff, cattleherd. But there was more. Above the other names was that of Michael Stieff, shepherd, the third brother of Friedrich and Heinrich. Beside it was the "widow of Hans Jerg Stieff," he being a fourth brother, apparently. Their land was located "below the Hungerberg Hill." Whether or not all three brothers and the widow Stieff owned the piece of land at the same time, the *Steuermessbuch* did not reveal.[6]

The *Steuermessbuch von 1720* had a complicated arrangement. Each plot of land was described according to its exact size and location relative to adjacent tracts. The names of the owners occupied the left-hand column of the page. When a plot was sold, the previous owner's name was simply crossed off the list, and the new name added. For plots that had traded hands repeatedly during the fifty-year life of the *Steuermessbuch*, the names were crowded together. At various times during the period, the tract owned by the Stiefs had seen four other owners.

At the time, the plots in the *Steuermessbuch* were rated according to a classification system indicating the quality of the land and fertility of the soil. The Stief brothers' land was classed as "7." What this signified, Roland did not know. Was a class "7" plot sufficiently fertile to grow enough food to feed four families? The question remains unanswered.[7]

Next, Roland described the size of the plot. According to the *Steuermessbuch*, the Stiefs' land consisted of three *viertel* plus eleven-and-a-half *ruten*. A *viertel* was equal to one-quarter of a *morgen*, and a *morgen* equivalent to 3,152 square metres—the standard amount of land a man could manage in one day. Since a single *rute* comprised twenty-one square metres, there were thirty-seven *ruten* in each *viertel*. Putting all these figures together, the Stief brothers' lot was approximately 2,612 square metres, or 167-feet square. It was large enough to accommodate a good-sized vegetable garden, but certainly not adequate for four families.

The last column of the *Steuermessbuch* carried the heading "*Liegen zwischen*" or "lying between." Listed were the names of the neighbouring owners. For the Stief brothers' land, the entry stated: "*Liegen zwischen dem*

Hungerberg u[nd] H. Jacob Lockhen Witwe, J[ung] Matthes Krehl." Translated, the plot was situated "between the [upper part of the] Hungerberg and the plots of H-., the widow of Jacob Lockhen [and] the young Matthias Krehl."

Each plot on the side of the Hungerberg Hill was thus described: its owners' names, its size, its quality, and the names of its neighbours. Although the *Steuermessbuch* had seen use for only fifty years, its cumbersome method presented the possibility of much confusion in a short period. It seems no wonder the system was eventually phased out.

The name *Hungerberg* is still common in parts of Germany, Roland explained, and is applied to places that seasonally dry up. The word *hunger* in German also means hunger in English, and hence *Hungerberg* might be translated as "hill of hunger." In fact, Münsingen's Hungerberg has been a reliable source of water in recent times. Whether that was always the case is not known. In times gone by, wooden pipelines ran down from the Hungerberg to supply the "great fountain" in the centre of town. Built in the style of the late Renaissance, the fountain dates to the early 1600s.

Great Fountain ca. 1850. The building on the right is today the Gasthof Herrmann, externally much unchanged. Courtesy Stadtarchiv, Münsingen

Today, a stone column rises elegantly from the centre of the fountain. At the top is perched a stone lion holding aloft the coat of arms of the Duke of Württemberg.

It wasn't difficult to imagine Heinrich and Regina Stief, making their way to the village market on a fine morning, and stopping beside the flowing waters of the fountain to chat with their neighbours. Perhaps it was beside the fountain that they had heard the stories from America—stories sent back in letters to friends and relatives about a new life in Pennsylvania, the land of opportunity and freedom.

"Where would this Hungerberg be found?" I wondered aloud.

"It is the hill overlooking Münsingen," Roland replied. He rose from his chair and pointed out the window. "There it is." It was the same hill I had seen earlier. Now, the broad green hill seemed to call me to explore.

Roland and I returned to the marriage record of February 25, 1745, which he proceeded to translate, word by word.

> *d[en] 25 Febr[uar] ist als früher Beyschläffer in einer Betstunde cop-*
> *ulieret worden Johann Heinrich Stieff, Augustin Stieffen, Kälberhirte,*
> *von hier eh[elich] lediger Sohn, s[eines] Handwerks ein Ziegler, mit*
> *Regina Staleggerin, Bauern Tochter von Honau, Pfullinger Amts.*

The word *Kälberhirte*—the occupation of Heinrich's father—seemed to give him pause. After a few moments he explained that Augustin had tended the village cows, without owning any of them. Augustin was the village cowherd, he said, and then added, "a cowboy." I had decided by then it was not the best word, but I was nevertheless amazed by the lasting impression made by Hollywood westerns on the European side of the Atlantic.

Roland elaborated that the Schlaitdorf term *viehhirte* more generally described a herder of animals. *Kälberhirte*, on the other hand, likely involved the tending of calves. Either way, cowherd or calfherd, Augustin's occupation was ranked very low on the social ladder. Did Augustin look after the village cattle in his retirement years or because of some disability? Or was Augustin Stieff the head of a poor family? Again, unanswered questions.

The *Betstunde*, or praying hour—the time when Heinrich and Regina were married—was a divine service, usually held on Wednesdays, with chanting, prayer, and the reading of psalms.

Heinrich had cultivated a garden plot on the Hungerberg, but his occupation was actually that of a *ziegler*, or brickmaker. Today, south of Münsingen, there is a low hill called the *Ziegelwäldle* or "brick-woods." The *Ziegelwäldle* had been occupied by brickmakers since the middle ages, and Heinrich Stief had chosen to pursue that trade. Perhaps Heinrich supported his father, the poor cattleherder.

Heinrich Stief's knowledge of brick-making would be invaluable when he and the other families began to establish themselves on the banks of the Petitcodiac River in 1766. In order to comply with the Articles of Agreement signed in Philadelphia, each settler would need to build a house with a stone or brick chimney. Maybe it was Heinrich Stief who showed teenaged Christian Trites how to make the bricks for his own house which he built, a few years later, at the edge of today's Albert Street marsh in Moncton. Until it was destroyed by fire in 1972, the house was one of the few remaining structures in New Brunswick built in the eighteenth century.[8]

One word remained for Herr Deigendesch to interpret: *beyschläffer*. He struggled to explain the meaning of the word. I struggled to understand it. Both the custom of the *beyschläffer* and the word have gone out of use in the 250-odd years since Heinrich and Regina Stief departed from Württemberg. And although the practice of the *beyschläffer* was not uncommon, it's doubtful if it was generally sanctioned. So what did it mean?

Heinrich and Regina Stief's descendants tend to think of them as an elderly couple. Many years have passed since their early days in Münsingen, and they both may have been well-advanced in years when they arrived on the Petitcodiac River. But Heinrich and Regina were young, once upon a time. And there may come a time in the lives of a young couple when the rules no longer matter. When love calls, both the young and the wise will answer. Suddenly, certain things become more important than human conventions, more urgent than society's rules, more pressing than the regulations of church and state. Perhaps Heinrich and Regina heard that call, when they knew each other, in the sight of God, a full four months before their marriage on February 25, 1745.

The meaning of the word *beyschläffer* became abundantly clear. Before their marriage, Heinrich Stief had lived in a common-law relationship with Regina Stalegger, his future wife. The child Katharina Barbara was conceived out-of-wedlock.

A flood of questions followed. How did Württemberg society view their unconventional relationship? Did their neighbours' reaction play any part in their decision to leave for America? I wondered how thousands of my Steeves cousins back in New Brunswick would respond to the news.

Dr. Yoder's comments on the subject of common-law arrangements and illegitimate children will be helpful:

> If the parents married shortly before or soon after the birth of the child, the pastors charitably considered the births legitimate. And here [in Pennsylvania] at least the pastors did not, as was the case in some German records I have studied in Europe, pretentiously reverse the book and inscribe illegitimate births upside down.[9]

The pastor in Münsingen was not so grudging as to inscribe the birth of Katharina Barbara upside down. Nevertheless, the telling notation was left for history: *ex premat: concub:* (*ex præmaturus concubitus*)—born out of premarital cohabitation.

Katharina Barbara Stieff, baptized July 28, 1745. Münsingen *Taufregister*
Courtesy of the Martinskirche

CHAPTER 21

A Walk on an Old Hill

On Tuesday evening, Dr. Rudolf Bütterlin strode into the reception area of the Gasthof Herrmann at precisely two minutes past seven. I was waiting near the front desk and we recognised each other at once. Probably in his fifties, he was nattily dressed in a sports coat and tie. Introductions completed, we went together to his car. A short drive brought us to the Bütterlins' house, situated below the Hungerberg—the hill Roland Deigendesch and I had been discussing only a few hours before.

Frau Bütterlin welcomed me into her home and introduced me to her son, Veit, as well as to her extended family of three cats, one large dog, six small birds, and two enormous turtles now relaxing in a sunken pond in the living room. The edge of a brown shell protruded from under a wet rock. Frau Bütterlin then withdrew to her kitchen, while her husband and I settled on the sofa and prepared for a dig into Münsingen genealogy.

I explained to Dr. Bütterlin that it seemed odd the birth-record for Heinrich Stief did not appear in the *Taufbuch*, even though his daughter was born in Münsingen. Had I overlooked the entry, or was Heinrich born elsewhere? Dr. Bütterlin attacked the problem with gusto. His genealogy library included copies of the Martinskirche baptismal records, and he was well acquainted with the contents. I felt certain I would get a definitive answer shortly. I browsed through some of his books on nineteenth-century emigration to Russia while I waited.

Fifteen or twenty minutes later, Dr. Bütterlin announced, "Heinrich Stief was not born in Münsingen." We discussed other possibilities, without arriving at an explanation about Heinrich's birth-place. It seemed his family had lived elsewhere when he was born. Then Frau Bütterlin called us to the table and we put the question aside.

I would have been happy to drink German wine that evening, but the Bütterlins considered the occasion to be worthy of their best French Beaujolais. The wine was excellent, and it complemented Frau Bütterlin's meal of roast, casserole, and salad. We were joined by their son, and the four of us entered into a stimulating dialogue that ran the gamut of current affairs: French-German relations; the perplexing challenges of international commerce; the present state of public education; and the deplorable outlook of German politics. At that point, Dr. Bütterlin uncorked another bottle of Beaujolais.

Coat of Arms of the Dukes of Württemberg, since 1495, showing (clockwise from upper left) original stag's antlers; the Wecken rhombuses; Barben fishes of Mömpelgart earldom; Markgröningen's imperial storm flag.
Courtesy of Dr. Rudolph Bütterlin

The most intriguing part of our discourse came when we turned to the history of Württemberg. Württemberg's long history, was, at times, confusing, dramatic, and violent. Decades in and out, European rulers fought each other for control, and old Swabia was never far from the centre of turmoil. The Peasants' War was brutally suppressed in 1526; Reformation was succeeded by counter-reformation; the power of the Habsburg family monopolized the political spectrum for centuries; the War of Spanish Succession lasted from 1701 to 1714; more turmoil ensued; the War of Austrian Succession followed from 1740 to 1748. Understandably, by the beginning of the eighteenth century, poor farmers and tradesmen were ready for a fundamental change in their lives.

It wasn't very late when we decided to bring the evening to a close. The Bütterlins anticipated another heavy work day, and I was somewhat bewildered from the combined effects of Württemberg history and French wine.

Wednesday morning saw me awake just after dawn. If my head was clear, the weather was not. The rain held off, but a smurry sky promised a wet day ahead.

After polishing off another Herrmann breakfast, I walked straight to Roland's office. It seemed he was anticipating my arrival; he had found something new relating to the Stieff brothers' land. In the archives, he had located an 1820s map that showed the village and the Hungerberg hill.

As if through the eyes of a bird soaring high above the nineteenth-century village, one sees the whole vista of Münsingen and environs—individual fields stretching away from the perimeter of the village, and the remains of the mediaeval moat, or *stadtgraben*, ringed about the houses. The streets and buildings are meticulously arranged inside the *stadtgraben*, with the dark shape of the Martinskirche positioned at the centre. Dominating the top portion of the map, the broad crest of the Hungerberg spreads back from the village. On the east and south sides of the hill, the terraced plots of land are clearly delineated.

Accompanying the 1820s map of Münsingen, and dating to the same period, was a finely detailed lithograph of the town, drawn by an unknown

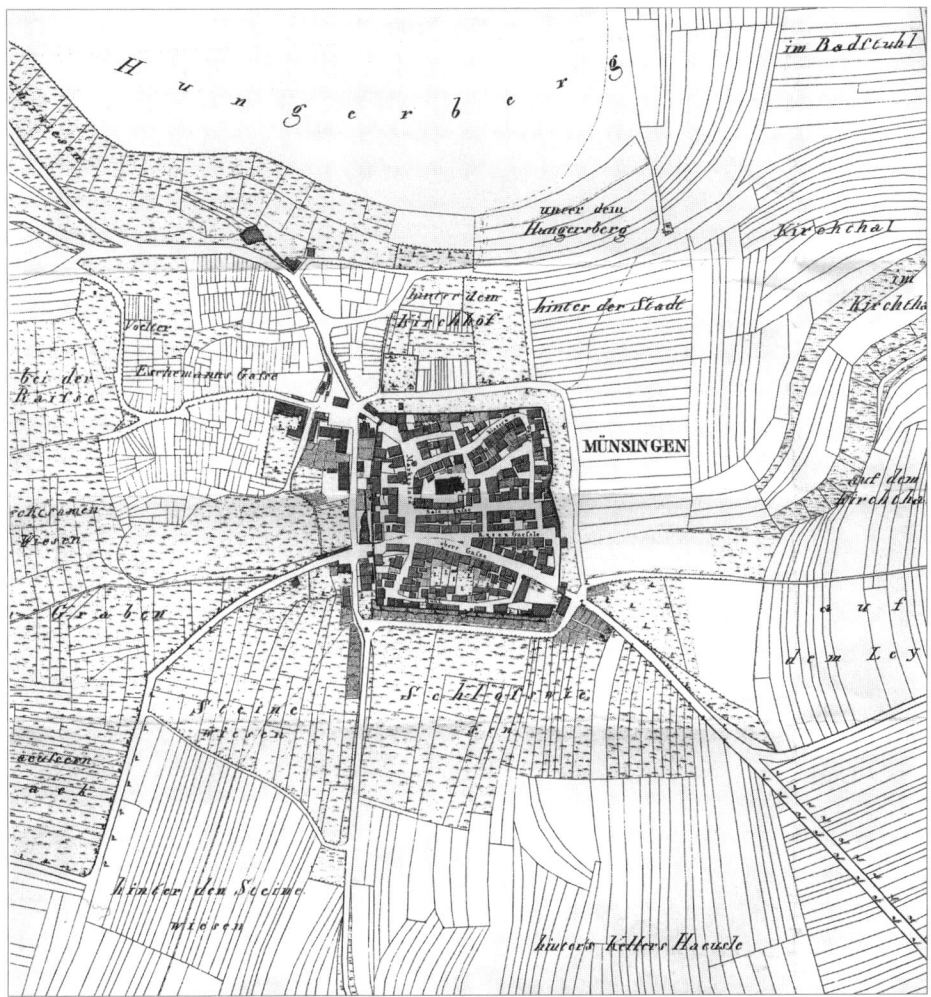

Münsingen 1820. "Unter dem Hungerberg" Flurkarte SO 11.29 (Ortslage Muensingen, 1820).
Courtesy of Stadtarchiv, Münsingen

"Münsingen sketch" Heimatmuseum Muensingen Inv.nr. O 54: Muensingen from the east, Lithography, ca. 1820.
Courtesy of Stadtarchiv, Münsingen

artist. Although the village is pictured as it might have looked seventy years after Heinrich and Regina's departure to America, the scene would not have changed a great deal in the interim.

In the foreground of the bucolic setting, viewed from the east, two men are conversing. One is a shepherd who rests on a boulder. The other, apparently a hunter or an official, leans on his gun; his dog waits beside him. Close by, a flock of sheep are grazing at the edge of a rise. Near the sheep, a flowering bush is in full summer bloom. Beyond them in the distance, enclosed by the remains of the mediaeval stone wall, the village of Münsingen expands across a wide, level space.

The buildings are crowded together, their steep roofs possibly built to withstand snow and ice in less temperate seasons. The upper lofts may have been used to store grain. Near the centre of the village rises the square tower of the Martinskirche. Three generations of villagers would come and go before a pointed stone steeple was added to the church in 1887. To the right of the village, beyond the *stadtgraben*, is a small cemetery with a tree at either end; tiny crosses represent the tombstones. On the left, rising above the village, stands the *Ziegelwäldle*, or "brick-woods," where Heinrich Stief plied his trade as a brickmaker.

Clearly, here was a community whose wall kept outsiders out. The villagers lived inside the walls and came outside to farm their fields. The place has a close, compact feel, and insularity comes to mind. What a different life Heinrich and Regina Stief were to encounter in America: open towns without walls, live-on farms scattered through the countryside, and the relative freedom that would allow a stranger to make a new start.[1]

The lithograph presents a perfect window on the past, and the rustic scene easily comes to life. On the left, a single plume of smoke rises undisturbed towards the billowy summer clouds. The sounds and smells can be imagined: bees droning above the flowers at the right; sheep bleating below the rise; perhaps a loaded wagon, somewhere unseen, grinding its wooden wheels on the dirt track as it makes its way toward the village. The hunter's mutt might be expected to look over its shoulder, pause thoughtfully, and begin scratching for fleas.

Imagined formulations aside, historical interpretation requires incontrovertible evidence on which to stand. The Martinskirche seemed the obvious place to go next. On that subject, however, Roland deferred my questions to a friend named Jürgen vom Grafen who was somewhat of an expert on the subject. Jürgen's office was located near the church.

After lunch, I found Jürgen vom Grafen's office a few paces from the front door of the Martinskirche. A middle-aged, urbane man who spoke flawless English, Jürgen explained that his advertising and promotions firm had participated in the preparation of a brochure about the Martinskirche. He suggested that we go to the church where we could discuss its history more appropriately.

Inside, a few parishioners were gathered with their pastor near the front of the nave. Jürgen and I walked to the back, where we stood out of earshot, and discussed the history of the church.

Martinskirche, dating from the eleventh century.

The oldest part of the building is the central nave, evidently dating to the eleventh century. The base of the tower dates to the mid-thirteenth century. Some of the adornments in the Martinskirche originally belonged to neighbouring Stephanuskirche, a church in the now-deserted village of Gruorn. These objects, including the crucifix and statues of the saints, date to about the year 1480. The baptismal font traces its origin to the year 1506, and the ornaments in the wooden ceiling date to 1558. The first organ was built at the end of the sixteenth century, and the frame of the second organ was built in 1758. That frame now holds the modern organ, constructed more recently in 1976.

During renovations in 1984, it was discovered that the Martinskirche was one of the few churches in post-Reformation Württemberg to be decorated with colour. For reasons unknown, the Martinskirche was an exception to the prevailing rule of austerity in Lutheran churches.

The upper part of the steeple, constructed of stone, holds four bells—the oldest cast in 1487, the most recent in 1952.[2]

I reflected on the provenance of the oldest bell—one that had been in use for a full 250 years before my Stief ancestors had wed here "in a praying hour." Jürgen and I were standing in the shadows at the back of the church, two-and-a-half centuries after that event had occurred in 1745. Just then, as if on cue, the oldest bell and its three companions began to ring in the hour.

But what I heard that afternoon wasn't simply the same fifteenth-century bell my ancestors had heard, it was *the same sound*. Every day for the past 500 years the oldest bell had pealed over the rooftops of the town, ringing its way into the hearts and minds of all and sundry—rich and poor, *Kälberhirte* and *Ziegler*, citizen and tourist alike.

As they toiled in their garden on the side of the Hungerberg, did the Stief brothers pause from their labours to listen to the magic of the great bell?

Did they lean thoughtfully on their hoes as it poured its heavenly music over the town and across the distant fields? Music it would have been to their eighteenth-century peasant ears, whose daily ration of music probably amounted to little more than the song of birds and the sound of the human voice.[3]

Later that afternoon, as the morning's fog changed to light rain, I grabbed my umbrella and headed up to the Hungerberg to scout around. Although the day didn't look promising for photography, I took my camera, hoping the high-speed film I had purchased in London would do the trick. I couldn't be fussy about the timing; my scheduled departure for Amsterdam was a mere eighteen hours away.

Dodging the puddles, I walked through the alleys and laneways, and headed toward the hill. Near the last of the houses at the base of the Hungerberg, a narrow trail led up through a thicket of birch and poplar trees. Rain dripped from the branches at the edge of the muddy track, and the last leaves of the year fell to the soggy ground.

Emerging from the woods at the end of the track, I made my way across the eastern side of the hill where a few solitary trees broke the monotony of a sloping field of dead grass. Along the hillside, running from north to south, traces of the former terraces were visible. In places where the rain had washed away the thin layer of snow, dead vegetation showed through, clearly revealing the pattern of the old earthworks. A disused cart track ran parallel to the terracing and disappeared into a stand of evergreens in the distance.

I stopped to fill my lungs with the damp air. Then I gazed at the trees and looked down at the ground, thinking. Somewhere near the spot—possibly right under my feet—was the place where Heinrich and his brothers had tilled their land in the mid-1700s. I walked along the hill for a short distance, observing the terraces and listening to the ground, trying to imagine the scene 250 years ago. Perhaps, with luck, I could conjure up the sound of their hoes scraping across the stony ground, or maybe envision an eighteenth-century crow, cawing at them from the branches of a tree. I got no help; the place had been abandoned long before.

Through the gloom, I snapped a few pictures of the landscape without being very optimistic about the results. To keep the rain off my camera, I had to aim and shoot with one hand while holding my umbrella aloft with the other. Anyone looking up from the houses at the foot of the hill must have thought it an odd sight.

Then, I picked my way across the sodden field, and headed back to the centre of town. It was well past four o'clock, but I wanted to look in on

Remains of terraces on the east side of the Hungerberg; looking north.

Roland who had said he would be working until six. Our meeting that morning had left us both enthused about the Stief brothers. Perhaps he had made some discoveries of his own.

Back at the town office, all was dark and deserted. I tried the main door, but found it locked. Unwilling to give up so easily, I went around to the side of the building where I guessed Roland's office would be. Light from a ground-floor window shone across the snow to the sidewalk. Maybe a well-placed snowball would get some attention. Missing my target with the first one, I threw another, this time making a direct hit. Roland's surprised face appeared behind the glass, and he left the office to investigate. His forbearance with my genealogical obsession was remarkable.

Inside his office, I could tell he had discovered something new about the Stief family. This time, the information wasn't about Heinrich and his brothers, but about their cattleherding father. The records of Münsingen's municipal court contained two stories about Augustin and his cows.

In the hot summer of 1750, Augustin had been tending his herd in the Tiefental valley, about two kilometres west of Münsingen. Seeking shade from the oppressive heat one day, some of the cows had escaped his watchful eye, and had strayed into a nearby woods belonging to the village. An agent of the Duke of Württemberg had seen the act, and reported the transgression to the court in Urach. Augustin was found guilty of an offence and ordered to pay a fine of 10 Gulden—probably more than he would earn in several months. But where would a poor man find such an amount of cash? He appealed to the Münsingen village council for help, since, as he stated, it wasn't his fault: cows will be cows. The council agreed that Augustin should not have to pay the fine, and offered to support him. The outcome was not recorded.[4]

It was not a good year for Augustin and his cows. Shortly after the first incident occurred, a conflict arose between him and a local horse herder named Ludwig Bosler. Their two herds had been competing for the same pasture, and Augustin and Ludwig had argued. In the heat of the moment, Ludwig had hit Augustin with the handle of his whip. When the two appeared before the court, Ludwig was fined, and Augustin was warned to keep the peace.[5]

There was still more about the Stiefs. Roland had also found a *Kaufbuch*, or record of land transactions, in which a 1746 document detailed the purchase of a portion of a house in Münsingen. One of the buyers was a Heinrich Stief.[6]

I doubted if my Stief ancestor would have made such an investment only a year or two before his departure to America. The record of sale was three pages long, and near the bottom of the final page was the signature of a Heinrich Stief.

I tried to recall the look of Heinrich's signature on the Articles of Agreement made in Philadelphia in 1766—the signature Esther Clark Wright described as his "careful, upright German script."

I thought the signature in the *Kaufbuch* looked familiar, but I knew I would need to see the Philadelphia agreement to determine whether or not both signatures had been made by the same man. Although a positive result was unlikely, it would be astounding to see Heinrich's signature here in Münsingen—possibly the only physical trace he himself had left behind in Württemberg. But how could I obtain a copy of the Articles of Agreement on such short notice?

Roland and I discussed the document a little further, after which I related my excursion up to the Hungerberg and my exploration of the old terracing. Finally, we wrapped up our investigations, arranging to meet one last time before my departure in the morning.

That evening, I packed my bags to be ready for a quick exit the next day. I wanted to retire early, since I knew Thursday would bring a full day of travelling. But, again I could not sleep; the events of the past several days flooded my mind. The scene on the Hungerberg flashed repeatedly on my internal screen, and I couldn't stop thinking about the signature on the house-sale document. Was it that of my ancestor? About one o'clock, I finally drifted off, the Articles of Agreement still on my mind.

Sometime in the middle of the night I awoke suddenly, with images of my Toronto office floating through my head. I recalled that several years before, I'd made a rough photocopy of the Articles of Agreement, taken from Dr. Wright's book, *The Petitcodiac*. The framed copy would be hanging on the wall above my desk in Toronto.

I looked at my watch: 2:30 in the morning. Back home, it would be only 8:30 of the previous evening. I suspected that Paul, who was managing the business in my absence, would be working late, as was his habit. There was no phone in the room, but I knew what I had to do. I jumped out of bed, threw on my clothes, and went outdoors.

The street was as hushed as the grave. I walked across the square and through a back alley where the sound of crunching snow underfoot echoed in the dark. Continuing past the town office, I reached a phone booth I had seen the day before. I fished out my phonecard and dialled Toronto.

Paul was still at work, surprised to hear from me at such an hour. He answered that he was standing in front of the framed photocopy of the 1766 agreement. He confirmed John Hughes Jr.'s clear, neat penmanship and the ten unreadable signatures with their seals, arranged in a column down the right side. At first, I remembered there being only nine signatures on the document—those of the one Welsh and eight German settlers who were preparing to leave Philadelphia for good. But I'd forgotten that the first signature was that of John Hughes, the Philadelphia merchant and land speculator who had made the whole thing possible.

Paul promised to fax the copy of the agreement to Roland's office, after which we briefly discussed business. When the phonecard expired, I replaced the receiver and headed back to my hotel room, confident I had done all I could that night.

CHAPTER 22

A Mistaken Signature

I managed to sleep until seven o'clock the next morning when the bells of the Martinskirche brazenly rang their way into my dreams. From the moment I awoke, I could think of little else but the fax from Toronto which, by then, should be in Roland's office. I dressed for my journey to Amsterdam, and went downstairs to gobble down some breakfast. Then I took care of business with my hosts, arranging to leave my luggage in the room for another hour. There was one other thing I needed to do before I saw Roland.

Frau Bader, the archivist at the *Dekanatamt*, had been so kind and helpful that now I wanted to say goodbye as well as to give her a token of my gratitude. Around the corner from the hotel was a small flower shop where I purchased a colourful bouquet. Then I dashed off to see Frau Bader in the church archives at 30 Karlstraße.

She welcomed me into her office as before, and accepted my gift with modest surprise. As I prepared to leave, thanking her for all the help she had freely given me over the previous three days, she replied, "Best wishes from Münsingen to all the Steeves descendants." I reflected that her wishes might be going out to upwards of 150,000 descendants of Heinrich and Regina Stief. It would be quite a crowd.

Now I walked straight back to the Gasthof Herrmann to collect my things. After a final look out the window at the old church spire, towering above the roof tops, I left the hotel.

When I arrived at Roland's office he was coming down the corridor, the fax from Toronto in his hand. My anticipation was acute. In the office, he opened the *Kaufbuch* to the Münsingen house-purchase document, and placed the faxed copy of the Articles of Agreement beside it. We compared the signature of a Heinrich Stief in 1746 with that of another—a pioneer who signed his name in Philadelphia twenty years later.

We saw immediately that the signatures were not the same. Unless my own Heinrich had changed his writing style remarkably in the intervening years, these were the signatures of two different men—probably cousins. It seemed unlikely that someone might have signed on Heinrich's behalf. Agreeing with Roland that the two signatures were different, I accepted the results. A graphic and dramatic conclusion to my quest on my last morning in Münsingen was not to be had. But, looking back on the events and discoveries of the past week, I could find no reason to complain. After years of research, I had found the German hometown of Heinrich and Regina Stief; there was little doubt about that. True, I hadn't found their birthplaces; and the fate of their daughter was still a mystery. But I was confident those answers would come, undramatically perhaps, in their own good time. I was working in the realm of genealogy and history, and dramatics would have to wait for another day.

But Roland was anxious to learn about the signatures on the Articles of Agreement. It was my turn to inform my Württemberg host.

I looked at the fax on his desk—an agreement that had irrevocably changed the lives of my ancestors on a mild winter day in 1766. How could I describe a document that had taken me so far from home—one that had sustained an interest in family history for more than thirty years? What could I say?

I tried to explain the role played by John Hughes, the Philadelphia merchant whose insatiable desire for recognition and accomplishment had precipitated the settlers' departure to the Petitcodiac River.

Then I went through the list of signatures, one by one, trying to provide Roland with the scraps of information about each man's background I had accumulated over the years.

Of Valentin Miller, Andrew Criner, Jacob Cline, and Matthias Lentz, I knew little, beyond the fact that they had stayed behind in Philadelphia when the other five sailed with John Hall that spring.

What could I say about Matthias Sommer, the first of the settlers to sign the agreement, the man from St. Peter's church who had encountered trouble with the quill pen during the signing ceremony?

Michael Lutz, who had arrived in Pennsylvania married and with a family of growing children, was a little easier. Thanks to Muriel Sikorski, his home village of Kreuzwertheim had been known for fifteen years.

If Michael Lutz was easier to describe, Jacob Treitz was impossible. How could I summarize my guesses about a signature that did not fit with the other eight? I still could not see clearly the events that had unfolded on that January day in John Hughes's office.

What about Charles Jones, the lone Welshman who couldn't sign his name? With all the dead ends I had come up against during the past two years, he had become more of a mystery figure than ever. I still didn't know if Charles Jones and John Hughes were related.

I had left the signature of Heinrich Stief for last. Roland Deigendesch now knew almost as much about my Stief ancestor as I did. What could I add about a man who had seen so many changes in his lifetime—a man whose memory is cherished by countless Steeves family members around the world, and whose pioneering spirit has fired the imaginations of so many of his descendants—a man who, as Dr. Wright suggests, founded a nation? Perhaps the fact that the legends of Heinrich Stief had brought an eighth-generation descendant all the way from Canada to a little town in the heart of Württemberg would suggest to Roland how important the life of Heinrich Stief was to the far-flung members of the Steeves family. I think he understood.

But time took care of further explanation; our conversation had gone on longer than we'd anticipated. It was approaching 10:30, when the bus would be leaving for Metzingen. It was one bus I could not afford to miss. I had worked out my schedule to put me in Amsterdam by seven o'clock that evening, but the scenario left no room for missed connections. Roland and I said our reluctant farewells, and he showed me out of the building into the cool Münsingen morning. We shook hands, and I marched off to the bus stop to begin my journey back to Canada. I never guessed how long a journey it would be.

The ride to Metzingen was the reverse of the one I had made three days before. Again, the bus travelled beside tree-lined hills and rode through frosty valleys where woodland streams rushed among the trees. Each time we came to a sign pointing to Metzingen, the bus went the opposite way. I knew enough to put aside my concerns this time, and devoted my attention to the countryside.

Several kilometres out of Münsingen, we passed the same limestone outcropping as before, where a gushing stream had worn a giant hole in the rock. The torrent of water momentarily passed out of sight and then reappeared on the other side of the cliff. This time I was struck by the resemblance to similar limestone caves in Albert County, N.B., a few miles from

Hillsborough where Heinrich and Regina finally settled. I wondered if they had been aware of the similarities between the two sites. Had they ever stood at the entrance to Underground Lake near Demoiselle Creek in New Brunswick, and reminisced about their old home in Münsingen from which they had begun their long journey years before?

When the bus reached Metzingen, I disembarked and drifted inside the station. A short queue of travellers waited at the ticket counter. With my mind reflecting on my last morning in Münsingen, I'd forgotten that I could have purchased a ticket on the train. Only a few minutes had elapsed when I stepped up to the counter and asked the woman for a ticket to Stuttgart.

"Stuttgart?" the clerk repeated sharply. She swung round in her chair to look toward the tracks behind her. "The train is here!"

Through the window beyond I could see the train standing in the station. I grabbed my bags and bolted for the platform. I ran down a flight of stairs in a panic, sprinted through a tunnel under the tracks, and came up on the other side. I wasn't even sure if I was going in the right direction. As I lunged across the platform, the doors of the train suddenly closed, and it began to move forward all at once. It quickly picked up speed and was soon gone. I could only stare in disbelief, gasping for breath, my heavy bags dead weight on my shoulders.

Still out of breath, I went to the schedule posted on the platform, and tried to re-orient myself. As best I could make out, I would need to take another bus across country to Stuttgart in order to get an Inter-City train to Amsterdam. Unwilling to rely solely on my own observation, I went back inside the station to get help.

The ticket seller, sympathetic to my plight, diligently set to work at her computer. The alternative wasn't as bad as I had feared; another train would be passing through Metzingen in just an hour. With a ninety minute stop-over in Stuttgart and a change of trains in Koblenz, I could be in Amsterdam by nine p.m.—only two hours behind schedule. I gratefully accepted the option and paid for a ticket, marvelling at my luck. The intervening hour gave me time to replenish some of my energies, and, when the next train arrived in the station, I was confidently waiting on the platform, ready to board.

I'd been seated for only a few minutes, when a bright-eyed, elderly gentleman wearing a bow tie sat down opposite me. Something about him made me smile, and he returned my glance. Without speaking, I reached in my briefcase and pulled out a large genealogy chart that showed my German ancestry—one that I had kept at my side during the past two years. Of course the chart did not include my latest discoveries in Münsingen, but the lines clearly showed my grandfather Jones's eighteenth-century German roots. I held the chart high, letting it fall open for him to see.

"*Forefatheren*," I said, pointing to the names Stief, Sommer, Lutz, Treitz, and Jones. His jaw dropped open and he took hold of the long chart to examine it, mouthing the names to himself. I tried my limited French on him, and soon we were stumbling along, *en français*, trying to establish his own possible relationship to Heinrich and Regina Stief through his French-Huguenot line. The other passengers eyed us with doubtful curiosity. The encounter was wonderful fun, but it ended almost as soon as it had begun. When the train arrived at Plochingen, he got up to leave, and I collected myself for the final, short ride to Stuttgart.

It was barely one o'clock when the train pulled into Stuttgart's giant station. After freshening up in the station restroom, I went into the great concourse to look for a bite to eat. At a little lunch place I ordered a take-out sandwich, and went off to eat it alone. At 2:30, I made my way among the foreign platforms, and boarded a long Inter-City train to Amsterdam. I was already feeling pangs of regret at having to leave Germany so soon. I had been in the country five short days, and I had made the most incredible discovery of my lifelong genealogical pursuits. I wasn't ready to move on to more worldly considerations just yet.

Metzingen station and the Swabian hills beyond.

House (on the right) in Münsingen once owned by Augustin Stief. The house was demolished early in 1997.

Courtesy of Stadtarchiv, Münsingen

CHAPTER 23

Journey to Another World

Around three o'clock, the train rolled into the great valley of the Rhine River, that ancient watercourse of legend and song which, forever and a day, has quietly observed mankind's often turbulent affairs as it flows unconcerned to the sea.

By the time we reached the city of Mainz, a wan winter sun was receding behind the hills. Every few kilometres, the remains of a ruined hillside castle came into view—the lasting physical evidence of the devastation brought on by nearly two centuries of warfare in the Palatinate. Now, somewhat restored to a former state of "feudal dignity and glory," as Beidelman says, these remnants of Palatine grandeur attract hordes of twentieth-century tourists who travel the Rhine valley every summer.[1]

Heinrich and Regina Stief journeyed down the same river long ago on their way to Rotterdam and the sea. For them, it was a one-way trip. From the deck of their river boat they had gazed at the same castles—mute relics standing silent witness to the past. Certainly they had beheld the same hills, already old, and narrowed their eyes at the same sun, gently setting on the day, as it was setting on their life in Württemberg forever.

Their final destination in Europe was the port of Rotterdam, six hundred kilometres distant from the junction of the Neckar and the Rhine. At the time, upwards of three dozen toll stations were situated along the Rhine River, where the boats' cargoes were inspected and customs duties paid. Delays at the toll stations slowed the river passage to as much as six weeks, further adding to the expense of the long trip down the Rhine.[2]

According to Gottlieb Mittelberger, the cost of the trip from Württemberg to Rotterdam "comes to at least forty florin no matter how economically one tries to live on the way." No cheap fare, it was as much money as an average craftsman might earn in three months.[3] Mittelberger came to Philadelphia in 1750, accompanying a new organ for St. Michael's Church—"the largest and finest organ in the Colonies." He stayed in Pennsylvania for four years as church organist and school teacher, but returned to Württemberg in 1754, disappointed with life in America.[4]

In Rotterdam, the emigrants were likely to encounter additional delays of several more weeks. During the wait, German ship's agents called *Neuländer* attempted to fleece the poor country-folk of their remaining money. The thieving hucksters came in for harsh criticism from Mittelberger who condemned their devious methods of painting a false picture of life in America and of misrepresenting the journey there. These "traffickers of human souls," as he calls them, were paid by their employers to go into towns and villages throughout the Palatinate and Württemberg, where they conned the naive country-folk into leaving home unprepared for the long journey ahead. Some emigrants prepaid the *Neuländer* to escort them to America, only to see the petty swindlers later vanish with all their money.[5]

By the time the emigrants reached Rotterdam, many had overspent themselves during the trip down the Rhine River. Those who were drained of their meagre savings were forced to sell themselves into bondage in order to obtain passage. Once they were in America, it would take years of indentured servitude to work off the debt. Poor families were separated, and many parents had to sell their children into certain slavery in order to pay the costs of the voyage. As many as 35,000 emigrants from the German regions became indentured servants in America. Often, their little chests containing extra food and possessions disappeared in Rotterdam, and when the passengers arrived in Philadelphia they had nothing to show but the dirty, vomit-stained clothes on their backs.[6]

Night descended quickly on the modern valley of the Rhine. In Koblenz, I waited for the connecting train that would take me on to Holland. It arrived on time, and departed with at least one Canadian family historian aboard. Finally, just before nine o'clock, the train rolled into Amsterdam's *Centraal Station*.

Tired from a long day of travel, my chief concern was to find a hotel. But more immediately, I needed to talk to someone about my discoveries in Münsingen. Ever since the breakthrough in the Martinskirche marriage register the previous Monday afternoon, I had searched in my mind for the best way to announce the news to the multitude of Steeves descendants who would be all ears. I was now anxious for advice.

I made a hasty phone call to John Lutz, a friend and distant cousin living back in Moncton. John had been involved in the unfolding saga of Muriel Sikorski's discovery of the Kreuzwertheim home of Michael Lutz, and as president of the Lutz Family Organization he would be able to fully appreciate my news. It was John who had told me the story of Mrs. Sikorski's find in Florida, and that story had set me searching for the clue that led, in the end, to the Württemberg home of Heinrich Stief.

Deerhide chest formerly belonging to the family of Heinrich Stief's fourth son, Frederick. Provenance unknown. Courtesy of Jane Wood

Although Mrs. Sikorski had made her find in 1982, more than ten years had elapsed before John related the tale to me. I wasn't sure my own story could wait ten minutes, let alone ten years. By then, I was so exhilarated that my news about Heinrich Stief was consuming me.

John brought me up to date on events in New Brunswick. His friend Dr. Rainer Hempel, professor of German Studies at Mt. Allison University, was in the process of finishing his all but definitive work, tentatively titled *Protestant German Settlers on the Petitcodiac*. I knew my news from Germany would have an impact on his book.[7]

"You'd better tell him to stop the press," I exclaimed to John, "I have found Heinrich Stief!"

There was a silence at the other end of the line, seven thousand kilometres and five time zones away.

"What do you mean?" John asked. I could hear the bewilderment in his voice.

"I've been researching in southern Germany and I have found the home of Heinrich Stief."

Then it hit him all at once, and he burst out with exclamation. I tried and failed to communicate my own excitement, and, for a while, we were both talking frantically at the same time. All the joys and frustrations of a wandering genealogist seemed to come to the surface in that hurried phone call.

Calming down, we discussed the broader implications of my discovery and the best way to deal with the news. A few options were broached and left to pursue later. When my phonecard signalled it was about to expire, we said our goodbyes, wishing each other the best of the Christmas season. Then I turned to face the more practical problem of finding some accommodation for the night.

Later that evening in Amsterdam, I attempted to entertain myself in that most entertaining city, but my mind was elsewhere. It seemed I was not ready to return to the present. At one point, very late, I found myself sitting in a darkened little bar, drinking a Heineken alone, staring at the floor—my thoughts far away in the Württemberg past.

On Friday morning I slept late and had to hurry to make the hotel's eleven o'clock check-out time. The train to the coast would depart at two o'clock, allowing me just enough time to find some food and drop in on my one-and-only business client in Amsterdam. With lunch in my stomach and my errand accomplished, I arrived at the train station without getting lost, and with half-an-hour to spare.

In the busy concourse, I found a place to sit and got out my writing pad. There, amid the bustle of Amsterdam's *Centraal Station*, with throngs of travellers milling about, and with the events of the past week fresh in my mind, I began to compose an account of my discovery of the Württemberg home of Heinrich Stief.

I continued writing on the train for the next hour until it arrived at Hoek van Holland—the final point of departure on the passage between the Netherlands and Britain. Here at Hoek, situated a few kilometres downriver from the great port of Rotterdam, the mighty Rhine finally gives up its life to the North Sea.

At this same place, 250-odd years ago, Heinrich and Regina Stief turned their backs on Europe and sailed away to America. For emigrants with enough money to pay the fare, the sea passage to Philadelphia would cost another sixty florin. Both those with money and those travelling in bondage quickly found, to their peril, that things were vastly different from what the *Neuländer* had promised. Many paid with their lives.

Once at sea, the first stop was at Cowes, off the south English coast. Further delays of one or two weeks were encountered at Cowes while the ship passed through English customs where additional stores were brought on board. By then, many of the passengers had exhausted their supply of extra provisions which they had brought for the Atlantic crossing.[8]

Finally, when the winds were favourable, the ship departed, passing Land's End on the coast of Cornwall a week later. Then, as Gottlieb Mittelberger ruefully remembered, "the long sea voyage and misery begin in earnest."9

For the luckless German passengers on the eighteenth-century vessels, conditions were often dreadful in the extreme. Most ships had inadequate food, little sanitation, and barely enough room to lie flat. Sickness and death were the travellers' constant companions throughout the two and often three months of the sea voyage. Typically, their journey was a living hell.

Countless passengers died while crossing the Atlantic, many of them simple, honest folk who had never before cast eyes on the sea. They were given "bad drinking water and putrid salt meat," says Morison: "they succumbed to dysentery, scurvy, typhus, canker, and mouth-rot." Rats "abounded," says Klees, and the lice were "so thick that they could be scraped off the body...." Typhus was so common that doctors of the day named the dread disease the Palatine fever.10

Often during storms, the sea was so rough that the poor passengers feared for their lives—often for days at a stretch. In 1733, the German Schwenckfelders were three months at sea during which they encountered at least six storms. On the morning of September 19, a week from the coast of America, a terrible storm elicited the following description from one passenger: "the waves were fearful, like rocky cliffs and high mountains. The noise of their roaring was horrible. It was a spectacle awful to witness."11

Passengers on the little emigrant ships were crammed together in the holds like sardines, reported Mittelberger, where they "pray and cry pitifully together." Sailor-historian Sam Morison knew from experience how cruel the sea could be. When the sea loosed it's fury, he wrote, "the hatches were battened down and everyone vomited in the foul air."12

Despite the poor odds, Mittelberger lived to tell his tale.

> *In the course of such a storm the sea begins to surge and rage so that the waves often seem to rise up like mountains, sometimes sweeping over the ship; and one thinks he is going to sink along with the ship. All the while the ship, tossed by storm and waves, moves constantly from one side to the other, so that nobody aboard can either walk, sit, or lie down and the tightly packed people on their cots, the sick as well as the healthy, are thrown every which way.*13

It was not a voyage anyone would look forward to with enthusiasm. Those who survived would not remember such a journey with fondness.

The life of the modern traveller, on the other hand, has become much simpler. All that remained for me to do was to check one piece of luggage, walk through Dutch passport control, and find a seat on the ferry to England. It seemed my adventure into the past was coming to a close.

On the crowded ferry, I found a seat in the non-smoking area and began to write again, trying to put down on paper a string of ideas and events that could later be expanded into a coherent narrative. I knew I had a story to tell. A three- or four-hour trip lay ahead. Knots of restless teenagers roamed the inner deck of the ferry in search of diversion, while noisy children dragged their parents about by the arms. The sound of the ship's engines echoed ponderously from below.

After a long wait, the big ferry began to move into the harbour of Hoek, the lights of the town twinkling through the late-afternoon dusk. A brisk wind blew in from the sea, and sober grey clouds scudded across a darkening sky.

As we cleared the harbour and moved into open water, the ferry began to roll from side to side, heaving into the wind and the waves. Soon, the voice of the Dutch captain came barking across the public-address system, announcing that the winds were gusting strongly down from the upper reaches of the North Sea. He added hastily that a heavy swell would delay our arrival. The part about the strong winds I had already guessed.

For some reason, the captain found it necessary to explain how he would steer the ship directly into the wind of the North Sea for the first half of the trip, then swing it sharply to port side and travel down-wind for the final half. Something that sounded like concern in his voice told me this wasn't going to be anything resembling a pleasant cruise along the Rhine. The ship pitched alarmingly as it crashed headlong into the huge waves, spraying sheets of sea water across the windows.

After an extremely unpleasant half-hour of the ship's incessant rocking, there began to appear a steady parade of passengers stumbling toward the washrooms. Travellers seated near me looked around nervously as the boat continued to sway severely. It wasn't long before several people were putting their seasickness bags to good use. The prospect was most disheartening.

The whole scene quickly degenerated, and people were getting sick anywhere they could. It was pathetic. The ship lurched madly, as a stray, empty pop can danced across the deck, adding to the melee with its insane clamour.

Perhaps I should have been paying more attention to my own situation, because my stomach began to complain distressfully. It was then that the lack of sleep over the previous few days made itself apparent: my energy reserves were badly depleted. Too late, I remembered that my supply of Gravol was safely stowed away in the hold.

My head spinning, I staggered on rubbery legs toward the nearest washroom, worried that it might already be full. Outside the washroom door, a dozen immobilised passengers were crouched on the floor, and half-conscious travellers were propped against each other for support.

Inside the washroom, every toilet stall was occupied by a body bent over in a wretched contortion. A sour stench hung in the warm air. I reached a vacant sink just as a great, sickening wave of nausea swept through me, stabbing my body with electrifying chills.

With the sinks on both sides of me in full use, I leaned over the basin, my mind reeling, and said good-bye to the sad remains of my meagre lunch. It was only the beginning. I stood vomiting into that sink for longer than I ever want to remember. All the while, an endless procession of seasick passengers groped their way into the washroom and left the contents of their stomachs behind.

My sickness would not abate. It went on and on as the ship continued to heave mightily. Waves of dizziness washed through my brain; my equilibrium had vanished. The torture was relentless; the minutes felt like days on a wide and lonely sea.

After a gruelling hour, the basin on my right had clogged and was filling fast with a horrid communal stew. Back and forth it sloshed, in rhythm with the rolling ship. It was a sight I will never forget.

After another vile hour of empty barfing, my arms and legs went numb, and I had to hang sideways over the sink to stop myself from collapsing on the slimy floor. I was far gone. Some well-meaning fool beside me had finished his pitiful routine, and asked "Are you okay?"

Without looking up, and still hanging over the sink, I sputtered an answer to his dumb question. "I'm fine," I mumbled through chattering teeth, "I do this all the time." Then I began to puke violently again.

With tears scalding my eyes, I muttered to myself, "Will this hellish trip never end?"

Suddenly, through the waves of nausea, there came a dark, distant spectre—an eighteenth-century apparition of a poor German couple facing a watery death on the high Atlantic. That's all I remember. It might as well have been Heinrich and Regina for all I knew, the two of them on their long and desperate journey across the Atlantic Ocean to America. The bleak reminder that they had endured a similar ordeal somehow made my agony a little easier to bear. They too would have been terribly sick, but their misery would have continued for weeks and probably months; mine would end in a few hours. In that moment, all my ancestral imaginings were wiped out. Whatever the price, I had gained a physical empathy for my ancestors' hardship—one that no documentary evidence could ever provide.

I gave humble thanks when the ship finally docked at Harrich on the coast of England. I thought I would need a wheelchair to disembark. Dreadfully weak and feeling wasted near death, I crept off the ship like a broken old man. Exhausted and dizzy, with a sharp, metallic taste in my mouth, I shuffled painfully through British Immigration and onto the train that would take me to London's Liverpool station.

Next trip I would take a bus through the chunnel.

If Heinrich and Regina had known beforehand of the nightmare ahead, would they have foregone their chance of a better life in America? Would they have chosen instead to remain in the little village of Münsingen, to face whatever difficulties they were leaving behind? Whether or not they guessed the horror that was to come, they somehow survived their long and dangerous voyage.

Following the pattern set by emigrants before them, those two pioneers reached America and settled in prosperous Pennsylvania. Then, after fifteen years of established life, Benjamin Franklin, John Hughes, and Alexander McNutt entered their lives, and the time arrived for them to choose whether to remain in Pennsylvania or to embark on another sea passage, this time to an uncertain future in the wilds of old Nova Scotia. By then they had seven young sons to add to their worries. Today, we can only imagine whether they recalled the memory of that first ghastly voyage.

Perhaps the sloop that took them and their friends to the Bay of Fundy in 1766 was better suited for transporting land-loving humans than were the filthy, overcrowded ships from Rotterdam. Possibly Heinrich and Regina put aside the memory of their Atlantic crossing and decided that the trip to the Petitcodiac River would be bearable. Maybe they knew they would be in good hands, and that the risk would be worth taking. A fellow passenger on that second voyage, the Reverend John Eagleson, reported later that Mr. Hall "saw every difficulty that might arise to them and did everything in his power to remedy it...." In any event, that voyage was far shorter than any transatlantic crossing might have been.[14]

Whether the journey to Nova Scotia was bearable or otherwise, on they came. Up the Bay of Fundy and into the muddy waters of the Petitcodiac River those settler families sailed as one, on a promising spring day in 1766.

The story of Heinrich Stief and his companions who settled on the Petitcodiac River is not over. I suspect that many details to the story remain undiscovered, waiting to be dug up from the depths of some distant archives—Canadian, American, or European—and brought into the light of day.

Will the log book from their as-yet-unnamed sloop eventually be found? Will we learn someday what happened to Heinrich Stief during the "lost years" from 1755 to 1764, during which, according to a vague legend, the family went to Virginia and suffered a crop failure? Will the baptismal records for Heinrich's youngest three sons eventually be uncovered? Did Heinrich Stief ever meet Benjamin Franklin?

Further examination of Dr. Yoder's *Pennsylvania German Immigrants* may one day lead a curious genealogist to the European homes of the other settlers who came to Monckton township with the Stief and the Lutz families. Someday we may discover how well those Pennsylvania-German families were previously acquainted, or if any of them were related. Perhaps we will learn the full story of why their Philadelphia sponsors abandoned them to almost certain starvation, or what happened to the four German signers of the Articles of Agreement who were left behind in Philadelphia when their friends departed to make a new beginning on the Petitcodiac River.

And what about Charles Jones, the enigma of the story, the lone Welshman who couldn't sign his name and who threw his and his family's fate in with a group of German farmers—the man who seems to have come and gone with hardly a trace? Now there's a mystery!

Epilogue

(two years later)

In the arcane world of genealogy, a single entry in an old document can change everything. An obscure marriage date, a scrawled signature on a land-settlement agreement, a lone baptismal entry in a church record book—any one of these can open the door to another dimension.

And what happens, in that complex and shadowy world, when an unsuspecting researcher stumbles upon the answer unawares? With no map to point one in the right direction, and nobody to offer guidance, one isn't always sure what to believe. What if, in that passionate and quirky world, Marguerite Yourcenar's poetic observation suddenly becomes apropos: "so eager are we to know the past that we wring from these poor relics more than they contain"?[1] And to carry that sentiment one step further—what if one's genealogical investigations take on a life of their own, and one is momentarily transported into the fleeting light of the past? What then?

In mid-October 1999, I returned to Philadelphia for one more dig into Pennsylvania-German genealogy. (I didn't go by boat.) The account was almost finished, but I went back to the Historical Society of Pennsylvania to look into a few troublesome areas of the story and to tidy up some loose footnotes. I had covered much ground in the two years since I'd begun writing, but there were still gaps in the story. I wanted to visit the American Philosophical Society, too, so I could look at William Franklin's original letters to his father. His descriptions of John Hall's dispute with the other Monckton proprietors were so important to the story that closer scrutiny of the letters seemed necessary. Also, a further reading of *Swedish Holsteins* had given me a hunch about John Hughes's family Bible and its possible location in New Jersey. Hopefully, the Bible would contain some Hughes or Jones genealogy. I hadn't entirely given up the search for Charles Jones, the elusive Welsh ancestor who had absorbed countless hours and days of my time over the previous five years. There would always be more clues to the story of the Petitcodiac settlers—maybe another surprise hiding around the next unexplored documentary corner. One never knows.

I thought I had seen all the evidence there was to see in St. Michael's baptismal records. Not long after I returned from Germany in 1997, I'd learned from Herb Steves, a distant cousin living in New Mexico, that Heinrich Stief had moved to the Germantown area north of Philadelphia after the birth of his son Jacob in 1749. Naturally I didn't expect to find any mention of the name Stief in Philadelphia records as late as 1766, the year the families departed for the Petitcodiac River. But it seems there was something Jacob Stief needed to do in St. Michael's Church before their departure from Philadelphia.

Parents	Children	Witnesses
Carl Schantz u[nd] s[eine] Fr[au] [and his wife] Margretha	Anna Margretha ist 5 Jahr u[nd] 4 Monath alt [5 years and 4 months old] Catharina Elisabeth ist 9 Monath alt [9 months old]	Jacob Stief und Anna Catharina Lutzin

Entry from St. Michael's *Taufbuch*, April 26/27 1766.[2]
Courtesy of Old Zion Evangelical Lutheran Church and the Lutheran Archives Center at Philadelphia

After I came home from Philadelphia late in 1999, I spent the better part of two months staring at the baptismal entry above. What did it mean? For two years, Roland Deigendesch had patiently answered a thousand questions via fax and email while I tried to compile the story, and now he had translated the entry. But still, it made no sense. Why would Jacob

Stief and Catherine Lutz be in St. Michael's Church in Philadelphia witnessing the baptism of two strangers, apparently, on the same day they were leaving for Nova Scotia? Who was Carl Schantz? Did his two daughters have some connection with the Stief or the Lutz families? Anna Margretha and Catharina Elisabeth...where had I heard those names before? I had to look at my own notes from Chapter 13.

> According to the faded inscription on her cracked and weathered tombstone, Margaret Jones, the eldest daughter of Charles Jones, died "April 16, 1806, in the 46th year of her age." Thus, she was born sometime in the twelve months before April 16, 1761. Her sister, Catherine, died April 1, 1854, aged 88 years. Thus, she was born sometime during the twelve months previous to April 1, 1766.

Those were my only substantial clues to the identity of the Philadelphia family of Charles Jones; I never suspected they'd be the only clues I'd need.

※

Heinrich Stief's eldest son, Jacob, was not yet seventeen years old when he and Catherine Lutz walked into St. Michael's Lutheran Church in Philadelphia sometime on the last weekend of April 1766. Jacob and Catherine weren't getting married that day, although those two would wed a few years later when their families settled beside the muddy banks of the Petitcodiac River at the head of the Bay of Fundy. Who knows, maybe on that day in St. Michael's Church those two sensed what the future held for them.

Actually, Jacob and Catherine were in St. Michael's that day to witness a baptism—in fact, a double baptism, according to the Taufbuch entry: that of Anna Margretha Schantz, five years and four months old, and her infant sister Catharina Elisabeth, nine months old. The parents were Carl Schantz (pronounced Shunts) and his wife of thirteen years, Margretha Lintz. The pastor officiating was the Reverend Heinrich Melchior Mühlenberg.[3]

There was a sense of urgency about the ceremony that day. Parents, children, and witnesses were about to embark on a sea journey to distant Nova Scotia. The excitement was so evident that Pastor Mühlenberg recorded the impending departure in the *Taufbuch*: "Leute die heute abreisen nach Neuschottland" [People who leave today for Nova Scotia].[4]

With a risky voyage ahead, it was natural that Carl would want his daughters baptized. He'd neglected to have it done until the last minute, and now their sloop was loaded and waiting at the wharf, just a few blocks away. Everyone was ready to go, the previous several months having taken up all their time in preparation for the journey. Much careful planning had been made for this trip because they wouldn't be coming back. The other families had already gone ahead to the wharf, and Carl Schantz had promised to follow soon. This ceremony wouldn't take long, he knew, but it was important.

Perhaps Carl had a habit of putting things off. He knew this trip was coming—had known about it for three months. Like the other families, he had anticipated this day ever since he'd walked into John Hughes's store back on the 27th of January.

There was something else Carl Schantz had neglected to do, although he'd had most of his life to do it. Just the same, he wouldn't need it where he was going. If all went well, he and the others would soon be standing at the edge of their new township on the Petitcodiac River trying to figure out where they would set themselves up.

No, Carl Schantz wouldn't need to know how to read and write where he was headed. No ink, no paper, no books—only Heinrich Stief's big Bible to look at once in a while. He liked to look at the strange and wonderful pictures in the Bible. They all liked the pictures, but he knew there wouldn't be much time for looking at pictures. Daylight hours would best be spent at farming; a hungry family would have more pressing things to do.

Carl had drifted off in thought. He remembered that mild day in January when John Hughes had called his name. It had sounded odd, the way Hughes said the name, but he hadn't cared. He'd made his "X" after Hughes's son had written his name, and then he'd handed the goose quill over to Heinrich Stief. Carl heard English spoken everywhere now, and his old German homeland was far away. He tried to remember what Hughes had said—something about the name sounding more in tune with English names. It didn't matter now.

Soon, Carl Schantz would sing his own kind of tune. With his two little daughters safely baptized, and two growing boys at his side, he could devote himself to building a new home on all the land he would have in Nova Scotia. Johannes was a strapping lad of nearly thirteen years, and little Heinrich was already past seven.[5] Carl would see his family grow and prosper. Soon, all the families would prosper. Maybe someday his children would learn to read and write as he had never done.

Now they were calling him to come. The baptism was finished. The sloop would be ready to leave.

And now Carl Schantz was walking down Mulberry Street with Jacob and Catherine and his family for the last time. He had walked down this same street before, but this time everything looked different—strange. People were busy with the day, and hardly noticed their passing.

Soon they had reached the wharf. All the families were there together, everyone hustling and bustling, talking and shouting, the last few barrels and sacks lying about.

Carl spotted John Hall on the deck of the sloop, talking to the captain. Carl liked Hall—a big, practical man who talked sense and cared for farming. Yes, they all liked Hall. Hall was their friend.

The sloop's captain was shouting orders to his men and directing traffic, trying to get everyone aboard. They had a long way to sail.

It wasn't a big sloop. Carl knew they would be very crowded. He looked at the gunwale and squinted his eyes as if it would help him to read the letters on the side of the battered old boat. He had heard the others say the name, but the letters made no sense to him. Anyway, it didn't matter now.

There was a parson from the English church coming with them too. He was standing on the deck, staring up at the roof-tops of the city.

The wharf was crowded with all their relatives and friends. He couldn't see John Hughes anywhere. Carl wanted to say good-bye to Hughes and thank him, but now it was too late. He knew Hughes would understand.

His wife, Margretha, was saying good-bye to her kin, all gathered around her. Matthias Lintz looked sad about being left behind. But the sloop was too small and they knew they couldn't all go together. Matthias and the rest would come after. Carl and the others would break the ground and get things started. It wouldn't be long. The Bay of Fundy was only two weeks away. Everything would work out fine—they would all be fine.

Finally, everyone was on board. The ropes were cast off and the sloop began to move away from the wharf. The sails were unfurled and quickly caught a little breeze. It was going to be a beautiful day on the big, wide Delaware River.

Now everyone was waving and shouting back and forth between the sloop and the wharf. Some of the women were crying. The children were very excited. So many children, thought Carl; he was proud of them all.

The breeze had picked up now. Seagulls soared above their heads, squawking at each other—calling and squawking. Carl liked the seagulls. He liked their loud, rough music. It was music he could understand.

Auf Wiedersehen!, said Carl Schantz to himself. Good-bye Philadelphia, good-bye.

Carl Schantz or Charles Jones... what did it matter? It was a beautiful day and they were going away together to a new home. Yes, they would all be fine.

A list of the settlers sent to Monckton township by John Hughes and Anthony Wayne, dated July 1, 1766. Nova Scotia Land Grant Records, Book 7, page 183.

Courtesy of Nova Scotia Crown Land Office, Halifax

Afterword:
A Late-Breaking Discovery

The Search for Heinrich Stief was almost finished when Nova Scotia genealogist and historian Dr. Allen Robertson discovered the opposite list of names in land-grant records at the Nova Scotia Archives in Halifax. The list is a genealogical gold mine—undoubtedly the earliest, and perhaps only, complete list of all the settlers sent to Monckton by John Hughes and Anthony Wayne. New Brunswick genealogists will want to sift and sort the names till the cows come home. A few particularly interesting points are worth noting here.

The list of names was compiled by John Huston, the Chignecto trader who provided John Hall and the settlers with supplies valued at £34:10. The settlers met Huston at Fort Cumberland, apparently, or else Huston met them at Monckton. On July 1, 1766, twenty-eight days after they landed at Hall's Creek, the names were appended to an unrelated land grant at Liscomb's Harbour on the eastern shore of Nova Scotia.

Several questions arise: Why did Huston omit the three families not sent by Hughes—the Wortmans, the Rickers, and the Copples? Moreover, why were the names recorded at all? And why was the list entered on an unrelated land grant?

For each family, Huston recorded the father, mother, and children in chronological order. I would say the spellings accurately reflect the contemporary pronunciation of the names. Huston anglicized Heinrich Stief's name to Henry Stief, as it was in the Articles of Agreement. His wife's name, however, had not made the transition to Rachel from the original Regina; Huston spelled it "Rekena." Of Michael Lutz's children, the youngest, John, born ca. 1761, is not mentioned, leading one to believe that John and Michael were the same person, possibly Johanne Michael. Margaret was the wife of Charles Jones; this is possibly the only recording of her name apart from the previously noted Schantz baptismal entry in St. Michael's records. The wife of Jacob Trites was Christiana, not Elisina as tradition states.

Endnotes

Introduction

1 Don Yoder, "Problems and Resources in Pennsylvania Genealogical Research," *The Pennsylvania Genealogical Magazine* (Philadelphia: Genealogical Society of Pennsylvania, 1979) Vol. 31, No. 1, 6.

2 For 1867, see Esther Clark Wright, *Samphire Greens, the Story of the Steeves* (1961) 82. The surname has evolved through various forms—from the original Stieff or Stief, through Stefe, Steef, Steve, Steves, and Stevz—until it settled on Steeves sometime in the middle of the nineteenth century. Several branches in the United States have retained the "Steves" version of the spelling. See *The Steeves Family Register*, Issue 2 (Hillsborough) 4. The Lutz surname experimented with Lootes and Lootz before arriving at Lutes, although some members of the family use the original form. Sommer became Summer, Somer, and eventually Somers. Treitz was occasionally Tritz before becoming Trites. Wortman was Workman, Workmann, Wartman, and Warterman. Ricker was sometimes Richter and Rickert. Jones was Johns and Johannes. Many variations exist.

3 Wright, *Samphire Greens*, 70. It should be noted that not all the Joneses in Moncton are descended from the Philadelphia settler. In 1971, Dr. Wright estimated there were about 125,000 descendants, of whom 75,000 were alive at the time. 'In Hillsborough, N.B., It's Not Who You Know But How Many You Know,' *Canadian Magazine*, Christmas Eve edition, 1971 (Toronto: Toronto Star) 18-20. In 1983, the estimate was revised to "maybe 250,000 descendants.' 'Heritage Moncton Salutes City's Early Settlers,' Special Supplement to the *Moncton Times and Transcript*, May 28, 1983, 7.

4 'In Hillsborough,' *Canadian Magazine*, 18.

5 Marjory Whitelaw encourages us to "remind ourselves of what 'America' meant in 1765, before the American Revolution: not only Nova Scotia (which until 1784 included what is now New Brunswick), Quebec and Newfoundland, but also the original thirteen colonies, East and West Florida, Bermuda, the Bahamas and the West Indian Islands." Marjory Whitelaw, *First Impressions: Early Printing in Nova Scotia* (Halifax: Nova Scotia Museum, 1987) 13. See also Richard Middleton, *Colonial America: A History, 1607-1760* (Cambridge: Blackwell Publishers, 1992) 362-3. Middleton states that the term "American" was first used in 1740 during the War of Jenkins Ear.

6 Marguerite Yourcenar, *Dear Departed*, Maria Louise Ascher, trans. (London: Aidan Ellis Publishing; HarperCollinsCanada, 1991; New York: Farrar, Straus, Giroux, 1991) 4; orig. pub. *Souvenirs pieux* (Editions Gallimard, 1974).

7 Peter Andrews, "Genealogy: The Search for a Personal Past," *American Heritage* (New York: American Heritage Publishing Co.) Vol. 33, No. 5 (Aug/Sep, 1982) 11.

8 Ron Messenger, past president of Southeastern Branch of the New Brunswick Genealogical Society, estimated in 1999 that approximately 70,000 genealogy sites were receiving as many as two million hits per day.

9 For example, "Osnaburg" is mentioned in "History of the Steeves (written 1907)," author unknown, possibly Rufus Palmer Steeves; see New Brunswick Museum Vertical File, (Provincial Archives of N.B. microfilm F11093). A good deal of this book was lifted from an unpublished 1867 account by Howard Steeves. Compare Fraser Robb, 'Steeves Family Early Pioneers of Albert," (undated manuscript) which states "The father was born in Osnastruck,

Germany in 1730." I am indebted to Judi Berry Steeves, past president of the New Brunswick Genealogical Society, for bringing these and a number of other related documents to my attention.

Chapter 1 Heinrich Stief: The Legend

1 For the date of Heinrich Stief's arrival, see my article, "The Signature(s) of Heinrich Stief," *Generations* (Fredericton: New Brunswick Genealogical Society) Vol. 21, No. 2 (Summer, 1999) 14-6. Contemporary estimates of the total number of German immigrants in Pennsylvania varied widely. Hirsching in 1742 estimated 100,000; Gov. Thomas in 1747, 72,000; Seidensticker in 1752, 90,000; Proud in 1770, 83,000; Benjamin Franklin in 1776, 53,000; Ebeling in 1790, 144,660. See Frank Reid Diffenderffer, *The German Immigration Into Pennsylvania, 1700-1775* (Baltimore: Genealogical Publishing Co., 1988) 98-100. See also Chessman A. Herrick, White *Servitude in Pennsylvania: Indentured and Redemption Labor in Colony and Commonwealth* (Freeport: Books for Libraries Press, 1970; orig. pub. 1926) 177-80.

2 Frederic Klees, *The Pennsylvania Dutch* (New York: The MacMillan Company, 1951) 146.

3 Oscar Kuhns, *The German and Swiss Settlements of Colonial Pennsylvania: A Study of the So-Called Pennsylvania Dutch* (Ann Arbor: Gryphon Books, 1971; orig. pub. 1901) 84. See also William H. Gehrke, "Beginnings of Pennsylvania-German Element in Rowan and Cabarrus Counties, North Carolina," *Pennsylvania Magazine of History and Biography* (Philadelphia: Historical Society of Pennsylvania) Vol. 58, 357; also Middleton, 347, 365. The charter of Pennsylvania was granted March 4, 1681; land sales began in July, 1681; William Penn reached the Delaware River on Oct. 28, 1682, and arrived in his new colony the next day. Jean R. Soderland, ed. *William Penn and the founding of Pennsylvania 1680-1684: A Documentary History* (Philadelphia: University of Pennsylvania Press, 1983) 38, 71, 185.

4 See James Logan to William Penn, 1727, Hon. Samuel Whitaker Pennypacker, LL.D., *Pennsylvania in American History* (Philadelphia: William J. Campbell, 1910) 202. Logan (1674-1751) was a friend and secretary of William Penn, scholar, statesman, Chief Justice, and President of the Provincial Council. See Townsend Ward, "The Germantown Road and its Associations," *Penn. Mag. Hist. & Bio*, Vol. 5, 128-133. See also Catherine Owens Peare, *William Penn* (Ann Arbor: University of Michigan Press, 1966) 367, 382. The first main body of Germans to arrive in William Penn's Philadelphia consisted of a colony of Mennonites who landed with their leader Francis Daniel Pastorius in 1683. See Ralph Beaver Strassburger, LL.D., William John Hinke, Ph.D., D.D., ed., *Pennsylvania German Pioneers* (Norristown: Pennsylvania German Society, 1934) Vol. 1, xv-xvi. Preceding them in 1643 were fifty families from Schleswig, Brandenberg, Holstein, and Switzerland under Swedish Governor Johan Printz. See Charles R. Barker, "The 'Old Dutch Church' in Lower Merion," *Bulletin of the Historical Society of Montgomery County Pennsylvania* (Norristown, Oct. 1954) Vol. IX, No. 3, 282. See also Diffenderffer who describes a colony established in 1638, as well a previous transient colony which left no traces, "and may therefore be dismissed with a mere allusion." Diffenderffer, 10.

5 Yoder, "Problems and Resources," 1.

Chapter 2 Beginnings

1 The upper Petitcodiac is today a normal-looking blue river, but until the Moncton-Riverview causeway was constructed in 1970 it was distinctly brown. Now, artificially choked with muddy silt, the down-river portion below the causeway has taken on the unfortunate appearance of a large ditch.

2 For a discussion of the erroneous term "expulsion," see Winthrop Pickard Bell, *The "Foreign Protestants" and the Settlement of Nova Scotia* (Toronto: University of Toronto Press, 1961) 15n.

Chapter 3 Dancing up a Terrible Storm

1 See Marjory Whitelaw, *The Wellington Dyke* (Halifax: Nimbus Publishing & Nova Scotia Museum, 1997) 19. In 1636, seventy-eight settlers arrived on the *Saint Jehan* from France— "farmers, peasants, carpenters and ship-builders, and a few women and children." Compare René Babineau, *Brief History of Acadia, 1604-1992*, (1992) 15: In 1620, "André Lasnier was probably the first child of European extraction to be born on the North American Continent."

2 Francis Parkman, *Montcalm and Wolfe* (Markham: Viking-Penguin Books Canada, 1984; orig. publ. Little, Brown, Boston, 1884) 138. The idea to remove the Acadians seems to have originated with Samuel Vetch (1668-1732) who, together with Col. Francis Nicholson, captured Port Royal in 1710. See Vetch to the Earl of Dartmouth, Jan. 22, 1711, cited in Francis Parkman, *A Half Century of Conflict*, 2 Vols. (Boston: Little, Brown, and Company, 1924) Vol. 1, 192n. Compare W. S. MacNutt, *The Atlantic Provinces: The Emergence of Colonial Society 1712-1785* (Toronto: McClelland and Stewart, 1965) 43, who states that "the idea of expulsion goes back to Nicholson in 1713...." Vetch became Gov. of Annapolis in 1710. Parkman, *Half Century*, 191n. William Shirley, born ca. 1693, England; came to Boston in 1735/6; planned the expedition to Louisbourg in 1745; Governor of Massachusetts from 1741; succeeded Braddock as Commander-in-Chief of the British forces in 1755; was later suspended and recalled to England; died 1771, Roxbury, MA. Thomas Akins, ed., *Nova Scotia Archives: Selections from the Public Documents of the Province of Nova Scotia* (Halifax: Charles Annand, 1869) 380.

3 George M. Wrong, *The Conquest of New France* (New Haven: Yale University Press; Toronto: Glasgow, Brook & Co.; London: Humphrey Milford; Oxford: Oxford University Press, 1918) 173. Charles Lawrence, born 1709, Portsmouth, England. Dominic Graham, "Charles Lawrence," *Dictionary of Canadian Biography* (Toronto: University of Toronto Press; Les Presses de l'université Laval) Vol. 3, 361; served under Warburton's Regiment of foot and saw garrison duty at Louisbourg in 1745 under Gov. Hopson. Akins, *Nova Scotia Archives*, 235; Lawrence was appointed Lieutenant-Governor of Nova Scotia, September 17, 1754; Governor from December 24, 1755 to October 19, 1760. Bona Arsenault, *History of the Acadians* (Montréal: Leméac, 1978; orig. pub. *Histoire et généalogie des acadiennes*, Book 2) 115; died of "inflammation of the lungs," Sunday, Oct. 19, 1760; unmarried. Akins, *Nova Scotia Archives*, 235. Lawrence was succeeded by Jonathan Belcher in 1760; Henry Ellis in 1761; Montague Wilmot in 1763; Michael Franklin in 1766. See *Canada and its Provinces*, (Toronto: Glasgow, Brook & Company, 1914) Vol. 23, 336. Compare A. James, S. Macdonald, "Life and Administration of Governor Charles Lawrence," *Collections of the Nova Scotia Historical Society* (Halifax: McAlpine Publishing Co., 1905) Vol. 12., 19-58. Whitelaw takes a brief but more balanced view. See *Wellington Dyke*, 25-6.

4 For Le Loutre's sordid life, see John Clarence Webster, *The Career of the Abbe Le Loutre in Nova Scotia* (Shediac: 1933).

5 Arsenault, 163, citing Hughes Graham to Dr. Andrew Browne, 1791, Andrew Browne Collection, British Museum, Add. 19,071. The bounties included £30 for native males over the age of 16 years captured alive, and £25 for native females and children. See also Gladys Trenholm, Miep Norden, Josephine Trenholm, *A History of Fort Lawrence: Times, Tides, and Towns* (Fort Lawrence, 1986) 97; James Dean Snowdon, *Footprints in the Marsh Mud: Politics and Land Settlement in the Township of Sackville 1760-1800* (Fredericton: University of New Brunswick, 1974; reprinted Tantramar Heritage Trust, n.d.) 15-16, 24.

6 See "1766 Account of Nova Scotia Lands," John Hughes Papers, Hist. Soc. of Penn. References to John Huston are scattered through the histories. He was born in New England, and traded with the Mi'kmaq and the Acadians. In Boston, Huston had befriended one-legged Brook Watson who later became New Brunswick's agent-general in London from 1786

to 1794 and Lord Mayor of London in 1796. See L. F. S. Upton, "Sir Brook Watson," *Dictionary of Canadian Biography*, Vol. 5, 842-4. Huston became a member of the second Assembly of Nova Scotia for Cumberland, Dec. 4, 1759, and was on military half-pay when he died in 1795 at Canard, Nova Scotia. See W. C. Milner, *The Basin of Minas and It's First Settlers* (n.d.; reprinted from the *Wolfville Acadian*) 105-6; see also John Clarence Webster, "Sir Brook Watson," in *The Argosy*, Vol. 3, No. 1, (Nov., 1924); also Akins, *Nova Scotia Archives*, 737.

7 See Lawrence Henry Gipson, *The British Empire before the American Revolution* (New York: Alfred A, Knopf, 1936 - 1970) Vol. 6, 292.

8 Akins, *Nova Scotia Archives*, 740.

9 Wright, *The Loyalists of New Brunswick* (Fredericton, 1955) 122. See also Raymond, 38.

10 See transcriptions of both proclamations in Raymond, 104-6. In 1759, the wording was changed to "never failing of crops nor needing to be manured." The second Proclamation was subsequently called "The Charter of Nova Scotia."

11 Forty-five families from Connecticut settled in Annapolis, Minas Basin, and Piziquid; fifty-eight went from Newport, Rhode Island to Falmouth; twenty vessels arrived in Cornwallis from Connecticut and six more arrived at Horton from New London, Connecticut. By 1763, sixty-five Rhode Island families had arrived in Chignecto. Sawtelle, 262-3. See also Raymond, 55, 71.

12 Parkman, *Montcalm and Wolfe*, 541-2. Louisiana was secretly transferred to Spain in 1762, then ceded back to France, and later sold by Napoleon to the United States to finance the war against England in 1812. Benjamin Franklin's 1760 pamphlet, "The Interest of Great Britain Considered with Regard to her Colonies and the Acquisitions of Canada and Guadaloupe," is thought to have influenced Britain's decision to retain Canada and give Guadaloupe to France at the Treaty of Paris in 1763. See Leonard W. Labaree & Whitfield J. Bell Jr., eds., *The Papers of Benjamin Franklin* (New Haven & London: Yale University Press) Vol. 9, 47-53. Compare Carl Van Doren, *Benjamin Franklin* (New York: The Viking Press, 1938) 288-90.

13 Archibald MacMechan, "Nova Scotia Under English Rule, 1713-1775," *Canada and its Provinces*, Vol. 13, 109. Compare Arsenault, 166; Raymond, 60.

Chapter 4 A Flamboyant Speculator

1 William Otis Sawtelle, "Acadia: The Pre-Loyalist Migration and the Philadelphia Plantation," *Pennsylvania Magazine of History and Biography*, (Philadelphia: Hist. Soc. of Penn., 1927) Vol. 51, 270.

2 John Bartlett Brebner, *Neutral Yankees of Nova Scotia* (Toronto: McClelland and Stewart, 1969) 30.

3 See W. O. Raymond, "Colonel Alexander McNutt and the Pre-Loyalist Settlements of Nova Scotia," *Proceedings and Transactions of the Royal Society of Canada*, Third Series, Vol. V, (1912) 29-30; see also Henrietta Hamilton McCormack, *Genealogies and Reminiscences* (Chicago: 1897) 53-65. Compare A. W. H. Eaton, "Alexander McNutt, the Colonizer," *Americana*, Vol. 8, No. 12, (Dec., 1913) 1074, 1093. Eaton discounts much of Raymond and McCormack: "In view of the actual facts of McNutt's life as we know them from reliable documents, most of these flattering statements have to be pronounced entirely untrue." He disputes McNutt's acquaintance with Dinwiddie, downplays "the obscure Shawnee raid," decides that the sword from King George was "next to impossible," and concludes that McNutt's "distinguished military service" was a fabrication. Eaton was unaware of John Hughes's dealings with McNutt in 1764.

4 Raymond, 30. The French and Indian War in North America (1756-1763) was part of the wider Seven Years' War and ended with the Peace of Paris.

5 MacNutt, 61-2. See also Raymond, 31.

6 For Carleton, see The Abbé H. R. Casgrain, *Wolfe and Montcalm* (University of Toronto Press, 1964; orig. pub. 1905) 79. For Cook, see R. T. Gould, *Captain Cook* (London: Gerald Duckworth & Co., 1978). Captain James Cook was born at Marton-in-Cleveland, Oct. 27, 1728; surveyed the lower St. Lawrence River, 1759-60; married Elizabeth Batts, Dec. 21, 1762; sailed the Endeavour around the world 1768-71; was killed at Kealakekua Bay, Hawaii, Feb. 14, 1779. The sailing master was responsible for navigating the ship. Regarding Cook in Acadia and on the St. Lawrence River, see Don W. Thomson, *Men and Meridians* (Ottawa: Department of Mines and Technical Surveys, 1966) Vol. I, 93-5.

Robert Monckton (1726-1782) commanded at the capture of Fort Beauséjour, 1755; played a leading role during the siege of Louisbourg in 1758 and at the defeat of Quebec in 1759; was appointed Governor of New York in 1761. See I. K. Steele, "Robert Monckton," *Dictionary of Canadian Biography*, Vol. 4, 540-2. Despite his role in the deportation, which Steele describes as performed "with characteristic efficiency but no apparent enthusiasm," he seems to have been a fair and decent man. Lawrence's response to the Acadians, on the other hand, Steele describes as one of "unprecedented severity." Compare Charles Henry Hart, ed., "Letters from William Franklin to William Strahan," *Penn. Mag. Hist. & Bio.*, (Philadelphia: Hist. Soc. of Penn., 1911) Vol 35, 429n. Hart states that at the opening of the Revolutionary War, Monckton "refused to fight against the colonists," but I have been unable to find any evidence to support such a claim.

7 See Raymond, 61-3, 70, 78, 81-5, 91-2. McNutt encouraged disbanded soldiers from Essex County, Massachusetts, to establish the first Protestant settlement at Maugerville on the St. John River near today's Fredericton. He was possibly involved with the first migration of planters from New London, Connecticut, who came to Horton (today Wolfville) and Chignecto (Westmorland and Cumberland Co.) in 1760. The following year, fifty families arrived in Cobequid from New Hampshire, while approximately 250 people from Londonderry, Ireland landed at Halifax, personally escorted by their zealous sponsor. McNutt played a role in founding numerous other settlements of the day: Cornwallis, Falmouth, Port Roseway (Shelburne), Onslow, Truro, Pictou, Liverpool, Bay Verte, Londonderry, St. Mary's Bay, Miramichi, and Monckton, as well as several sites on the St. John River. McNutt claimed to have served as a volunteer in twenty military expeditions at his own expense. See Raymond, 75. See also Phyllis R. Blakeley, "Alexander McNutt," *Dictionary of Canadian Biography* (Toronto: University of Toronto Press; Les Presses de l'université Laval) Vol. 5, 553-7. McNutt apparently spent the winter of 1761-2 in Halifax, was in Ireland the following June, and returned to Halifax late that year, threatening to remove his 170 immigrants to Philadelphia for lack of government support.

8 Raymond, 60, 31, quoting McCormack, 64.

9 Raymond, 61 (Raymond's italics).

10 Exactly how and when Hughes and McNutt were introduced is difficult to determine. See Raymond, 77, 83, 85; also Hugh Hughes, James Parker, and Benj. Blagge in New York, to John Hughes, May 20, 1764, Hughes Papers, Hist. Soc. of Penn. Raymond's statements regarding Monckton and Hillsborough have since been superseded by Dr. Wright's investigations.

11 Maurice W. Armstrong, *The Great Awakening in Nova Scotia 1776-1809* (Hartford: The American Society of Church History, 1948) 23, quoting Roy Hidemichi Akagi, *The Town Proprietors of the New England Colonies* (Philadelphia: University of Pennsylvania, 1924; repub.

Gloucester: Peter Smith, 1963) 2. See also "The State of the late Grants of Townships, with the Numbers propos'd to be settled in each Township, and the time of Settlement. Halifax," Aug. 8, 1766. Colonial Office Records: CO 217, Vol. 43, No. 28. Raymond, 83-5. For biographical sketches of McNutt's twenty-two partners, see Appendix D.

12 Joseph F. W. DesBarres to the King's Most Excellent Majesty, *The Atlantic Neptune* (London: 1775-81).

13 See Hugh Hughes, et. al. to John Hughes, May 20, 1764, Hughes Papers, Hist. Soc. of Penn.: "In Pursuance of Coll. McNutts Advertisements and your Letters to your brother and us, we have agree'd with many of our friends, Relations, and Neighbours to Remove to Nova Scotia and settle there, and we have reason to believe that at least thirty families will follow our Example...."

14 Brebner, *Neutral Yankees*, 30.

15 John Hughes to Alexander McNutt, Philada, May 29th, 1764, Hughes Papers, Hist. Soc. of Penn.; see also Sawtelle, 272; Esther Clark Wright, *The Petitcodiac* (Sackville: The Tribune Press, 1945) 18.

16 Thomas Raddall, *Halifax: Warden of the North* (Toronto: McClelland and Stewart Limited, 1971) 74; Raymond, 102.

17 Labaree, Vol. 12, 346n. See also William Franklin to Benjamin Franklin, Oct. 23, 1767, Willcox, Vol. 14, 291-4. Apparently Benjamin Franklin advanced some fees in London for the project.

18 See their advertisements in the *Pennsylvania Journal or Weekly Advertiser* (Philadelphia: William Bradford) Oct. 25, 1764, Nov. 5, 1767, and other dates. The difficulty in identifying John Cox prompted historian Willcox to label him a "mysterious figure." See William B. Willcox, ed., *The Papers of Benjamin Franklin* (New Haven & London: Yale University Press)Vol. 16, 116n.

19 See Anthony Wayne to John Hughes, Oct. 7, 1765, Hughes Papers, Hist. Soc. of Penn. See also Pennypacker, *Pennsylvania in American History* 5. Pennypacker was a former president of the Historical Society of Pennsylvania, and Governor of Pennsylvania from 1903 to 1907; see also Wright, *The Petitcodiac*, 21.

20 Anthony Wayne to John Hughes, May 30, 1765, Anthony Wayne Papers, Vol. 1, Hist. Soc. of Penn.

21 Alexr. McNutt to Messrs. Benjamin Franklin, John Foxcraft, John Hughes, John Cox, John Reed, Samuel Miles and Benjamin Davis. Philada., Jan'y 1st, 1765. Hughes Papers, Hist. Soc. of Penn.; Wayne to Hughes, July 9, 1765, Hughes Papers, Hist. Soc. of Penn.

22 Wayne to Hughes, Aug. 5, 1765, Hughes Papers, Hist. Soc. of Penn. Wayne's punctuation is open to interpretation since he tended to employ a dash in place of a period.

23 Wayne to Hughes, Oct. 7, 1765. Hughes Papers, Hist. Soc. of Penn.; Wright, *The Petitcodiac*, 21-2.

24 Robert Shackleton, *The Book of Philadelphia* (Philadelphia: The Penn Publishing Company, 1920) 323; Hugh F. Rankin, "Anthony Wayne: Military Romanticist," *George Washington's Generals*, George Ethan Billias, ed. (New York: William Morrow and Co., 1964) 260. See also Paul David Nelson, *Anthony Wayne: Soldier of the Early Republic* (Bloomington: Indiana

University Press, 1985) 1-2.

25 Raymond, 74, 89; Labaree, Vol. 12, 346.

26 See Margaret Ells's complex and instructive study, "Clearing the Decks for the Loyalists," *The Canadian Historical Association Report* (Ottawa, 1933) 43-58. By 1765, Governor Lawrence and the Board of Trade had reached a deadlock over the granting of land, an impasse that was resolved when the Nova Scotia Council took matters into its own hands. "Thus it came about that the last seventeen days before the coming into force of the Stamp Act witnessed the granting away of three million acres of land in Nova Scotia. McNutt and his associates alone received one and a half millions." Ells, 50. In her explanatory note, Ells calculated that the total cost of a 100,000-acre grant would be £15:16s:3d. See *The Canadian Historical Association Report* (Ottawa, 1934) 109.

27 Monckton lost its "k" as a result of a government clerical error in 1784 but was officially changed to Moncton when the town was incorporated in 1855. See Lloyd Machum, *A History of Moncton Town and City 1855-1965* (City of Moncton, 1965) 45. Compare C. Alexander Pincombe, and Edward W. Larracey, Resurgo: *The History of Moncton* (Moncton: The City of Moncton, 1990) Vol. 1, 317.

28 Wright, *Samphire Greens*, 3. The supposition that the agreement was actually signed in Hughes's office has yet to be proved.

Chapter 5 Searching For Ancestors

1 For the founding of the Society, see Penn. Mag. Hist. & Bio., Vol. 34, 263.

2 For Ganong, see Wright, preface to *Samphire Greens*.

3 See Esther Wright to Harriet Wright, Apr. 5, 1942, Wright Papers, Acadia University Archives. Esther Isabelle Clark Wright, born May 4, 1895, Fredericton, the daughter of William George Wright and Harriet Hannah (Richardson) Clark. Wright, *The Steeves Descendants*, (1965) 867. Dr. Wright authored fifteen books and numerous articles on Maritime history; married Dr. Conrad Payling Wright, July 31, 1924; died June 17, 1990 in Wolfville, N.S.; was buried in Fredericton. *Steeves Family Register*, No. 81, 15. For an extensive bibliography see Patricia Townsend, "Esther Clark Wright: A Bibliography, 1914-1988," *Acadiensis* (Fredericton: University of New Brunswick, 1998) (Spring, 1998) 167-76. For a look at Wright's early years, see Barry M. Moody, "A View from the Front Steps: Esther Clark Wright and the Making of a Maritime Historian," *Creating Historical Memory: English Canadian Women and the Work of History* (Vancouver: UBC Press, 1997) 233-53.

4 Wright, *Samphire Greens*, 3.

5 Statistics gleaned in conversation with Dr. Daniel Rolph, Historical Society of Pennsylvania.

6 The cover jacket of Pincombe's *Resurgo* shows the document to be a continuous, one-sided sheet, that rendition being the authors' reconstruction, possibly done to portray the agreement in its entirety.

7 Articles of Agreement, John Hughes Papers, Hist. Soc. of Penn. See also Wright, *Samphire Greens*, Appendix A. A quarter of an acre was apparently a standard unit of land, equivalent to one rood or forty square perches. The quit-rent was a vestige of the days when mediaeval overlords collected rents from their tenant farmers in lieu of services that the landholder might otherwise be obligated to perform. See *Oxford English Dictionary*, 2nd ed. (Oxford: Clarendon Press, 1989).

8 Wright, *Samphire Greens*, 6.

9 An unsigned copy of the Articles of Agreement intended for William Smith & Co., with some modifications but without settlers' names, can be found in the Jacobs Papers, Vol. 1, 173, Hist. Soc. of Penn. See also Pincombe, 373-77; Wright, *The Petitcodiac*, 38-9.

10 For Hughes & Son, see below.

11 Deborah Franklin to Benjamin Franklin, January 12, 1766, Labaree, Vol. 13, 33; Elizabeth Forman Crane, ed., *The Diary of Elizabeth Drinker*, 3 Vols. (Boston: Northeastern University Press, 1991) Vol. 1, 126.

12 Wright, *Samphire Greens*, 10.

13 Pincombe, Vol. 1, 97.

14 See Wright, *Samphire Greens*, 6-7. Dr. Wright suggests they changed their minds. I have not been able to fully identify "Matthias Lintz aüf Bärnhill" buried Jan 27, 1775, aged 93. See *Records of St. Michael's Evangelical Lutheran Church, Germantown: Collections of the Genealogical Society of Pennsylvania* (Philadelphia, 1896) Vol XVI, 1102. On March 27, 1754, a Michael Lintz married Christiana Sophia Wistenloven in St. Michael's Lutheran Church, Philadelphia. Witnesses were Carl Johns and Jacob Klein. Sachse, 618, 622.

15 Regarding Wortman, Copple, and Ricker, see W. C. Milner, "Records of Chignecto," *Collections of the Nova Scotia Historical Society* (Halifax: Wm. MacNab & Son, 1911) Vol. 15, 81-2; also Wright, *The Petitcodiac*, 40; Sawtelle, 276n. Caton and Co. apparently sent no settlers.

Chapter 6 "A Herd of Hogs"

1 Labaree, Vol. 4, 469n. See also Melvin H. Buxbaum, *Benjamin Franklin and the Zealous Presbyterians* (University Park: Pennsylvania State Press, 1975); Hart, "Letters," 424n. Smith's involvement with the "English Society for Propagating Christian Knowledge Among the Germans in Pennsylvania," whose objective was to teach English to German children, put him out of favour with most Germans who wished to retain their own language and customs. See Joseph Jackson, "A Philadelphia Schoolmaster of the Eighteenth Century," *Penn. Mag. Hist. & Bio.*, Vol. 35, 322.

2 Labaree, Vol. 8, 35. See also William S. Hanna, *Benjamin Franklin and Pennsylvania Politics* (Stanford: Stanford University Press, 1964) 134-6; also Robert Middlekauff, *Benjamin Franklin and His Enemies* (Berkeley: University of California, 1996) 54, 67-8.

3 Benjamin Franklin to Mary Stevenson, Mar. 25, 1763, Labaree, Vol. 10, 234. See also Ralph L. Ketchum, "Benjamin Franklin and William Smith: New Light on an Old Philadelphia Quarrel," *Penn. Mag. Hist. & Bio.*, Vol. 88, 143, 151.

4 Labaree, Vol. 4, 468n citing Franklin B. Dexter, ed., *Literary Diary of Ezra Stiles* (New York: 1901) II, 338.

5 Labaree, Vol. 8, 320n. See Albert F. Gegenheimer, *William Smith Educator and Churchman 1727-1803* (Philadelphia, 1943) 149-50.

6 Van Doren, 300.

7 Labaree, Vol. 10, 78n, 146n, 152n; also Van Doren, 300-304. Elizabeth Downes, born ca. 1729; died New York, July 28, 1778. Hart, "Letters," 419-21.

8 Franklin to Strahan, April 25, 1763. Hart, "Letters," 424, 426. Strahan was a London publisher and printer; born April, 1715, Scotland; died July 9, 1785; William Franklin, born ca. Sept 1, 1730, Philadelphia; was a Captain in the British army during the French and Indian War; comptroller of the Post Office for two years; died a Loyalist in England, Nov 17, 1813. Hart, "Letters," 420, 415, 425-6. Readers in the Atlantic provinces will be interested to learn that the Franklin family enjoyed playing a card game called cribbage. William told his friend Strahan that if he could convince his wife to return to England some day, they would "take Revenge for the last Drubbing you & Mrs Hughes gave us at Cribbage." Hart, "Letters," 422.

9 Franklin to Strahan, Oct. 14, 1763. Hart, "Letters," 431.

10 See *Pennsylvania Journal*, April 22, 1756, cited in Ketchum, 150n, who states that Smith "sought frequently to abuse William Franklin." See also 142-163. The best source for William Franklin is undoubtedly Sheila L. Skemp, *William Franklin, Son of a Patriot, Servant of a King* (New York: Oxford University Press, 1990). For his parentage, see 4, 62-3. See also Van Doren, 91-3, 231. Compare Charles Henry Hart, "Who Was the Mother of Franklin's Son.[?]" *Penn. Mag. Hist. & Bio.*, Vol. 35, 308. Hart argues that William's birth mother was Franklin's wife, Deborah. For the elusive Barbara, see Claude-Anne Lopez and Eugenia W. Herbert, *The Private Franklin, the Man and his Family* (New York: W. W. Norton & Co., 1975) 22-24; also Labaree, Vol. 11. 370-1.

11 Joan de Lourdes Leonard, "Elections in Colonial Pennsylvania," *William and Mary Quarterly*, Vol. 11 (Ser. 3) 1954, 399. For William's campaign, see Skemp, 62-3.

12 Esmond Wright, *Franklin of Philadelphia* (Cambridge: Belknap Press of Harvard University Press, 1986) 83. For "Hogs," see Benjamin Franklin to Richard Jackson, Oct. 11, 1764, Labaree, Vol. 11, 397. See also Alfred Owen Aldridge, *Benjamin Franklin, Philosopher & Man* (Philadelphia: J. B. Lippincott Company, 1965) 167. For Franklin's "Observations Concerning the Increase of Mankind," see Labaree, Vol. 4, 225-234, and Vol. 11, 370; also Van Doren, 218, 315-6; Middlekauff, 98-9; Philip J. Gleason, "A Scurrilous Colonial Election and Franklin's Reputation," *William and Mary Quarterly* (Williamsburg: Institute of Early American History and Culture, 1961) Vol. 18, 78-9. For Smith, see Newcomb, *Franklin and Galloway*, 94-8. See also Richard H. Shryock, "The Pennsylvania Germans in American History," *Penn. Mag. Hist. & Bio.*, Vol. 63, 262; Samuel W. Pennypacker, "The Settlement of Germantown and the Causes which led to it," *Penn. Mag. Hist. & Bio.*, Vol. 4, 2. For the vote count, see Labaree, Vol. 11, 397; Van Doren, 316. For more on the role of the Germans in the 1764 election, see Dietmar Rothermund, "The German Problem of Colonial Pennsylvania, *Penn. Mag. Hist. & Bio.*, Vol. 84, 18-20; also Theodore Thayer, *Pennsylvania Politics and the Growth of Democracy 1740 - 1776* (Harrisburg: Pennsylvania Historical and Museum Commission, 1953) 94-5. Thayer notes that many Lutheran and Reformed Germans favoured the Proprietary Party.

13 Edmund S. Morgan & Helen M. Morgan, *The Stamp Act Crisis, Prologue to Revolution* (Chapel Hill: The University of North Carolina Press, 1953) 245-6. The authors have written one of the better histories of the Stamp Act. See also "A letter from John Hughes, Esq. to the Commissioners of the Stamp office in London, Philadelphia, Oct. 12, 1765," Supplement to the *Pennsylvania Journal*, Sept. 4, 1766; also Middlekauff, 100-3.

14 William Franklin to William Strahan, Feb 18, 1765, Hart, "Letters," 441-2. William Allen Sr. (1710-1780) Chief Justice of Pennsylvania from 1750 to 1774; died in England, a Loyalist. Hart, "Letters," 441n. For Nov. 7, see Labaree, Vol. 11, 427, 447. Morgan & Morgan, 245.

15 *Pennsylvania Journal*, Dec. 20, 1764; see also William Cabell Bruce, *Benjamin Franklin Self-Revealed*, 3 Vols. (New York: G.P. Putnam's Sons, 1917) Vol. 1, 337; Compare Thomas F.

Gordon, *The History of Pennsylvania From Its Discovery by Europeans to the Declaration of Independence in 1776* (Philadelphia: Carey, Lea & Carey Publishers, 1829) 432. Gordon states it was £5 per accusation; Aldridge, 168, states it was £10 and £15; Morgan & Morgan agree it was £10 and £5, but cite issues of the *Pennsylvania Gazette* and *Pennsylvania Journal* twelve months after the event. For pies and cakes, see Thayer, 107.

Chapter 7 Charles Jones, his Mark

1 Paul A. W. Wallace, *The Muhlenbergs of Pennsylvania* (Freeport: Books for Libraries Press, 1950) 44, quoting Henry Melchior Mühlenberg, 3 Vols., *The Journals of Henry Melchior Muhlenberg*, Theodore G. Tappert and John W. Doberstein, trans. (Philadelphia: The Evangelical Lutheran Ministerium of Pennsylvania, 1945) Vol. 1, 577.

2 Mühlenberg, Vol 2, 143. Although his name is usually given as Henry Melchior Muhlenberg, in 1742 he signed "Heinrich Melchior Mühlenberg." See Diffenderffer, 191.

3 For the battle between Franklin and the Proprietors, see Middlekauff, 82-101.

4 Mühlenberg, Vol. 2, 190-2. See also Alan W. Tully, "Ethnicity, Religion, and Politics in Early America," *Penn. Mag. Hist. & Bio.*, Vol. 107, 519.

5 Wayland Fuller Dunaway, Ph.D., *A History of Pennsylvania* (New York: Prentice-Hall, 1935) 346; Middleton, 252.

6 Julius Friedrich Sachse, "The Records of St. Michael's and Zion Lutheran Congregation of Philadelphia," *Pennsylvania German Church Records of Births, Baptisms, Marriages, Burials, Etc. From The Pennsylvania German Society Proceedings and Addresses* (Baltimore: Genealogical Publishing Co., 1983) Vol. 1, 514.

7 See William S. Hoar, *Steeves and Colpitts Pioneers of the Upper Petitcodiac* (1988) 31. Hoar quotes Roland H. Hutchinson who states that W. B. Oulton wrote about the 1749 baptismal record of Jacob Steeves as early as 1986.

8 For the anglicization of German names and other aspects of acculturation, see Stephanie Grauman Wolfe, *Urban Village: Population, Community, and Family Structure in Germantown, Pennsylvania 1783-1800* (Princeton: Princeton University Press, 1976) 127-153. See also G. Elmore Reaman, *The Trail of the Black Walnut* (McClelland & Stewart Ltd., 1957) 169; also Leslie Alan Dunkling, *First Names First* (Detroit, Gale Research Co., 1977) 69. Dunkling points to a Biblical source for eighteenth-century use of the name Rachel. For the declining use of the German language in speech and signatures in Germantown specifically, see Wolfe, 142-3.

9 Esther Clark Wright to William Hoar, July 21, 1987. See Esther Clark Wright Papers, Acadia University Archives.

10 Wright, *Samphire Greens*, 84-5. See also Leon Parkin Steeves, "Early Settlement of the Steeves Family in New Brunswick," 7-8. This eleven-page report was "copied from an old document on foolscap," the author of which was Howard Steeves. The original work has apparently disappeared, although transcriptions possibly survive in the collections of the St. John Museum.

11 *Steward's Book*, Sept. 12, 1790, "Trueman Family Papers," Ralph Picard Bell Library, Mt. Allison University, cited in Shirley Dobson, *Methodism at the Bend and the Free Meeting House* (1989) 7. For a comprehensive look at the coming and goings of Methodist preachers in the area, see Neil Semple, *The Lord's Dominion* (Montréal: McGill Queens University Press, 1996);

see also Roland H. Hutchinson, *The Early Methodist Connection of the Steeves Family* (Wallace: 1981).

12 Arch St. was originally named Holmes St. after William Penn's chief surveyor. From the *Pennsylvania Gazette*, Roy Goodman has determined that the transition from Mulberry to Arch was underway by 1766. Mulberry continued to be used as late as 1796. See Grant Miles Simon, *Part of Old Philadelphia: A Map Showing Historic Buildings & Sites from the Founding until the Early Nineteenth Century* (Philadelphia: G. Simon, 1973).

13 John T. Faris, *Old Churches and Meeting Houses in and Around Philadelphia* (Philadelphia: J. B. Lippincott Co., 1926) 139. For St. Michael's corporate name see Sachse, Vol. 1, 537.

14 Don Yoder, introduction to *Pennsylvania German Church Records of Births, Baptisms, Marriages, Burials, Etc. From The Pennsylvania German Society Proceedings and Addresses* (Baltimore: Genealogical Publishing Co., 1983) Vol. 1, vi, 530. See also Mühlenberg, Vol. 2, 301. For a concise overview of St. Michael's and Zion, see Joseph Henry Dubbs, "The Founding of the German Churches of Pennsylvania," *Penn. Mag. Hist. & Bio.*, Vol. 17, 241-262. See also Ells Paxson Oberholtzer, *Philadelphia: A History of the City and its People* (Philadelphia: S. J. Clarke Publishing Co., 1893) Vol. 1, 189.

15 Sachse, Vol. 1, 573.

16 Sachse, Vol. 1, 593, 519, 544. The bride and groom's name are transcribed as Mathias Summer and Christina Nullin. Witnesses were Jacob Schütt, Hans Jürg Null, Johan. Jurg Kurtz, Philipp Haller, John Dorett. Matthias Sommer witnessed at least two marriages in St. Michael's: Jacob Schitt to Maria Cathrina Antonin on April 1, 1749; and Mathias Haase to Margretha Jacklerin on Nov. 20, 1752. On Oct. 7, 1753, Matthias and his wife Christina witnessed the baptism of Margretha Sommer, daughter of Hans-George and Anna Barbara Sommer. Sachse, 595, 610, 551.

17 "A Muhlenberg Manuscript," *Bulletin of the Historical Society of Montgomery County* (Norristown: The Society) Vol. XI, No. 4 (Spring, 1959) 286. See also Mühlenberg, Vol. 1, 685; Vol. 2, 206, 303. Valentin Müller and Lewis Kolb (303) may have been related. In 1751, Johann Valentin Müller's marriage to Eva Kolb was witnessed by Ludwig Kolbe. See Sachse, Vol. 1, 600. The Barren Hill connection to the name Sommer was possibly first discovered by Dr. Rainer L. Hempel, who mentioned it to me in 1996. For more about churchgoing in Germantown see Wolfe, 213-5.

18 On the subject of name variations, Dr Wright comments: "Eighteenth century spelling created many problems, because names were apt to be spelled differently by every person who had occasion to write them down." Esther Clark Wright, *Planters and Pioneers*, rev. ed. (Wolfville, 1978) 9.

19 Sachse, Vol. 1, 696.

20 Geneva Jones Emberley, "Descendants of Charles Jones of N.B. from 1766 and Ellis Descendants from 1739" (1977); Esther Clark Wright, *Planters and Pioneers* (Wolfville, 1978) rev. ed., 173; Pincombe, Vol. 1, 67. I am indebted to Judi Berry Steeves for providing this information.

21 Wright, *Samphire Greens*, 10, 25. See also Wright, *The Petitcodiac*, 45.

22 "Jones marriages in early southeast Pennsylvania," XR 120.16, EE 192, Sheet No. 7. For David and Letitia Jones, see GEN Jo8. For James J. Levick, see VoM 65, Vol. 13. For Francis

Jones Senior, see Jones Bible Records, BR Jo; also GEN, Ro49.

23 "Genealogy of John ap Thomas," GEN BA 16; "Jones Bible Records," BR Jo. Thomas's genealogy is delineated in James J. Levick, M.D., "An Old Welsh Pedigree," *Penn. Mag. Hist. & Bio.*, Vol. 4, 471-83; see also Charles H. Browning, *Welsh Settlements of Pennsylvania* (Genealogical Publishing Company: Baltimore, 1967) 109-123. The Welsh terms "ap" and "ab" mean "son of."

24 D. Michael Hughes, *The Hughes Family History* (Ingram: 1994).

Chapter 8 Bedbunts and Faggathies, Candlesticks and Chocolate

1 See *St. Peter's Lutheran Church, Barren Hill, Montgomery, PA, 1851-1919* (Philadelphia, Genealogical Society of Pennsylvania, 1919) Vol. 370.

2 Dickey Betts, (Allman Brothers Band), "In Memory of Elizabeth Reed," *Idlewild South* (New York: Atlantic Recording Corporation/ATCO Records, 1970).

3 Anna M. Holstein, *Swedish Holsteins in America* (Norristown: M. R. Willis, 1892). In 1995, the family history room was located on the second floor beside the research room. Called "the hallway" by the staff, the room was demolished in 1999 as part of the general renovations to the building, and the collection was moved to a larger room beside the new research area on the main floor. In 1998, I was able to purchase from a Vermont antiquarian bookseller a copy of *Swedish Holstiens* from which the title page is reproduced.

4 See Holstein, 46-7. John's paternal grandparents died at Walnut Grove and are thought to be buried in the cemetery of St. David's in Radnor where Anthony Wayne and his ancestors are also buried. Walnut Grove was located near present-day Gulf Mills. For Hughes Family genealogy, see Appendix B.

5 See Hon. Judge Botsford, "The Pioneers of Westmorland," *The Daily Times* (Moncton) Jan. 19, 1885.

6 For 1751, see Hannah Benner Roach, "Benjamin Franklin Slept Here" *Penn. Mag. Hist. & Bio.*, Vol. 84, 162-3. The house, and probably the store later, was located at 38 Fourth St. The three-storey building was eighteen feet wide by thirty-one feet deep, and built of nine-inch bricks. Roach believes Hughes moved to Dock Ward in 1756, during the year the Franklins occupied the house.

7 Holstein, 48.

8 Jonathan Roberts, "Memoirs of a Senator from Pennsylvania (1771-1854)" *Penn. Mag. Hist. & Bio.*, Vol. 61, 468-70, cited in Holstein, 48.

9 Holstein, 261, 270-8. The originals can be found in the papers of Anthony Wayne and John Hughes, Hist. Soc. of Penn.

10 For appointees to the militia, see J. Thomas Scharf and Thompson Westcott, *History of Philadelphia, 1609-1884*, 2 Vols. (Philadelphia: L. H. Everts & Co., 1884) Vol. 1, 215.

11 *Pennsylvania Gazette* (Philadelphia: Benjamin Franklin & David Hall) Oct. 20, 1748. See also Labaree, Vol. 11, 371n. The Indian King was located on the south-west corner of Market and Elbow Lane, about two blocks from Hughes's house on Fourth St. See Simon, *Part of Old Philadelphia*.

12 *Pennsylvania Gazette*, Dec. 29, 1749.

13 Benjamin H. Newcomb, *Franklin and Galloway: A Political Partnership* (New Haven: Yale University Press, 1972) 26.

14 *Pennsylvania Gazette*, June 2, 1757; *Pennsylvania Gazette*, June 5, 1759. See also Thayer, 122, who refers to Hughes's "fortitude and courage."

15 Newcomb, *Franklin and Galloway*, 61-2; See also Donna Bingham Munger, *Pennsylvania Land Records: A History and Guide for Research* (Wilmington: Scholarly Resources, Inc., 1991) 54-7. Compare Merrill Jensen, *The Founding of a Nation: A History of the American Revolution 1763-1776* (New York: Oxford University Press, 1968) 88. The Proprietary Party accused Hughes of stealing land warrants from the state house. For one of Hughes's land flips involving the Germans in Merion, see Browning, 485.

16 *Pennsylvania Gazette*, Dec. 2, 1762. Compare Holstein, 259-60. Many of the terms, now obsolete, refer to varieties of linen and woollen fabric. *Oxford English Dictionary* defines diaper primarily as linen table cloth but also as "baby's napkin" or "clout." Raven's duck was a heavy fabric, probably made from hemp, and used for tents, sails, and sailors' clothing. For a list of items sold in Benjamin Franklin's store, twenty years earlier, see Van Doren, 128.

17 See "Debts due to John Hughes in Ledger B" & "An Account of Outstanding Debts," John Hughes Papers, Hist. Soc. of Penn. Joseph Galloway was Franklin's friend, a lawyer, first lieutenant in the Pennsylvania Assembly, and his successor after 1764; born ca. 1730; died a Tory in England, 1803. Scharf & Westcott, Vol. 1, 274. For Israel Jacobs, see James G. Barnwell, "Some of the Alleys, Courts and Inns of Philadelphia, 1767-1790," *Penn. Mag. Hist. & Bio.* (Philadelphia: Hist. Soc. of Penn.) Vol. 37, 108.

Chapter 9 A Crisis Over Stamps

1 Samuel Eliot Morison, *Oxford History of the American People* (New York: Oxford University Press, 1965) 176. William Penn, it will be sadly noted, fared worse than the colony he founded in 1682. Pennsylvania affairs taxed his every resource, until the year 1708 saw him in debtor's prison in England. Nearly bankrupt, he suffered a paralytic stroke in 1712, and died on July 30, 1718 at the age of 74. Peare, 402, 411-14. For population counts, see Billy G. Smith, *The "Lower Sort": Philadelphia's Laboring People, 1750-1800* (Ithaca: Cornell University Press, 1990) 206-7. The 1750 census count of 12,736 people did not include 1000 Black slaves, a number that by 1760 had increased to 1,700. Smith, 193n. See also James Mease, MD., *The Picture of Philadelphia* (Philadelphia: B. & T. Kite, 1811) 31; Middleton, 354-5; Holstein, 49.

2 Penn's instructions to his land commissioners, Sept. 30, 1681. Richard S. Dunn and Mary Maples Dunn, *The Papers of William Penn* (Philadelphia: University of Pennsylvania Press, 1982) Vol. 2, 122, cited in Peare, 225.

3 Lord Adam Gordon, "Journal of an Officer who Travelled in America and the West Indies in 1764 and 1765," Newton D. Mereness, ed., *Travels in the American Colonies*, 1690-1783 (New York: The MacMillan Co., 1916) 410-11.

4 Morison, 176; Van Doren, 316-7.

5 See Adolph Koeppel, *The Stamps That Caused the American Revolution* (The Town of North Hempstead, NY, 1976) 34-5. Koeppel credits Henry McCulloh with raising the act with Grenville in 1763. Compare John C. Miller, *Origins of the American Revolution* (Boston: Little, Brown & Company, 1943) 112; also Scharf and Westcott, Vol. 1, 270. Scharf suggests that the idea originated with Governor Keith and Joshua Gee in Philadelphia in 1739.

6 See *Journals of the House of Commons* (Gr. Britain), Vol. 30 (March 22, 1765) 293. Also Van Doren, 321, who states, in an apparent double entendre, that the act "received the king's assent by commission, the king having had his first attack of insanity."

7 Koeppel, 59-80.

8 Arthur M. Schlesinger, "The Colonial Newspapers and the Stamp Act," *The New England Quarterly*, Vol. VIII (Plimpton Press, 1935; New York: AMS Reprint Co., 1963) 70. Mueller's paper was named *Der Wöchentliche Philadelphische Staatsbote*. See also Labaree, Vol. 12, 347.

9 Koeppel, 84.

10 Morison, 197; Van Doren, 365-6; Labaree, Vol. 13, 257n. Thayer, 93-4. See also Jared Sparks, *The Works of Benjamin Franklin*, Vol. IV (London: Benjamin Franklin Stevens, 1882) 233, 302-3. The Walpole Company was also called the Grand Ohio Company, or Vandalia. The land companies' complex history is delineated in Shaw Livermore, *Early American Land Companies - Their Influence on Corporate Development* (New York: Octagon Books, 1968) 111-22.

11 Benjamin Franklin to Richard Jackson, May 1, 1764, Labaree, Vol. 11, 186-7; see also Vol. 12, 345-7.

12 Van Doren, viii; Labaree, Vol. 1, xii. For a radically divergent view, see D. H. Lawrence, "Benjamin Franklin," *Critical Essays on Benjamin Franklin*, Melvin H. Buxbaum, ed. (Boston: G. K. Hall, 1987) 41-60. Lawrence's emotional outpouring is briefly countered by Esmond Wright, 81.

13 Kenneth Silverman, *Benjamin Franklin: The Autobiography and Other Writings* (New York: Penguin, 1986) 3-28. See also Russel B. Nye, ed., *Benjamin Franklin, Autobiography and Other Writings* (Boston: Houghton Mifflin Company, 1958). Franklin was born January 17, 1706, new style. Josiah Franklin, born Jan. 1657; married Ann(e) Child; arrived Boston, Oct. 1683; dyer, candle and soap maker, and prominent member of the Church of England in Boston. Van Doren, 4; Labaree, Vol. 8, 135n.

14 Silverman, 28; Van Doren, 39.

15 Silverman, 53; Van Doren, 55.

16 John F. Watson, *Annals of Philadelphia and Pennsylvania in the Olden Time*, (Philadelphia: Edwin S. Stuart, 1897) Vol. 1, 532. See also Thomas Fleming, ed., *Benjamin Franklin: A Biography in His Own Words*, The Founding Fathers series (New York: Newsweek, 1972) Vol. 1, 88-98, 173. For Franklin's armonica, see Van Doren, 297-9, 305.

17 Van Doren, 189, 731.

18 Skemp, 33. See also John W. Jordan, "Franklin As A Genealogist," *Penn. Mag. Hist. & Bio.*, Vol. 23, 1-22; also Labaree, Vol. 8, 114-21, 133-46. For Franklin's quote, see Silverman, 5.

19 Benjamin Franklin to Deborah Franklin, London, June 10, 1758, Labaree, Vol. 8, 90.

20 Morgan & Morgan, 246-7. See also Hart, 442n; Scharf & Westcott, Vol. 1, 271.

21 Watson, Vol. 2, 269-70. For October 7, see Bernhard Knollenberg, *Origin of the American Revolution*, rev. ed. (New York: The Free Press, 1960) 210. For the boycotts, see Scharf & Westcott, Vol. 1, 272-3. See also Thomas M. Doerflinger, *A Vigorous Spirit of Enterprise* (Williamsburg: Institute of Early American History and Culture, 1986) 167-196. Doerflinger

argues that the merchants' interests were as much pecuniary as political. For the members of McNutt's syndicate who signed the Philadelphia boycott agreement see the end of Appendix D.

22 Scharf & Westcott, Vol. 1, 272; Van Doren, 351.

23 Schlesinger, 75, states that the latter slogan was used as a motto by newspapers in Boston and New York. Knollenberg, 215, describes a New York mob on Nov. 28, 1765 carrying banners with the same slogan. For the important role of colonial tavern-keepers in the revolutionary movement, see David W. Conroy, *In Public Houses: Drink and the Revolution of Authority in Colonial Massachusetts* (Chapel Hill: University of North Carolina Press, 1995) especially Chapter 6.

24 For May 30, see Scharf & Westcott, Vol. 1, 271.

25 See Theodore Draper, *A Struggle for Power, The American Revolution* (Toronto: Random House, 1996) 243-52. The term "Sons of Liberty" was coined by Col. Isaac Barré, that "towering, one-eyed veteran of the wars," during a speech to the House of Commons on February 6, 1765. Miller, 112. See also Knollenberg, 206.

26 Miller, 131-132.

27 Joseph J. Kelly Jr., *Pennsylvania: The Colonial Years* (Garden City: Doubleday & Company, 1980) 557.

28 Miller, 135; Draper, 243-6; Morgan & Morgan, 122-5. See also G. B. Warden, *Boston 1689-1776* (Boston: Little, Brown and Company, 1970) 163-173.

29 Alice Dickinson, *The Stamp Act* (New York: Franklin, Watts, 1970) 45. For Philadelphia newspapers, see Watson, Vol. 2, 270.

30 Wilfred B. Kerr, "The Stamp Act in Nova Scotia," *The New England Quarterly*, Vol. VI (1933) 556. Hinshelwood was clerk under Edward Cornwallis and other governors, and assemblyman for Lunenberg in 1759 and 1765. Thomas Akins, *History of Halifax City* (Belleville: Mika Publishing, 1973; orig. pub. Nova Scotia Historical Society, 1895) 230.

31 Whitelaw, 13-4. See also Brebner, *Neutral Yankees*, 140.

32 *Halifax Gazette*, Feb. 13, 1766.

33 Brebner, *Neutral Yankees*, 139; Koeppel, 99-101. Henry was born Anton Heinrich and originated in Alsace. Bell, 213-4. In 1766, publication of the *Gazette* was suspended until August when the paper was reborn with a new name under Robert Fletcher. In 1770, Henry bought Fletcher's paper and renamed it *Nova Scotia Gazette and Weekly Chronicle*. Gertrude E. N. Tratt, *A Survey and Listing of Nova Scotia Newspapers 1752-1957* (Halifax: Dalhousie University, 1979) 71-3. See a complete listing of stamp distributors and inspectors in Koeppel, 14, 41; also Gipson, Vol. 10, 277. For Thomas's description of events, see Isaiah Thomas, *The History of Printing in America* (Worcester, 1810) Vol. 1, 368; Vol. 2, 175-9, cited in Brebner, *Neutral Yankees*, 135n.

34 Franklin to Hughes, London, Aug. 9, 1765. Labaree, Vol. 12, 235. See also Van Doren, 327.

35 W. P. [William John Potts], "Book Notices," *Penn. Mag. Hist. & Bio.*, Vol. 17, 126-7. Thirteen years after it appeared in *Swedish Holsteins*, Franklin's letter was published in Albert Henry

Smyth, *The Writings of Benjamin Franklin* (London: The MacMillan Company, 1906) Vol. IV, 391-2.

Chapter 10 A Loyal Englishman

1 See Thayer, 119; Scharf & Westcott, Vol. 1, 271.

2 Samuel Wharton to Benjamin Franklin, Oct. 13, 1765, Labaree, Vol. 12, 315-6. Franklin's house was located on Market Street between Third and Fourth. According to Deborah Franklin's descriptions, Hughes's home was nearby, probably on Fourth above Market Street, and possibly in the same building as his dry-goods store. See Roach, 162, 173; also John Hughes's will in Holstein, 244-5.

3 Deborah Franklin to Benjamin Franklin, September 22, 1765, Labaree, Vol. 12, 270-4. See also Lopez, 122-130.

4 Extracts of Hughes letters to Franklin, Sept. 8-17, 1765. Labaree, Vol. 12, 264-6; printed in the *Pennsylvania Journal*, Sept. 4, 1766. See also Morgan & Morgan, 247-8.

5 Deborah Franklin to Benjamin Franklin, Oct. 8, 1765, Labaree, Vol. 12, 300. Holstein, 50. Steadman and Mosby describe a carbuncle as a deep, festering staphylococcal skin infection, accompanied by fever, malaise and prostration, common on the back of the neck and the buttocks, and possibly related to anthrax. *Steadman's Medical Dictionary*, 26th ed. (Baltimore: Williams and Wilkins, 1995) 276; *Mosby's Medical, Nursing and Allied Health Dictionary*, 5th ed. (St. Louis: Mosby Year Book, Inc., 1998) 263.

6 Samuel Wharton to Benjamin Franklin, Oct. 13, 1765, Labaree, Vol. 12, 316; Thayer, 120.

7 The above names are listed with approximately 1700 other "jurors," or oath-takers in *Naturalizations of Foreign Protestants in the American Colonies and West Indies*, M. S. Giuseppe, ed. (Baltimore: Genealogical Publishing Co., 1964; orig. pub. London: Publications of the Huguenot Society of London Vol. XXIV, 1921) 105-6, 118, 145; Criner is spelled Kryner. See also Wright, *The Petitcodiac*, 55; *Samphire Greens*, 3. See elections standings in Labaree, Vol. 12, 290-1n.

8 Benjamin H. Newcomb, "Effects of the Stamp Act on Colonial Pennsylvania Politics," *The William and Mary Quarterly* (Williamsburg: Institute of Early American History and Culture, 1966) Third Series, Vol. XXIII (October, 1966) 268. For the fire company, see Carl and Jessica Bridenbaugh, *Rebels and Gentlemen* (New York: Reynal & Hitchcock, 1942) 206; see also Miller, 137.

9 "A letter from John Hughes, Esq. to the Commissioners of the Stamp office," Supplement to the *Pennsylvania Journal*, Sept. 4, 1766; See also John Hughes to Mr. Dickeson Stamps, 1765, Samuel Hazard, *Pennsylvania Archives* (Philadelphia, 1865) Series 1, Vol. 4, 241-2.

10 Deborah Franklin to Benjamin Franklin, Oct. 9, 1765, Labaree, Vol. 12, 301. See *Pennsylvania Journal*, Oct. 10, 1765; Morgan & Morgan, 249-250; Mühlenberg, Vol. 2, 273.

11 Mühlenberg, Vol. 2, 274; Morgan & Morgan, 250.

12 Morgan & Morgan, 251. Compare Watson, Vol. 2, 269. See also Scharf & Westcott, Vol. 1, 271. William Bradford was a local printer who operated the Old London Coffeehouse at Front and Market Streets where many of the plans of the Philadelphia Sons of Liberty were hatched. See Peter Thompson, *Rum Punch and Revolution, Taverngoing and Public Life in Eighteenth*

Century Philadelphia (Philadelphia: University of Pennsylvania Press, 1999) 108-9. See also Morgan & Morgan, 249. For Bradford's further adventures, see Frederick D. Stone, "How the Landing of Tea was Opposed in Philadelphia," *Penn. Mag. Hist. & Bio.*, Vol. 15, 386-393.

13 *Pennsylvania Journal*, Oct. 10, 1765. The mob action is described in Morgan & Morgan, 250-2. See also *Pennsylvania Gazette*, Oct. 10, 1765; *Halifax Gazette*, Nov. 7, 1765; Gipson, Vol. 10, 310.

14 Margaret Ells, "Loyalist Attitudes," *Historical Essays on the Atlantic Provinces*, G. A. Rawlyk, ed. (McClelland and Stewart Ltd., 1967) (Carleton Library No. 35) 48. Reprinted from *Dalhousie Review*, Vol. XV (October 1935) 320-334.

15 Deborah Franklin to Benjamin Franklin, Oct. 9, 1765, Labaree, Vol. 12, 301; Nov. 3, 1765, Labaree, Vol. 12, 352.

16 "A letter from John Hughes, Esq. to the Commissioners of the Stamp office," Supplement to the *Pennsylvania Journal*, Sept. 4, 1766. See Scharf & Westcott, Vol. 1, 271-2, where the Germans are called Dutch. Seeming to contradict Scharf and Westcott's statement, Pastor Mühlenberg recorded that he implored the members of his congregation to avoid "any uprising or tumult. And this was what was done by our people." Mühlenberg, Vol. 2, 273. The Germans, or *deitsch*, as they called themselves, continued to be referred to as Pennsylvania Dutch well into the twentieth century. See Klees, 7-9. Eschewing the more precise term "Pennsylvania Germans," Klees has followed the long-standing tradition attached to the original expression. Klees's *deitsch* is a dialect variant of *deutsch*, and was used by Swabians of south Germany in conversation. I am obliged to Roland Deigendesch for elaborating on this subject. See also Shryock, 261-281.

17 Morgan & Morgan, 252-5.

18 See Van Doren, 332, who states that Franklin "had somehow gone underground...."

19 James C. Humes, *The Wit and Wisdom of Benjamin Franklin*, (New York: HarperPerennial, 1996) 33. Watson, Vol. 1, 534; Van Doren, 731.

20 *Pennsylvania Gazette*, Feb. 6, 1766, cited in Sawtelle, 276n; See also *Penn. Mag. Hist. & Bio.*, Vol. 37, 113-4. For Jacobs's house, see James G. Barnwell, "Some of the Alleys, Courts and Inns of Philadelphia, 1767-1790," *Penn. Mag. Hist. & Bio.* (Philadelphia: Hist. Soc. of Penn.) Vol. 37, 108; for the White Horse Inn see also *Pennsylvania Gazette*, Sept. 18, 1766.

21 "A letter from John Hughes, Esq. to the Commissioners of the Stamp office," Supplement to the *Pennsylvania Journal*, Sept. 4, 1766; see also Morgan & Morgan, 256.

22 See Labaree, Vol. 12, 263n. A school teacher named Hugh Williamson, one of Franklin's many enemies, and who historian Benjamin Newcomb describes as a "refuse spreader," is blamed for intercepting the sealed letters and sending copies back to Philadelphia. Labaree, Vol. 13, 425n, 480n. Newcomb, *Franklin and Galloway*, 95. See also Newcomb, "Effects of the Stamp Act," 270n.

23 Alexander McNutt to John Hughes, July 18, 1766, John Hughes Papers, Hist. Soc. of Penn.

24 Joseph Galloway to Benjamin Franklin, October 17, 1768. William B. Willcox, ed., *The Papers of Benjamin Franklin*, (New Haven: Yale University Press, 1972) Vol. 15, 232.

25 William Franklin to Benjamin Franklin, Jan. 31, 1769, Willcox, Vol. 16, 37.

26 Morgan & Morgan, 298. See also Hart, 442. Hart erroneously states that Hughes sold Walnut Grove, whereas Holstein, 46-7, notes that the farm was bequeathed to his son Isaac in 1772. Tradition holds that George Washington headquartered there for a week in December, 1777. See William S. Baker, "The Itinerary of General Washington, 1777," *Penn. Mag. Hist. & Bio.*, Vol. 14, 276n.

27 John Hughes to William Franklin, Walnut Grove, June 11, 1769, American Philosophical Society, XLVIII, 137.

28 Roberts, 468. Compare Holstein, 50, who states with nineteenth-century patriotic revisionism that Hughes later changed his loyalties.

Chapter 11 Into a Dungeon of Fog

1 See Wright, *The Petitcodiac*, 44-5; *Samphire Greens*, 8. It seems Parson Eagleson didn't tell the story of the accusing servant girl to the Reverend Mr. Breynton, who later wrote that Eagleson was leaving the Presbyterian fold for the Church of England, not "through disgust, quarrel or any other sinister practice, but from real conviction...." C. W. Vernon, *Bicentenary Sketches and Early Days of the Church in Nova Scotia* (1910) 216. For more on Eagleson, see Ernest A. Clarke, *The Siege of Fort Cumberland, 1776: An Episode in the American Revolution* (Montréal: McGill-Queens University Press, 1995) 97-8; 106-8. See also Gertrude Tratt, "John Eagleson," *Dictionary of Canadian Biography* (Toronto: University of Toronto Press; Les Presses de l'université Laval) Vol. 4, 258-9.

2 Matthew Clarkson and Michael Hillegas to John Hall, Apr. 26, 1766, American Philosophical Society, Vol. 47, Folio 34, Misc. Papers. With no existing mail service between Philadelphia and the Bay of Fundy, Clarkson's letter was certainly delivered personally to Hall before departure. Dr. Wright refers to this letter, but doesn't indicate where Hall was on April 26. See Wright, *St. John River*, 106. The date was included in the McClelland and Stewart edition of *The St. John River and its Tributaries* (1949) but omitted in the self-published edition in 1966. The voyage and the accompanying legends are examined in Wright, *Samphire Greens*, 8-17 and Pincombe, Vol. 1, 60-70.

3 Sawtelle, 274, 266, citing D. R. Jack, ed., *Acadiensis* (Saint John, 1901) Vol. 1, 186. (I have not been able to verify Sawtelle's source.) See also Wayne to Hughes, April 10, 1765, Hughes Papers, Hist. Soc. of Penn.

4 For June 8, see John Hughes Esq. in Acct. Current with Anthony Wayne 1765-6, John Hughes Papers, Hist. Soc. of Penn. For the *Leopard*, see Halifax Naval Office Records, Public Record Office, CO 217, Vol. 44, 243. See more below.

5 Harry Emmerson Wildes, *Anthony Wayne, Trouble Shooter of the American Revolution* (New York: Harcourt, Brace and Co., 1941) 27-8; see also a Bill of Lading at Philadelphia for the Schooner *Charming Nancy*, Dec. 20, 1766, Wayne Family Papers, Waynesborough, Paoli, PA. Compare Pincombe, Vol. 1, 63. For Wayne's supposed departure at Digby, see Wright, *Samphire Greens*, 11. For more on the Wayne Family Papers, see below.

6 John Eagleson to Francis Alison, Halifax, 23 Oct., 1767, American Philosophical Society, Vol. 47, Folio 42. See also Wright, *The Petitcodiac*, 44. For the *Elizabeth*, see Halifax Naval Office Records, Public Record Office, CO 217, Vol. 44, 259.

7 For Larracey's fantasy account of the voyage, see *The First Hundred*, 6-44.

8 Fra[nci]s Peabody to John Hall, August 16, 1767. American Philosophical Society, Fol. XLVII, No. 35; see also Wright, *The St. John River and its Tributaries* (1966) 122-3. Hall's grant on the St. John's River may be the same one referred to in Lt. Gov. Michael Franklin to John Hall, Nov. 26, 1766, Colonial Office Records CO 217, Vol. 44, 367.

9 Compare Wright, *Samphire Greens*, 11-2. The Wolastoqewiyik came to be called Maliseet, a Mi'kmaq term meaning "broken talkers." See Olive Patricia Dickason, *Canada's First Nations: A History of Founding Peoples from Earliest Times* (Toronto: McClelland & Stewart, 1992) 107-8, 446n. Professor Dickason states: "The Maliseets were known to Champlain and the early Jesuits as Etchemin or Eteminquois."

10 Today spelled Cape Maringouin. See J. F. W. DesBarres, "Isthmus of Nova Scotia" in *The Atlantic Neptune* (1777).

11 Thos. Crowley, Feb. 24, 1766, "American Politics Discussed in Commercial Letters, 1764-1766," *Penn. Mag. Hist. & Bio.*, Vol. 17, 212. See also *Journals of the House of Commons*, (Gr. Britain), (Jan. 10, 1765 - Sept. 16, 1766) Vol. 30, 293, 667; Knollenberg, 218.

12 Harold A. Innis, ed. *The Diary of Simeon Perkins 1766-1780* (Toronto: Champlain Society, 1948) 3.

13 John Hall to William Smith, June 13, 1766, University of Pennsylvania Archives, William Smith Papers, UPT 50; S664. The original was previously located at the Hist. Soc. of Penn. The entire letter is transcribed in Pincombe, Vol. 1, 61-2. It should be noted that Hall used the same spelling for Petitcoodiac as did Matthew Clarkson in his letter to Hall on April 26. Hall likely carried the letter with him to Nova Scotia.

Chapter 12 "NovaScosha or sum such plase"

1 William Franklin to Benjamin Franklin, Oct. 23, 1767. American Philosophical Society. See Labaree, Vol. 14, 291-4. Franklin's letter was possibly first published in William Duane, ed., *Letters to Benjamin Franklin from his Family and Friends, 1751-1791* (Freeport: Books for Libraries Press, 1858; repub. 1970) 36-38. Duane's transcription saw numerous changes to Franklin's original, including added punctuation, the removal of capital letters, and a land grant of only 2,000 acres. The letter is torn through the last "0," making the number appear as "20,00"; hence Duane's misreading. For more on Franklin's grant, see below. The above version of the letter incorporates Duane, Labaree, and my own examination of the original. Parts of the letter are quoted in Sawtelle, 276-8.

2 Labaree, Vol. 14, 291n; Willcox, Vol. 15, 121n. Willcox seems to have taken at face value William Franklin's statement that Jacob Hall was involved in the Nova Scotia land venture. Regarding John Hall, the author comments: "He is not there identified, and cannot be beyond all doubt. But he was almost certainly the son of Joseph Hall of Tacony (1688-1731)...." See Hall family genealogy, Appendix C.

3 John C. Mendenball, "Old Frankford from Advertisements in the Colonial Newspapers," *Papers Read before the Historical Society of Frankford* (Gettysburg: Times and News Publishing Co., 1937) Vol. 3, No. 5, 116.

4 1766 Nova Scotia Lands, John Hughes Papers, Hist. Soc. of Penn. For Wethered, see Ernest A. Clarke, "Cumberland Planters and the Aftermath of the Attack on Fort Cumberland," Margaret Conrad, ed. *They Planted Well: New England Planters in Maritime Canada* (Fredericton: Acadiensis Press, 1988) 47. Thomas Dickson, born May 3, 1733, married Catherine Wethered, died Nov. 8, 1809; his half brother Charles Dickson came from Connecticut and was a grantee

at Horton township. See Shirley B. Elliot, *Legislative Assembly of Nova Scotia* (Province of Nova Scotia, 1984) 56. See also Katharine Dickson, *Downeast Dicksons* (Henniker: 1987) 18, 31.

5 Deborah Franklin to Benjamin Franklin, Jan. 12, 1766; see Labaree, Vol. 13, 32. The amount allocated to Benjamin Franklin in Holstein, 261 reads £28:10:72. For Wayne's father and John Cox Jr., see 1766 Nova Scotia Lands, John Hughes Papers, Hist. Soc. of Penn. For the "Flower," see John Hughes Esq. in Acct. Current with Anthony Wayne 1765-6, John Hughes Papers, Hist. Soc. of Penn.

6 For Moore vs. Wayne, see Glenn Tucker, *Mad Anthony Wayne and The New Nation* (Harrisburg: Stackpole Books, 1973) 22.

7 Jacobs Papers, Vol. 1, 191a. Hist. Soc. of Penn. Thomas Church was Captain of the schooner *Leopard* which made regular trips between Philadelphia and Halifax. Anthony Wayne possibly travelled to Halifax on the *Leopard*, arriving June 4. See Halifax Naval Office Records, CO 217, Vol. 44, 243, etc. See more above.

8 Jacobs Papers, Vol. 1, 207b, Hist. Soc. of Penn.

9 Jacobs Papers, Vol. 1, 291, Hist. Soc. of Penn. For Rev. Paulus Bryzelius and his visit to The *Petitcodiac*, see Bell, 215.

10 See Petition of Benjamin Franklin to King George III in Colonial Office Records, Feb. 10, 1766, CO 217, Vol. 23, No. 2. The conditions for settlement were similar to those given to Hughes and Co., viz. one Protestant person to be settled per 200 acres, and a quit rent of two shillings per hundred acres. In Franklin's grant, pine trees greater than twenty-four inches in diameter were reserved for His Majesty's navy. See also CO 218, Vol. 7, 210, Privy Council to Benjamin Franklin, June 26, 1767. Labaree, Vol. 14, 202-4. As Labaree points out, the peninsular portion of the colony became Nova Scotia proper, thus the continental part likely refers to present-day New Brunswick.

11 "Dr. Franklin's Answer to the Foregoing Report," on the "Settlement on the Ohio River," (ca. May 1, 1772), Smyth, Vol. V, 508-9 (Report's italics). See also Jared Sparks, ed., *The Works of Benjamin Franklin* (London: B. F. Stevens, 1882) Vol. IV, 354-5. Compare Willcox, Vol. 19, 123-5. Although several Franklin biographers have attributed the Ohio report to Franklin, Willcox argues that the report—also called "the Walpole Company's Rejoinder to a Report from the Board of Trade"—was actually prepared by his two partners, Samuel Wharton and Thomas Walpole, with some factual information contributed by Franklin. Franklin was certainly aware of the unsuccessful results of his partners' settlement venture at Monckton.

12 Mühlenberg, Vol. 2, 160-1.

13 James Parker to Benjamin Franklin, Jan. 14, 1765, Labaree, Vol. 12, 21; *Pennsylvania Journal*, Jan. 10, 1765.

14 Deborah Franklin to Benjamin Franklin, Jan. 8, 1765, Labaree, Vol. 12, 13. For a look at the popular sport of sleigh-riding, see Louis B. Wright, *Life in Colonial America* (New York: Capricorn Books, 1965) 202-4; also Clarke, *The Siege of Fort Cumberland*, 19.

15 William Franklin to Benjamin Franklin, May 10, 1768, Willcox, Vol. 15, 121. Their advertisement for new settlers appeared in the *Pennsylvania Chronicle*, Mar 14-21, 1768, and the *Pennsylvania Gazette*, March 17. Not to be confused with an advertisement in the *Pennsylvania Chronicle*, Mar 3, 1768 for the Philadelphia township on the north side of the basin of Minas.

16 *Pennsylvania Gazette*, March 17, 1768. See also Wright, *The Petitcodiac*, 39.

17 Jacobs Papers, Vol. 2, 449. Hist. Soc. of Penn. Charles Baker was hired by the syndicate to survey the township. See below.

18 Jacobs Papers, Vol. 2, 455. Hist. Soc. of Penn.

19 One perch equalled 16.5 linear feet. See *Oxford English Dictionary*.

20 Scharf & Westcott, Vol. 1, 215; Compare Minutes of Provincial Council of Pennsylvania, *Pennsylvania Archives* (Harrisburg, 1851) Vol. 5, 247, 193. For King George's War, see Morison, 158.

21 See John W. Jordan, LL.D., *Colonial and Revolutionary Families of Pennsylvania* (Baltimore: Genealogical Publishing Company, 1978) Vol. 1, 442. See also Arthur C. Bining, *Pennsylvania Iron Manufacture in the Eighteenth Century* (New York: Augustus M. Kelley, 1970; orig. pub. 1938) 188.

22 *Pennsylvania Gazette*, Nov. 10, 1763. Hughes's friend and fellow-assemblyman Joseph Galloway also had concerns in the steel industry. See Holstein, 256.

23 By my calculations, Wayne measured the township in nautical miles. I am grateful to my brother, Bob, for his suggestions about the map and Wayne's surveying methods.

24 See Wildes, 468-9. Some of the author's assertions are wildly inaccurate to the point of being loopy. Monckton township, for example, is positioned on an island in Northumberland Strait.

25 Samuel Pennypacker's 1873 reminiscences in the Jacobs Papers, Hist. Soc. of Penn. are cited in Wright, *The Petitcodiac*, 39-40. Because Pennypacker got the story from his father and wrote a century after the event, his account must be attended by the proverbial grain of salt.

26 John Eagleson to Francis Alison, Halifax, 23 Oct., 1767, American Philosophical Society, Vol. 47, Folio 42. See also Wright, *The Petitcodiac*, 44. Dr. Wright followed Eagleson's spelling of "Allison."

27 Labaree, Vol. 13, 31n; Vol. 4, 470n. See also Thayer, 100, who states that Alison, the "Presbyterian Pope," encouraged Presbyterian ministers to "[turn] their pulpits into political rostrums."

28 Sept. 1, 1769, "An Account of Fees Received in the Customs House - Piscataqua to Sept. 4, 1770," Hughes Papers, Hist. Soc. of Penn. See also Hart, 442n. Hughes's appointment was noted in the *Pennsylvania Gazette*, Aug, 3, 1769. For Customs districts, see *Atlas of Early American History: The Revolutionary Era 1760 - 1790*, Lester J. Cappin, editor-in-chief (Princeton: Princeton University Press, 1976) 40, 119-20.

29 Charles Baker to John Hughes, July 24, 1769, John Hughes Papers, Hist. Soc. of Penn.; see also Wright, *Samphire Greens*, 20-2.

30 Willcox, Vol. 17, 157n. Charles Town or Charlestown became Charleston after the Revolution.

31 John Hughes to Jonathan Roberts, Charles Town, Feb. 1, 1771, John Hughes Papers, Hist. Soc. of Penn. Compare Holstein, 59; Morgan, 298.

32 Holstein, 60-1. For Benjamin Franklin and silk-worm culture, see Van Doren, 428-9.

33 A Return of the State of the Township of Hillsborough, January 1, 1770 (MG 9, B10, M5219, Vol. 443, Bell Library, Mt. Allison University). For background on the Hillsborough township, see Wright, *Samphire Greens*, 20-30.

34 Wright, *The Petitcodiac*, 48. According to the census report for 1783, George Wortman (or Warterman) had moved to Hillsborough, apparently sometime between 1770 and 1773. See A General Return of the number of families that had been settled in the township of Hillsboro in the county of Cumberland 1 June 1783: "George Warterman, resides on premises... no wife, 5 children under age." I am indebted to Judi Berry Steeves for bringing these facts to my attention.

35 Holstein, 61. See John Hughes to Isaac Hughes, July 25, 1771, John Hughes Papers, Hist. Soc. of Penn.

36 Roberts, 470, who adds, "he was neither own'd by Whigs, nor Tories."

37 John Hughes to Jonathan Roberts, Charles Town, Sept. 25, 1771, Hughes Papers, Hist. Soc. of Penn.

38 Holstein, 51. The Hughes family Bible has not been found.

39 Holstein, 51.

40 Skemp, 221-3, quoting William Franklin, 334n.

41 Skemp, 216-7, 233. For a compelling description of events leading up to the American Revolution, see Christopher Moore, *The Loyalists: Revolution, Exile, Settlement* (Toronto: McClelland & Stewart, 1984) 39-64.

42 Skemp, 265, 269, 273. See also Middlekauff, 208-9. "To my son, William Franklin, late Governor of the Jerseys, I give and devise all the lands I hold or have a right to, in the province of Nova Scotia, to hold to him, his heirs, and assigns forever....The part he acted against me in the late war, which is of public notoriety, will account for my leaving him no more of an estate he endeavoured to deprive me of." Smyth, Vol. X, 493-4.

43 Tucker, 28. See also Charles J. Stillé, *Major-General Anthony Wayne and the Pennsylvania Line in the Continental Army* (Port Washington: Kennikat Press, 1893) 10. Stillé erroneously believed that Wayne, "as superintendent of the Nova Scotia lands...had led into the wilderness and settled in their new home a colony abundantly provided with implements of husbandry and provisions."

Chapter 13 A Chance Discovery

1 *The Works of Michael Drayton*, J. William Hebel, ed. (Oxford: Basil Blackwell & Mott, Ltd., 1961) Vol. IV, 382.

2 See William F. Ganong, "Place-Nomenclature of New Brunswick," *Transactions of the Royal Society of Canada* (Second Series) Vol. 2 (1896) 239. Hall's Creek "said by tradition to be for the captain of the ship which brought the German settlers here in 1763. Earlier, *Panaccadie Creek*, which in 1765, is in the description of the bounds of the township of Moncton; doubtless Micmac, as the *accadie* shows." (Ganong's italics).

3 John Eagleson to Rev. Doctor Hind, Cumberland, Jan. 16, 1775, Society for the Propagation of the Gospel in Foreign Parts. Public Archives of Canada: SPGFP, B-25, No. 186 (MG 17, B 1/1, Vol. 2, page 549) [PANS film #14847]. Eagleson's records have not been found. Compare Vernon, 217. For the Acadian chapel, see Edward W. Larracey, *Chocolate River, A Story of The Petitcodiac River* (1985) 32, 46; Pincombe, Vol. 1, 27-8.

4 John Eagleson to Rev. Doct. Morice, July 13, 1785, Society for the Propagation of the Gospel in Foreign Parts, Public Archives of Canada: SPGFP, Letters Received, B-25, Nova Scotia, "C" Series 1752-1858, letter 110 (MG 17, B.1 to B 1/1 fo. 1-27-) [PANS film #14793].

5 Joseph Bouchette, *The British Dominions in North America; or a Topographical and Statistical Description of the Provinces of Lower and Upper Canada, New Brunswick, Nova Scotia, The Islands of Newfoundland, Prince Edward, and Cape Breton* (London: Colburn & Bentley, 1831; repub. New York: AMS Press, 1968) Vol. 2, 129.

6 For Simon Outhouse, see Larracey, *The First Hundred*, 272.

7 Hoar, *Steeves and Colpitts Pioneers*, 40. See also Larracey, *Chocolate River*, 48. Larracey states that Belliveau's first name was Pierre, although this be may be as imaginary as the rest of his account. Whether Belliveau had survived in hiding, or whether he had left the area in 1755 and later returned, is not known. A work-in-progress that may hold some clues to Belliveau's identity is Stephen A. White, *Dictionnaire généalogique des familles acadienne* (Moncton: Centre d'études acadiennes, Université de Moncton, 1999). Five Belliveau families are included in "Part 1 - 1636 to 1714." See also Gesner, who wrote in 1847 of a "Monsieur Belliveaux, who lived to the advanced age of one hundred and ten years." Abraham Gesner, *New Brunswick; with Notes for Emigrants* (London: Simmonds & Ward, 1847) 136.

8 Apparently there survives no documentation that the Acadians or their French ancestors actually used marsh greens. Nevertheless, "between 1632 and 1637 sixty families from La Rochelle, Saintonge and Poitou, where dykes were familiar, were settled in the Port Royal area." E. L. Eaton, "The Dyke Lands," *Nova Scotia Historical Quarterly* (Halifax: Public Archives of Nova Scotia) Vol. 10, Nos. 3 & 4 (December, 1980) 199. Marsh greens are included in Marielle Cormier-Boudreau and Melvin Gallant's *A Taste of Acadia* (Fredericton: Goose Lane Editions, 1991) 102, 114; orig. publ. *La Cuisine Traditionnelle en Acadie* (Moncton: éditions d'acadie, 1978). For the comparative nutritional values of wild and cultivated vegetables, including goosetongues and samphires, see W. S. Hoar, Marjorie Barberie, D. W. Davidson, "Wild Greens as Dietary Supplements to Commercial Vegetables," *Journal of the Canadian Dietetic Association*, Vol. 8, No. 1, June 1948, (Toronto) 14-28. The greens can also be found on Northumberland Strait, along the lower reaches of the St. Lawrence River, and in many other sea-side areas.

9 Roméo LeBlanc to The Senate, Installation Speech, Feb. 8, 1995.

10 See Ken Kanner, *Early Families Revisited* (Moncton: 1993) 155. Henry died Jan. 20, 1840, aged 82. Compare David Christopher, *Cemeteries of Albert County New Brunswick* (Riverview: 1988) 142, where Henry's death is listed as 1860. The stone is badly worn. Henry married Matthias Sommer's daughter Christenah, noted in the 1851 census as "Dutch, widow, infirm, aged 89." *New Brunswick Census of 1851: Westmorland County*, Wayne A. Gillcash, ed. (Fredericton: Provincial Archives of New Brunswick, 1981) Vol. 1, 33. For Catherine (Jones) Trites, see also Brenda & Lloyd Parsons, *Moncton's Civic Treasure: The Free Meeting House* (Moncton: Betson's Publishing, 1997) 99; also Moncton Free Meeting House Cemetery Records at the Moncton Museum.

11 Strassburger & Hinke, Vol. 1, 508, 531.

12 *Pennsylvania German Immigrants*, 1709-1786, Don Yoder, ed. (Baltimore: Genealogical Publishing Co., 1980) 227.

13 *Pennsylvania German Immigrants*, 118, 194. It should be noted that two different ships named Phoenix arrived in 1752: on Nov 2, 1752, the *Phoenix*, John Spurrier, Commander, from Portsmouth England; three weeks later on November 22, the *Phoenix*, Captain Rueben Honor, from Cowes, England. See Strassburger & Hinke, Vol. 1, 508; Vol. 2, 610. For more on Martin Beck, see Wright, *Samphire Greens*, 54; also Wright, *Planters and Pioneers*, 51. See also Terrence M. Punch, trans., "'Hörte ich daß...' ; Travels of a Rhinelander in Nova Scotia in 1807," *Journal of the Royal Nova Scotia Historical Society*, Vol. 3 (Dartmouth, 2000) 128.

14 *Pennsylvania German Immigrants*, 122.

15 The Toronto Reference Library holds two copies of Yoder's *Pennsylvania German Immigrants*. The second copy, unknown to me until six months later, bears a date stamp of April 11, 1983.

Chapter 14 Across the Pond

1 Many sources exist, but a history of Shrewsbury written closer to the time it describes can be found in B. Owen and J. B. Blakeway's two volume *A History of Shrewsbury* (London: Harding, Lepard, and Co., 1825). I encourage readers unfamiliar with Ellis Peters to begin with *A Morbid Taste for Bones* (published in several editions), and then read all nineteen subsequent Cadfael stories.

Chapter 15 A Hidden History

1 Rowan Robinson, *The Great Book of Hemp* (Rochester: Park Street Press, 1996) 74-101; see also Ernest L. Abel, *The First Twelve Thousand Years* (New York: Plenum Press, 1980) 10-35. Possibly the earliest references to the sacred properties of the hemp plant or bhanga occur about 1400 B.C. in the Sanskrit Atharvaveda. See Tod H. Mikuriya, M.D., *Excerpts from the Indian Hemp Drugs Commission Report with Centennial Thoughts on Indian Hemp and the Dope Fiends of Old England* (San Francisco: Last Gasp of San Francisco, 1994) 32. See also *Histories of Herodotus*, Book IV, Chapter 75.

2 Richard Bulkeley, "Nova Scotia, at a Councill Holden at Halifax the 30th of April, 1765," John Hughes Papers, Hist. Soc. of Penn. "The Council," Bulkeley wrote, "were further of opinion that it should be recommended to the Lords of Trade & Plantation to procure such Conditions of Settlement for these people as may be most Likely to induce them to come into the province in order to put the Country into a Condition of Yielding the many advantages it would peculiarely afford from it being well Peopled, particularly the Cultivation of Hemp & Cureing of Fish both which Articles of Export seemed to be the Principles object they had in View and which Could never be obtained to any Considerable Degree until the Country was so well peopled...." Bulkeley's entire sentence is a marathon 254 words long. See also Pincombe, Vol. 1, 52; Middleton, 343.

3 Walter Allen Knittle, *Early Eighteenth-Century Palatine Emigration* (Baltimore: Genealogical Publishing Co., 1970) 88-9. For Lancaster Co., see James T. Lemon, *The Best Poor Man's Country: A Geographical Study of Early Southeastern Pennsylvania*, (New York: W. W. Norton & Company, 1976) 215, citing *American Weekly Mercury* (Philadelphia) Dec. 27, 1720.

4 John W. Roulac, *Hemp Horizons* (White River Junction: Chelsea Green Publishing Company, 1997) 27 Compare Abel, 4-5. Abel refers to documentary evidence dating to ca. 2350 BC and speculative theory to 8000 BC.

5 *The History of Herodotus*, Book IV, Chapter 74.

6 Roulac, 30.

7 Roulac, 32.

8 Raymond, 104. For the Acadians and hemp, see J.C. Webster, "Sir Brook Watson," *The Argosy*, Vol. 3, No. 1, Nov., 1924; also in *Nova Scotia Historical Society Journal*, Vol. 2, (June, 1924) 135, quoted in Arsenault, 94. See also M. de Goutin au Ministre, Dec. 22, 1707 cited in Francis Parkman, *A Half Century of Conflict*, Vol. 1, (London: MacMillan and Co., 1894) 115. For a good, general description of hemp in Acadia, see Jonas Howe, "Early Attempts to Introduce the Cultivation of Hemp in Eastern British North America," *New Brunswick Historical Society Collections* (1892).

9 Charles Morris, "Description and State of the New Settlements in Nova Scotia in 1761," Sessional Paper No. 18, *Report Concerning Canadian Archives for the Year 1904* (Ottawa, 1905) 300. During a subsequent visit to Maugerville in the summer of 1767, Morris observed that the settlers' "tryals" of hemp on the alluvial lands of the intervale had "succeeded beyond their Expectation." When Morris viewed the crop in late July, the plants were already nine feet tall. Charles Morris, "Description of the Harbour and River of Saint John's in Nova-Scotia, and the townships of Sunbury, Burton, Gage, and Conway, lying on said river, as received from Charles Morris, Esq; surveyor-general of Halifax, and contained in a letter wrote to Capt. W. William Spry, one of the proprietors of said township, dated 25th of January, 1768." See also David Russell Jack, ed., *Acadiensis*, Vol. 3, No. 1 (January, 1903) 122-4. It may be interesting to note that Morris's son Charles Jr. married a sister of Rev. John Eagleson's wife. See Clarke, "Cumberland Planters," 54n.

10 DesBarres, Preface to *The Atlantic Neptune*. See more about DesBarres in Don W. Thomson, 91-5. See also Marc Debard, "The Family Origins of Joseph Frederick Wallet DesBarres: A Riddle Finally Solved," *Nova Scotia Historical Review*, Vol. 14, No. 2 (Halifax: Public Archives of Nova Scotia, 1994) 108-122.

11 Wilmot to Lords of Trade and Plantations cited in Raymond, 86, who adds, "Under the instructions to Governor Wilmot a condition of the land grants was that every grantee should plant one rood of every 100 acres with hemp, and continue to plant a like quantity year by year. The condition doubtless originated in the desire of the British Government to be independent of foreign nations in providing cordage for their marine." Raymond, 88n. A rood was equivalent to one quarter acre. See *Oxford English Dictionary*, 2nd ed. (Oxford: Clarendon Press, 1989).

12 Wayne to Hughes, Apr. 10, 1765, Hughes Papers, Hist. Soc. of Penn. See also Pincombe, Vol. 1, 54.

13 Lords of Trade to George III. April 8, 1762, cited in Raymond, 69-70, 113-4.

14 John Hall to William Smith, June 13, 1766, William Smith Papers, Hist. Soc. of Penn.

15 D. Allison, Esq., LL.D., "A General Return of the Several Townships in the Province of Nova Scotia, the first day of January, 1767," *Collections of the Nova Scotia Historical Society* (Halifax: 1891) Vol. VII, 69. The 1767 census return is also reproduced in Raymond, 114x. Total hempseed amounted to 64.75 bushels; total hemp fibre, 3,400 lbs. By comparison, flax yielded 1,716.5 bushels of seed and 42,250 pounds of fibre. Dr. Sumach advises that 1200 lbs. of hemp probably referred to the finished product, the ratio of finished rope to crude stalk being as

much as 1:10. Two people might have spent several hours per day for two weeks working up the raw hemp into 1200 lbs. of finished rope. The leftover tow was sold for shipbuilding, and woven into canvas or gunny. The gunny was stitched to make sacks—for coal, ore, grain, etc—or used as wrapping for cotton bales. Some of it may have been used to insulate houses.

16 A Return of the State of the Township of Hillsborough, January 1, 1770. (See MG 9, B10, M5219, Vol. 443, Bell Library, Mt. Allison University). For Benjamin Franklin and hemp, see Lopez, 43; see also Benjamin Franklin to Jared Eliot, July 16, 1747, Labaree, Vol. 3, 148. See also "Dr. Franklin's Answer to the Foregoing Report," on the "Settlement on the Ohio River," (ca. May 1, 1772), Smyth, Vol. V, 505; see also Sparks, Vol. IV, 351; compare Willcox, Vol. 19, 123-5. As noted previously, the Ohio report may have been composed by his two partners, Samuel Wharton and Thomas Walpole, with some factual information contributed by Franklin.

17 Charles A. Armour and Thomas Lackey, *Sailing Ships of the Maritimes* (Toronto: McGraw-Hill Ryerson Ltd., 1975) 10.

18 See Wright, *Samphire Greens*, 62, 72. W. H. Steeves, born May 20, 1814, died Dec. 9, 1873; represented Albert Co. in the New Brunswick House of Assembly, 1846-51; Surveyor General, 1854; delegate to the Charlottetown conference, 1864; Senator, 1867. See W. A. Spray, *Dictionary of Canadian Biography*, (Toronto: University of Toronto Press and Les Presses de l'université Laval, 1972) Vol. 10, 665-6. Compare *Steeves Family Register*, No. 63 (July 1985).

19 Roulac, 13.

20 Jack Herer, *The Emperor Wears No Clothes*, Chris Conrad, Lynn Osburn, Judy Osburn, Ellen Komp, eds. (Van Nuys: 1995) 23-32. See also Abel, 237-47. For the temporary re-emergence of hemp during the Second World War, see Raymond Evans, Brittain B. Robinson, *Hemp for Victory Video* (U. S. Dept. Agriculture, 1942); Herer, 120-3. See also "New Billion-Dollar Crop," *Popular Mechanics Magazine* (Feb., 1938) 238-9; "The Most Profitable and Desireable Crop that can be Grown," *Mechanical Engineering* (Feb. 26, 1937).

21 See "Factfile - Hemp," *New Internationalist* (Oxford: New Internationalist Publications) July, 2000, 4 where the figure is 25,000. A much lower estimate was revealed in my conversations with book author John Roulac, former Hempworld Magazine publisher Mary Kane, Hemp Industries Assoc. International Vice President Larry Duprey, and Canada's Hemp Future Studies Group director Dr. Alexander Sumach.

22 *Coffeeshop* has become the accepted euphemism for a bar or club which offers cannabis; one which serves coffee and alcoholic beverages is called a *koffie shop* or café. Joe Pauker, *Get Lost: The Cool Guide to Amsterdam*, (Amsterdam: Get Lost Publishing, 1997) 51. By 1999, there were as many as 1500 coffeeshops in Holland. See Robert J. MacCoun and Peter Reuter, "Does Europe Do It Better? Lessons From Holland, Britain and Switzerland," *The Nation*, Sept. 20, 1999 (New York: The Nation Company, L.P., 1999) 28. Hemp cultivation is encouraged and cannabis use is tolerated by several European governments including those of Holland, France, Italy, Germany and Spain, as well as of some countries in eastern Europe. Canada legalized industrial hemp in 1999.

Chapter 16 A Castle in the Sky

1 Georg Zobl, *Landeck auf alten Ansichtskarten*, Bücherreihe Auf alten Ansichten; James A. Brundage, Richard Lion Heart (New York: Charles Scribner's Sons, 1974) 108-136; 174-195.

2 See Rev. Allen Stewart Hartigan, M.A., *A Short Account of the Family of Eyre of Eyrecourt and Eyre of Eyreville in the County of Galway* (Dublin: Trinity College); also Steven Beckweth Ayres, *Genealogy of the Ayres Family* (New York City, 1902).

3 Elijah Ayer, born April 30, 1727, Norwich; son of Joseph and Dorothy (Bailey) Ayer; married[1] Content Werden, died 1749; married[2] Mar. 26, 1752 Abigail Merrill; died November 13, 1799; buried in the Four Corners/Tantramar Cemetery, Upper Sackville, N.B. Wright, *Planters and Pioneers*, 42-3. For Noah Steeves, see Wright, *The Steeves Descendants*, 466.

4 The ship's passenger list has never been found, and the exact date of George and Mary Dobson's arrival is still subject to some debate. Compare Howard Trueman, *The Chignecto Isthmus And Its First Settlers* (Toronto: William Briggs, 1902; repr. Mika Publishing Co., 1975) 245-7. See also W. C. Milner, "Records of Chignecto," *Collections of the Nova Scotia Historical Society* (Halifax: Wm. MacNab & Son, 1911) Vol. 15.

5 For the source of Bob's information, see www.mapquest.com.

Chapter 17 In the Neckar Valley

1 *Pennsylvania German Immigrants*, 3; see also William H. Gehrke, "Beginnings of Pennsylvania-German Element in Rowan and Cabarrus Counties, North Carolina," *Penn. Mag. Hist. & Bio.*, Vol. 58, 352, citing P. J. Bruns, *Geographisches Handbuch in Hinsicht auf Industrie und Handlung* (Leipzig: 1788) 117. Herr Deigendesch informs me that eighteenth-century Württemberg extended south only as far as the Danube. Today, Württemberg encompasses approximately 7,500 square miles. Pennsylvania's boundaries expanded numerous times after it was founded in 1682. By 1768, the area of the colony was approximately 30,000 square miles. See Munger, i.

2 *Pennsylvania German Immigrants*, 9, ix. The figure of 2000 immigrants includes only arrivals from Württemberg, not all of whom landed at Philadelphia. In 1749, at least twenty-two ships arrived in Philadelphia with an average of 308 passengers per vessel. Strassburger calculated the total number of passengers recorded for that year to be 6,787. He compiled lists of 324 ships between 1727 and 1775, with a total of more than 65,000 passengers. Strassburger & Hinke, Vol. 1, xxx-xxxii. Compare Abbot Emerson Smith, "Some New Facts about Eighteenth-Century German Immigration," *Pennsylvania History* (Pennsylvania Historical Association) Vol. X, No. 1 (June, 1943) 114-117.

3 Gottlieb Mittelberger, *Journey to Pennsylvania*, Oscar Handlin and John Clive, eds. & trans., (Cambridge: Belknap Press of Harvard University, 1960) 7. Mittelberger's work was originally published on his return to Württemberg, and first translated into English in 1898 as *Journey to Pennsylvania in the Year 1750 and Return to Germany in the Year 1754*, Carl Theo. Eben, trans. (Philadelphia: John Jos. McVey, 1898). The two translations are noticeably different. For the origins of the term Palatinate, see Sanford H. Cobb, *The Story of the Palatines: An Episode in Colonial History* (New York: G. P. Putnam's Sons, 1897) 22-5.

4 William Beidelman, *The Story of the Pennsylvania Germans* (Easton: Express Book Print, 1898; repub. Detroit: Gale Research, 1969) 20. See also Kuhns, 2-29.

5 Kuhns, 3, citing Gustav Freytag, *Bilder aus der deutschen Vergangenheit* (Leipzig, 1867) Vol. III, 115. Beidelman, 18.

6 Klees, 137-8. Pennypacker, *Pennsylvania in American History*, 198.

7 *Pennsylvania German Immigrants*, 156; see also Knittle, 5.

8 Klees, 138, quoting Franz Löher, *Geschichte und Zustände der Deutschen in Amerika* (Leipzig: beir. F. Rohler, & Cincinnati: Eggers, 1847) 42. See also Knittle, 4; Dubbs, 251.

9 Paul Kapff, *Schwaben in Amerika seit der Entdeckung des Weltteils* (Stuttgart: D. Gundert, 1893) quoted in *Pennsylvania German Immigrants*, 9-10.

10 *Pennsylvania German Immigrants*, 15. Compare Herrick, 170. Regarding the early years from 1683 to 1708, Herrick states: "The numerous appeals of Penn and his agents had slight immediate response, probably because they were looked upon with suspicion." After 1709, the influence of the *Neuländer* must be taken into account. See below.

11 *Pennsylvania German Immigrants*, 185.

12 *Pennsylvania German Immigrants*, 191-254, 203.

13 *Pennsylvania German Immigrants*, 185-8. A farrier was a smith who shoed horses; a cooper made barrels and casks.

14 *Pennsylvania German Immigrants*, 29, 117.

15 *Pennsylvania German Immigrants*, 56. Gajer has been identified as a stonecutter who prospered in Philadelphia from 1763 to 1772. Gary B. Nash, "Up From the Bottom in Franklin's Philadelphia," *The Private Side of American History* (New York: Harcourt Brace Javanovitch, Inc., 1975) 176.

16 *Pennsylvania German Immigrants*, 32-137.

17 Genealogist Terrence Punch, describing Irish immigration to Nova Scotia, states: "According to this model, people tend to follow the route taken by relatives, neighbours and friends to the new world, and to settle where possible near one another." Terrence M. Punch, "Finding Our Irish," *Nova Scotia Historical Review* (Halifax: Public Archives of Nova Scotia, 1986) Vol. 6, No. 1, 53.

18 *Pennsylvania German Immigrants*, 28. For a comparative look at eighteenth-century German agriculture in Europe, Pennsylvania, and Upper Canada, see Reaman, 126-136.

Chapter 18 A Travelling Shoemaker

1 D. H. Lawrence, *Movements in European History* (Oxford: Oxford University Press, 1981; orig. pub. 1921) 209.

2 See Roland H. Bainton, *Here I Stand: A Life of Martin Luther* (New York: New American Library, 1950). See also Kuhns, 3. For a divergent view, see Herbert J. Muller, *The Uses of the Past* (New York: Oxford University Press, 1952) 282-294.

3 See *Pennsylvania German Immigrants*, 10-11; Klees, 72-90; also Dubbs, 248-9.

4 The Stief Bible measures 27.5 cm. x 40.5 cm. x 12.5 cm., (11" x 16" x 5" thick) and weighs 5.23 kg. It today occupies an honourable place near the front door of the Moncton Museum/Le Musé de Moncton, where it is on extended loan from the Provincial Archives of New Brunswick. See also M. A. MacDonald, *Rebels & Royalists, The Lives and Material Culture of New Brunswick's Early English-Speaking Settlers 1758-1783* (Fredericton: New Ireland Press, 1990) 53. According to MacDonald, the Bible was identified by the American Bible Society as a 1747 Lutheran edition, printed by Johann Andre Endters in Nüremberg.

5 Dr. Wright discounted the Bible as evidence of Heinrich's religion, stating that the Bible contains only a "list of the names of the seven sons." Whether Dr. Wright was told this, or whether she examined the Bible herself is not known. From my examination, at any rate, the Bible contains only the names of Heinrich and his first three sons: Jacob, Johannes, and Christian. See Wright, *Samphire Greens*, 4, 82-3.

6 I am obliged to Dr. Rainer L. Hempel for elaborating on the subject of trade guilds in eighteenth-century Württemberg. Dr. Hempel believes that, in this case, a cattleherder's son could only have entered the shoemaker's guild through marriage.

7 Mittelberger adds: "They also raise good cattle, fast horses, and many bees. Sheep, bigger than those in Germany, generally produce two lambs a year. Almost everyone raises pigs and poultry, especially turkeys." Chickens were so plentiful that they roosted in the trees, and a tree loaded with fowl would often bow the branches to the ground. See Mittelberger, xiv, 48. For more on the subject of farming and home life in the German regions see Kuhns, 83-114.

8 Wright, *Samphire Greens*, 19. Compare two variations: "Well boys, we'd better go back to our turnip mush." Margaret Ells, "The Philadelphia Merchants and The Petitcodiac," *Nova Scotia Historical Review*, Vol. II, No. 2, 109; also "We'll go home and eat our turnip mush a while longer." "History of the Steeves Family," *The Moncton Transcript*, Jan. 8, 1966; reprinted Jul. 23, 1966. For an expanded discussion of mush and related dishes in Pennsylvania-German cuisine, see Don Yoder, *Discovering American Folklore, Studies in Ethnic, Religious and Regional Culture* (Ann Arbour: UMI Research Press, 1990) 131-2.

9 *The Royal Society for the Encouragement of Arts Manufactures and Commerce* (London: The Royal Society of Arts, 1938) 12-4. Founded in 1754, the society was variously called the Premium Society and the Society of Arts; not to be confused with the Royal Society, founded in 1660, whose membership comprised many scientists including Franklin. See Van Doren, 271; see also Bruce G. Wilson, ed., *Manuscripts and Government Records in the United Kingdom and Ireland Relating to Canada* (Ottawa: National Archives of Canada, 1992) 262, 268-9. For John Hughes's participation in the Premium Society, see Frank R. Lewis, "Benjamin Franklin and the Society of Arts, *Pennsylvania History* (University Park: Pennsylvania Historical Association, 1979) Vol. VI, No. 1 (Jan., 1939) 14-19. For Benjamin Franklin's interest in kohlrabi, see Van Doren, 429.

10 Wright, *Samphire Greens*, 70.

11 Revelation 12: 1-2, King James Version.

Chapter 20 In America

1 Donations to the Martinskirche steeple repair fund (in German Deutsche Mark) may be sent to Renovierung des Kirchturms der Martinskirche Münsingen, Karlstraße 32, 72525 Münsingen, Germany.

2 Sulpicius Severus, "The Life of St. Martin," *The Western Fathers*, F. R. Hoare, trans. & ed. (New York: Harper & Row, 1954) 12-44; 42-43. For Martin's dream, see Hoare, 14-5. See also Christopher Donaldson, *Martin of Tours: Parish Priest, Mystic and Exorcist* (London: Routledge & Kegan Paul, 1980). Omer Englebert, *The Lives of the Saints* (New York: David McKay Company, 1951) 429. Englebert adds that four thousand churches in France are dedicated to St. Martin.

3 Wright, *Samphire Greens*, 35.

4 Mittelberger, 14-5. See also Morison, 142. The ship *Osgood*, Captain William Wilkie, from Rotterdam and Cowes, arrived in Philadelphia on September 29, 1750, with 486 passengers. Ship list 157C, Strassburger & Hinke, Vol. 1, 445. Compare "Narrative of the Journey of the Schwenckfelders to Pennsylvania, 1733," *Penn. Mag. Hist. & Bio.*, Vol. 10, 167-179. During the Schwenckfelders three-month crossing, at least seven children and three adults died, and two children were born.

5 *Steuermessbuch von 1720*, Stadtarchiv Münsingen B 128.

6 The name Friderich Stief in Münsingen's *Steuermessbuch* appears as Georg Friedrich Stieff in Schalitdorf's *Famlien-Register*. The second name in German carries the same importance as the first name in English, thus explaining why the name Georg had been omitted in the first instance. The spelling variations of "Friedrich" and "Friderich" can be compared to the same variety one finds in contemporary English records. As Dr. Hempel has pointed out, Georg Friedrich Stieff's presence at the baptism, in Philadelphia, of Heinrich Stief's fourth son, Friederich, further confirms the family relationship. Michael apparently died young, for his widow's name appears in subsequent Münsingen land records. For Hans Jerg Stieff (Johann Georg Stieff) see Stief family genealogy, Appendix A.

7 In her comprehensive look at German settlements in Renfrew County, Ontario, Brenda Lee-Whiting describes seven classes in Canada's land-classification system, type one being the best land, types 4-6 marginal, and type 7 unsuitable for agriculture. Brenda Lee-Whiting, *Harvest of Stones* (Toronto: University of Toronto Press, 1985) 6-7. I have been unable to find any correlation between Canadian and German systems.

8 Christian Trites, born in Philadelphia, 1759[?]; died in Moncton, June 22, 1836; married Catherine Jones, born in Philadelphia, ca. 1766; died in Moncton, April 1, 1854. See "Family Roots of Jacob Trites," Lutz Mountain Meeting House. The couple are buried at the Moncton Free Meeting House; a brick from Christian's house is on display at the Moncton Museum. See descriptions of the house in Larracey, *The First Hundred*, 217-9; also Pincombe, Vol. 1, 97-9.

9 Don Yoder, introduction to *Pennsylvania German Church Records of Births, Baptisms, Marriages, Burials, Etc. From The Pennsylvania German Society Proceedings and Addresses* (Baltimore: Genealogical Publishing Co., 1983) Vol. 1, vi-vii. I am grateful to Terrence Punch for his subsequent translation of the Latin.

Chapter 21 A Walk on an Old Hill

1 I am grateful to Roland Deigendesch for supplying most of the facts noted, and to Marylee MacDonald for her subsequent collaborative interpretation of the 1820 sketch. Dr. and Frau Bütterlin supplied the facts relating to Württemburg's Coat of Arms.

2 *Begleiter durch die Martinskirche Münsingen* (Münsingen: Evangelische Kirchengemeinde Münsingen, 1998), with additional information provided by Sonja Bader.

3 Herr Deigendesch informs me that one source of music was a wind instrument called a *zinken*, periodically played from the church tower by an official called the *Stadtzinkenist*.

4 Stadtarchiv Münsingen B 15, Minutes of the Municipal Court Council for Justice and Administration, 1750, Stadtgesichtsprotokoll 1750, Folio 58-9. Ten Gulden or florin equalled 600 Kreuzer. According to Herr Deigendesch, a craftsman earned approximately 10 to 30 Kreuzer for one day's labour. A Bible might have cost two Gulden.

5 Stadtarchiv Münsingen B 15, Minutes of the Municipal Court 1750, Fol. 30-1.

6 Stadtarchiv Münsingen B 101, Kaufbuch 1735-1745.

Chapter 23 Journey to Another World

1 Beidelman, 17-8.

2 Mittelberger, 11; Klees, 142.

3 Mittelberger, 17. As noted above, a craftsman earned approximately 10 to 30 kreuzer for one day's labour (60 kreuzer equalled one florin). At the time, a book cost 10 to 30 kreuzer and a small house 200 florin. Mittelberger states that in Philadelphia a hen sold for 6 kreuzer, a pound of sugar for 10 kreuzer, a pound of rice for 3 kreuzer, and a bushel of salt for 15 kreuzer. A bushel of wheat sold for just under one florin, equivalent to 3 Philadelphia shillings. Mittelberger, 49-50, 66-7. For an in-depth discussion of transatlantic fares and currency ratios see Bell, 260-3; also A. E. Smith, 112-117. By comparison, the fare from Michael Lutz's Wertheim to Rotterdam was 8 1/2 florin. For children under fourteen years, the cost was half as much. At those rates, it would cost the typical family of a craftsman, his wife, and three children as much as five months wages to travel from Wertheim to Rotterdam. *Pennsylvania German Immigrants*, 178.

4 Faris, 140.

5 Mittelberger, 9, 26-32. Also spelled Newlander, and called *Zeilverkoopers* by the Dutch; see Herrick, 184; *Pennsylvania German Immigrants*, 166-74; Brigette Burkett, *Emigrants from Baden and Württemberg in the Eighteenth Century*, 2 Vols. (Camden: Picton Press, 1996) Vol. 1, xv-xvi.

6 See Middleton, 198, 344, who states that bondage was not always a regrettable experience, and that some emigrants benefited from the system. He estimates that almost 100,000 indentured servants came from Britain as well. See also Mittelberger, 17, 21; William T. Parsons, *The Pennsylvania Dutch: A Persistent Minority* (Boston: Twayne Publishers, 1976) 45; also Herrick, 174-80 and 186-94.

7 See Rainer L. Hempel, *New Voices on the Shores* (Toronto: German-Canadian Historical Assoc., 2000).

8 Although Cowes was "the favorite stopping place," other ports included Deal, Dover, Portsmouth, Gosport, Porte, Plymouth, and Falmouth. Ships also embarked from Amsterdam, Hamburg, London, and Lisbon. See Strassburger, Vol. 1, xxxiv.

9 Mittelberger, 12. One should keep in mind Oscar Kuhn's remark that of the "contemporaneous accounts of these abuses...Mühlenberg is the most temperate....Mittelberger the most lurid. The book of the latter must be read with a great deal of allowance." Kuhns, 77; see also Strassburger, Vol. 1, xxxiv-xxxv.

10 Morison, 141-2. Klees, 142. For typhus, see Knittle, 147.

11 "Narrative of the Schwenckfelders," 178.

12 Mittelberger, 13. Morison, 141-2.

13 Mittelberger, 13.

14 John Eagleson in Halifax to Rev. Dr. Alison in Philad., Oct. 23, 1767. American Philosophical Society, Vol. 47, Folio 42, cited in Wright, *Samphire Greens*, 9.

Epilogue

1 Yourcenar, 4.

2 *Taufbuch*, April 27[?], 1766, *St. Michaelis & Zion, Philadelphia* (Philadelphia: Genealogical Society of Pennsylvania, 1898) Vol. 36, 361. See also Humphrey, 429.

3 Johan Carl Schantz married Dec. 6, 1752, Margretha Lintzin; witnesses: Christoph Weber, Michael Lintz, Maria Barbara Copin. Sachse, Vol. 1, 610. I am grateful to Rev. Robyn Kulp and her colleagues at the Lutheran Archives Center at Philadelphia for advising me that Rev. Mühlenberg performed the baptism.

4 Apparently Rev. Mühlenberg was so overwhelmed by the excitement that he forgot to include the date in the baptismal entry. The subsequent entry in Mühlenberg's hand is dated April 27 (Sunday).

5 Johannes Schantz, born Aug. 23, 1753, baptized Dec. 16, 1754, son of Carl & Margaretha Schantz. *Taufbuch, St. Michael's Lutheran Church*, Germantown. It seems the parents acted as witnesses because the entry states the witnesses were "lui même." The baptismal record for Heinrich Schantz has not been found.

Appendix A

Stief Family Genealogy

First Generation

1. Hans Heinrich STIEF[1] Died October 6, 1699 in Münsingen. Occupation Stricker (Knitter). He married Anna. They had the following children:

    2   i.   Augustin STIEF
    3   ii.   Johan Heinrich STIEF
    4   iii.   Susanna Barbara STIEF
    5   iv.   Johan Heinrich STIEF
    6   v.   Georg Friedrich STIEF
    7   vi.   Ferdinand STIEF
    8   vii.   Anna Marie STIEF

Second Generation

2. Augustin STIEF[1] Born November 30, 1683 in Münsingen; died October 1761. Occupation Kälberhertin (Cowherd). He first married Anna Barbara WORNER.[3] Born 1683 in Ohnastetten;[5] died May 24, 1746 in Münsingen. They had the following children:

    9   i.   Johann Heinrich STIEF
    10   ii.   Michael STIEF
    11   iii.   Johan Georg STIEF
    12   iv.   Georg Friedrich STIEFF

He married 2nd Anna Barbara[2] HAUSEN, January 23, 1747 in Münsingen.

3. Johan Heinrich STIEF[1] Born January 1, 1685 in Münsingen; died July 20, 1685 in Münsingen.

4. Susanna Barbara STIEF[1] Born February 9, 1686 in Münsingen.

5. Johan Heinrich STIEF[1] Born May 21, 1687; died 1744 in Münsingen. Occupation Stricker (knitter). He married Maria Barbara.[2] They had the following children:

    13   i.   Anna Catharina STIEF
    14   ii.   Johann Heinrich STIEF
    15   iii.   Maria Barbara STIEF
    16   iv.   Johann STIEF
    17   v.   Augustin STIEF
    18   vi.   Lawrentius STIEF
    19   vii.   Johann Jacob STIEF

6. Georg Friedrich STIEF[1] Born January 31, 1690 in Münsingen.

7. Ferdinand STIEF[1] Born November 16, 1692 in Münsingen; died March 18, 1693 in Münsingen.

8. Anna Marie STIEF[1]

Third Generation

    2. Children of **Augustin** and **Anna Barbara STIEF**:

9. **Johann Heinrich STIEF** Born Circa 1720; died Circa 1778.[14] Buried in Hillsborough. Occupation Ziegler (Brickmaker). Resided in: Münsingen, Seissen, Philadelphia, Monckton, and Hillsborough. He married Regina STAHLEKER,[2] daughter of David STAHLEKER & Agnes WENER, February 25, 1745 in Münsingen. Born September 3, 1719 in Honau; died after August 21, 1782. Buried in Hillsborough. They had the following children:

20	i.	Katharina Barbara STIEF
21	ii.	Heinrich STIEF
22	iii.	Christina STIEF
23	iv.	Jacob STEVES
24	v.	John STEVES
25	vi.	Christian STEEVES
26	vii.	Frederick STEEVES
27	viii.	Henry STEEVES
28	ix.	Lewis STEEVES
29	x.	Matthias STEEVES

10. **Michael STIEF**[2] He married Barbara WALTER, January 11, 1746 in Münsingen.

11. **Johan Georg STIEF**[1]

12. **Georg Friedrich STIEFF**[6] Born 1712; arrived in Pennsylvania in 1753; died November 15, 1795 in Reading, PA. Occupation Farmer and shoemaker. He first married Maria Katharina HAUBENSACK, February 4, 1744 in Schlaitdorf. She was born April 6, 1712 in Schlaitdorf; died December 22, 1770[7] in Reading, PA. They had the following children:

30	i.	Regina STIEFF
31	ii.	Georg Friedrich STIEFF
32	iii.	Anna Maria STIEFF
33	iv.	Jacob Friedrich STIEFF
34	v.	Maria Katarina STIEFF

He married second Magdelena HELLER,[7] February 10, 1771 in Reading, PA. He married third Mrs. Elisabeth FUESS,[7] July 30, 1782 in Reading, PA.

5. Children of **Johan Heinrich** and **Maria Barbara STIEF**:

13. **Anna Catharina STIEF**[1] Born May 6, 1716 in Münsingen.

14. **Johann Heinrich STIEF**[1] Born July 13, 1717 in Münsingen; died March 27, 1767 in Münsingen.[3] He married Anna Maria.[3] They had the following children:

35	i.	Maria Barbara STIEFF Born June 14, 1749 in Münsingen; died Circa June 14, 1749.

15. **Maria Barbara STIEF**[1] Born April 1, 1720 in Münsingen; died April, 1743.

16. **Johann STIEF**[1] Born March 13, 1722 in Münsingen; died December 13, 1793[4] in Münsingen. Occupation Knitter. He married Rosina Barbara,[2] April 18, 1747 in Münsingen. Born July 6, 1723 in Münsingen; died October 27, 1809[4] in Münsingen. They had the following children:

36	i.	Elizabeth Catharine STIEF
37	ii.	Jacob Friderich STIEF
38	iii.	Johan Conrad STIEF
39	iv.	Johannes STIEF
40	v.	Joannes STIEF

17. Augustin STIEF[1] Born January 23, 1725 in Münsingen; died Circa January 23, 1725 in Münsingen.

18. Lawrentius STIEF[1] Born October 31, 1726 in Münsingen.

19. Johann Jacob STIEF[1] Born July 21, 1729 in Münsingen; died February 29, 1732 in Münsingen.

Fourth Generation
        9.   Children of **Johann Heinrich STIEF** and **Regina STAHLEKER**:

20. Katharina Barbara STIEF[1] Born July 28, 1745 in Münsingen.

21. Heinrich STIEF[8] Born July 5, 1747 in Seissen.

22. Christina STIEF[8] Born June 16, 1748 in Seissen.

23. Jacob STEVES Born November 14, 1749 in Philadelphia;[9] died October 9, 1803. Buried in Hillsborough. He married Anna Catharina LUTZ, daughter of Georg Michael LUTZ & Anna Walburga WIESSLER, Circa 1772. Born January 11, 1749[11] in Kreuzwertheim; died 1827. They had the following children:

        41   i.   'King' John STEEVES
        42   ii.   Leonard STEEVES
        43   iii.   Rachel STEEVES
        44   iv.   Nancy STEEVES
        45   v.   William STEEVES
        46   vi.   'Squire' George STEEVES

24. John STEEVES Born June 25, 1751[10] in Germantown, PA; died February 1, 1821 in Hillsborough. Buried in Hillsborough. He married Anna Margretha LUTZ, daughter of Georg Michael LUTZ & Anna Walburga WIESSLER, April 30, 1774. Born March 4, 1755[9] in Philadelphia; died January 2, 1828. They had the following children:

        47   i.   Michael STEEVES
        48   ii.   Rachel STEEVES
        49   iii.   Henry STEEVES
        50   iv.   David STEEVES
        51   v.   Abraham STEEVES
        52   vi.   John 'under-the-hill' STEEVES
        53   vii.   Katherine STEEVES
        54   viii.   Isaac STEEVES
        55   ix.   Thomas STEEVES
        56   x.   Joel STEEVES
        57   xi.   Stephen STEEVES

25. Christian STEEVES Born November 9, 1752[10] in Germantown, PA; died October 1820. He lived on the Monckton property with Frederick Steeves.[14] Christian married Rosanna TRITES, daughter of Jacob TREITZ & Elisina, Circa 1778. Born ca. 1753; died October 1820. They had the following children:

        58   i.   Henry STEEVES
        59   ii.   Rachel STEEVES
        60   iii.   Mary STEEVES
        61   iv.   Susanna STEEVES
        62   v.   Jacob STEEVES

63	vi.	Ann STEEVES
64	vii.	Christian STEEVES
65	viii.	Job STEEVES

26. Frederick STEEVES Born October 8, 1755[10] in Germantown, PA; died May 7, 1830[13] possibly in Salisbury. He first married Rachel SOMERS, daughter of Matthias SOMERS & Maria Christiana NULL, June 25, 1780.[10] She was born January 31, 1764;[10] died 1814. They had the following children:

66	i.	Andrew STEEVES
67	ii.	Hannah STEEVES
68	iii.	Lewis STEEVES
69	iv.	Moses STEEVES
70	v.	Reuben (Preston) STEEVES
71	vi.	Charles STEEVES
72	vii.	Joshua STEEVES
73	viii.	Rosanna STEEVES
74	ix.	Margaret STEEVES
75	x.	Ann (Nancy) STEEVES
76	xi.	Ephraim STEEVES
77	xii.	Daniel STEEVES

He married 2nd Rosanna RICKER, daughter of Jacob RICKER, January 16, 1816. Born ca. 1758.

27. Henry STEEVES Born Circa 1758; died May 1, 1826.[12] Buried in Hillsborough. He married Mary BECK, ca 1781, daughter of Martin BECK & Johanna[?]. Born 1761; died June 3, 1826. They had the following children:

78	i.	John (Cupboard) STEEVES
79	ii.	Martin STEEVES
80	iii.	Hannah STEEVES
81	iv.	James STEEVES
82	v.	Joseph STEEVES

28. Lewis STEEVES Born Circa 1760;[14] died March 15, 1827. Buried in Turtle Creek.[12] He married Elizabeth PORTER,[4] daughter of Samuel [?] PORTER. Born 1771; died January 17, 1850.[12] They had the following children:

83	i.	Margaret STEEVES
84	ii.	Miriam STEEVES
85	iii.	Samuel STEEVES
86	iv.	Rhoda STEEVES
87	v.	Frederick STEEVES
88	vi.	Susannah STEEVES
89	vii.	Rachel STEEVES
90	viii.	Lewis STEEVES
91	ix.	Elisha STEEVES
92	x.	John Enoch STEEVES
93	xi.	Elizabeth STEEVES
94	xii.	David STEEVES
95	xiii.	Abigail STEEVES
96	xiv.	Henry STEEVES
97	xv.	Arizena STEEVES

29. Matthias STEEVES Born Circa 1761; died May 12, 1848.[12] Buried in Hillsborough. He married Sophia BECK, daughter of Martin BECK & Johanna, Circa 1785. She was born 1768; died August 25, 1844. They had the following children:

98	i.	Aaron STEEVES
99	ii.	Jacob STEEVES
100	iii.	Alexander STEEVES
101	iv.	Elizabeth STEEVES
102	v.	William STEEVES
103	vi.	Annie STEEVES
104	vii.	Allan STEEVES
105	viii.	Charles STEEVES
106	ix.	Hannah STEEVES
107	x.	Simon STEEVES
108	xi.	Mansfield STEEVES
109	xii.	Mary STEEVES
110	xiii.	Matthias STEEVES

12. Children of **Georg Friedrich STIEFF** and **Maria Katharina HAUBENSACK**:

30. Regina STIEF[6] Born October 7, 1744 in Schlaitdorf. She married Jacob GRAFF,[7] April 16, 1765 in Reading, PA. They had the following children:

111	i.	Juliana GRAFF
112	ii.	Anna Catharina GRAFF
113	iii.	Jacob GRAFF
114	iv.	Johannes Michael GRAFF
115	v.	Maria Elizabeth GRAFF
116	vi.	Maria Magdalena GRAFF

31. Georg Friedrich STIEFF[6] Born January 23, 1746 in Schlaitdorf; died November 3, 1746 in Schlaitdorf.

32. Anna Maria STIEFF[6] Born December 9, 1747 in Schlaitdorf; died April 15, 1748 in Schlaitdorf.

33. Jacob Friedrich STIEFF[6] Born May 5, 1749 in Schlaitdorf; died February 26, 1751 in Schlaitdorf.

34. Maria Katarina STIEFF[6] Born May 22, 1751 in Schlaitdorf; died in Pennsylvania.

16. Children of **Johann STIEF** and **Rosina Barbara**:

36. Elizabeth Catharine STIEF[4] Born January 11, 1749.

37. Jacob Friderich STIEF[4] Born October 7, 1752; died March 30, 1792. Occupation Knitter. He married Maria Magdelena, May 12, 1778 in Münsingen. Born March 17, 1754; died June 20, 1810. They had the following children:

117	i.	Johan Friderich STIEF
118	ii.	Johannes STIEF
119	iii.	Rosina Catharina STIEF
120	iv.	Jacob STIEF
121	v.	Johann Friderich STIEF
122	vi.	Augustin STIEF

38. Johan Conrad STIEF[4] Born October 25, 1754; died June 16, 1828. He married Maria Catharina, May 9, 1779 in Münsingen. Born September 4, 1755; died September 17, 1827. They had the following children:

123	i.	Rosina Barbara STIEF
124	ii.	Joh. Conrad STIEF
125	iii.	Johan STIEF
126	iv.	Johann Conrad STIEF
127	v.	Johannes STIEF
128	vi.	Maria Catharina STIEF
129	vii.	Maria STIEF
130	viii.	Maria Magdalena STIEF
131	ix.	Maria Salome STIEF

39. Johannes STIEF[4] Born April 13, 1761; died December 29, 1763.

40. Joannes STIEF[4] Born December 29, 1763; died 1807.

Sources:

1. Martinskirche Lutheran Church (Münsingen) Register No. 502: Taufbuch (baptisms)1631-1736; Totenbuch (deaths)1631-1737.

2. Martinskirche Lutheran Church (Münsingen) Register No. 509: Ehebuch (marriages)1662-1785; Seelenreg (communion) 1661-1704.

3. Martinskirche Lutheran Church (Münsingen) Register No. 503:
Taufregster (baptisms) 1736-1785; Totenregster (deaths) 1736-1785; Konfirmandregstr 1745-1785.

4. Münsingen Famlien-Register.

5. Ohnastetten (Württemberg) Church Records. Information supplied by Bill Steeves.

6. Schlaitdorf Famlien-Register.

7. Jacqueline B. Nein & Gail H. Hesser, *Trinity Lutheran Church, Reading PA: Alphabetical compilation of baptisms, marriages, & deaths, 1751-1904* (1988).

8. Seissen (Württemberg) Church Records. Information supplied by Bill Steeves.

9. St Michael's and Zion Lutheran (Philadelphia) Church Records, Vol. XLVI (Philadelphia: Collections of the Genealogical Society of Pennsylvania, 1899).

10. St Michael's Evangelical Lutheran (Germantown) Church Records, Vol. XVI (Philadelphia: Collections of the Genealogical Society of Pennsylvania, 1896).

11. "The Lutz Books," Lutz Mountain Meeting House.

12. David F. Christopher, *Cemeteries of Albert County*.

13. William S. Hoar, *Steeves and Colpitts Pioneers of the Upper Petitcodiac*.

14. E. C. Wright, *The Steeves Descendants*.

Appendix B

Hughes Family Genealogy

First Generation
1. John HUGHES Sr. Born ca. 1640. Said to be buried at St David's Episcopal Church, "but no marked graves of the family are now to be found there." "The name Radnor was no doubt given by the early Welsh settlers in that vicinity in loving remembrance of the county of that name in Wales..." He married Jane EVANS. They had the following children:
    2   i.   Hugh HUGHES

Second Generation
2. Hugh HUGHES Born 1671 in Merionethshire, Wales. Occupation: tanner. Resided at Third Street, Philadelphia, and Walnut Grove, Upper Merion. He was an only child, and came to Pennsylvania in 1680 at the age of 9. He married Martha JONES, daughter of Hugh JONES & Martha, who resided in Lower Merion, Montgomery Co. They had the following children:
    3   i.   John HUGHES
    4   ii.   William HUGHES
    5   iii.   Sarah HUGHES
    6   iv.   Hugh HUGHES

Third Generation
3. John HUGHES Born 1712; died February 1, 1772 in Charles Town, SC. Occupation: Merchant, Assemblyman, Ironmaster, Collector of Customs. Resided at Philadelphia and Walnut Grove, Upper Merion. Baptised at Christ Church, PA: "John, ye son of Hugh and Sarah Hughes, baptized August ye 1, aged 3 weeks and 3 days, 1711." He married Sarah JONES, 1738. Born 1721; died October 1774. They had the following children:
    7   i.   Prudence HUGHES
    8   ii.   Jane HUGHES
    9   iii.   Hugh HUGHES
    10   iv.   Ruth HUGHES
    11   v.   John HUGHES Jr.
    12   vi.   Isaac HUGHES
    13   vii.   Catherine HUGHES
    14   viii.   James HUGHES

4. William HUGHES

5. Sarah HUGHES Married Peter DEHAVEN. Resided in Philadelphia. They had the following children:
    15   i.   Hugh DEHAVEN

6. Hugh HUGHES Born April 20, 1727 in Upper Merion. Resided in New Jersey in 1765; taught grammar school in New York in 1766; was a colonel in the Revolutionary army. He married Charity SMITH (nee PORTER), July 14, 1748 in New York.

Fourth Generation

7. Prudence HUGHES Born July 7, 1740.

8. Jane HUGHES Born June 15, 1741.

9. Hugh HUGHES Born September 7, 1742. Resided in New Jersey.

10. Ruth HUGHES Born November 16, 1743. She married Lindsay COATES, a Lawyer, May 1, 1765 in Christ Church, Philadelphia. They had the following children:
        16   i.   Ruth COATES
        17   ii.   Sarah COATES
        18   iii.   Mary COATES
        19   iv.   Lindsay COATES Jr.

11. John HUGHES Jr. Born December 14, 1745. He married Margaret PASCHALL, June 11, 1767. He was a partner in his father's store on Fourth St., Philadelphia.

12. Isaac HUGHES Born Circa December 1747; died April 26, 1782. He married Hannah HOLSTIEN, daughter of Matthias HOLSTIEN & Magdalena HULINGS, October 5, 1769. Born December 4, 1748; died June 13, 1832. Buried at Christ Swedes Church, Upper Merion. They had the following children:
        20   i.   Sarah HUGHES
        21   ii.   John HUGHES
        22   iii.   Rachel HUGHES
        23   iv.   Ruth HUGHES
        24   v.   Sarah HUGHES
        25   vi.   Hannah HUGHES

13. Catherine HUGHES Born June 29, 1750. She married Mr. PRITNER. They had the following children:
        26   i.   Elizabeth PRITNER

14. James HUGHES Born November 29, 1752.

15. Hugh DEHAVEN Born 1750. He married Sarah HOLSTIEN, daughter of Matthias HOLSTIEN & Magdalena HULINGS, April 27, 1775.

Source:

Anna M. Holstein, *Swedish Holsteins in America* (Norristown: M. R. Willis, 1892).

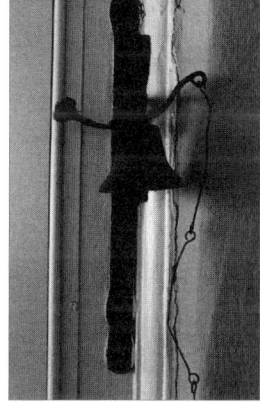

Colonial door bell at the house of John Hughes's grandson, in Upper Merion. November, 1999

Courtesy of Arthur Keyser

Appendix C

Hall Family Genealogy

First Generation
1. Joseph HALL.[1,2] Born February 11, 1686/1687,[2] son of Jacob Hall.[4] Died before June 17, 1731.[2] Occupation Brewer; land-owner; Vestryman in Trinity Church, Oxford.[1] Immigrated to Pennsylvania on the Amity.[4] Residence: Tacony, Oxford Township.[4] He married Rebecca RUTTER[1,2] daughter of Thomas RUTTER & Rebecca STAPLES, Circa 1707.[2] Born November 9, 1688.[2] They had the following children:

2	i.	Joseph HALL
3	ii.	Rebecca HALL
4	iii.	Theodore HALL
5	iv.	Thomas HALL
6	v.	Sarah HALL
7	vi.	Susannah HALL
8	vii.	Jacob HALL
9	viii.	John HALL
10	ix.	Hannah HALL
11	x.	Ruth HALL
12	xi.	Charlesworth HALL
13	xii.	Mary HALL

Second Generation
2. Joseph HALL[2] Born Circa 1707. Died 1743/1749. Occupation Tanner.[1] He married Mary FISHER,[2] daughter of Joseph FISHER, January 18, 1733.

3. Rebecca HALL[2] Born 1709. Died July 1, 1785. She first married Isaac LEECH, son of Toby LEECH & Esther ASHMEAD. Died December 10, 1744. She married 2nd. Rev. Richard TREAT, Minister of Abington Presbyterian Church, 1731-77.[6]

4. Theodore HALL[2] Born ca. 1710. Drowned in the Delaware River[6] ca. 1759. Residence Kingwood, Hunterdon Co., NJ. He married Gertrude GOODWIN,[2] April 29, 1729.

5. Thomas HALL[2] Died before 1742/1743.

6. Sarah HALL[2] Born 1717/1718. Died July 30, 1760. She married Rev. Samuel FINLEY, September 26, 1744. Died 1766. Occupation President of Princeton College.[1]

7. Susannah HALL[2] Born 1717/18. Died July 2, 1795. She married 1st. Joseph HARVEY, January 18, 1733. Died Circa 1735. She married 2nd. John RUSH, before 1743. Died 1751. They had the following children:

14	i.	Dr. Benjamin RUSH
15	ii.	Hon. Jacob RUSH
16	iii.	Rebecca RUSH

She married 3rd. Richard MORRIS, Circa 1755. Died 1771.

8. Jacob HALL[2] Born before 1720. Died 1783/1785. Occupation Capt. in Prov. Militia, 1748; Justice of the Peace.[1] He married 1st. Mary PARRY,[2] daughter of John PARRY & Hannah

ARMITAGE, before 1739. Born 1717.[3] Died August 26, 1762. They had the following children:

  17 i. Rebecca HALL
  18 ii. Jacob HALL, MD
  19 iii. Margaret HALL
  20 iv. Sarah HALL

He married 2nd. Harmina (DORLAND) WOOD,[2] April 3, 1768.

9. John HALL,[2] Born before 1722. Died ?1798. Occupation Iron Master; Capt. in Prov. Militia; blacksmith. Residence Byberry, Philad. Co.[1] "John Hall was a blacksmith and also ran a foundry in Philadelphia."[4] He married Sarah PERRY, daughter of John PARRY & Hannah ARMITAGE, May 28, 1747[2] in Trinity Church, Oxford. They had the following children:

  21 i. John HALL Christened October 16, 1748 in Trinity Oxford Church.
  22 ii. Rev. Thomas HALL[5] Born April 1750. Christened October 19, 1752 in Trinity Oxford Church. Died in Leghorn. Occupation Chaplain to British Colony at Leghorn ("accused of Tory sympathies") Resided in Virginia.
  23 iii. Mary HALL Born May 26, 1752. Christened October 19, 1752 in Trinity Oxford Church.
  24 iv. Martha HALL Born Circa December 18, 1754. Christened March 2, 1755 in Trinity Oxford Church. Died August 1759.

10. Hannah HALL[2] Born before 1727. Died before 1743.

11. Ruth HALL[2] Born before 1727. Died before August 7, 1794. She married 1st. Dr. Elisha HALL, son of Elihu HALL & Sarah HARRISON, May 27, 1746 in Trinity Church, Oxford. Died 1757? She married 2nd. Rev. James HUNT, before 1768. He was a school teacher and Presbyterian clergyman. Resided at Montgomery Co, MD; Rockville from 1761. Died June 2, 1793.

12. Charlesworth HALL[2] Born 1729/1730. Died before 1742/1743.

13. Mary HALL[2] Died before 1743.

Reference Notes:

Note 1
Josiah Granville Leach, LLB, *Chronicle of the Yerkes Family* (Philadelphia: J.B. Lippincott Co., 1904) 230-31.
Note 2
Dr. J. Hall Pleasants, "Hall Family of Tacony, Philadelphia County, Pennsylvania," *William and Mary Quarterly*, Series I, Vol. 22 (1913-1914) 134-9.
Note 3
Records of Trinity P.E. Church of Oxford, Philadelphia Co. (1711-1855).
Note 4
Daniel A. Graham, *Thomas Rutter I (c1660-1730) of Germantown, Pennsylvania, and the Birth of the Pennsylvania Iron Industry* (Aug, 1996) 21, 67.
Note 5
J. Hall Pleasants, MD, "Jacob Hall, Surgeon and Educator, 1747-1812," *Maryland Historical Magazine*, Vol. VIII, No. 3, Sept. 1913.
Note 6
John W. Jordan, LL.D., *Colonial and Revolutionary Families of Pennsylvania* (Baltimore: Genealogical Publishing Company, 1978,1911) Vol. 1.

Appendix D

The Twenty-two Philadelphia Proprietors

Following are the men named in Alexander McNutt's land grants at Frankfort and Monckton. One twelfth of the Monckton grant was reserved for Alexander McNutt, around whom was loosely organized the Philadelphia land syndicate. The remaining portion of the grant was allocated among four companies:[1]

1. Matthew Clarkson, Edward Duffield, Gerardus Clarkson, and John Naglee
2. Benjamin Franklin, Anthony Wayne, John Hughes, and John Cox Jr.
3. Isaac Caton, John Relfe, and James Caton
4. William Smith, Hugh Neil, Thomas Barton, William Moore, Joseph Richardson, John Hall, William Craig, Joseph Jacobs, John Bayley, Israel Jacobs, and Benjamin Jacobs

Matthew Clarkson was a prominent Philadelphia merchant and surveyor. In 1764, his grocery-and-dry-goods store, located on Second Street opposite the Baptist meeting house, stocked British herring, split peas, pickled walnuts, anchovies, onions, olives, nuts, dried fruit, chocolate, spices, spirits, beer, and tea.[2] Clarkson was part-owner of the schooner *Adventure*, Capt. Benj. Keen, registered at Philadelphia June 25, 1757, as well as the schooner *Experiment*, Capt. Jno. Wells, registered Nov. 2, 1758.[3] He was later the mayor of Philadelphia and served during the yellow fever epidemic in 1793.[4] Clarkson was in Halifax in the fall of 1765 with Anthony Wayne, "Mr. Jacobs," and "Capt. Caton," to obtain land grants from the Nova Scotia Council.[5] When John Hall (see below) accompanied their settlers up the Saint John's River in 1766, Clarkson asked Hall to take note of the condition of a private grant situated "between the Washademoak and Grand Lake."[6]

Gerardus Clarkson, brother of Matthew, was a medical doctor and a founder of the Philadelphia Medical Society. Both brothers were members of the American Philosophical Society.[7]

Edward Duffield was a Philadelphia clock and watchmaker. He was a friend of the Franklin family and an executor of Benjamin Franklin's will.[8]

John Naglee, or **Nagle**, may have been descended from the namesake of Naglee's Hill located on the road from Philadelphia to Germantown where a John Nagle lived in 1808.[9] In 1748, a silversmith of the same name lived at Front Street in Philadelphia.[10] He was possibly the assemblyman named John Naglee who received 284 votes in the 1750 Pennsylvania election.[11]

Benjamin Franklin (1706-1790) was, at various periods, a soldier, writer, printer, inventor, land speculator, philosopher, politician, and diplomat. He was an architect of the Declaration of Independence, and negotiated peace with England in 1783. Historian Leonard W. Labaree describes his Nova Scotia land dealings as "clouded in obscurity."[12]

Anthony Wayne (1745-1796) was a surveyor for the Philadelphia syndicate and land agent for John Hughes and Benjamin Franklin. He was afterwards a general under George Washington during the American Revolution, and was called "mad Anthony" by his troops.[13]

John Hughes (1712-1772) was a merchant, farmer, land owner, Judge of the Court of Common Pleas for Philadelphia, and member of the Pennsylvania Assembly from 1755 to 1765.[14] John Hughes, Jacob Hall, and John Hall (see below) were commissioned captains in the Pennsylvania militia in 1748.[15] On January 27, 1766, John Hughes and Anthony Wayne signed the Articles of Agreement with nine Pennsylvania farmers who were to settle at Monckton township. His store was probably located at 38 Fourth Street north of Market Street.[16]

John Cox Jr. sold general merchandise at his "store in Third Street, four doors above Market Street."[17] Three years previously, Cox's father advertised that his dry goods store in the same location was "now opening." John Cox Jr. may have been one of the "suffering traders" who petitioned London for redress after losses sustained in the French and Indian War.[18] John Cox attended the bedside resignation of John Hughes in October, 1765.[19] This same Cox was likely a member, in 1775, of the pre-Revolutionary "Committee of Safety" for Berks County, Pennsylvania, when he brought information to the committee's attention that William Walton "had drunk damnation to the Congress and uttered expressions derogatory to that Honorable Body and disrespectful to the present public measures."[20] The difficulty in distinguishing John Cox Jr. from other contemporaries named Cox or Coxe prompted historian William Willcox to label him a "mysterious figure."[21]

Isaac Caton was a ship's captain, possibly of the *Myrtella* which sailed from Philadelphia to London in Sept., 1764.[22] A year later, the ship *Myrtilla* arrived in Philadelphia during the Stamp Act crisis.[23] Isaac Caton went to Halifax in 1765 with Anthony Wayne and Benjamin Jacobs.[24] In 1765, Isaac and James Caton (see below) were granted 2000 acres of land at Long Reach plus the island in the St. John River which today bears their name.[25]

John Relfe was a Quaker merchant[26] who operated a dry-goods store on the south side of the Market Street wharf.[27] Relfe was one-third owner of the ship *Rachell*, Capt. Thomas Grant, registered at Philadelphia, Feb. 26, 1760, as well as part owner of at least two other vessels.[28] Relfe was Benjamin Franklin's neighbour in Philadelphia. He was declared a bankrupt while in London in 1767.[29]

James Caton was likely a relative of Isaac Caton[30] (see above).

William Smith (1727-1803) was a well-known educator, clergyman, and Provost of the College of Philadelphia (subsequently the University of Pennsylvania) from 1755 to 1791.[31] In addition to his interests in Nova Scotia, he had extensive land holdings in Pennsylvania.[32] Smith's long-standing quarrel with Benjamin Franklin cast a shadow on Pennsylvania politics for many years.

Rev. Hugh Neil was a Rector of Oxford (Episcopalian)[33] Church, Philadelphia. On March 26, 1761, he advertised for sale a sixty-three-acre plantation "convenient for the two Churches of Oxford and White Marsh."[34]

Rev. Thomas Barton (1730-1780) was a member of the Juliana Library Company and, in 1759, a Rector of St. James Episcopal Church in Lancaster, Pennsylvania. He married Esther Rittenhouse, a sister of astronomer David Rittenhouse who, in turn, married a sister of the three Jacobs brothers (see below).[35] Barton died a Loyalist in New York on May 25, 1780.[36]

William Moore, the son of Robert Moore of Moore Hall, held various public offices during his lifetime. He was a leading Anglican, a Proprietary Magistrate, and the father-in-law of William Smith.[37] In 1758, Smith and Moore were jailed by the Pennsylvania Assembly for libel.[38] Moore was a neighbour of the Wayne family of Waynesborough, PA, and was involved in a perennial feud with Anthony Wayne's father.[39] He was appointed to the first

United States Congress in 1777 but declined to serve.[40]

Joseph Richardson (1707-1770) was an army captain during the French and Indian War.[41] From 1763 to 1770, he was a political moderate in the Pennsylvania Assembly, but opposed Franklin's appointment as agent to London in 1764.[42] Richardson was half-owner of the fifty-ton brig *Greyhound*, Capt. Lester Faulkner, registered at Philadelphia Nov. 12, 1751.[43]

John Hall (1722?-1798?) was the son of Joseph and Rebecca (Rutter) Hall of Tacony. His brother Jacob Hall kept the Wheat Sheaf Inn near Frankford.[44] Their sister Susannah was the mother of Dr. Benjamin Rush, noted Philadelphia physician and a signer of the Declaration of Independence. In 1748, the Hall brothers were appointed Captains in the Pennsylvania militia.[45] John Hall accompanied the Philadelphia settlers to The Petitcodiac River in 1766.

William Craig was possibly the Lieutenant of the same name who fought at the Battle of Three Rivers in Canada during the American Revolution.[46] In 1765, Craig owned land "over the Blue Mountain."[47] He was a manager of the Philadelphia Almshouse in 1776.[48]

Joseph Jacobs was a Philadelphia merchant. In addition to his interest in Monckton township, Jacobs was a proprietor, in 1768, of the Philadelphia township on Minas Basin.[49]

John Bayley, with John Hughes, was a charter member of the Union Library Company of Philadelphia, founded in 1746.[50] A Quaker, Bayley was described as "broke" by 1770.[51]

Israel Jacobs lived at Elbow Lane, Philadelphia, where Matthew Clarkson (see above) called the proprietors of Monckton township to meet on Feb. 14, 1766[52] Jacobs was a member of the second United States Congress.[53] He owned the White Horse tavern, located near Market St. and Elbow Lane.[54]

Benjamin Jacobs was a surveyor and an associate judge of the Court of Common Pleas.[55] In 1775, he was a member of the Committee of Safety for Philadelphia County.[56] He was likely the same Jacobs who accompanied Clarkson, Wayne, and Caton (see above) to Halifax in the fall of 1765. Brothers Joseph (b. 1728), Israel (b. 1726), and Benjamin (b. 1731) were the sons of John Jacobs Jr., a Quaker descendant. Their sister Hannah (b. 1735) married David Rittenhouse, whose own sister married Thomas Barton (see above).[57]

The eight members of Alexander McNutt's land syndicate who signed the Philadelphia non-importation agreements in 1765:[58]
    Joseph Richardson
    William Craig
    John Bayly
    John Relfe
    William Moore
    John Cox Jr.
    Joseph Jacobs
    John Hughes

Sources:

1 Gov. Montague Wilmot, "Nova Scotia Land Grant," Oct. 31, 1765. Nova Scotia Crown Land Office, Book 7, 98. See also Margaret Ells, "The Philadelphia Merchants and The Petitcodiac," 105; Wright, *The Petitcodiac*, 38; Compare Labaree, Vol. 12, 348-9 where the name John Naglee is omitted.

2 *Pennsylvania Journal*, Oct. 25, 1764.

3 "Ship Registers for the Port of Philadelphia, 1726-1775," *Penn. Mag. Hist. & Bio.*, Vol. 26, 128, 140.

4 J. H. Powell, *Bring out Your Dead* (New York: Time Inc., 1949).

5 Anthony Wayne to John Hughes, Oct. 7, 1765, Hughes Papers, Hist. Soc. of Penn.; cited in Pincombe, 55.

6 Wright, *St. John River*, 106.

7 Sawtelle, 274; Labaree, Vol. 12, 274n. See Clarkson family biography and genealogy in "Memoirs of Matthew Clarkson of Philadelphia, 1735-1800 by his great-grandson, John Hall; and of His Brother, Gerardus Clarkson 1737-1790 by his Samuel Clarkson." (1890) in Walter W. Spooner, ed., *Historic Families of America* (New York: n.d.).

8 Watson, Vol. 1, 533; Labaree, Vol. 7, 211n; Vol. 13, 198n; Mary Parry, "Philadelphia Clockmakers," *Penn. Mag. Hist. & Bio.*, Vol. 56, 225-27. See also Rev. Edward Duffield, "Rev. Jacob Duché, the First Chaplin of Congress," *Penn. Mag. Hist. & Bio.* Vol. 2, 61-2n.

9 Ward, 241-3.

10 "Extracts of the Diary of Jacob Hiltzheimer of Philadelphia, 1768-1798," *Penn. Mag. Hist. & Bio.*, Vol. 16, 93.

11 Scharf & Westcott, 218.

12 Labaree, Vol. 11, 186n.

13 Nelson, 1; Shackleton, 329.

14 Charles Henry Hart, ed., "Letters from William Franklin," 442n.

15 Scharf & Westcott, Vol. 1, 215.

16 Roach, 162.

17 *Pennsylvania Journal*, Nov. 5, 1767.

18 Willcox, Vol. 15, 265n; Vol. 16, 116n.

19 *Pennsylvania Journal*, Sept. 4, 1766.

20 "Minutes of the Committee of Safety," Dec. 26, 1775; Jan 6, 1776. *Penn. Mag. Hist. & Bio.*, Vol. 15, 270-3.

21 Willcox, Vol. 16, 116n.

22 "Notes and Queries," *Penn. Mag. Hist. & Bio.*, Vol. 6, 251; also *Pennsylvania Journal*, Sept. 6, 1764.

23 Sept. 21, 1765, Labaree, Vol. 12, 270n.

24 Wayne to John Hughes, Aug. 5, 1765, John Hughes Papers; Caton to Jacobs and Wayne, Aug. 15, 1765, Anthony Wayne Papers, Vol. 1, Hist. Soc. of Penn.

25 Wright, *St. John River*, 82. See also James Andrew Fraser, *A History of Caton's Island* (Chatham: Miramichi Historical Society, 1967) 25-7.

26 Bridenbaugh, 182.

27 *Pennsylvania Journal*, Aug. 16, 1764.

28 "Ship Registers," Vol. 26, 472.

29 Labaree, Vol. 14, 279n; Vol. 7, 276n.

30 See Wright, *St. John River*, 82.

31 Labaree, Vol. 4, 467-9n; Hart, 420, 415, 425-6.

32 Bertha Sprague Fox, "Provost William Smith and His Land Investments in Pennsylvania," *Pennsylvania History*, Vol. VIII, No. 3—June, 1941, 189-209. No mention is made of Monckton township.

33 Thayer, 91.

34 Mendenball, 119.

35 Hon. Charles I. Landis, "The Juliana Library Company in Lancaster," *Penn. Mag. Hist. & Bio.*, Vol. 43, 240.

36 Marvin F. Russell, "Thomas Barton and Pennsylvania's Colonial Frontier," *Pennsylvania History* (University Park: Pennsylvania Historical Association, 1979) Vol. XLVI, No. 4—Oct. 1979, 333.

37 Robert Lawson-Peebles, "William Moore," *American National Biography* (Oxford: Oxford University Press, 1999) Vol. 15, 788-9. See also Thayer, 63-4; 68-71.

38 Hanna, 134-6.

39 Tucker, 22.

40 "Diary of James Allen, Esq., of Philadelphia, Counsellor-at-Law, 1770-1778," *Penn. Mag. Hist. & Bio.*, Vol. 9, 279.

41 Samuel W. Pennypacker, "Anthony Wayne," *Penn. Mag. Hist. & Bio.*, Vol. 32, 259.

42 Labaree, Vol. 11, 526n.

43 "Ship Registers for the Port of Philadelphia, 1726-1775," *Penn. Mag. Hist. & Bio.*, Vol. 25, 268. See also Labaree, Vol. 11, 526n.

44 Labaree, Vol. 14, 291. See also Gregory B. Keen, "The Descendants of Jöran Kyn, the Founder of Upland," *Penn. Mag. Hist. & Bio.*, Vol. 4, 243, 353, 355; Josiah Granville Leach, LL.B, *Chronicle of the Yerkes Family* (Philadelphia: J. B. Lippincott Co., 1904) 230-31; Dr. J. Hall Pleasants, "Hall Family of Tacony, Philadelphia County, Pennsylvania," *William and Mary Quarterly*, Series I, Vol. 22 (1913-1914) 134-5; John W. Jordan, *Colonial and Revolutionary Families of Pennsylvania* (Baltimore: Genealogical Publishing Company, 1978; orig. pub. Lewis Publishing Company, 1911) Vol. 1, 441-3.

45 Scharf & Westcott, Vol. 1, 215.

46 Mrs. Harry Rogers and Mrs. A. H. Lane, "Pennsylvania Pensioners of the Revolution," *Penn. Mag. Hist. & Bio.*, Vol. 42, 267.

47 "John Okley to Abel James," June 21, 1765, *Penn. Mag. Hist. & Bio.*, Vol. 18, 267.

48 Robert J. Hunter, MD., "The Origin of the Philadelphia General Hospital," *Penn. Mag. Hist. & Bio.* Vol. 57, 46-7. See also *Pennsylvania Gazette*, Oct. 23, 1760 and Mar. 17, 1763.

49 "Notes and Queries," *Penn. Mag. Hist. & Bio.*, Vol. 13, 254. See also Hon. Samuel W. Pennypacker, LL.D., "Bebber's Township and the Dutch Patroons of Pennsylvania," *Penn. Mag. Hist. & Bio.*, Vol. 31, 4.

50 E. V. Lamberton, "Colonial Libraries of Pennsylvania," *Penn. Mag. Hist. & Bio.* Vol. 42, 195, 196n. See also *Pennsylvania Gazette*, Oct 11, 1783.

51 Bridenbaugh, 182.

52 *Pennsylvania Gazette*, Feb. 6, 1766, cited in Sawtelle, 276n (erroneously cited as 1776).

53 Pennypacker, "Bebber's Township," 4.

54 *Pennsylvania Gazette*, Feb. 6, 1766, cited in Sawtelle, 276n; *Penn. Mag. Hist. & Bio.*, Vol. 37, 113-4.

55 Wm. H. Egle, "The Constitutional Convention of 1776, Biographical Sketches of its Members." *Penn. Mag. Hist. & Bio.*, Vol. 3, 444.

56 Pennypacker, "Bebber's Township," 4.

57 J. Smith Futhey and Gilbert Cope, *History of Chester County, Pennsylvania* (Philadelphia: Louis H. Everts, 1881) 612.

58 Scharf & Westcott, Vol. 1, 272-3.

Bibliography

Abbreviations

    American Philosophical Society: Amer. Phil. Soc.

    Historical Society of Pennsylvania: Hist. Soc. of Penn.

    Nova Scotia Archives and Records Management: NSARM

    Pennsylvania Magazine of History and Biography: Penn. Mag. Hist. & Bio.

    Provincial Archives of New Brunswick: PANB

Unpublished Works

"A Return of the State of the Township of Hillsborough, January 1, 1770"

Brown, Marion Steelman Hughes, "Earliest Record of Ancestors: Hughes" (Lancaster Historical Society)

Collections of the American Philosophical Society, Philadelphia: Franklin Papers

Collections of the Historical Society of Pennsylvania, Philadelphia: Anthony Wayne Papers, Vol. 1; "Genealogy of David and Letitia Jones" ; Jacobs Papers; "James J. Levick Collection"; John Hughes Papers; "Jones Bible Records"; "Jones Family notes"; Lea C. Steeves, "The Steeves Family"

Colonial Office Records, 1766, CO 217, Vols. 23 & 44

Emberley, Geneva Jones, "Descendants of Charles Jones of N.B. from 1766 and Ellis Descendants from 1739" (1977) (Lutz Mountain Museum)

"Esther Clark Wright Papers" (Acadian University Archives)

"Family Roots of Jacob Trites." (Lutz Mountain Museum)

Famlien-Register Schlaitdorf (Wendelinkirche)

"History of the Steeves [written 1907]" (PANB)

Leon Parkin Steeves, "Early Settlement of the Steeves Family in New Brunswick" (PANB)

Morris, Charles, "Description of the Harbour and River of Saint John's in Nova-Scotia...25th of January, 1768"

Münsingen Ehebüch, Totenregister, Taufregister, Famlien-Register (Martinskirche)

Robb, Fraser, "Steeves Family Early Pioneers of Albert" (PANB)

Society for the Propagation of the Gospel in Foreign Parts, Public Archives of Canada, B-25, No. 186 (MG 17, B 1/1, Vol. 2); Letters Received, B-25, Nova Scotia, "C" Series 1752-1858 (MG 17, B.1 to B 1/1 fo. 1-27-)

Stadtarchiv Münsingen B 15, Minutes of the Municipal Court

Steward's Book, Sept. 12, 1790, "Trueman Family Papers," (Ralph Picard Bell Library, Mt. Allison University)

Wayne Family Papers (Waynesborough, Paoli, PA)

William Smith Papers (University of Pennsylvania)

Published Works

"A letter from John Hughes, Esq. to the Commissioners of the Stamp office in London, Philadelphia, Oct. 12, 1765," Supplement to the *Pennsylvania Journal*, Sept. 4, 1766

"A Remarkable Record in Provincial History," *Saint John Sun*, ca. March 1, 1893

Abel, Ernest L., *The First Twelve Thousand Years* (New York: Plenum Press, 1980)

Akagi, Roy Hidemichi, PhD., *The Town Proprietors of the New England Colonies* (Philadelphia: University of Pennsylvania, 1924; repub. Gloucester: Peter Smith, 1963)

Akins, Thomas, *History of Halifax City* (Belleville: Mika Publishing, 1973; orig. pub. Nova Scotia Historical Society, 1895)

Akins, Thomas, ed., *Nova Scotia Archives: Selections from the Public Documents of the Province on Nova Scotia* (Halifax: Charles Annand, 1869)

Aldridge, Alfred Owen, *Benjamin Franklin: Philosopher & Man* (Philadelphia: J. B. Lippincott Company, 1965)

Allison, D., Esq., LL.D., "A General Return of the Several Townships in the Province of Nova Scotia, the first day of January, 1767," *Collections of the Nova Scotia Historical Society* (Halifax: 1891) Vol. VII

Andrews, Peter, "Genealogy: The Search for a Personal Past," *American Heritage* (New York: American Heritage Publishing Co.) Aug./Sep., 1982; Vol. 33, No. 5

Armour, Charles A. and Thomas Lackey, *Sailing Ships of the Maritimes* (Toronto: McGraw-Hill Ryerson Ltd., 1975)

Armstrong, Maurice W., *The Great Awakening in Nova Scotia 1776 - 1809* (Hartford: The American Society of Church History, 1948)

Arsenault, Bona, *History of the Acadians* (Montréal: Leméac, 1978; orig. pub. *Histoire et généalogie des acadiennes*, Book 2)

Atlas of Early American History, Lester J. Cappin, editor-in-chief (Princeton: Princeton University Press, 1976)

Ayres, Steven Beckweth, *Genealogy of the Ayres Family* (New York City, 1902)

Babineau, René, *Brief History of Acadia*, 1604-1992, (1992)

Bainton, Roland H., *Here I Stand: A Life of Martin Luther* (New York: New American Library, 1950)

Baker, William S., "The Itinerary of General Washington, 1777," *Penn. Mag. Hist. & Bio.*, Vol. 14

Barker, Charles R., "The 'Old Dutch Church' in Lower Merion," *Bulletin of the Historical Society of Montgomery County Pennsylvania* (Norristown, Oct. 1954) Vol. IX, No. 3

Barnwell, James G., "Some of the Alleys, Courts and Inns of Philadelphia, 1767-1790," *Penn. Mag. Hist. & Bio.* (Philadelphia: Hist. Soc. of Penn.) Vol. 37

Bean, Theodore W., ed. *History of Montgomery County* (Philadelphia: Everts & Peale, 1884) Vol. 2

Begleiter durch die Martinskirche Münsingen (Münsingen: Evangelische Kirchengemeinde Münsingen, 1998)

Beidelman, William, *The Story of the Pennsylvania Germans* (Easton: Express Book Print, 1898: repub. Detroit: Gale Research, 1969)

Bell, Winthrop Pickard, *The "Foreign Protestants" and the Settlement of Nova Scotia* (Toronto: University of Toronto Press, 1961)

Betts, Dickey, "In Memory of Elizabeth Reed," *Idlewild South*, The Allman Brothers Band (New York: Atlantic Recording Corporation/ATCO Records, 1970)

Bining, Arthur C., *Pennsylvania Iron Manufacture in the Eighteenth Century* (New York: Augustus M. Kelley, 1970: orig. pub. 1938)

Blakeley, Phyllis R., "Alexander McNutt," *Dictionary of Canadian Biography* (Toronto: University of Toronto Press; Les Presses de l'université Laval) Vol. 5

Blum, John M., Bruce Catton, Edmund S. Morgan, Arthur M. Schlesinger, Jr., Kenneth M. Stampp, C. Vann Woodward, eds., *The National Experience: A History of the United States* (New York: Harcourt, Brace & World, Inc., 1963)

Botsford, Bliss, "The Pioneers of Westmorland," *The Daily Times* (Moncton) Jan. 19, 1885

Bouchette, Joseph, *The British Dominions in North America; or a Topographical and Statistical Description of the Provinces of Lower and Upper Canada, New Brunswick, Nova Scotia, The Islands of Newfoundland, Prince Edward, and Cape Breton* (London: Colburn & Bentley, 1831; repub. New York: AMS Press, 1968) Vol. 2

Bowser, Les, "The Signature(s) of Heinrich Stief," *Generations* (Fredericton: New Brunswick Genealogical Society, 1999) Vol. 21, No. 2 (Summer, 1999)

Brebner, John Bartlet, *Neutral Yankees of Nova Scotia* (McClelland and Stewart Limited, Carleton Library, No. 45, 1969; orig. pub. New York: Columbia University Press, 1937)

Brebner, John Bartlet, *North Atlantic Triangle* (McClelland and Stewart Limited, Carleton Library No 30, 1966)

Bridenbaugh, Carl and Jessica, *Rebels and Gentlemen* (New York: Reynal & Hitchcock, 1942)

Browning, Charles H., *Welsh Settlements of Pennsylvania* (Baltimore: Genealogical Publishing Company, 1967)

Bruce, William Cabell, *Benjamin Franklin Self-Revealed* (New York: G. P. Putnam's Sons, 1917) Vol. 1

Brundage, James A., *Richard Lion Heart* (New York: Charles Scribner's Sons, 1974)

Bruns, P. J., *Geographisches Handbuch in Hinsicht auf Industrie und Handlung* (Leipzig: 1788)

Burkett, Brigette, *Emigrants from Baden and Württemberg in the Eighteenth Century*, 2 Vols. (Camden: Picton Press, 1996)

Buxbaum, Melvin H., *Benjamin Franklin and the Zealous Presbyterians* (University Park: Pennsylvania State Press, 1975)

Casgrain, Abbé H. R., *Wolfe and Montcalm* (University of Toronto Press, 1964; orig. pub. 1905)

Canada and its Provinces (Toronto: Glasgow, Brook & Company, 1914) Vol. 23

Christopher, David, *Cemeteries of Albert County New Brunswick* (Riverview: 1988)

Clarke, Ernest A., "Cumberland Planters and the Aftermath of the Attack on Fort Cumberland," Margaret Conrad, ed. *They Planted Well: New England Planters in Maritime Canada* (Fredericton: Acadiensis Press, 1988)

Clarke, Ernest A., *The Siege of Fort Cumberland, 1776: An Episode in the American Revolution* (Montréal: McGill-Queens University Press, 1995)

Cobb, Sanford H., *The Story of the Palatines: An Episode in Colonial History* (New York: G. P. Putnam's Sons, 1897)

Conroy, David W., *In Public Houses: Drink and the Revolution of Authority in Colonial Massachusetts* (Chapel Hill: University of North Carolina Press, 1995)

Cormier-Boudreau, Marielle and Melvin Gallant, *A Taste of Acadia* (Fredericton: Goose Lane Editions, 1991); orig. publ. *La Cuisine Traditionnelle en Acadie* (Moncton: Editions d'Acadie, 1978)

Crane, Elizabeth Forman, ed., *The Diary of Elizabeth Drinker* (Boston: Northeastern University Press, 1991) Vol. 1

Crowley, Thos., Feb. 24, 1766, "American Politics Discussed in Commercial Letters, 1764-1766," *Penn. Mag. Hist. & Bio.*, Vol. 17

Cunningham, Caroline, *Jones Records*, Vol. I, Pennsylvania Marriages (Hist. Soc. of Penn.)

Debard, Marc, "The Family Origins of Joseph Frederick Wallet DesBarres: A Riddle Finally Solved," *Nova Scotia Historical Review*, Vol. 14, No. 2 (Halifax: Public Archives of Nova Scotia, 1994)

DesBarres, Joseph F. W., *The Atlantic Neptune* (London: 1775-81)

Dexter, Franklin B., ed., *Literary Diary of Ezra Stiles* (New York: 1901)

"Diary of James Allen, Esq., of Philadelphia, Counsellor-at-Law, 1770-1778," *Penn. Mag. Hist. & Bio.*, Vol. 9

Dickason, Olive Patricia, *Canada's First Nations: A History of Founding Peoples from Earliest Times* (Toronto: McClelland & Stewart, 1992)

Dickinson, Alice, *The Stamp Act* (New York: Franklin, Watts, 1970)

Dickson, Katharine, *Downeast Dicksons* (Henniker: 1987)

Diffenderffer, Frank Reid, *The German Immigration Into Pennsylvania, Through the Port of Philadelphia from 1700-1775* (Baltimore: Genealogical Publishing Co., 1988; orig. publ. 1900)

Dobson, Shirley, *Methodism at the Bend and the Free Meeting House* (1989)

Doerflinger, Thomas M., *A Vigorous Spirit of Enterprise* (Williamsburg: Institute of Early American History and Culture, 1986)

Donaldson, Christopher, *Martin of Tours: Parish Priest, Mystic and Exorcist* (London: Routledge & Kegan Paul, 1980)

Draper, Theodore, *A Struggle for Power: The American Revolution* (Toronto: Random House, 1996)

Drayton, Michael, *Polyolbion*, xviii, J. William Hebel, ed. (Oxford: Basil Blackwell & Mott, Ltd., 1961) Vol. IV

Duane, William, ed., *Letters to Benjamin Franklin from his Family and Friends*, 1751-1791 (Freeport: Books for Libraries Press, 1858)

Dubbs, Joseph Henry, "The Founding of the German Churches of Pennsylvania," *Penn. Mag. Hist. & Bio.*, Vol. 17

Duffield, Rev. Edward, "Rev. Jacob Duché, the First Chaplin of Congress," *Penn. Mag. Hist. & Bio.*, Vol. 2

Dunaway, Wayland Fuller, Ph.D., *A History of Pennsylvania* (New York: Prentice-Hall, 1935)

Dunn, Richard S. and Mary Maples Dunn, *The Papers of William Penn* (Philadelphia: University of Pennsylvania Press, 1982) Vol. 2

Dunkling, Leslie Alan, *First Names First* (Detroit, Gale Research Co., 1977)

Eaton, A. W. H. "Alexander McNutt, the Colonizer," *Americana*, Vol. 8, No. 12 (Dec, 1913)

Eaton, E. L., "The Dyke Lands," *Nova Scotia Historical Quarterly* (Halifax: Public Archives of Nova Scotia) Vol. 10, Nos. 3 & 4 (December, 1980)

Egle, Wm. H., "The Constitutional Convention of 1776, Biographical Sketches of its Members." *Penn. Mag. Hist. & Bio.*, Vol. 3

Elliot, Shirley B., *Legislative Assembly of Nova Scotia* (Province of Nova Scotia, 1984)

Ells, Margaret, "Clearing the Decks for the Loyalists," *The Canadian Historical Association Report* (Ottawa, 1933)

Ells, Margaret, "Explanatory Note to 'Clearing the Decks for the Loyalists,'" *The Canadian Historical Association Report* (Ottawa, 1934)

Ells, Margaret, "Loyalist Attitudes," *Historical Essays on the Atlantic Provinces*, G. A. Rawlyk, ed. (Carleton Library No. 35, McClelland and Stewart Ltd., 1967)

Ells, Margaret, "The Philadelphia Merchants and The Petitcodiac," *Nova Scotia Historical Review*, Vol. II, No. 2

Englebert, Omer, *The Lives of the Saints* (New York: David McKay Company, 1951)

Evans, Raymond and Brittain B. Robinson, *Hemp for Victory* [Video] (U. S. Dept. Agriculture, 1942)

"Extracts of the Diary of Jacob Hiltzheimer of Philadelphia, 1768-1798," *Penn. Mag. Hist. & Bio.*, Vol. 16

"Factfile - Hemp" *New Internationalist* (Oxford: New Internationalist Publications) July, 2000

Faris, John T., *Old Churches and Meeting Houses in and Around Philadelphia* (Philadelphia: J. B. Lippincott Co., 1926)

Fleming, Thomas, ed., *Benjamin Franklin: A Biography in His Own Words*, The Founding Fathers series, 2 Vols. (New York: Newsweek, 1972)

Fox, Bertha Sprague, "Provost William Smith and His Land Investments in Pennsylvania," *Pennsylvania History* (University Park: Pennsylvania Historical Association, 1941) Vol. VIII, No. 3—June, 1941

Fraser, James Andrew, *A History of Caton's Island* (Chatham: Miramichi Historical Society, 1967)

Freytag, Gustav, *Bilder aus der deutschen Vergangenheit* (Leipzig, 1867) Vol. III

Futhey, J. Smith and Gilbert Cope, *History of Chester County, Pennsylvania, with Genealogical and Biographical Sketches* (Philadelphia: Louis H. Everts, 1881)

Ganong, William F., "A Monograph of the Cartography of the Province of New Brunswick," *Transactions of the Royal Society of Canada* (Second Series) Vol. 3 (1897)

Ganong, William F., "Place-Nomenclature of New Brunswick," *Transactions of the Royal Society of Canada* (Second Series) Vol. 2 (1896)

Gegenheimer, Albert F., *William Smith Educator and Churchman 1727-1803* (Philadelphia, 1943)

Gehrke, William H., "Beginnings of Pennsylvania-German Element in Rowan and Cabarrus Counties, North Carolina," *Penn. Mag. Hist. & Bio.*, Vol. 58

Gesner, Abraham, *New Brunswick; with Notes for Emigrants* (London: Simmonds & Ward, 1847)

Gipson, Lawrence Henry, *The British Empire before the American Revolution*, 15 Vols. (New York: Alfred A, Knopf, 1936 - 1970) Vols. 6 & 10

Gleason, Philip J. "A Scurrilous Colonial Election and Franklin's Reputation," *William and Mary Quarterly* (Williamsburg: Institute of Early American History and Culture) Vol. 18 (1961)

Gordon, Lord Adam, "Journal of an Officer who Travelled in America and the West Indies in 1764 and 1765," Newton D. Mereness, ed., *Travels in the American Colonies*, 1690-1783 (New

York: The MacMillan Co., 1916)

Gordon, Thomas F., *The History of Pennsylvania From Its Discovery by Europeans to the Declaration of Independence in 1776* (Philadelphia: Carey, Lea & Carey Publishers, 1829)

Gould, R. T., *Captain Cook* (London: Gerald Duckworth & Co., 1978)

Graham, Dominic, *Dictionary of Canadian Biography* (Toronto: University of Toronto Press; Les Presses de l'université Laval) Vol. 3

Hacker, Werner, ed. *Eighteenth-Century Register of Emigrants from South West Germany* (Apollo: Closson Press, 1994)

Halifax Gazette, 1765-66

Hall, John, "Memoirs of Matthew Clarkson of Philadelphia, 1735-1800 by his great-grandson, John Hall; and of His Brother, Gerardus Clarkson, 1737-1790 by his great-grandson, Samuel Clarkson," (1890), Walter W Spooner, ed., *Historic Families of America* (New York: n.d.)

Hanna, William S., *Benjamin Franklin and Pennsylvania Politics* (Stanford: Stanford University Press, 1964)

Hannay, James, *The History of New Brunswick*, 2 Vols. (St. John: John A. Bowes, 1909)

Hart, Charles Henry, ed., "Letters from William Franklin to William Strahan," *Penn. Mag. Hist. & Bio.* Vol. 35

Hart, Charles Henry, "Who Was the Mother of Franklin's Son.," *Penn. Mag. Hist. & Bio.*, Vol. 35

Hartigan, Rev. Allen Stewart, M.A., *A Short Account of the Family of Eyre of Eyrecourt and Eyre of Eyreville in the County of Galway* (Dublin: Trinity College)

Hazard, Samuel, *Pennsylvania Archives*, Series 1, Vol. 4 (Philadelphia, 1865)

Herer, Jack, *The Emperor Wears No Clothes*, Chris Conrad, Lynn Osburn, Judy Osburn, Ellen Komp, eds. (Van Nuys, 1995)

"Heritage Moncton Salutes City's Early Settlers," Special Supplement to the *Moncton Times and Transcript*, May 28, 1983

Herrick, Chessman A., *White Servitude in Pennsylvania: Indentured and Redemption Labor in Colony and Commonwealth* (Freeport: Books for Libraries Press, 1970; orig. pub. 1926)

"History of the Steeves Family," *The Moncton Transcript*, Jan. 8, 1966 and reprinted Jul. 23, 1966

Hoar, W. S., Marjorie Barberie, D. W. Davidson, "Wild Greens as Dietary Supplements to Commercial Vegetables," *Journal of the Canadian Dietetic Association* (Toronto) Vol. 8, No. 1 (June, 1948)

Hoar, William S., *Steeves and Colpitts Pioneers of the Upper Petitcodiac* (Vancouver: Tangled Roots Press, 1988)

Holstein, Anna M., *Swedish Holsteins in America from 1644 to 1892* (Norristown: M. R. Willis, 1892)

Howe, Jonas, "Early Attempts to Introduce the Cultivation of Hemp in Eastern British North America," *New Brunswick Historical Society Collections* (1892)

Hughes, D. Michael, *The Hughes Family History* (Ingram: 1994)

Humes, James C., *The Wit and Wisdom of Benjamin Franklin* (New York: HarperPerennial, 1996)

Humphrey, John T., *Pennsylvania Births, Philadelphia County*, 1644-1765 (Washington: Humphrey Publications, 1994)

Hunter, Robert J., MD., "The Origin of the Philadelphia General Hospital," *Penn. Mag. Hist. & Bio.*, Vol. 57

Hutchinson, Roland H., *The Early Methodist Connection of the Steeves Family* (Wallace: 1981)

"In Hillsborough, N.B., It's Not Who You Know But How Many You Know," "Canadian Magazine," *Toronto Star,* Dec. 24, 1971

Innis, Harold A., ed. *The Diary of Simeon Perkins 1766-1780* (Toronto: Champlain Society, 1948)

Jack, David Russell, ed., *Acadiensis* (Saint John) Vol. 1 (1901); Vol. 3, No. 1 (1903)

Jackson, Joseph, "A Philadelphia Schoolmaster of the Eighteenth Century," *Penn. Mag. Hist. & Bio.*, Vol. 35

Jensen, Merrill, *The Founding of a Nation: A History of the American Revolution 1763-1776* (New York: Oxford University Press, 1968)

Johnson, Thomas H., *Oxford Companion to American History* (Oxford: Oxford University Press, 1966)

Jordan, John W., LL.D., "Franklin As A Genealogist," *Penn. Mag. Hist. & Bio.*, Vol. 23

Jordan, John W., LL.D., *Colonial and Revolutionary Families of Pennsylvania*, 3 Vols. (Baltimore: Genealogical Publishing Company, 1978; orig publ. Lewis Publishing Company, 1911)

Journals of the House of Commons (Gr. Britain) Vol. 30 [Jan. 10, 1765 - Sept. 16, 1766] (London: House of Commons)

Kanner, Ken, *Early Families Revisited* (Moncton: 1993)

Kapff, Paul, *Schwaben in Amerika seit der Entdeckung des Weltteils* (Stuttgart: D. Gundert, 1893)

Keen, Gregory B., "The Descendants of Jöran Kyn, the Founder of Upland," *Penn. Mag. Hist. & Bio.*, Vol. 4

Kelly, Joseph J., Jr., *Pennsylvania: The Colonial Years* (Garden City: Doubleday & Company, 1980)

Kerr, Wilfred B., "The Stamp Act in Nova Scotia," *The New England Quarterly*, Vol. VI (1933)

Ketchum, Ralph L., "Benjamin Franklin and William Smith, New Light on an Old Philadelphia Quarrel," *Penn. Mag. Hist. & Bio.*, Vol. 88

Klees, Frederic, *The Pennsylvania Dutch* (New York: The MacMillan Company, 1951)

Knittle, Walter Allen, *Early Eighteenth-Century Palatine Emigration* (Baltimore: Genealogical Publishing Co., 1970)

Knollenberg, Bernhard, *Origin of the American Revolution*, rev. ed. (New York: The Free Press, 1960)

Koeppel, Adolph, *The Stamps That Caused the American Revolution* (The Town of North Hempstead, 1976)

Kuhns, Oscar, *The German and Swiss Settlements of Colonial Pennsylvania: A Study of the So-Called Pennsylvania Dutch* (Ann Arbor: Gryphon Books, 1971; orig. pub. 1901)

Labaree, Leonard W., & Whitfield J. Bell Jr., eds., *The Papers of Benjamin Franklin* (Philadelphia: American Philosophical Society; New Haven: Yale University Press, 1959-1970) Vols. 1-14

Lamberton, E. V., "Colonial Libraries of Pennsylvania," *Penn. Mag. Hist. & Bio.* Vol. 42

Landis, Charles I., "The Juliana Library Company in Lancaster," *Penn. Mag. Hist. & Bio.*, Vol. 43

Larracey, Edward W., *Chocolate River: A Story of the Petitcodiac River* (1985)

Larracey, Edward W., *The First Hundred* (Moncton, 1970)

Lawrence, D. H., "Benjamin Franklin," *Critical Essays on Benjamin Franklin*, Melvin H. Buxbaum, ed. (Boston: G. K. Hall, 1987)

Lawrence, D. H., *Movements in European History* (Oxford: Oxford University Press, 1981; orig. pub. 1921)

Lawson-Peebles, Robert, "William Moore,"*American National Biography* (Oxford: Oxford University Press, 1999) Vol. 15

Leach, Josiah Granville, LL.B., *Chronicle of the Yerkes Family* (Philadelphia: J. B. Lippincott Co., 1904)

LeBlanc, Roméo, "Installation Speech to Parliament," Feb. 8, 1995

Lee-Whiting, Brenda, *Harvest of Stones* (Toronto: University of Toronto Press, 1985)

Lemon, James T., *The Best Poor Man's Country: A Geographical Study of Early Southeastern Pennsylvania* (New York: W. W. Norton & Company, 1976)

Leonard, Joan de Lourdes, "Elections in Colonial Pennsylvania," *William and Mary Quarterly* (Williamsburg: Institute of Early American History and Culture) Ser. 3, Vol. 11 (1954)

Levick, James J., M.D., "An Old Welsh Pedigree," *Penn. Mag. Hist. & Bio.*, Vol. 4

Lewis, Frank R., "Benjamin Franklin and the Society of Arts," *Pennsylvania History* (University Park: Pennsylvania Historical Association, 1939) Vol. VI, No. 1—Jan., 1939

Livermore, Shaw, *Early American Land Companies: Their Influence on Corporate Development* (New York: Octagon Books, 1968)

Löher, Franz, *Geschichte und Zustände der Deutschen in Amerika* (Leipzig: beir. F. Rohler, & Cincinnati: Eggers, 1847)

Lopez, Claude-Anne and Eugenia W. Herbert, *The Private Franklin: the Man and his Family* (New York: W. W. Norton & Co., 1975)

Lossing, Benson J., *The Pictorial Field-Book of the Revolution: or, Illustrations, by Pen and Pencil, of the History, Biography, Scenery, Relics, and Traditions of the War for Independence*, 2 Vols. (New York: Harper Brothers, 1860) Vol. 2

MacCoun, Robert J. and Peter Reuter, "Does Europe Do It Better? Lessons From Holland, Britain and Switzerland," *The Nation* (New York: The Nation Company, L.P., 1999) Sept. 20, 1999

McCormack, Henrietta Hamilton, *Genealogies and Reminiscences* (Chicago: 1897)

Macdonald, James, S. "Life and Administration of Governor Charles Lawrence," *Collections of the Nova Scotia Historical Society* (Halifax: McAlpine Publishing Co., 1905) Vol. 12

MacDonald, M. A., *Rebels & Royalists: The Lives and Material Culture of New Brunswick's Early English-Speaking Settlers 1758-1783* (Fredericton: New Ireland Press, 1990)

Machum, Lloyd, *A History of Moncton Town and City 1855-1965* (City of Moncton, 1965)

MacMechan, Archibald, "Nova Scotia Under English Rule, 1713-1775," *Canada and its Provinces*, 23 Vols. (Toronto: Glasgow, Brook & Company, 1914) Vol. 13

MacNutt, W. S., *The Atlantic Provinces: The Emergence of Colonial Society 1712-1785* (McClelland and Stewart, Toronto, 1965)

Mease, James, MD., *The Picture of Philadelphia* (Philadelphia: B. & T. Kite, 1811)

Mendenball, John C., "Old Frankford from Advertisements in the Colonial Newspapers," *Papers Read before the Historical Society of Frankford* (Gettysburg: Times and News Publishing Co., 1937) Vol. 3, No. 5

Middlekauff, Robert, *Benjamin Franklin and His Enemies* (Beley: University of California, 1996)

Middleton, Richard, *Colonial America: a History, 1607 - 1760* (Cambridge: Blackwell Publishers, 1992)

Mikuriya, Tod H., M.D., *Excerpts from the Indian Hemp Drugs Commission Report with Centennial Thoughts on Indian Hemp and the Dope Fiends of Old England* (San Francisco: Last Gasp of San Francisco, 1994)

Miller, John C., *Origins of the American Revolution* (Boston: Little, Brown & Company, 1943)

Milner, W. C., "The Basin of Minas and It's First Settlers" (*Wolfville Acadian*)

Milner, W. C. , "Records of Chignecto," *Collections of the Nova Scotia Historical Society* (Halifax: Wm. MacNab & Son, 1911) Vol. 15

"Minutes of Provincial Council of Pennsylvania," *Pennsylvania Archives*, Vol. 5 (Harrisburg, 1851)

"Minutes of the Committee of Safety," Dec. 26, 1775; Jan 6, 1776. *Penn. Mag. Hist. & Bio.*, Vol. 15

Mittelberger, Gottlieb, *Journey to Pennsylvania*, Oscar Handlin and John Clive, eds. & trans. (Cambridge: Belknap Press of Harvard University, 1960) also pub. as *Journey to Pennsylvania in the Year 1750 and Return to Germany in the Year 1754*, Carl Theo. Eben, trans. (Philadelphia: John Jos. McVey, 1898)

Moody, Barry M., "A View from the Front Steps: Esther Clark Wright and the Making of a Maritime Historian," *Creating Historical Memory: English Canadian Women and the Work of History* (Vancouver: UBC Press, 1997)

Moore, Christopher, *The Loyalists: Revolution, Exile, Settlement* (Toronto: McClelland & Stewart, 1984)

Morgan, Edmund S. and Helen M. Morgan, *The Stamp Act Crisis: Prologue to Revolution* (Chapel Hill: The University of North Carolina Press, 1953)

Morison, Samuel Eliot, *Oxford History of the American People* (New York: Oxford University Press, 1965)

Morris, Charles, "Description and State of the New Settlements in Nova Scotia in 1761," Sessional Paper No. 18, *Report Concerning Canadian Archives for the Year 1904* (Ottawa, 1905)

Mosby's Medical, Nursing and Allied Health Dictionary, 5th ed. (St. Louis: Mosby Year Book, Inc., 1998)

Mühlenberg, Henry Melchior, *The Journals of Henry Melchior Muhlenberg*, Tappert, Theodore G. and John W. Doberstein, trans., 3 Vols. (Philadelphia: The Evangelical Lutheran Ministerium of Pennsylvania, 1945)

"A Muhlenberg Manuscript," *Bulletin of the Historical Society of Montgomery County*, Vol. XI, No. 4, Spring, 1959 (Norristown: The Society)

Muller, Herbert J., *The Uses of the Past* (New York: Oxford University Press, 1952)

Munger, Donna Bingham, *Pennsylvania Land Records: A History and Guide for Research* (Wilmington: Scholarly Resources, Inc., 1991)

"Narrative of the Journey of the Schwenckfelders to Pennsylvania, 1733," *Penn. Mag. Hist. & Bio.* , Vol. 10

Nash, Gary B., "Up From the Bottom in Franklin's Philadelphia," *The Private Side of American History: Readings in Everyday Life*, Gary B. Nash, ed. (New York: Harcourt Brace Jovanovich, Inc., 1983)

Naturalizations of Foreign Protestants in the American Colonies and West Indies, M. S. Giuseppe, ed. (Baltimore: Genealogical Publishing Co., 1964; orig. pub. London: Publications of the Huguenot Society of London, Vol. XXIV, 1921)

Nelson, Paul David, *Anthony Wayne: Soldier of the Early Republic* (Bloomington: Indiana University Press, 1985)

"New Billion-Dollar Crop," *Popular Mechanics Magazine*, February, 1938

New Brunswick Census of 1851: Westmorland County, Vol. 1, Wayne A. Gillcash, ed. (Fredericton: Provincial Archives of New Brunswick, 1981)

Newcomb, Benjamin H., "Effects of the Stamp Act on Colonial Pennsylvania Politics," *William and Mary Quarterly*, Series 3, Vol. XXIII (October, 1966)

Newcomb, Benjamin H., *Franklin and Galloway: A Political Partnership* (New Haven: Yale University Press, 1972)

"Notes and Queries," *Penn. Mag. Hist. & Bio.*, Vols. 6 & 13

Nye, Russel B., ed., *Benjamin Franklin: Autobiography and Other Writings* (Boston: Houghton Mifflin Company, 1958)

Oberholtzer, Ells Paxson, *Philadelphia: A History of the City and its People*, 3 Vols. (Philadelphia: S. J. Clarke Publishing Co., 1893)

"Okley, John to Abel James," June 21, 1765, *Penn. Mag. Hist. & Bio.*, Vol. 18

Owen, B. and J. B. Blakeway, *A History of Shrewsbury*, 2 Vols. (London: Harding, Lepard, and Co., 1825)

Oxford English Dictionary, 2nd ed. (Oxford: Clarendon Press, 1989)

Parkman, Francis, *A Half Century of Conflict*, Vol. 1 (Boston: Little, Brown, and Company, 1924; orig. pub. London: MacMillan and Co., 1894)

Parkman, Francis, *La Salle and the Discovery of the Great West* (Toronto: New American Library of Canada: Signet Classic, 1963: orig. publ. 1879)

Parkman, Francis, *Montcalm and Wolfe* (Markham: Viking - Penguin Books Canada, 1984: orig. publ. Little, Brown, Boston, 1884)

Parry, Mary, "Philadelphia Clockmakers," *Penn. Mag. Hist. & Bio.*, Vol. 56

Parsons, Brenda & Lloyd, *Moncton's Civic Treasure: The Free Meeting House* (Moncton: Betson's Publishing, 1997)

Parsons, William T., *The Pennsylvania Dutch: A Persistent Minority* (Boston: Twayne Publishers, 1976)

Pauker, Joe, *Get Lost: The Cool Guide to Amsterdam* (Amsterdam: Get Lost Publishing, 1997)

Peare, Catherine Owens, *William Penn* (Ann Arbor: University of Michigan Press, 1966)

Pennsylvania Chronicle, 1766

Pennsylvania Gazette (Philadelphia: Benjamin Franklin & David Hall) 1748-66

Pennsylvania German Church Records of Births, Baptisms, Marriages, Burials, Etc. From The Pennsylvania German Society Proceedings and Addresses, 3 Vols. (Baltimore: Genealogical Publishing Co., 1983) Vol. 1

Pennsylvania German Immigrants, 1709-1786, Don Yoder, ed. (Baltimore: Genealogical Publishing Co., 1980; orig. pub. Pennsylvania German Folklore Society, 1947)

Pennsylvania Journal or Weekly Advertiser (Philadelphia: William Bradford) 1765-66

Pennsylvania Magazine of History and Biography (Philadelphia: Historical Society of Pennsylvania)

Pennypacker, Samuel W., LL.D, "Anthony Wayne," *Penn. Mag. Hist. & Bio.*, Vol. 32

Pennypacker, Samuel W., LL.D, "Bebber's Township and the Dutch Patroons of Pennsylvania," *Penn. Mag. Hist. & Bio.*, Vol. 31

Pennypacker, Samuel W., LL.D., *Pennsylvania in American History* (Philadelphia: William J. Campbell, 1910)

Pennypacker, Samuel W., LL.D, "The Settlement of Germantown and the Causes which led to it," *Penn. Mag. Hist. & Bio.*, Vol. 4

Pincombe, C. Alexander, and Edward W. Larracey, *Resurgo: The History of Moncton*, 2 Vols. (Moncton: The City of Moncton, 1990) Vol. 1

Pleasants, J. Hall, "Hall Family of Tacony, Philadelphia County, Pennsylvania," *William and Mary Quarterly*, Series 1, Vol. 22 (1913-1914)

Potts, William (W. P.), "Book Notices," *Penn. Mag. Hist. & Bio.*, Vol. 17

Powell, J. H., *Bring out Your Dead* (New York: Time Inc., 1949)

Punch, Terrence, M., "Finding Our Irish," *Nova Scotia Historical Review* (Halifax: Public Archives of Nova Scotia, 1986)

Punch, Terrence M., trans., "'Hörte ich daß...' ; Travels of a Rhinelander in Nova Scotia in 1807," *Journal of the Royal Nova Scotia Historical Society*, Vol. 3 (Dartmouth, 2000)

Raddall, Thomas H., *Halifax: Warden of the North* (Toronto: McClelland and Stewart Limited, 1971)

Rankin, Hugh F., "Anthony Wayne: Military Romanticist," *George Washington's Generals*, George Ethan Billias, ed. (New York: William Morrow and Co., 1964)

Raymond, W. O., "Colonel Alexander McNutt and the Pre-Loyalist Settlements of Nova Scotia," *Proceedings and Transactions of the Royal Society of Canada*, Third Series—Vol. V (1912)

Reaman, G. Elmore, *The Trail of the Black Walnut* (McClelland & Stewart Ltd., 1957)

Records of St. Michael's Evangelical Lutheran Church, Germantown: Collections of the Genealogical Society of Pennsylvania (Philadelphia, 1896) Vol. XVI

Roach, Hannah Benner, "Benjamin Franklin Slept Here" *Penn. Mag. Hist. & Bio.*, Vol. 84

Roberts, Jonathan, "Memoirs of a Senator from Pennsylvania (1771-1854)," *Penn. Mag. Hist. & Bio.*, Vol. 61

Robinson, Rowan, *The Great Book of Hemp* (Rochester: Park Street Press, 1996)

Rogers, Mrs. Harry, and Mrs. A. H. Lane, "Pennsylvania Pensioners of the Revolution," *Penn. Mag. Hist. & Bio.*, Vol. 42

Rolater, Fred S., "Charles Thomson, 'Prime Minister' of the United States," *Penn. Mag. Hist. & Bio.*, Vol. 101

Rothermund, Dietmar, "The German Problem of Colonial Pennsylvania, *Penn. Mag. Hist. & Bio.*, Vol. 84

Roulac, John W., *Hemp Horizons* (White River Junction: Chelsea Green Publishing Company, 1997)

The Royal Society for the Encouragement of Arts Manufactures and Commerce (London, Adelphi: The Royal Society of Arts, 1938)

Russell, Marvin F., "Thomas Barton and Pennsylvania's Colonial Frontier," *Pennsylvania*

History (University Park: Pennsylvania Historical Association, 1979) Vol. XLVI, No. 4—Oct. 1979

Sachse, Julius Friedrich, "The Records of St. Michaelis and Zion Lutheran Congregation of Philadelphia," *Pennsylvania German Church Records of Births, Baptisms, Marriages, Burials, Etc. From The Pennsylvania German Society Proceedings and Addresses,* 3 Vols. (Baltimore: Genealogical Publishing Co., 1983) Vol. 1

St. Michael's & Zion, Philadelphia (Philadelphia: Genealogical Society of Pennsylvania, 1898) Vol. 36

St. Peter's Lutheran Church, Barren Hill, Montgomery, PA, 1851-1919 (Philadelphia, Genealogical Society of Pennsylvania, 1919) Vol. 370

Sawtelle, William Otis, "Acadia: The Pre-Loyalist Migration and the Philadelphia Plantation," *Penn. Mag. Hist. & Bio.,* Vol. 51

Scharf, J. Thomas and Thompson Westcott, *History of Philadelphia, 1609-1884* (Philadelphia: L.H. Everts & Co., 1884) Vol. 1

Schlesenger, Arthur M., "The Colonial Newspapers and the Stamp Act," *The New England Quarterly* (Plimpton Press, 1935; New York: AMS Reprint Co., 1963) Vol. VIII

Schmauk, Theodore Emanuel, "Pennsylvania-the German Influence in its Settlement and Development: Part IX, The Lutheran Church in Pennsylvania 1636-1800," The Pennsylvania-German Society Proceedings and Addresses at Easton, Oct. 26, 1900, Vol XI (The Society, 1902)

Semple, Neil, *The Lord's Dominion* (Montréal: McGill Queens University Press, 1996)

Severus, Sulpicius, "The Life of St. Martin," *The Western Fathers,* F.R. Hoare, trans. & ed. (New York: Harper & Row, 1954)

Shackleton, Robert, *The Book of Philadelphia* (Philadelphia: The Penn Publishing Company, 1920)

"Ship Registers for the Port of Philadelphia, 1726-1775," *Penn. Mag. Hist. & Bio.,* Vols. 25 & 26

Shryock, Richard H., "The Pennsylvania Germans in American History," *Penn. Mag. Hist. & Bio.,* Vol. 63

Shuckburgh, E. S., ed., *Herodotus* (Cambridge: Cambridge Press, 1906)

Silverman, Kenneth, *Benjamin Franklin: The Autobiography and Other Writings* (New York: Penguin, 1986)

Simon, Grant Miles, *Part of Old Philadelphia: A Map Showing Historic Buildings & Sites from the Founding until the Early Nineteenth Century* (Philadelphia: G. Simon, 1973)

Skemp, Sheila L., *William Franklin: Son of a Patriot, Servant of a King* (New York: Oxford University Press, 1990)

Smith, Abbot Emerson, "Some New Facts about Eighteenth-Century German Immigration," *Pennsylvania History,* (University Park: Pennsylvania Historical Association, 1943) Vol. X, No. 1 (June, 1943)

Smith, Billy G., *The "Lower Sort": Philadelphia's Laboring People,* 1750-1800 (Ithaca: Cornell University Press, 1990)

Smyth, Albert Henry, *The Writings of Benjamin Franklin,* 10 Vols. (London: The MacMillan Company, 1906) Vols. 5 & 10

Snowdon, James Dean, *Footprints in the Marsh Mud: Politics and Land Settlement in the Township of Sackville 1760-1800* (Fredericton: University of New Brunswick, 1974; reprinted Tantramar Heritage Trust, n.d.)

Soderland, Jean R., ed. *William Penn and the founding of Pennsylvania 1680-1684: A Documentary History* (Philadelphia: University of Pennsylvania Press, 1983)

Sparks, Jared, *The Works of Benjamin Franklin* (London: Benjamin Franklin Stevens, 1882) Vol. 10.

Spray, W. A., *Dictionary of Canadian Biography* (Toronto: University of Toronto Press; Les Presses de l'université Laval) Vol. 10

Steadman's Medical Dictionary, 26th ed. (Baltimore: Williams and Wilkins, 1995)

Steele, I. K., "Robert Monckton," *Dictionary of Canadian Biography*, Vol. 4.

Steeves Family Register (Hillsborough: The Steeves Family)

Stillé, Charles J., *Major-General Anthony Wayne and the Pennsylvania Line in the Continental Army* (Port Washington: Kennikat Press, 1893)

Stone, Frederick D., "How the Landing of Tea was Opposed in Philadelphia," *Penn. Mag. Hist. & Bio.*, Vol. 15

Strassburger, Ralph Beaver, L.L.D. *Pennsylvania German Pioneers*, 3 Vols., William John Hinke, Ph.D., D.D., ed. (Norristown: Pennsylvania German Society, 1934)

Thayer, Theodore, *Pennsylvania Politics and the Growth of Democracy 1740 - 1776* (Harrisburg: Pennsylvania Historical and Museum Commission, 1953)

"The Most Profitable and Desireable Crop that can be Grown," *Mechanical Engineering*, February 26, 1937

Thomas, C. E., "The First Half-Century of the Work of the Society for the Propagation of the Gospel in Nova Scotia," *Collections of the Nova Scotia Historical Society* (Halifax: 1963) Vol. 34

Thomas, Isaiah, *The History of Printing in America* (Worcester, 1810) Vol. 1

Thompson, Peter, *Rum Punch and Revolution: Taverngoing and Public Life in Eighteenth Century Philadelphia* (Philadelphia: University of Pennsylvania Press, 1999)

Thomson, Don W., *Men and Meridians* (Ottawa: Department of Mines and Technical Surveys, 1966) Vol. 1

Townsend, Patricia, "Esther Clark Wright: A Bibliography, 1914-1988," *Acadiensis* (Fredericton: University of New Brunswick, 1998) Spring, 1998

Tratt, Gertrude E. N., *A Survey and Listing of Nova Scotia Newspapers 1752-1957* (Halifax: Dalhousie University, 1979)

Tratt, Gertrude, "John Eagleson," *Dictionary of Canadian Biography* (Toronto: University of Toronto Press; Les Presses de l'université Laval) Vol. 4

Trenholm, Gladys, Miep Norden, Josephine Trenholm, *A History of Fort Lawrence - Times, Tides, and Towns* (Fort Lawrence, 1986)

Tucker, Glenn, *Mad Anthony Wayne and The New Nation* (Harrisburg: Stackpole Books, 1973)

Tully, Alan W., "Ethnicity, Religion, and Politics in Early America," *Penn. Mag. Hist. & Bio.*, Vol. 107

Upton, L. F. S., "Sir Brook Watson," *Dictionary of Canadian Biography*, Vol. 5

Van Doren, Carl, *Benjamin Franklin* (New York: The Viking Press, 1938)

Vernon, C. W., *Bicentenary Sketches and Early Days of the Church in Nova Scotia* (1910)

Wallace, Paul A. W., *The Muhlenbergs of Pennsylvania* (Freeport: Books for Libraries Press, 1950)

Ward, Townsend, "The Germantown Road and its Associations," *Penn. Mag. Hist. & Bio.*, Vol. 5

Warden, G. B., *Boston 1689-1776* (Boston: Little, Brown and Company, 1970)

Watson, John F., *Annals of Philadelphia and Pennsylvania in the Olden Time*, 2 Vols. (Philadelphia: Edwin S. Stuart, 1897)

Webster, John Clarence, ed. *The Career of the Abbe Le Loutre in Nova Scotia* (Shediac: 1933)

Webster, John Clarence, ed. "Sir Brook Watson," *The Argosy*, Vol. 3, No. 1, Nov., 1924; also in Nova Scotia Historical Society Journal, Vol. 2, June, 1924

White, Stephen A., *Dictionnaire généalogique des familles acadienne: Part 1 — 1636 to 1714* (Moncton: Centre d'études acadiennes, Université de Moncton, 1999)

Whitelaw, Marjory, *First Impressions: Early Printing in Nova Scotia* (Halifax: Nova Scotia Museum, 1987)

Wildes, Harry Emmerson, *Anthony Wayne: Trouble Shooter of the American Revolution* (New York: Harcourt, Brace and Co., 1941)

Willcox, William B., ed., *The Papers of Benjamin Franklin* (Philadelphia: American Philosophical Society; New Haven: Yale University Press, 1972-1987) Vols. 15-26

Wolfe, Stephanie Grauman, *Urban Village: Population, Community, and Family Structure in Germantown, Pennsylvania 1783-1800* (Princeton: Princeton University Press, 1976)

Wright, Esmond, *Franklin of Philadelphia* (Cambridge: Belknap Press of Harvard University Press, 1986)

Wright, Esther Clark, *The Loyalists of New Brunswick* (Fredericton: 1955)

Wright, Esther Clark, *The Petitcodiac* (Sackville: The Tribune Press, 1945)

Wright, Esther Clark, *Planters and Pioneers*, rev. ed. (Wolfville: 1978)

Wright, Esther Clark, *The St. John River and Its Tributaries* (1966)

Wright, Esther Clark, *Samphire Greens: the Story of the Steeves* (1961)

Wright, Esther Clark, *The Steeves Descendants* (1965)

Wright, Louis B., *Life in Colonial America* (New York: Capricorn Books, 1965)

Wrong, George M., *The Conquest of New France* (New Haven: Yale University Press; Toronto: Glasgow, Brook & Co.; London: Humphrey Milford; Oxford: Oxford University Press, 1918)

Yoder, Don, *Discovering American Folklore: Studies in Ethnic, Religious and Regional Culture* (Ann Arbour: UMI Research Press, 1990)

Yoder, Don, "Problems and Resources in Pennsylvania Genealogical Research," *The Pennsylvania Genealogical Magazine*, Vol. 31, No. 1 (Philadelphia: Genealogical Society of Pennsylvania, 1979)

Yourcenar, Marguerite, *Dear Departed* (London: Aidan Ellis Publishing; *HarperCollins*Canada, 1991; New York: Farrar, Straus, Giroux, 1991) trans. Maria Louise Ascher (orig. pub. *Souvenirs pieux*, Editions Gallimard, 1974)

Zobl, Georg, *Landeck auf alten Ansichtskarten*, Bücherreihe Auf alten Ansichten

Acknowledgements

This book would not have been possible without the help of numerous individuals who provided information, encouragement, and sometimes a bed and a meal along the way. In keeping with the scope of the book, I have tried to thank or acknowledge all those who played a part. Knowing that such an endeavour comes at the risk of forgetting someone, I nevertheless make the attempt. Here are but some of the individuals who became involved, one way or another, in *The Search for Heinrich Stief*.

First, I send my thanks to Roland Deigendesch, archivist for the town of Münsingen, at whose suggestion this book was begun. Without his initial discoveries in 1997, plus his expertise, enthusiasm, and encouragement during three years of research and writing, the end result would be but a shadow of its present self.

I am especially indebted to Lisa Darrach for her patient editing during the two and a half years it took me to learn how to construct a readable sentence. May our long-winded debates become renowned in the annals of editor-writer relations.

My friend Stewart Donovan has earned my deep gratitude for pulling the manuscript out of the ditch at a crucial stage, and giving it some needed direction.

I am thankful to my friend Wiltrud Steinacker for her generous hospitality in Landeck, and for getting me back on the road. Although neither of us knew it at the time, the project teetered on the brink of failure.

I would have liked to thank Jürgen vom Grafen personally for his warm sociability and for taking time to educate me about the history of the Martinskirche, but I say with regret that Jürgen passed away shortly after we met in 1997.

Sonja Bader, archivist at the *Dekanatamt* in Münsingen, willingly opened her church records to an amateur genealogist from Canada. Dr. and Frau Rudolph Bütterlin graciously entertained and educated me about Württemberg history, and supplied information about the Dukes of Württemburg Coat of Arms; the timing was perfect. Kristina Reichle, Pastor of the Wendelinkirche in Schlaitdorf, was instrumental in providing the missing key to the puzzle.

Moncton *Times and Transcript* writer Sandra Devlin, herself a Steeves descendant, took me under her wing shortly after my discovery in Münsingen, and reported the news to the world.

Paul Smith, Blair Eveleigh, Ed Pussar, David Meslin, & Co. kept my business afloat while I gallivanted around North America and Europe in search of ancestors. Had it not been for their competence and loyalty, this book would likely be another two years in the future.

My brother Bob read the manuscript and advised me on a number of technical matters. He also pointed the way to Schlaitdorf when I was completely lost. My other siblings, Eric, Don, and Diane, read portions of the manuscript and made helpful comments.

Judi Berry Steeves read the manuscript and offered many practical suggestions; she also supported my efforts with periodic background research into many obscure and difficult areas of the history.

Although the story took on a life of its own, I began the account for my cousins and comrades in the New Brunswick Genealogical Society. I trust they will enjoy the reading as much as I enjoyed the writing. Ron Messenger and several of his colleagues examined several genealogy conundrums. Special thanks go to George Hayward, Ivan Edgett, Eleanor Goggin, Bing Geldart, Ken Kanner, Dawn Lutes, Shirley Dobson, Rev. Armand and Mrs. Steeves, Sharon Steeves, and Bev Land.

Joyce and Malcolm Wortman refreshed my faded memory on the subject of spear fishing on The Petitcodiac River. Jane Wood shared her Steeves family photographs and records. Tony Steele allowed me to reproduce the 1755 d'Anville map from his collection. Alvin Edgett showed me Howard Steeves's 1867 sketch book.

Herb and Charlene Steves, distant cousins in New Mexico, provided collaborative ideas regarding several murky areas of family history. Bill Steeves in Cincinnati shared the results of his own research into many areas of the story, especially Heinrich Stief's departure from Württemberg in 1749.

In Fredericton, Marylee MacDonald introduced me to the world of Marguerite Yourcenar. Ted and Anita Jones encouraged me to write the history I wanted to write. William Spray encouraged me to write the history the way I wanted to write it. My friend Craig Schneider clarified a detail concerning a fundamental aspect of trains. In less than five minutes, Elizabeth Hamilton found an important document at the Harriet Irving Library for which I had searched eighteen months. Eric Swanick and his staff at the New Brunswick Legislative Library assisted with DesBarres's maps in *The Atlantic Neptune*. Fred Ferrell at the Provincial Archives of New Brunswick allowed me to weigh and measure Heinrich Stief's Bible. Brenda Orr and Philip Oliver at the Moncton Museum offered their thoughts about the Stief Bible. Eric Miller made suggestions about Heinrich Stief's signature(s). Piet Defraeye urged me to show particular appreciation to those individuals who helped me with this enormous project, his affectionate advice on that point being the reason for the lengthiness of these acknowledgements.

I am happy to be able to share my discoveries with Dr. William Hoar, whose own writing of Steeves family history was inspiring. Arthur Cox encouraged Judi Steeves and myself to poke around on his marsh near Moncton in search of the home of Charles Jones.

Nick Gamble offered insightful direction when the manuscript was at a very rough stage. Looking back, I don't see how he made any sense of it. Arthur and Merion Bourns read the manuscript and recommended pertinent modifications. Sarah Ives made a number of improvements to the manuscript. Allen Robertson read the manuscript and offered useful criticism on the early chapters. Near the end of the process, Carol Dobson edited the entire manuscript for content and style.

Uli Menzefricke translated German excerpts and advised about certain statistical problems. Cordula Quint translated part of Franz Löher's account and other German passages. Patricia Townsend at Acadia University burrowed through one hundred boxes of Dr. Wright's papers to find a single letter. In 1995, Alex Groper's passion for archaeology rekindled my own appetite for genealogy like nothing since my early days reading Esther Clark Wright. My long-time friend Dr. Alexander Sumach read and commented on the hemp portion of the story. I was surprised when my former business partner, Mary Lou Morgan, an Upper Canadian, taught me something new about those Maritime exotics, samphire and goosetongue greens. Regis Brun at the Musé acadien shared his knowledge about Outhouse Point. Author and friend Jacques Gauthier offered insights into Acadian history. Dael Wilson encouraged me to honour the legends.

Special thanks are extended to Dorothy Beveridge and friends in Belize who facilitated my e-mail connection to Toronto while I was entrenched in a Hemmingway-esque beach house (sans rum) on Caye Caulker in 1998. Guy Montgomery shared his hearth and home in London while I explored the Society of Genealogists.

Patricia Kosco Cossard will remember a morning at the Historical Society of Pennsylvania when a happy camper made several discoveries about the Articles of Agreement. Dr. Don Yoder advised me on a key document; his alacrity for all things relating to Pennsylvania-German genealogy was inspirational. Sheila Skemp at the University of Mississippi commented on the Franklin portions of the manuscript; I highly value her interest.

Jim Stokes and Kevin Shue at the Lancaster Historical Society encouraged me to keep going when all hope of discovery seemed lost. Michael Hughes and Robert Braun gave long-distance advice. Fran Gleason, Rosalie Zimmermann, and Wayne Lewis at Waynesborough Museum provided assistance with Anthony Wayne's map. As this book goes to press, I have not yet found Wayne's missing papers.

Arthur Koestler showed me through his home in Upper Merion, PA, originally belonging to the grandson of John Hughes. Jerry and Laura Heebner in North Wales, PA acquainted me with their German Schwenkfelder ancestry (and delivered me to the train station on time). Rev. Robyn Kulp at the Lutheran Archives at Philadelphia shared ideas about Rev. Mühlenberg and the records of St. Michael's Church in Philadelphia. At the American Philosophical Society, Rob Cox advised me on William Franklin's letters; Roy Goodman directed my inquiries into areas where I would never have thought to venture.

John Lutz encouraged my endeavours at a crucial moment, and subsequently provided superior organizing skills. Dr. Rainer Hempel kindly corroborated some of my Württemberg discoveries with his own research. Chris Chambers had the grace to treat me like a fellow writer long before I could pretend to be such a creature. Tom Kemple enlightened me about the art and mechanics of the footnote.

Though I never anticipated the thought of a governor-general of Canada tramping around a New Brunswick marsh in rubber boots, I now have the pleasure of that image courtesy of Roméo LeBlanc, who kindly conveyed some of his memories to me about picking goosetongue greens on the Memramcook River.

It will seem odd for me to be remembering my grade-school teachers in New Brunswick, but I am nevertheless grateful for their founding inspiration: Winifred Coffey, my fifth-grade history teacher, demonstrated to me that a balanced sense of time can be its own reward; Phyllis Hall impressed me with her own love of history; Helen Renouf fostered a new understanding about the health of The Petitcodiac River; Joan McNutt taught me that creative writing was both easier and more difficult than I imagined it to be.

Helpful encouragement came from numerous librarians and archivists at institutions in Moncton, Toronto, Ottawa, Philadelphia, Los Angeles, New York, and London—help that was sometimes unsolicited and often unrewarded. For their unstinting assistance, I am grateful to numerous librarians at family history centres in the Church of Jesus Christ of Latter-Day Saints. I am further indebted, in many small ways, to a legion of unnamed hotel clerks, bus and taxi drivers, bed-and-breakfast operators, church pastors—all of these in cities from Los Angeles to London, England. You all have my heartfelt thanks for your help and hospitality.

Rona Moreau helped me find a publisher. Dorothy Blythe, my publisher at Nimbus, took a chance with an untried writer. Stephanie Domet, my editor at Nimbus, coaxed the manuscript into what I hope is a more coherent text. Towards the end of the project, Jim Barnes read the manuscript and offered valuable editorial comments. Terrence Punch offered last-minute clarification on several important points. Ditte Haarlov-Johnson made suggestions about the pictures. Mary Chalifour offered her home in Dartmouth while I finished the manuscript. Abraham Rotstein suggested the title.

I wish to acknowledge several historians and genealogists whose guiding spirit was central to my search; although they are now deceased, their ideas live on: William Orober Raymond, Esther Clark Wright, William Francis Ganong, Alexander Pincombe, Francis Parkman, Samuel Eliot Morison, Carl Van Doren.

Finally, I wish to express my gratitude to my distant ancestors, named and unnamed, who were the reason for this story. I hope, above all, that they would not be unhappy with the way a twentieth-century descendant has poked around in their lives and prodded their stories loose from the recesses of history. He's still not sure the reason for it all. May you be at peace, all of you.

Index

Aberystwyth, Wales, 113, 115
Acadians, x, xiii, 2, 15–16, 59, 80, 102–105
    Belliveau, 3, 104–105; deportation, 10, 11–14, 19, 52, 59, 102, 118; dykes, 11, 102; hemp, 118; "Neutrals," 12
Acre, (Holy Land), 129
Adam, Hans Jacob, 137
"Ages of Francis Jones Senior's Sons," 43
Aire, Humphrey le, 127–129
Akins, Thomas, 13
Albert County, NB, 4, 10, 103, 120, 183
Alison, Rev. Dr. Francis, 95–96
Allen, Chief Justice William, 34, 70
Alternriet, 141
America, vii, xiii, 1, 4, 11–14, 16, 32, 57–60, 63–66, 72, 99, 118, 123, 129, 131, 133–134, 137–138, 142, 145–146, 150, 162–163, 165, 168, 170, 174, 179, 188, 190–191, 193–194
American Philosophical Society, 38, 197
American Revolution, 2, 21, 72, 94, 100
Amiens (Gaul), 160
Amsterdam, 116, 121–124, 127, 129–130, 138, 151, 158, 177, 183–185, 188, 190
    Cannabis Cup, 116, 121; *Centraal Station*, 122–124, 188, 190; coffeeshops, 122
Ancestor Quest (1997), 108
Annapolis Royal, NS, 80
Arlberg Pass, Austria, 131
Articles of Agreement, 24–30, 39–42, 44, 48, 54, 58, 72, 86, 89, 102, 109–110, 117, 169, 179–180, 182, 195
Atlantic Neptune, The, 76, 118
Atlantic Ocean, 11, 14, 79, 104, 112, 132, 137, 147, 162, 169, 190–191, 193–194
Austria, 122–124, 126–129, 131
Ayer, Elijah, 127
Bad Urach, Württemberg, 152, 163, 179
Bader, Sonja, 149, 152–153, 156, 161, 163, 181
Bailey (Bayley), John, 88, 91, Appendix D
Baker, Charles, 91, 97
Barton, Rev. Thomas, 91, Appendix D
Barzilles, see Bryzelius, Rev.
Bay of Fundy, x, 1, 3, 7, 10–12, 15, 19, 22, 29, 59, 71, 78–80, 89, 103, 105, 118, 194, 199, 201
Beck,
    Hans Michel, 109–110; Johannes, 109–110; Martin (King's baker), 9, 109; Mary, 9
Beidelman, William, 133, 187
Belliveau, 3, 104–105
Bible, 39, 98, 142–143
    Book of Revelation, 149; Heinrich Stief, 142–143; John Hughes, 98, 198
Board of Trade, London, 21, 89
Bosler, Ludwig, 179
Boston, 11, 63–65, 70, 72
Bouchette, Joseph, 103
Boundary Creek, 5–10
    Baptist Church, 5; Cemetery, 5, 10, 48
Bowser, Bob, 130, 132
Braddock, General, 16

Bradford, William, 70, 74
Braun, Robert, 45
Brebner, John, 15
Bristol, 83, 85
British government, 10–11, 13, 33, 58, 65, 81, 117–118
Brother Cadfael, 113–114
Brown, Marion Steelman Hughes, 44–45, 48, 50
Brown, Patricia Steelman (Walz), 45
Bryzelius, Rev., 83
Bulkeley, Richard, 117
Burlington, NJ, 32, 83, 96
Bütterlin, Dr. Rudolf and Frau, 163, 171–172
Candes-St. Martin, 160
Cape Marangouin, 80
Carleton, Lieut.-Col. Guy, 16
Caton, Isaac, Appendix D
Caton, James, Appendix D
chain migration, 137
Charles Town, SC., x, 97–98
Charlotiana Company, 59
Chignecto, 22, 86, 95, 127, 130
Chignecto Bay, 80
Church, Captain Thomas, 78, 88
Church of St. Martin, see Martinskirche
Clarkson and Company, 29, Appendix D
Clarkson, Gerardus, Appendix D
Clarkson, Matthew, 29, 72, 77, 79, 86–87, Appendix D
Cline, Jacob, 26, 29, 54, 85, 182
Coates, Lindsay, 99
College of Philadelphia, 31
Commissioners for Trade and Plantations, 89
Committee of Safety, 70
Cook, Capt. James, 16
Copple, John, 29, 98, 186
Cowes, England, 190
Cox, John Jr., 19, 70, 87–88, Appendix D
Cox, John Sr., 70, Appendix D
Craig, William, 88, 91, Appendix D
Criner, Andrew, 26, 28–29, 54, 69, 85, 182
Criner, Jacob, 54–55
Cumberland, 37, 119, see also Fort Cumberland
Cumberland Basin, 4, 22, 180
Davenport, Josiah, 83
Declaration of Independence, 72
Deigendesch, Roland, 164–165, 167–169, 172, 175, 178–183, 198
Dekanatamt (Martinskirche archives), 159, 181
    Ehebuch, 153–156, 158–159, 164; *Taufbuch*, 153, 159, 161, 171; *Taufregister*, 161, 163; *Totenregister*, 163
Delaware River, 69, 73–74, 85, 90, 201
DesBarres, Joseph F. W., 18, 76, 118
Dettingen, Württemberg, 152
Deutsch (German), 71
Dickson, Charles, 81–82, 86–87
Dickson, Major Thomas, 86
Dinkel, Nicholaus, 135
Dinwiddie, Gov. Robert, 16
Dobson, George and Mary (Barker), 130

Index   269

Doggett, Major, 81
Dovey River (Afon Dyfi), 114–115
Downes, Elizabeth, 32, 99
Drayton, Michael, 101
Drinker, Elizabeth, 28
Duffield, Edward, 91, Appendix D
Duval (Philadelphia baker), 52
Eagleson, Rev. John, 77–80, 86, 95–96, 102-03, 194
"Earliest Record of Ancestors," 44
Ecton, Northamptonshire, 61
Elbow Lane, Philadelphia, 72–73
Ells, Margaret, 71
Emberley, Geneva Jones, 41
England, 15, 20, 28, 32, 88, 92, 99–100, 123, 129, 147, 192, 194
Europe, vii–xiii, 12, 23, 40, 57, 72, 101–102, 112, 116, 121–122, 142, 157–158, 170, 187, 190
Fachwerk, 146, 158, 163
Family History Holstein, 44–45, 49–50
Fischer, Pfarrer Siegfried, 160
Florida, 94, 101–102, 107–109, 189
Folger, Abiah, 60
Fort Beauséjour, 4, 16, 22
Fort Cumberland, 3, 22, 79–80, 82, 86, 104, 109
Fort Duquesne, 16
France, 15–16, 72, 92, 104, 160–161
Frankford, Tacony, PA, 56, 84–85, 92
Frankfort township, 72, 79–80, 90
Frankfurt, 72, see Frankfort township
Franklin, Benjamin, ix, 10, 16, 19–20, 28, 30ff., 41–42, 51–52, 54, 57ff., 78, 87–88, 93, 95–97, 99–100, 107, 194–195, Appendix D
  Boston, 60; genealogy, 61; inventions, 61; land settlement, 2, 16, 89; London, 35–36, 58, 60, 71–72, 74; maidservant Barbara, 33; Market Street, 67, 72; Monckton township, 16, 33, 59, 66, 83, 87, 93; Oxford University, 32; Paris, 100; Peter (Black servant), 61; Philadelphia, 31–34, 57, 60–61, 73; Philadelphia tombstone, 38; private land grant in Nova Scotia, 84, 89; Society of Arts, 148; Stamp Act, 62ff.; Stief, Heinrich, 2, 59–60, 148, 195
Franklin, Deborah (Read), ix, 28, 60, 67, 69–71, 87, 90
Franklin, Gov. Michael, 84
Franklin, William, ix, 32–34, 59, 61, 75, 78, 83–86, 90, 96, 99–100, 197
  disinherited, 100; governor of New Jersey, 32, 78, 99; John Hall, 78, 84–85, 90; Monckton township, 33, 83–85, 90
Franklin family, 60–61
Fredericton, 79
French and Indian War, 16, 52
French Huguenots, 13, 185
French West Indies, 12, 14
Friend, Capt., 68
Funk, Elizabeth and Jacob, 48
Gajer, Johann Caspar and Anna Maria (née Walther), 137
Galloway, Joseph, 54, 67, 75
Ganong, W. F., 23–24
Gasthof Herrmann, 157–158, 163, 168, 171–172, 181
genealogy, xii–xiii, 6, 37, 41, 43, 49, 61, 102–103, 107–109, 112, 115, 122, 137, 148, 171, 197
"Genealogy of David and Letitia Jones," 43
George II, 16–17

George III, 63, 81, 84, 119
Gerber, Adolf, 109, 145
Germans,
  ancestry, xiii; emigration, 1–2, 13, 107–110, 142, 190–191; hemp farmers, 117–121; indentured servants (bondage), 188; names, 37–38, 110; in Pennsylvania, x, 2, 33, 36–40, 57, 102, 107, 110, 147; voters (1764-1765), 33–34, 36, 69
Germantown, 33, 40, 54, 56, 69, 198
Germany, vii, ix, xiii–xiv, 2–3, 101, 108, 113, 127, 129, 131, 150, 155–156, 185
Gleason, Fran, 95
Glynndene, 113
goosetongue greens, 7, 103–105
Grayson, Mrs., 86–87
Grenville, Lord George, 58, 62
Gurrbach, Mayor of Schlaitdorf, 130
Habsburg (Hapsburg) family, 172
Halifax, 10, 13–14, 17, 19–21, 27, 64, 78–79, 86, 88, 95–96, 119
Halifax Gazette, 58, 64
Hall, Jacob, 83–85, 91–92, 244
Hall, John (or Jonathan), ix, 55, 77–78, 81–88, 91–93, 96, 101–102, 119, 147, 182, 194, 197, 201, 245, Appendices C & D
  and farming, 79, 82, 91; Frankford, 84–85, 92; iron and steel, 79, 92; June 3, 1766, 80–81, 100, 102–103, 119; Justice of the Peace, 79; Maugerville, 77–79; Pennsylvania militia, 92–93; sloop captain, 3, 77, 79–80, 85, 92–93; Wheat Sheaf Tavern, 84–85, 91
Hall, Joseph and Rebecca (Rutter), 85, 244
Hall's Creek, 94, 102–103, 111, see also Panaccadie Creek
Harmon, Captain Lebot, 78
Harrich, England, 194
Haubensack, Martin and Anna (Auckberlin), 145
Haubensacker, Catharina (Maria Katharina), 110, 140, 144
Heart and Hand Fire Company, 69
Heidelberg, Germany, 133
Heilbronn, Germany, 133
hemp, 26, 116–121
Hempel, Dr. Rainer, 189
Henry, Anthony, 64
"Herd of Hogs," 31, 34
Herodotus (*Histories*), 117
Hillegas, Michael, 91
Hillsborough, NB, xii, 37–38, 97, 102, 119, 142, 184
Hinke, William John, 107
Hinshelwood, Archibald, 64
Historical Society of Pennsylvania, 23–24, 38, 43–44, 47, 52, 101, 197
History of the Province of Massachusetts Bay, 64
Hoar, William, 37
Hoek van Holland, 190, 192
Holland (Netherlands), 116, 127, 148, 188, 190
Holstein, Hannah, 44, 50, 68, 98
Holstein, Matthias, and Magdalena (Hulings), 44
Honau, Württemberg, 156, 159, 163–165, 169
Hughes and Company, 27–28, 84, 86–87, Appendix D
Hughes, D. Michael, 44–45, 47–49
Hughes, Hanah, 50
Hughes, Hugh and Martha (Jones), 44–45, 51
Hughes, Col. Isaac, 44, 50, 97–98
Hughes, John, ix, 10, 13, 15ff., 23–30, 34, 36, 41ff., 57–59, 62, 65ff., 82, 84ff., 96–99, 107, 112–113, 117, 119, 180, 182–183,

194, 198, 200–201, Appendices B & D
    ancestry, 50; Articles of Agreement, 25ff., 58, 72, 89, 117, 180, 182; assemblyman, 34, 54, 62, 85, 96; baker, 52; Bible, 98, 198; Charles Town, 97–98; Heart and Hand Fire Company, 69; illness (1765), 68–71; iron and steel, 18, 92; Jones, Sarah, 41, 44–45, 51, 96–97, 99; land speculation, 36, 52, 62; Lower Merion, 45; merchant, 17, 53–54, 62, 75; Monckton township, 16, 42, 59, 66, 87, 93; Mühlenberg, 36; Pennsylvania militia, 52; pies and cakes, 34; residence in Philadelphia, 51, 57, 70; Stamp Act riots, 52, 67ff., 88; stamp distributor, 44–45, 49–50, 62ff.; store on Fourth Street, 27, 53, 70, 72, 92, 200; Upper Merion, 51–52, 75, 91, 97; Walnut Grove, 44, 51, 75, 85, 96–97
Hughes, John, Jr., 26–28, 41, 53, 69, 180, 200
Hughes, John, Sr. and Jane (Evans), 50
Hughes family, 23, 44–45, 50, Appendix B
Hughes Family History, 44
Hungerberg Hill, 152, 167–169, 171–173, 176ff.
Huston, Capt. John, 13, 84, 86–87
Hutchinson, Lieut-Gov. Thomas, 64, 70
"In Memory of Elizabeth Reed," 48
Indian King, 52
Inn River, Austria, 126–127, 130
Ireland, 16, 42, 117, 119, 149
Isthmus of Chignecto, 127
Jacobs, Benjamin, 88, 91, Appendix D
Jacobs, Israel, 54, 72–73, Appendix D
Jacobs, Joseph, 88, Appendix D
Jacobs Papers, 88
Johnson, Sir William, 59
"Jones Bible Records," 43
Jones, Charles, 6, 9–10, 26, 29, 41ff., 53, 55, 86–87, 96–98, 105–107, 110, 112–113, 115, 183, 195, 198–199, 201
Jones,
    Abel Saunders, 5, 8, 105, 185; Abel Sr., 8; Calvin Abel, 8, 10; Catherine, 9, 106, 199; Dr. Edward, 42; family, xi, 43–44, 47, 49, 106; Henry, 9, 106; Hugh and Martha, 44–45, 113; John, 106; Lena (Copp), 7; Lucy Anne, 8; Margaret, 9, 106, 199; Sarah, 44–45, 51, 96–97; Solomon, 7–8
"Jones Family notes," 43
Kälberhirte (calfherd), 154–156, 159, 169, 176
Kaufbuch, (land record book), 179, 182
Kent County, England, 147
King George's War, 92
Klees, Frederic, 1, 133, 191
Koblenz, Germany, 184, 188
kohlrabi, 148
Kolb, Ludwig (Lewis), 41
Kredenbach, Germany, 109
Krehl, J[ung] Matthes, 168
Kreuzwertheim (Germany), 101, 108–109, 129, 135, 182, 189
Kuhn, Johannes and Anna Barbara (Adam), 137
Kuhns, Oscar, 133
Labaree, Leonard, 32, 60
Lancaster, PA, 48–50, 91, 117
Lancaster Historical Society, 44, 48
Landeck, Austria, 122, 126–130
Land's End, Cornwall, 191
Lawrence, Gov. Charles, 11ff., 27, 59, 86, 118
Le Loutre, Abbé, 13
LeBlanc, Governor General Roméo, 104–105

Lentz, Matthias, 26, 29, 85, 182, 201
Leopold of Austria, 127
Levick, James, J., 43
Lewis, Major, 16
Liverpool, NS, 81
Lockhen, H. Jacob, 168
London, England, 11–12, 32–33, 36, 58–60, 65–67, 71, 81, 83, 89, 96, 112, 116, 118, 129, 138, 177, 194
Lords of Trade, 17, 118–119
Louis XIV, 13, 133
Louisiana, 12
Loyalists, xiii, 71
Lutes (Lutz) family, xi, 189, 195
Luther, Martin, 141–143
Lutheran Church, 36, 39–40, 69, 141–142, 176
Lutz, Georg Michael, 9–10, 26–27, 29, 40, 55, 69, 86–87, 97–98, 101–102, 107–110, 120, 129, 134–136, 182–183, 189
Lutz,
    Anna Margretha, 40; Anna Walburga, 40, 109; (Anna) Catherine, 120, 162, 199–201; Catharina Lutzin, 198; Johann Wilhelm, 9; John, 9, 189; Margaret, 7–8
Lutz Mountain Museum, 107
Machynlleth, Wales, 114–115
MacIntosh, Ebenezer, 64
McNutt, Col. Alexander, x, 15–21, 27, 29, 35–36, 51, 54, 59, 66, 70, 74, 79, 119, 194
McNutt (McNaught) family, 16
Main River, Germany, 101, 135
Mainz, Germany, 133, 187
Maison Rouge, Lancaster, PA, 48–49
Mann, James, 37–38
Mannheim, Germany, 133
Maritimes, 7, 23, 25, 107, 120, 148
Martinskirche (Church of St. Martin), 149, 152, 154, 157–158, 160–161, 171, 173–175, 181, 188, see also *Dekanatamt* (Martinskirche archives)
Massachusetts, 11, 58, 62, 78, 119
Matthew, John, 41–43
Maugerville, NB, 79, 119
Mayhew, Capt., 81
Memramcook River, NB, 104–105
Mendenball, John C., 85
Meole Brook, Shrewsbury, 114
Merionethshire, Wales, 42, 51
Metzingen, Württemberg, vii, 133, 150–152, 183–185
Mi'kmaq, iv, 13, 102, 105
Miller, John, 63
Miller (Müller), Vallentin, iv, 26, 29, 40–41, 47, 85, 182
Miramichi River, 12
Mittelberger, Gottlieb, 147, 162–163, 188, 191
Mitton, Jane, 6, 8
Mitton, Ralph Blakely Johnson, 9
Monckton, Lieut-Col. Robert, 16
Monckton township, iv, 19, 21, 29, 33, 37, 41, 51, 66, 72-73, 79ff., 106, 119, 127, 195, 197
    Anthony Wayne, 16, 20–22, 93–95; Wayne's map, 93–95
Moncton (city), iv, xi, 5, 21, 29, 100–103, 108, 189
    Albert Street, 169; Bore Park, 103; Hall's Creek, 93, 102–103, see also Panacadie Creek; Magnetic Hill, 93, Moncton Museum, 92; Public Library, 107
Moncton Daily Times, xii

Moore, William, 31, 88, 91, Appendix D
Morgan, Edmund and Helen, 71, 75
Morison, Samuel Eliot, 191
Mormon Family History Centres, 102, 111
Morris, Charles, 118
Mueller, Heinrich, 59
Mühlenberg, Reverend Heinrich Melchior, 35–36, 38, 40–41, 44, 70, 89, 107, 199
    Alexander McNutt, 35–36; St. Michael's Church, 35, 38–39; Stamp Act riots, 70; Trappe, 35
Müller, Henry, 41
München, Germany, 126
Münsingen, vii, 133, 145, 149ff., 157ff., 188, 194, see also Dekanatamt
    Famlien-Register, 149, 154; great fountain, 157, 168; Karlstraße, 150, 152, 157, 159, 181; Martinskirche, 149, 152, 160–161, 173; stadtgraben (moat), 173–174; Ziegelwäldle, 174
Murphy family, 42
Museum of London, 112
Naglee, John, Appendix D
National Library of Wales, 113, 115
Neckar River, 132–133, 137–138, 141, 187
Neckartenzlingen, Germany, 136–138, 141
Neil, Hugh, Appendix D
Neuhaussen, Württemberg, 152
Neuländer, 188, 190
New Brunswick, iv, vii, x–xiii, 10, 37, 82, 101, 103–104, 115, 125, 131, 148, 169, 170, 184, 189
New England, xi, 11, 13–14, 64, 71, 118
New Jersey, 32, 71, 198
New York, 62–63, 71, 83, 90, 99
Newfoundland, x, 14
Newtown, Wales, 114
North America, x–xi, xiii, 2–3, 11, 37, 52, 57, 102, 117, 121, 143
North Sea, 190, 192
Northumberland Strait, 12
North York Public Library, 107
(old) Nova Scotia, iv, ix–x, 10–11, 13–14, 17, 19, 21, 24, 27, 33, 35–36, 42, 54–55, 58–60, 64ff., 84, 87–90, 94, 100, 104, 109, 117–119, 127, 164, 194, 199–200
Nova Scotia Council, 17, 66
Null, Christina, 40
Null, Maria Christiana, 9
Nüremberg, Germany, 126
Nürtingen, Germany, 132–133, 136–140, 145–146, 150–151
Oberboihingen, Germany, 109
Offa's Dyke, 114
Oliver, Andrew, 64
Osnabruck, xiii, 3, 116, 123, 167
Oulton, William, 37
Outhouse, Lucretia, 128
Outhouse, Simon Jr., 103, 127–128
Outhouse Point, 103–104
Oxford University, 32
Palatinate (Rhine River), 2, 13, 109, 117, 131, 133, 135, 142, 187–188
"Palatine Boors," 34
Panaccadie Creek, 80, 102, see also Hall's Creek
Parry, Mary and Sarah, 85, Appendix C

Peabody, Francis, 79, 92
Peasants' War, 172
Pembrokeshire, Wales, 43, 51, 113
Penn, William, 1, 38, 42–43, 57, 92, 134
Penn family, 36, 52
Pennsylvania, x–xii, 1–2, 4–5, 10–12, 21, 31, 36, 42–44, 47, 50–52, 58–59, 62, 66, 69, 72, 89, 92, 94, 96, 102, 107, 109, 115, 131, 135, 137, 142, 145, 147, 153, 156, 161–164, 167–168, 170, 182, 188, 194
    elections, 33–34, 36, 69; and the Germans, 36, 113; land settlement, x, 1–2, 42, 59; provincial Assembly, 31, 36, 52, 58, 69; Royal government, 36, 59
Pennsylvania Gazette, 52–53, 62, 72, 90
Pennsylvania-Germans, ix, 3, 23, 33, 41, 48, 108–109, 112, 117, 129, 195
Pennsylvania German Folklore Society, 109
Pennsylvania German Immigrants, 1709-1786, 109–111, 131, 137, 144, 150, 195
Pennsylvania German Pioneers, 107
Pennsylvania Journal, 74, 89
Pennsylvania Magazine of History and Biography, 65
Pennypacker, Samuel, 133
Perkins, Simeon, 81
Peters, Ellis, 113
Petitcodiac, The, 24, 180
Petitcodiac River, iv, x–xii, 2–4, 7, 10, 12–13, 16, 21–22, 37, 51, 53–54, 58–59, 72, 74, 77, 80–83, 86, 89–91, 93–96, 99–109, 112, 115, 117, 120–121, 127–128, 142, 147–148, 162, 164, 167, 169–170, 182, 194–195, 198–200
Pet-koat-kwee'-ak, iv
Pflum, Werner, 147–148, 151
Pflum Hotel, 138–139, 146–147, 151
Pfullingen county, Württemberg, 156, 164, 169
Philadelphia, iv, ix–xi, xiii, 1–3, 10ff., 27ff., 70–74, 77ff., 106–110, 112, 119, 123, 132, 140, 142, 145, 147, 150, 153, 161, 169, 179–180, 182, 188, 190, 195, 197–199, 201
    Anglicans, 31, 71, 88; Antique Row, 47; Appletree Alley, 38–39; Arch Street, 38; Baptists, 71; Bodine Street (Biddle Alley), 73; Cherry Street, 39; Elbow Lane, 72–73; Fifth Street, 38–39; Fourth Street, 27, 39, 51, 53, 92; Independence Park, 38; Locust Street, 24, 38; Market Street, 51–53, 60–61, 67, 72–73; Mulberry Street, 38, 200; Philosophical Society, 38, 197; Presbyterians, 68, 71, 88, 96; Stamp Act riots, 67ff.; Third Street, 51, 73; trade boycotts, 62, Appendix D; Washington Square, 38
Philadelphia land speculators, 10, 17–19, 21–22, 29–30, 33, 36, 54, 59, 66, 72–74, 77, 83ff., 100, 119, 197, Appendix D
Pincombe, C. Alexander, 41
Piscataqua Customs district, NH, 96
Plochingen, Germany, 132, 185
Point Laurence, 81
Portsmouth, NH, 96–97
Presbyterians, 68, 71, 88, 96
Proprietary Party of Pennsylvania, 31, 33–34, 69
Protestant German Settlers on the Petitcodiac, 189
Protestantism, 141, 160
Protestants, 13, 15
Quaker Party, 33–34, 69, 88
Quakers, 2, 31, 36, 41, 58, 68–69, 71, 75, 88, 92
Quebec, 12, 14, 58
Quebec Gazette, 59

Raben, Christopher, 40
Radcliffe College, 23
Raddall, Thomas, 19
Radford, Anna, 41–43
Raymond, W. O., xii, 17, 19
Read, Deborah, see Franklin, Deborah (Read)
Reading Town, Berks Co., PA, 110
Reformation (1534), 133, 142, 160, 172, 176
Reformed Lutherans, 142
Reichle, Pfarrer Kristina, 143–145, 149–150
Relfe, John, Appendix D
Reutlingen, Württemberg, 132–133, 164
Reynolds, John, 147–148
Rhine River, 2, 51, 123, 133–134, 187–188, 190, 192
Richard the Lion-Heart, 127, 129
Richardson, Joseph, 88, 91, Appendix D
Ricker, Jacob, 29, 86, 97–98
Roberts, Jonathan and Mrs., 51, 75, 97
Roman Catholic Church, 141–142, 160
"Roots Surname List," (Internet), 108
Rosanna River, Austria, 130–131
Rotterdam, 123, 133, 187–188, 190, 194
Roulac, John, 117
Rutter, Thomas, 92
Saarland, 149
Saint John, NB, xii, 5, 78
Saint Martin of Tours, 160–161
Saint Wendelin, 141
St. Anne's (Fredericton), 79–80
St. James Street, London, 32
St. John River (St. John's River), iv, 3, 35, 77–80, 90, 92, 118
St. Michael's German Lutheran Church, Philadelphia, 19, 35–36, 38–44, 53, 70, 142, 167, 188, 198–199
St. Michael's and Zion Lutheran Congregation, 39
St. Peter and St. Paul's Church, Shrewsbury, 113
St. Peter's Lutheran Church, Barren Hill, PA, 40, 47, 182
St. Pierre and Miquelon, 14
Sachsenhausen, 109
Sackville, NB, 119, 127
Salisbury Pioneer Cemetery, 106
Samphire Greens, 24, 162
samphire greens, 7, 10, 103–105, 115, 147
Saxons, 2, 113–114
Schantz,
    Anna Margretha, 200; Carl and Margretha, 198–201; Catharina Elisabeth, 200; Heinrich, 200; Johanne, 200
Scharff, J. Thomas, 71
Schlaitdorf, 110–112, 116, 122–123, 129ff., 152, 154, 156–158, 169
    Famlien-Register Schlaitdorf, 144–145, 149
Schrofenstein (Ruine), 127–128
Schuylkill River, 51–52
Schwenckfelders, 191
Second Presbytery of Philadelphia, 77
Seeburg, Württemberg, 152
Seven Years' War, 2
Severn River, 113–114
Shawnee Indians, 16
Shepody Bay, 3, 22, 80, 105
Shirley, Gov. William, 11
Shrewsbury, 113–114

Siglin, Johannes, 137
Sikorski, Muriel Lutes, 101–102, 107–109, 182, 189
Smith, Dr. William, 29–34, 81–83, 86–88, 91, 96, 119, Appendix D
    Oxford University, 32; paymaster, 32, 87; William Smith Papers, 101
Smith and Company, 88, 91, 96, Appendix D
Society of Arts, London, 148
Society of Genealogists, 112–113
Somers,
    Anna Catharina, 40; Christenah, 9, 106; Eva Magdalena, 40; family, xi; Rachel, 9
Sommer, Joseph, 109
Sommer, Matthias, 6, 9–10, 26, 29, 40–41, 47, 55, 69, 86–87, 98, 101, 106, 109, 182
Sons of Liberty, x, 63–64
Speier, Ella, 149
Speyer, Germany, 133
Stag Inn (Neckarntzlingen), 137–138
Stalegger, Regina, 155–156, 159–160, 164–165, 167–170, see also Stief (Stieff), Regina
Stamp Act, 21, 27, 52, 58–59, 62–72, 74, 77, 81, 85, 88, 107
Stamp Act Congress (1765), 62
Stamp Commissioners (London), 74
Staunton, Virginia, 16
Steeves (Steves),
    Catherine, 8; Ephraim, 6, 8; Frederick, 9; Henry, 9; James, 37; Jane (Mitton), 8; John, 8; John, George, and Leonard, 120; Lewis Edward, 8; Margaret, 37; Matthias, 120; Maude Clara, 8; Noah, 128; Rachel, 162–163; William, 108; William Henry, 120
Steeves Descendants, The, xii, 113
Steeves family, viii–xii, 3, 37, 108
    descendants, xi, 120, 154, 181, 189; gathering in 1867, viii–xii, 37; history, 142; legends, xiii, 3–4, 51, 78, 91, 104, 147, 162; members, xiii, 183
Steeves Family Register, 108
Steevescote, NB, xi
Steinacker, Wiltrud, 122, 127–130
Stephanuskirche (Gruorn), 176
Steuermessbuch von 1720, 165–168
    viertel, ruten, morgen, 167
Steves, Herb, 198
Steveston, BC, xi
Sthieff, Jurg Fredk, 108, 110
Stief (Stieff),
    Anna Catharina, 159; Frederick, 189
    Hans Jerg, 166–167; Heinrich and Barbara, 159; Jacob, 36–38, 110, 120, 153, 161–162, 167, 198–201; Jacob Friderich, 150; Joh. Heinrich, 150; Johañ Conrad, 150; Johann Heinrich, 150; Johann Heinrich and Maria Barbara, 159; Johañne, 150; Johannes and Rosina Barbara, 150, 154; John, 40, 142; Katharina Barbara, 161–163, 170; Matthias, 120; Michael, 154, 156, 166–167
Stief (Stieff), (Johannes) Heinrich, iv, vii, x–xiii, 1–3, 6, 9–10, 19, 23ff., 36–39, 41–42, 47, 51, 53, 55, 69, 73, 86–87, 98, 101–102, 107ff., 116, 119–121, 123, 127–129, 140ff., 159–171, 174, 177ff., 193–195, 198–200, Appendix A
    Articles of Agreement, 26–27, 39, 41, 183; Benjamin Franklin, 2, 59–60, 148, 195; *Betstunde*, (praying hour), 164, 169, 176; *beyschläffer*, 164, 169–170; Bible, 142–143,

200; birth-place, 159–160, 171–172, 182; Hillsborough, xii, 37, 97, 184; Hungerberg, 165–169, 177; legends, xiii, 3–4, 51, 78, 91, 104, 147, 162; marriage record, 155, 164, 169–170; Münsingen, 154–156, 159ff.; signature, 24, 179–182; Steeve, Henry, 119; turnips, 146–147; *ziegler* (brickmaker), 169, 174, 176

Stief (Stieff) Regina (Rachel), iv, 1, 9, 37–38, 110, 150, 152, 155–156, 161–163, 167–170, 174, 181ff., Appendix A, see also Stalegger, Regina

Stieff, Augustin, 145, 149, 156, 159–160, 167, 169, 178–179, 186, Appendix A

    Anna Barbara, 154; Augustinus, 154; house in Münsingen, 186

Stieff, Georg Friedrich, 110, 112, 116, 122–123, 129, 132, 135, 137, 140, 143ff., 149, 153–154, 156, 165–167, Appendix A

    Maria and Regina, 145; *schuster*, (cobbler), 110, 144–145; in Philadelphia, 110; in Schlaitdorf, 110, 114

Stieve, Rachel, iv, 38
Stiles, Ezra, 32
Stoever, J. Caspar, 38
Strasbourg, Germany, 133
Strassburger, Ralph, 107–110
Stumpp, Michael, 145
Stuttgart, Germany, 130, 132–133, 184–185
Sulpicius Severus, 160–161
Swabia (Württemberg), vii, 135, 141, 151, 158, 172, 185
Sweden, 35, 44
Swedish Holsteins in America 1644–1892, 49, 51, 65, 113, 198
Switzerland, 13, 109, 131, 135
Tauber River, Germany, 101
tétines de souris, 104
Third Crusade, 127–129
Thirty Years War, 133
Thomas, Isaiah, 64–65
Thomas, John ap, 43
Tiefental valley, 178
Tilghman, James, 70
Tindal, Thomas, 41
Toronto, xi, 44, 107–109, 111–112, 123, 180–181
Toronto Reference Library, vii, 108, 129, 148
Tours, France (Gaul), 160
Trailfingen, Württemberg, 152
Treaty of Aix-la-Chappelle, 52
Treitz, (Trites) Jacob, 3, 6, 9–10, 26–29, 55, 86–87, 92, 98, 101, 106, 183

    "father of Moncton," 29

Trites (Treitz),

    Abraham, 9, 106; Catherine, 9; Christian, 9, 106, 169; Nancy, 8

Tubingen, Württemberg, 130, 132–133
Tucker, Glen, 100
Turenne, Marshall, 133
turnips, 3, 82, 147–148
typhus (Palatine fever), 191
Underground Lake (Demoiselle Creek, NB), 184
U.S. Mint, Philadelphia, 38
University of Pennsylvania, 61
University of Wittemberg, 141
Upper Merion, PA, 51–52, 56, 75, 91, 97
Van Doren, Carl, 60
Vaugundy (map), 135

vessels,

    Elizabeth, 78–79; *Hillsborough*, 120; *Leopard*, 98; *Mary Jane*, 120; *Minerva*, 81; *Osgood*, 162; *Pembroke*, 16; *Phoenix*, 107, 110; *Richard and Mary*, 108, 110, 132, 138; *Royal Charlotte*, 69; *Sardine*, 70; *Sophie*, 120; *Three Brothers*, 120

viehhirte (cowherd), 145, 156, 169
Virginia, 15–16, 37, 195
vom Grafen, Jürgen, 175–176
Walen, Mr., 86–87
Wales, 41–43, 51, 113–116
Walnut Grove, 44, 51, 56, 85, 96–97
Walpole Company, 59
Walter, Anna Barbara, 154
War of 1812, 121
War of Austrian Succession, 172
War of the Palatinate, 133
War of Spanish Succession, 172
Washademoak, 79
Washington, George, 16, 21, 99
Wayne, Anthony, ix, 19–21, 26, 29, 51, 55, 59, 70, 78–79, 86–88, 91, 93–96, 119, 147, Appendix D

    Anthony Sr., 87–88; Burlington pork, 78–79, 95; family papers, 78; map of Monckton, 93–94; Petitcodiac River, 16, 19–21, 59, 87, 93; Revolutionary War general, 21

Waynesborough Museum, 93–95
Welsh and German settlers, ix, xi, 10, 21, 23, 28, 41–42, 45, 47, 53, 58, 112, 195
Wendelinkirche (Church of Saint Wendelin), 139, 141, 143, 149
Wertheim, 101, 109–110, 129, 134–136
Westmorland County, NB, 10
Wetherhed, Samuel, 86–87, 95–96
Wheat Sheaf Tavern, 84–85, 91
Wheatland Estate, 48
Wiessler, Anna Walburga, 9
Wiessler, Peter, 9
Wildes, Harry Emmerson, 94
William and Mary, 58
William the Conqueror, 113
Wilmot, Gov. Montague, 118
Wittemberg Castle Church, 142
Wolastoqewiyik Indians, 80
Wood, James, 37
Worms, Germany, 133
Wortman, George, 29, 86, 98
Wortman family, xi
Wright, Dr. Esther Clark, xii, 10, 14, 21ff., 37, 41, 44–45, 77, 79, 107, 112–113, 148, 162, 179–180, 183
Wright, Esmond, 33
Wrong, George, 12
Württemberg, vii, 109, 111, 122–123, 129ff., 142, 145–147, 160–161, 163, 169–170, 172, 176, 179, 182–183, 187–190

    dukes, 134, 168; emigrants' occupations, 137; Mennonites, 142; Moravians, 142; Plain People, 142; Reformed Lutherans, 142; winter of 1708-9, 134

Yoder, Dr. Don, ix, 3, 39, 108, 110–111, 122, 131, 135, 137–138, 140, 144–145, 148, 170, 195
Yorkshire, xiii, 16, 113
Ziegelwäldle, 169, 174
Zimmermann, Rosalie, 94
Zion Church, Philadelphia, 39